UK Economic Decline

UK Economic Decline
Key Texts

edited by

David Coates
and
John Hillard

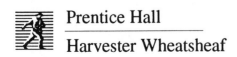
Prentice Hall
Harvester Wheatsheaf

London New York Toronto Sydney Tokyo Singapore
Madrid Mexico City Munich

First published 1995 by
Prentice Hall/Harvester Wheatsheaf
Campus 400, Maylands Avenue
Hemel Hempstead
Hertfordshire, HP2 7EZ
A division of
Simon & Schuster International Group

Printed and bound in Great Britain by
T. J. Press Ltd, Padstow

Library of Congress Cataloging-in-Publication Data

Available from the publisher

British Library Cataloguing in Publication Data

A catalogue record for this book is available
from the British Library

ISBN 0-13-342775-7

1 2 3 4 5   99 98 97 96 95

Contents

INTRODUCTION

I

The British economic 'problem' is elusive, difficult to define but unmistakable. But also, the problem under review in this book is not exactly new. For the past 100 years (at least) there has been a vision of the UK political economy as displaying symptoms of decline, degeneration and decay. The texts assembled in this volume represent an anthology of perspectives that hopefully give some clues towards understanding the origins of Britain's long slide from economic preeminence to that of a middle-ranking industrialised economy. A great deal of intellectual energy has been expended, and millions of words have been written and spoken, trying to come to terms with the so-called British Disease. These introductory remarks are designed to set the tone for what follows and to give some justification for (re)producing yet more words!

II

The main objective of this collection is to make a positive contribution to the debate on decline which, despite an ever-growing sophistication, remains as unresolved as the 'problem' itself. As Michael Dintenfass (1992: 71) concluded his recent survey:

> The decline of industrial Britain now has a long history and so too does its interpretation. Our understanding of Britain's relative economic failure, however, remains incomplete and unsatisfactory.

Why this should be the case is an important question. One reason for the lack of consensus on the British Disease is because, as we noted in Coates and Hillard (1986), the differences of opinion in the literature reflect broad ideological and political disagreements. Secondly, self-contained debates have evolved in disciplinary 'furrows' largely oblivious to the findings of other specialisms. The confusion is further compounded because of differences within the various disciplines. Finally, not only is it difficult to specify the relevant variables but also the connecting principles weave multifarious patterns, depending on the method and theory employed.

In all, the fuzzy nature of the problem makes its specification, and hence its resolution, largely beyond the pale of conventional explanation. This is not the place to explore methodological questions except to underline that, since the 1970s, academia has faced its own crisis. In neoclassical economics, for example, the present generation continues to deny and repress the implications of 20th century science for the orthodox paradigm (Ormerod, 1994). The world of neoclassical economics is static, closed and timeless. To put it mildly, this poses difficulties for understanding the impact of past events on current performance. In consequence, there is profound disagreement in the literature about the extent to which 'the failures of the post-war economy are deeply rooted in the past' (Crafts, 1988: i). Of necessity, therefore, the 'historical' dimension constitutes an underlying theme throughout the collection.

But also the dominance of the 'Manchester School' mentality, which, as David Marquand argues in Chapter 24, permeates the entire fabric of British society, can be regarded as a major barrier to an understanding of its late 20th century predicament. The political supremacy of free-market solutions has been mirrored in the academic debate by the resurgence of pre-Keynesian economics. The belief that the economy, if it is left to its own devices, gravitates naturally to its optimal state, has regained the intellectual high ground that it lost during the so-called Keynesian era. J. M. Keynes's critique of neoclassical dogma – that the economy is not innately self-regulating – is ignored, while the patent failure of neoclassical solutions is blamed not on the solutions themselves but on the government's reluctance to take them to their logical extreme.

Moreover, the 'imperial' status of neoclassical economics has hindered the development of alternative 'ways of seeing' the problem. In sum, the way in which the problem is conceptualised has been bounded by the dominant vision of the economy as operating independently from historical, social and political factors. An alternative vision is emerging, however, taking inspiration from the 'new view' of science (Prigigone and Nicolis, 1989). This heterodox approach stresses the recursive nature of social phenomena, where the problem is seen as an *open, complex* and *interdependent* process. In particular, the complex nature of the problem implies that its resolution demands much more than the quick-fix solutions of the type which promised so much yet delivered so little in the recent past. The texts below have thus been deliberately chosen to transcend traditional disciplinary boundaries and, whereas the reader is unlikely to reach the 'holy grail' of an all-embracing explanation of British economic decline, the modest aim of what follows is to deepen your understanding of the problem by bringing together key arguments from a variety of vantage points.

III

De-industrialisation is perhaps *the* key word in the decline debate but it is a somewhat unsatisfactory term to capture the factors and processes embodied in UK underperformance. Since 1988, for example, the clearing banks have liquidated over 50,000 jobs. In the 1990s the *service* sector, both public and private, is being 'de-industrialised' along the same lines as the manufacturing sector has been since the 1960s. Taking on board that a process of rationalisation is occurring across all sectors of the British economy, 'the main question is whether de-industrialisation can be regarded simply as a normal response to changing technology and tastes or does it signify some structural disequilibrium in the economy as a whole?' (Singh, 1987: 302). The cumulative outcome of the process of de-industrialisation has been described by Ajit Singh (*ibid.*: 304) as follows:

> The weaknesses of British industry have led to a slow overall growth of the economy over the last quarter century relative to that of the competitor countries. This, in turn, is responsible for the lack of dynamism in the country's productive system. Economies that grow quickly have higher investment, achieve faster technical progress, more product innovation and improvements in other non-price spheres of competition. In addition the take-home pay of workers in a fast growing economy will generally also be growing more quickly. Other things being equal, this is likely to lead to better relations between workers and managers with consequent benefits to productivity and performance. On account of slow growth UK industry has suffered on both these counts. The result has been a vicious circle of causation by which industry is increasingly unable to hold its own in either overseas or home markets.

Although this narrative is a fair description of the pattern of events in recent UK economic history, it still begs the question as to the *sources* of the 'weaknesses' and it is upon this issue that the debate on decline has generated a multiplicity of contradictory explanations.

In the decline literature, the term 'negative' de-industrialisation is used as a shorthand to capture the *consequences* of the UK's weak economic performance. This weakness is reflected in both the largest absolute and relative decline in industrial employment in all OECD countries and a barely rising trend of manufacturing output since 1973. In the late 1970s Tom Nairn summarised the problem as follows:

A constantly weakening industrial base, a dominant financial sector oriented towards foreign investment rather than the restructuring of British industries, a non-technocratic state quite unable to bring about the 'revolution from above' needed to redress the balance; everything conspired to cause an inexorable spiral of decline. (Nairn, 1977: 5)

During the 1980s, there followed a sort of 'revolution from above' (Hillard, 1986) but during the decade manufacturing output rose by only 8 per cent, while domestic spending on manufactures increased by 28 per cent. The productivity gap (Matthews, 1988) between Britain and other advanced capitalist economies was not bridged in the 1980s. The Thatcherite promise of a Greater Britain never quite materialised and the achievement of her regime represented simply a tortured return to the trend line of growth which had been interrupted by the 'shocks' of the 1970s (Reddaway, 1992). There is little talk any more of an 'economic miracle' (Buxton *et al.*, 1994). The 'hollowing out of British manufacturing' (Williams *et al.*, 1990) has continued apace, so that by the mid-1990s 'the UK has ceased to be a specialist net manufacturing exporter and now incurs a substantial deficit in manufacturing trade – even at levels of domestic expenditure far below that required to attain full employment' (Wells, 1994: 73).

IV

As David Coates shows in Part 1, the legacy of economic underperformance is the commanding feature of the British political landscape in the late 20th century. The question posed in the 1950s by Andrew Shonfield (Chapter 2), as to why Britain's wealth grows so much more slowly than the wealth of most other industrialised countries, is still the burning issue of the 1990s. This signifies a structural deficiency in the domestic economy which has proved resistant to the various 'remedies' aimed at reversing the downward trend.

Part 2 of the collection is devoted to a series of classic views which set the parameters of the present debate. Whereas it is impossible to 'prove' the salience of one factor (or set of factors) as *the* generative mechanism of British economic underperformance, Parts 3, 4, 5 and 6 bring together analyses of 'factors' which have been prioritised in the debate – the respective roles of labour and training, culture and education, capital and the state. Since the mid-1980s, the focus of the debate has shifted away from a pre-occupation with the effects of organised labour on economic performance. The Thatcherite onslaught against the trade unions reflected a blind faith in monocausality that failed to deliver the intended economic rejuvenation. If labour is accorded a minor part in the present debate, it is still strategic, if only in terms of its appalling neglect. Predictably, recent research reported by Peter Nolan (Chapter 12) has revealed that, after all, trade unions may make a positive contribution to the generation of economic wealth.

Such findings merely reinforce a growing realisation that, notwithstanding the rhetoric and hype, the past fifteen years of British economic history have represented another twist in the 20th century spiral of relative decline. The short-lived confidence generated by the Thatcherite conviction that a trickle-down economy would deliver a British renaissance has been replaced by an increasing sense of uncertainty. In the absence of any alternative hegemonic project à la Thatcher, and at a time when the crown-in-parliament is ceasing to provide a stable foundation for the British constitution, the orderly management of decline is but a rapidly fading memory.

John Hillard
Leeds

Part 1

UK economic underperformance

CHAPTER 1

UK underperformance: claim and reality[*]

David Coates

When, in March 1994, the Centre for Industrial Policy and Performance (CIPP) at the University of Leeds called a one-day conference on the causes and cures of UK economic underperformance, an audience of over 500 people heard Bryan Gould, MP open his remarks by saying:

> It is not surprising ... that our share of world trade could not be maintained at its pre-eminent level when other powerful economies began to industrialise and take part in international trade ... But what ... is not so clear is why it should have been the case that Britain should not have fallen back to a position of equality with other comparable economies, but should now be doing so much worse than they are doing. Why is the German share in world manufacturing twice that of Britain's? Why are we now exceeded not just by the Americans and the Japanese and the Germans – which you might have expected – but now by the French, the Italians, and perhaps shortly by the Spanish and the Benelux countries as well? Why should our national output not just have fallen back from its pre-eminent position but is now overtaken by, for example, Italy? To make these points is not, I think, to indulge in any form of xenophobia, but is simply to try to see more clearly than perhaps we are accustomed to seeing quite what has happened to our economy over a very long period.

The size of Bryan Gould's audience that day was itself an indication of how widespread in contemporary Britain is his sense of the frailty of the UK's economic performance and position. The size of his audience was also a sign of

---

[*] This reader updates Coates and Hillard (1986, 1987); and is intended to accompany the survey of explanations published as Coates (1994).

how concerned so many of us have become with the likely impact of this frailty on key elements of post-war UK life: on things like full employment, rising prosperity, decent welfare provision and generalised social peace. Bryan Gould was not the only speaker that day, nor was he by any means the most pessimistic of those who addressed the conference.[**] But he – like the rest – shared a recognition that if underperformance was ever to be corrected, it had first to be understood. The purpose of this text is to bring within easy reach of a concerned audience the major explanations now available in the academic literature on which such an understanding ought properly to be built.

The scale of the problem

The scale of the problem of UK economic underperformance is itself a matter of intense academic and political debate. It is not unusual for commentators and politicians sympathetic to the policies of the Conservative governments in power in the UK since 1979 to decry those who talk of economic underperformance as guilty of 'talking Britain down' (Lamont, 1993). Even more charitable voices from that persuasion tend to insist that underperformance needs dating, needs re-specifying as 'yesterday's problem', needs treating as something endemic to UK economic life before 1979 but not since. Indeed there is a general tendency in government circles to talk up the contemporary economic record, and to soften the significance of any current signs of underperformance. Government ministers often invoke an image of *a dark age in the past* (an age of corporatism, government intervention, trade union strength and winters of discontent) against which to set the Tory record of the 1980s – a record they describe as one of *seven years of unbroken economic growth*. Ministers regularly speak of the UK in the mid-1990s *leading Europe out of recession,* and as the one economy in the European community now *creating jobs without inflation*. And they invariably characterise the UK's recent economic performance as one of recovery and strength, by making statistically based claims of the following kinds:

- that the 1982–89 economic recovery was the longest period of continuous UK expansion in the post-war period;
- that UK output growth in that recovery outstripped growth in Germany, France and Italy, and in doing so, turned the tide on relative industrial decline;
- that take-home pay for the average family rose by at least a third after 1979;

[**] The text of the conference is available from CIPP, Economics and Social Studies Building, University of Leeds LS2 9JT.

- that annual rates of labour productivity accelerated sharply through the 1980s, and rose more quickly here than in the rest of continental Europe;
- that total investment rose by 1989 to levels well above those achieved in even the best of the years under Labour;
- that the UK's share of world trade in manufactures – after years of decline – stabilised in the mid-1980s; and
- that employment in the UK revived in the 1980s, as the economy expanded to create more than 1.5 million extra jobs, to take the UK unemployment rate to under the European average, and to give the UK the best job-creation record in the European Union (cited in Wells, 1991: 178).

The latest, and rather splendid, example of this judicious use of statistics on growth and performance is to be found in the Government's own White Paper, *Competitiveness: Helping Business to Win* (DTI, 1994), published in May 1994 in part as a response to the earlier, more critical report of the Select Committee on Trade and Industry, *Competitiveness of UK Manufacturing Industry* (Select Committee, 1994). The White Paper 'had to negotiate a fine line between being honest about the UK's problems while remaining positive about how they have been tackled over the past 15 years' (*Financial Times*, 25.5.1994), a balancing act it achieved by a repeated emphasis on the need persistently to respond to strong international competitive pressures. Scattered throughout the White Paper are clear indications of continuing competitive weakness: discreet recognitions that after 1945 Britain's standard of living rose faster than ever before, but that other countries did better still; and discreet admissions that – since policy initiatives were required now – existing policy could no longer suffice. There was even an open confession of goals not yet achieved: in that 'although we have many world-beating companies, average productivity levels in manufacturing have not yet risen to those of our major competitors and our overall share of world trade in services has continued to fall', and 'our GDP per head remains below that of many other advanced countries' (DTI, 1994: 13–14).

But all this self-criticism was buried within an overall representation of the UK as an economy on the move – forward and upward – one in which, throughout the 1980s:

- manufacturing productivity grew faster in the UK than in the US, France and Germany;
- our share of the volume of world trade in manufactures stabilised after decades of decline;
- our overall growth rate was similar to that in France, Germany and Italy, whereas we had grown significantly more slowly in previous economic cycles;
- employment rose by over 1.25 million over the last economic cycle, faster than at any time for at least 30 years;

- the climate of industrial relations was transformed – working days lost in 1993 were the lowest since records began 100 years ago;
- the business sector invested a proportion of its value added similar to our major competitors after lagging behind in previous cycles;
- we succeeded in attracting the lion's share of US and Japanese investment in the EC in the 1980s; and
- there was a dramatic rise in the number of small firms – at the end of 1991 there were around 900,000 more small businesses than in 1979 – and in self-employment (DTI, 1994: 10–12).

When governments speak in this way, they appear to speak with authority, and with the weight of official statistics on their side. But in this instance they do not. The statistical claims made in the White Paper and in other Government/Conservative Party research papers need to be treated with considerable scepticism and caution. For as John Wells among others has noted, though such statistics are, with occasional exceptions, 'broadly correct, albeit subject to ... detailed qualifications, some of them quite substantial ... The picture they present of the development of the British economy during the past decade is ... extremely partial and, in many crucial respects, quite misleading' (Wells, 1991: 179). It is hard to realise, for example, from the kind of listing made in the White Paper, that the 1980s began with the deepest recession in UK industrial history: one characterised by a 20% loss of manufacturing capacity, and a destruction of 1.7 million manufacturing jobs. It is hard to realise too, from claims of this sort, that the 1980s ended with the UK economy immersed in its longest unbroken recession in recent times (with UK GDP falling for 7 successive quarters); or to see that, between the two recessions, investment levels did not return to their 1979 levels until 1988, and did so only to restore productivity levels to those commonplace in the UK in the 1960s.

In fact, the key feature of the 'productivity miracle' of the 1980s – on which so much of the Conservatives' defence of their industrial policy ultimately depends – was that it did *not* take UK industry up to US, German or Japanese levels; and that the growth in labour output it engendered came largely from an intensification of the work process (from making people work faster, longer and harder) and not from providing them with new technology on anything like a sufficient scale. (The White Paper, if you look back, does quietly concede the first of these quite crucial dimensions of recent UK economic underperformance, while gliding over the second.) It is true that investment, as a percentage of GDP (at 19.9% in 1989 and 20.2% in 1990), had by the end of the decade risen beyond its 1979 level of 18.1%, and that investment in manufacturing industry did rise – by some 12.8% – over the decade 1979–89; but that figure looks paltry when set against comparable investment in Western Europe manufacturing industry, and positively minuscule when set against the 320.3% growth in the volume of investment in financial services in the UK in the same period.

The biggest distortion of the actual record associated with the public defence of government policy comes in the claims made about employment growth during the Thatcherite and post-Thatcherite period. The record is invariably presented by Government ministers as one of long-term job creation. The reality is entirely the reverse. The years since 1978 have seen a veritable culling of full-time jobs, a culling which has reached dramatic proportions in the 1990s.

- In 1971, there were 21,648,000 people in civilian employment: of whom 85% (some 18,299,000) were in full-time work.
- By 1978 the number of full-time employees still stood at 17,854,000.
- By 1985, total civilian employment had fallen to 20,910,000 of whom only 16,141,000 were full-time.
- By 1989 the total had risen (to 22,143,000), with the number working full-time roughly constant (at 16,750,000).
- By 1993, the total had fallen to 20,787,000 and the number working full-time to 14,980,000.

In other words, since the Conservatives came to power in 1979 *the number of full-time jobs in civilian employment in the UK economy has been reduced by some 3 million – 1.8 million of which have gone since 1989* – as manufacturing industry shed employment in total, and as large firms in the service sector restructured their employment patterns from full-time to part-time work. And of the part-time jobs created (4.7 million in 1985, 5.4 million in 1989, 5.8 million in 1993), at least 70% involve people working for less than 16 hours a week (and many for less than 8 hours). So when we calculate the number of hours worked in the UK economy since 1979, we find that total reduced by many millions. The 1984 figure for hours worked per week in the UK economy stood at 850 million. It is now some 780 million (*Guardian*, 26.2.1994). Against this background therefore, no amount of political rhetoric should be allowed to persuade us that, through the creation of a labour force of low-paid, low-skilled part-time workers, the UK has suddenly and miraculously acquired a secure base for long-term economic recovery.

These counter-weights to an over-optimistic assessment of recent UK economic performance need then to be reinforced by statistical material rooted in a longer and less partisan reading of our circumstances. For if we just drop back even as little as two decades rather than one, we find:

- that in 1970, UK manufacturing industry contributed over 30% of the country's GDP. It now contributes only 22%. In 1960 manufacturing industry in the UK captured 16.3% of total world exports of manufactured goods. By 1990 that percentage was down to 8.4%;
- that at its peak in 1966 UK manufacturing industry employed 8.5 million people. It now employs less than half that number, just over 4 million;

- that until 1983 the UK was a net exporter of manufactured goods – and had been in peace-time ever since the industrial revolution.   The UK now imports more manufactured goods than it exports – a gap which reached £20.9 billion in 1989, or 4% of GDP;
- that prior to the 1980s, the UK's deficit on its total foreign payments just hovered on the edge of solvency – sometimes positive, sometimes falling into deficit – and going into deficit only when the UK economy itself was buoyant, over-heated even, sucking in imports.   The great achievement of government policy in recent years has been to put the UK into *permanent* balance of payments deficit, to do so in spite of North Sea oil, and to do so even when the internal economy is itself in recession.
- Little wonder then that a gap has opened up between government expenditures and the revenues available to finance them – a gap created by large-scale unemployment on the one side, and a shrinking tax base (in industrial output and employment) on the other.   It is salutary to remember that in 1960 the UK was the second most successful capitalist economy: exceeded in output, living standards and market share only by the USA.   It now stands 18 out of 24 in the OECD's table of GDP per head, with a standard of life (and a quality of welfare provision) akin only to those found in Western Europe's weakest industrial players: Spain, Portugal, Ireland and Greece.

As Karel Williams and his colleagues correctly observed, 'in social and national terms, what matters is the aggregate of output and employment generated inside the national economy by all manufacturing firms'.   When those aggregates are calculated and compared – with British manufacturing set against other leading industrial economies:

> Britain has two melancholy distinguishing characteristics. Firstly, Britain is the only advanced country where real manufacturing output shows no sustained growth over the past twenty years. In 1989, UK real manufacturing output was less than 10 per cent up on the level of the cyclical peak of 1973; other European national manufacturing sectors show growth rates of 17–75 per cent over the same period. Secondly, the British record is dominated by unusually sharp cyclical fluctuations and severe downturns after 1973 and 1979. In the post-1979 downturn, British real net manufacturing output fell by nearly 15 per cent, a fall which was twice as large as in any other OECD country. The British pattern is that recovery on the upswing restores output loss, but the manufacturing sector then turns down when the level of the previous cyclical peak has been regained. The pattern seems likely to be repeated in the early 1990s. (Williams *et al.*, 1990: 461–2)

GDP/head in the UK rose by 24.4% between 1960 and 1970, and by 19.1% in the 10 years that followed. The equivalent figures for West Germany were 38.7% and 30.2%, for France 54.6% and 36.1%, for Italy 58.2% and 39.2%, and for Japan a staggering 159.2% and 48.2% (Reddaway, 1983: 223). Gaps of a similar kind can be recorded for GDP, for manufacturing output, for gross fixed capital formation, for trade performance, for industrial R&D, for wage growth and so on. The UK has slipped not simply from its nineteenth-century position of world economic leadership. That, as Bryan Gould said, was to be expected. It has slipped, and slipped much more recently, from the first division of industrial nations into the second; and has done so as the global linkages between economies have intensified, and as new international divisions of labour have emerged to locate industrial power in Asia as well as in the Americas and Western Europe. The UK was once the world's leading manufacturing economy and financier of world trade. It has now slipped to become simply one of Western Europe's least competitive industrial economies. To quote M. W. Kirby:

> unprecedented levels of consumer affluence not withstanding, the post-war decades ... were an era of unremitting national economic decline, the inevitable consequence of the progressive weakening in Britain's status as an advanced industrial and trading nation. No matter which index of economic performance is taken – the rate of growth of GDP, of industrial production, of labour productivity, and Britain's share of world trade in manufactured goods – all of these statistics make depressing reading when compared with the achievements of other countries, notably the founder members of the EEC, Britain's partners in EFTA, and Japan. Only the USA has a comparable record of relative failure, but that could be no source of comfort to Britain in view of the higher absolute level of the American standard of living. (Kirby, 1991: 11–12)

It is salutary to set the tone and detail of a reading of UK performance such as this by Kirby against that presented earlier in the Government's 1994 White Paper, and to compare both with the understanding of contemporary UK economic difficulties expressed in the opening section of the Select Committee on Trade and Industry's report on the *Competitiveness of UK Manufacturing Industry*. In the comparison, the Select Committee stand far nearer to Kirby than to Heseltine, even though the membership of the Committee was cross-party and Conservative-dominated. This is how the Select Committee began their report on UK competitiveness:

> Public concern about the state of the UK's manufacturing sector has grown significantly in recent years, for four main reasons. First, following decades of deterioration, the UK's trade balance in manufactured goods moved into deficit in 1983 for the first time since the Industrial Revolution. It has remained in deficit ever since. Secondly, some argue that the UK's manufacturing sector is now too small to sustain a strong national economy or allow rapid economic growth. The recession of the early 1990s and the slow pace of recovery have heightened this perception. Thirdly, growing competition, particularly from the rapidly expanding low-wage countries in the Far East, is seen as a threat to the UK's remaining manufacturing industry. Fourthly, it is widely believed that the UK Government has been less supportive of domestic manufacturing than governments overseas have been. (Select Committee, 1994: 13)

The Select Committee then added their own specification of the trends and evidence justifying apprehensions of this kind. While conceding the achievement of some improvement in relative competitiveness and performance in the 1980s, they insisted that, nevertheless:

- The improvement in the UK's performance in terms of value added per hour between 1979 and 1989 was from a low base, and the gap remains wide. In 1989, taking value added per hour worked in manufacturing in the UK as 100, the figure was 125.3 in France, 130.4 in Germany, 133.7 in Japan and 165.3 in the US.
- The improvement in productivity has not yet given rise to substantial increases in manufacturing output ...
- The performance of UK manufacturing has been distinctive in several major respects ... Taking the [last] two decades as a whole, the UK is the only major industrial country whose manufacturing output has remained virtually static, although there has been some catching up in respect of France and Germany since the early 1980s. Not until 1988 did UK manufacturing output recover its level in the peak year of 1973, and in 1992 it was less than 1% higher than in 1973, whereas output increased by 27% in France, 25% in Germany, 85% in Italy and 119% in Japan during the same period.
- Another measure [of manufacturing competitiveness] is the UK's share of exports of manufactures by the 11 major manufacturing countries. From 1962 to 1991 the UK's share almost halved. From 1973 to the present it has varied between 7.5% and 9.6%, the lowest point being in 1984; in 1991 it was 8.5%.
- The UK's balance of trade in manufactures has steadily worsened, and the deterioration has been more severe than in most other major industrial countries ...

- A further measure of performance is the UK manufacturing sector's rate of return on capital, which has been consistently lower than elsewhere in the past two decades. The gap widened in the second half of the 1980s.
- Recent decades have also seen a decline in the *range* of manufacturing carried out in the UK. This is not necessarily peculiar to the UK, but it does mean that there is a smaller base of existing industries to develop, and that economic recovery gives rise to extra imports of manufactured goods no longer made in the UK. (*ibid.*: 13–20)

This slippage in the international standing of the UK economy – if it continues – will do many things to the UK's social fabric, and will call into question many of the social institutions and practices whose stability and continuance we take for granted. The UK in the mid-1990s is already a more divided society – with greater class, ethnic and regional differences of income, job security and prospects than at any time this century – divisions built around a solid white middle-class access to private affluence and public welfare. But this access is likely to be threatened too, and the social differences we now know are likely to be accentuated, if economic underperformance cannot be reversed. At the very least, the failure to widen and strengthen the competitiveness of the UK's manufacturing base will threaten the capacity of even this generation of workers to enjoy their pensions, and will erode the ability of their children to know a life style as bountiful and as secure as that enjoyed by the majority of their parents. Economic decline will, in this sense, open up political tensions between generations, as well as between social classes, regions and ethnic groupings; and because it will, the need to understand why it has occurred and how it can be reversed is fast becoming *the* economic and political issue of our time.

The limits of the problem

As we explore the possible origins of recent UK economic underperformance, we need to control for two possible over-statements of the problem. We need to avoid over-stating the scale and dangers of *de-industrialisation*, and we need to avoid over-generalising *the range of industries* caught up in it.

De-industrialisation

To take 'de-industrialisation' first, we need to absorb elements of conceptual control laid out more fully in the extract from the work of Rowthorn and Wells (see below, Ch. 11). It is too easy to look at the size of the manufacturing sector, note its loss of employment and market share, and take those losses as unambiguous evidence of diminished competitiveness. They are not. For there is plenty of comparative evidence to show – for *successful* economies as well as for weakening ones – a diminution over time in the share of GDP provided by manufacturing industry (a diminution caused by the rise of service industries), and a corresponding reduction in both the share (and the absolute levels) of employment provided by the manufacturing sector. There is, after all, nothing morally superior to manufacturing over services, or to work in a factory over work in an office. On the contrary, it is a measure of a civilised society that more of its people spend their time servicing the needs of others, and that fewer of its workforce find themselves trapped in the alienation of factory work.

Rowthorn and Wells remind us that de-industrialisation measured in this way (as shares of output and employment provided by manufacturing industry) can be generated for two quite different sets of reasons. It can be generated by economic success – caused by the enhanced maturity of an economy, its involvement in developing patterns of trade specialisation, and its ability to produce manufactured goods ever more productively. Or it can occur because the economy's manufacturing sector is out-competed by others, and thereby obliged to shut down plant and lay off workers. De-industrialisation, that is, can be either *positive* or *negative*. If positive, the shedding of labour can be the base for the expansion of non-inflationary welfare provision, and rising employment in the service sector. If negative, it heralds erosion of welfare provision, inflationary pressures, and rising unemployment. What we have to ask of the UK is whether its de-industrialisation since 1966 has been positive or negative in kind.

For their part, Rowthorn and Wells do not believe that the level of manufacturing employment could have been maintained at its 1966 level indefinitely. They feel that processes of economic maturity and trade specialisation must have eroded that number, no matter how competitively powerful UK-based manufacturing industry had remained. But they argue too that a more competitive manufacturing sector could have sustained more employment across the economy as a whole – and that a weak manufacturing sector holds the key to the emergence of internationally low levels of income in the UK over time. This is how Rowthorn put the case in a slightly earlier essay:

> The weakness of manufacturing industry is certainly the main reason why Britain has become a relatively poor country, why per capita incomes in Britain are now among the lowest in northern Europe. It also helps to explain why the unemployment rate is so high. Consider what it would mean if Britain's manufacturing industry were much stronger and more competitive than it is at present, having more equipment, using more advanced methods of production, and producing a wider range of higher quality of output. For a start, manufacturing output would obviously be much greater. Part of this additional output would go directly to meet domestic requirements, and part would be exported in payment for goods and services purchased from other countries. Some of these additional imports would be non-manufactures, such as raw materials or services; but there would also be a large increase in manufactured imports. Taking account of both the additional supplies from

domestic industry and the additional imports from elsewhere, the total amount of manufactured goods available for home use would rise considerably. Since the production and distribution of manufactured goods involves a wide range of complementary activities, output would also rise in such areas as construction, mining, consulting, finance, transport and retail distribution. Moreover real incomes would be higher and, consequently, consumers' expenditure of almost every kind would be greater; as, indeed, would public expenditure on items such as health and education. Thus, with a stronger manufacturing sector, output would be greater in almost every sector of the economy. (Rowthorn, 1986: 23–4)

Here then is a clear position in the ongoing debate about whether manufacturing matters. Most commentators now seem to recognise, as did the Select Committee on Trade and Industry, that 'the percentage of employment in manufacturing ... declined in most (but not all) industrialised countries during the 1970s and 1980s' and that 'given the continuing rise in productivity, the jobs lost in manufacturing in developed countries in recent years are unlikely ever to be fully restored' (Select Committee, 1994: 15). Like Rowthorn in the quotation above, the Select Committee believed that 'growth in the UK manufacturing sector should be viewed primarily as a way of increasing the creation of national wealth and thus of jobs elsewhere in the economy, rather than of creating jobs in manufacturing itself' (*ibid.*). But there is another view. It is one built around a series of linked propositions:

- that de-industrialisation in many rich countries seems set to intensify;
- that the world economy is experiencing both a sectoral shift (within OECD economies from manufacturing to services) and a geographical one (the consequence of the growing comparative advantage of developing countries in producing manufactured goods);
- that the trend to manufacturing is a desirable and natural phenomenon; and
- that manufacturing businesses will increasingly have to locate in low cost developing countries (McWilliams, 1994, citing Julius-Brown).

Rowthorn is on record as rejecting that view (Rowthorn, 1994). So too is the Select Committee on Trade and Industry. Faced with arguments specific to the UK case – that service expansion will compensate manufacturing decline, that the UK was never particularly good at manufacturing anyway and should therefore play to its strengths, and that policy should recognise the inevitability of a relocation of mass manufacturing industry to low-wage economies in East Asia and elsewhere – this was the Committee's response:

We believe that there are three crucial reasons for regarding manufacturing industry as especially important. The first is that manufacturing, though only about 20% of GDP, provides over 60% of UK exports, compared to less than 25% in the case of services ... Secondly, a significant proportion of the service sector is dependent on manufacturing ... Thirdly, the notion that services can substitute for a substantial part of the UK's manufacturing base does not appear to be borne out by serious analysis. (Select Committee, 1994: 21)

The Select Committee did 'not take the view that *only* manufacturing matters, or that it should be promoted at the expense of service industries'; and nor should we. 'What matters, as has often been emphasised is *tradeable items*. At present the bulk of these are manufactures' (*ibid*.: 22); and in an economy with the UK's structure of exports, we simply need to remember that 'every 1% decline in exports of manufactures requires more than a 2.5% rise in exports of services to compensate'. This, in a situation in which 'only about 20% of service output *can* be exported' (*ibid*.). It is data like this which led the Select Committee to 'regard the health of the UK's manufacturing industry as crucial to the health of the UK economy as a whole' (*ibid*.); and which should require of us a sensitivity to the extent to which any further UK de-industrialisation is negative or positive in kind.

Sectoral variations

So first we require explanations of UK economic underperformance that are sensitive to the importance of maintaining a strong UK manufacturing base. Secondly we require explanations of underperformance that are sensitive to variations in competitiveness between various industrial sectors within that base. For it is not the case that every UK company, or every UK sector, has underperformed (or underperformed to the same degree) in these last three decades.   On the contrary, a whole range of academic commentators has commented on the variation of performance between companies and/or sectors over time; and as you read on, you will do well to keep some sense of the variation with you.

One important source for the specification of sectoral variation is the work of Michael Porter. Surveying *the competitive advantage of nations* in 1990, Porter had this to say of the UK case:

Many strong British positions are in consumer goods of various sorts. British strength is also significant in trading ... Along with these successes are a wide smattering of other industries that range broadly across the economy, including chemicals, engines and textiles ... The largest concentration of British competitive advantage is in consumer packaged goods ... Related to this strength in consumer goods is a strong position in many areas of consumer goods retailing. Another important cluster is financial or financially related services ... Another important cluster, looming large in export volume, is petroleum and chemicals, including paint (where ICI and Courtaulds are world leaders). Significant clusters are also present in pharmaceuticals, entertainment and leisure products ... publishing ... aircraft, defence goods, motors and engines, and textiles (largely fibres). Other pockets of advantage lie in radio transmitters and radar apparatus, electrical generating equipment, glass and scrap metal. (Porter, 1990: 484–94)

It was Porter's view that few of these clusters were 'unusually strong ones. There are scarcely any industries with the high shares that characterise leading Japanese, American and German industries'. The 'vertical depth of clusters [was also] less than in nations such as Italy, Sweden or even Switzerland' (*ibid.*: 494). He found the economy as a whole losing competitive ground in the 1980s, with 'far more competitive industries in Britain [having] lost world export share than have gained it' – a pattern signalling, for him at least, 'an inability to upgrade, a shrinkage of clusters, and a narrowing of competitive industries in the economy' (*ibid.*: 494, 496).

Other commentators have produced similar readings of sectoral variation and overall performance for the UK economy of late. William Walker, noting the persistence of competitive strength *outside* manufacturing in the UK – in 'agriculture, energy and tradable services – and in areas of manufacturing that are linked to resource trading (e.g. food processing, petrochemicals)' used this as the reason why 'the priority given to advanced manufacturing and thus to technological development has been less evident in Britain than in other European countries' (Walker, 1993: 160–61). The Walker list of sectoral strengths *outside manufacturing* included:

1. *agriculture* – though the UK remains a net importer of food;
2. international commerce in foodstuffs – home to some of the world's largest *food, drink and tobacco* companies;
3. *energy* – once coal, now oil and natural gas: with BP and Shell as global actors and the largest companies based outside the US;
4. *international financial services,* based in the City of London;
5. *international services* (in industries such as hotels, retail, air transport, and advertising).

The Walker list for the *manufacturing base* distinguished sectors where the strength is indigenous and where it derives from the presence of foreign multinationals. Among the former, three stand out:

1. *Chemicals and pharmaceuticals* ... Here Britain possesses some of the world's leading companies (ICI, Glaxo, Beecham) ... This sector gains

additional strength from the chemical and petrochemical activities of the major British oil companies.

2. *Aerospace* ... Strength in this sector derives largely from Britain's heavy post-war commitment to defence procurement. The leading firms are British Aerospace (airframes and guided weapons), Rolls-Royce (aero-engines) and Lucas Aerospace, Dowty and Smiths Industries (engine controls, hydraulics and other sub-assemblies). For the same reason, Britain has a strong international presence in *defence electronics* – (GEC, now incorporating Ferranti and Plessey – and British Aerospace Dynamics). None of these firms is strongly multinational in the sense that they locate significant R&D and production abroad. However, all are notable participants in collaborative aerospace projects within Europe and across the Atlantic.

3. *Food, drink and tobacco* ... The firms have long been strongly multinational, having large production bases outside the United Kingdom. (Walker, 1993: 168–9)

Walker also noted a residual indigenous capacity in *telecommunications*, and in *electrical and mechanical engineering* – though in neither case could he find a widely-based UK comparative advantage. Then, 'to the areas of indigenous capability [he] added those in which production in Britain relies heavily on foreign investment'. Two stand out:

1. *Motor vehicles* ... Ford and General Motors (Vauxhall) have had large production facilities in Britain since the 1920s (their design and R&D centres have, however, largely been moved to Germany). Ford have recently acquired Jaguar, and General Motors has acquired Lotus ... The remaining British volume-car manufacturer, Rover, [has recently been acquired by BMW] ... The automobile industry in Britain is about to experience a period of strong expansion because of the decisions by Nissan and Toyota to locate their main European production bases in northern England.

2. *Electronics* ... Companies with large manufacturing facilities in Britain include IBM, DEC and Fujitsu following its recent takeover of ICL (computers); Hitachi, Sony, Matsushita, and Toshiba (consumer electronics); Motorola, NEC and Intel (semi-conductors); and Rank Xerox and Cannon (office electronics). Scotland now has the largest concentration of semi-conductor manufacturing in Europe ('silicon glen'). In semiconductors there is no internationally significant capability remaining in British hands. (Walker, 1993: 168)

So overall – as the Select Committee on Trade and Industry confirmed in 1994,

the performance of different sectors of manufacturing, as measured by the balance of payments, has varied greatly. At the most general level, the UK is considerably more successful with capital goods (£1489 million surplus in 1991) than consumer goods (£6907 million deficit in 1991). It has had a deficit in consumer goods since the 1970s. The only manufacturing sectors with substantial surpluses in 1991 were chemicals and other transport equipment (chiefly aerospace). There are [however] areas of strength, such as medical equipment and measuring instruments, within sectors which have an overall deficit. (Select Committee, 1994: 19)

In fact one important feature of the recent weakening of UK manufacturing overall has been what the Select Committee called 'the stagnation of particular sectors'. Between 1978 and 1989 'three-quarters of the deterioration in the UK's trade balance was caused by just three sectors: motor vehicles, machinery and textiles' and 'the partial recovery since then has resulted not just from development of the UK's areas of strength but from revival in two of those sectors – motor vehicles and machinery (in both cases chiefly due to inward investment)' (*ibid.*: 20, 26).

Equipped with this information on sectoral variation, it is possible to specify with greater precision where the UK's competitive advantage now lies. In rank order it lies with '*aerospace, pharmaceuticals, food products, coal and petroleum, chemicals and mechanical engineering*' (Walker, 1993: 168) – a pattern and a ranking similar to that operating in France and the USA, but not in Japan and Germany.

The future of the problem

These sectoral differences also offer pointers to the critical issue of how overall manufacturing competitiveness is likely to develop over time. They make clear that patterns holding in one sector do not automatically apply to others; and that in consequence the future performance of UK manufacturing as a whole will be fixed by the extent to which successful sectors can flourish and unsuccessful ones regroup and reform. An analysis of the UK's industrial future therefore requires sensitivity to questions of industrial structure and to the dynamics of industrial change.

On the first of these, the Select Committee on Trade and Industry, in its 1994 report, made a number of observations on aspects of UK industrial structure, to set against structural dimensions of key competitor economies. The Select Committee reproduced data, for example, to indicate that

- in the balance between high, medium and low technology sectors, the UK's industrial profile was very similar to that of its main competitors;
- a similar balance existed when the UK was compared to other equivalent economies on the size of its low value-added and high value-added

sectors, even on its low wage and high wage sectoral distribution (though the Committee did report that 'UK industry appears to have specialised in lower unit-value items within sectors such as clothing, wood-working and food manufacturing' (Select Committee, 1994: 26);

- no similar balance, however, was found between the UK industrial structure and those of its major competitors on three other key dimensions: on the weight of defence industries in the whole (where the UK scored disproportionately high), the size of the medium-firm sector (where the UK scored low), and the involvement of UK manufacturers in the fastest growing parts of the world market (from which they seemed disproportionately to have been deflected).

The Select Committee did not make great play of these distinctions in its own analysis of economic underperformance; but other scholars have. Mike Smith, for example, (writing in 1986) explored the trade performance of industries in three broad manufacturing sectors: those with high research intensity, those with medium research intensity, and those with low research intensity. The industries to be included in each category, and their overall contribution to UK GDP, are given in Table 1.1.

Using these categories, Smith reported the following, of the situation in the mid-1980s:

High research intensity industries

Products of high research intensity industries account for half of the UK's manufactured exports and 45% of imports. The trading position has worsened in all of the constituent industries since the mid-1970s, with the exception of office and data-processing machinery ... The UK now trades at a surplus in only two such high research intensity industries – *chemicals and aerospace equipment*. Of the others, trade in motor vehicles, electrical and electronic equipment and instrument engineering have moved into deficit during the past ten years. The net result is that the level of import penetration has almost doubled since 1975.

Medium research intensity industries

This segment largely comprises the traditional engineering industries ... During the last ten years the vulnerability of the medium research intensity segment to the generally sluggish demand for industrial products has been compounded by an accelerating loss of international competitiveness. Not only was the performance of the ... segment markedly worse than the average for manufacturing as a whole, but the volume of all the individual industries, rubber and plastic products excepted, was lower in 1985 than in 1975.

Table 1.1   Output trends of manufacturing industries, 1975–85

	Annual average change	Share of GDP	
	1975–85 %	1975 %	1985 %
High research intensity			
Chemicals & allied products	2.8	2.3	2.6
Office & data-processing equipment	16.4	0.2	0.9
Electronic & electrical engineering	1.4	2.9	2.8
Motor vehicles	– 2.9	1.9	1.2
Instrument engineering	1.9	0.4	0.4
Total	**1.8**	**8.5**	**8.6**
Medium research intensity			
Basic metal industries	– 0.8	1.2	0.9
Non-metallic minerals & products	– 1.5	1.8	1.3
Finished metal products	– 2.2	2.7	1.5
Mechanical engineering	– 2.6	5.0	3.2
Shipbuilding & marine engineering	– 3.9	0.5	0.3
Rubber & plastic products	1.5	1.0	1.0
Total	**– 1.8**	**12.2**	**8.5**
Low research intensity			
Food	1.2	2.5	2.3
Drink and tobacco	0.4	1.2	1.0
Textiles & synthetic fibres	– 2.7	1.3	0.8
Clothing, footwear & leather goods	– 0.3	1.2	1.0
Timber products	– 2.1	1.0	0.7
Paper goods, printing & publishing	0.4	2.5	2.2
Total	**– 0.1**	**9.7**	**8.0**
Total manufacturing	**– 0.1**	**30.4**	**25.1**

Low research intensity industries
Most of the goods produced by low research intensity industries are demanded by individuals rather than by other industrial sectors, and include products such as food and clothing which are essential items of consumption. The demand facing most low research intensity industries has therefore been insulated to some degree from the effects of economic recession ... The UK

Table 1.2   UK trade balance by sector 1978–86 (£m)

	Exports minus imports 1978	Exports minus imports 1986	Change in balance 1978–86
Medium and high technology			
chemicals, drugs	+ 1206	+ 2306	+ 1100
electricals, electronics	+ 486	– 2183	– 2669
mech. engineering	+ 2298	+ 1725	– 573
motor vehicles	+ 311	– 4127	– 4438
aerospace	+ 237	+ 1634	+ 1397
other	+ 376	– 1332	– 1708
sub total	+ 4914	– 1977	– 6891
Low technology			
food, drink, tobacco	– 1644	– 3252	– 1608
textiles etc.	– 707	– 3289	– 2582
metals	– 400	– 652	– 252
paper and printing	– 773	– 2088	– 1315
other	– 1290	– 3071	– 1781
sub total	– 4814	– 12352	– 7538
Total	+ 100	– 14329	– 14429

trades at a deficit in all but one of the low research intensity product groups. The extent of this imbalance – as measured by the ratio of exports to imports – in 1985 was little different from a decade earlier (Smith, 1986, *passim*).

The Walker results, published nearly a decade later, are similar, though more aware than Smith's of diminishing competitiveness even in the low technology sector. He reproduced the UK trade balance by sector as in Table 1.2.

As Walker said, the 'important question in relation to Britain's recent industrial performance is, therefore, why the chemical and aerospace industries have done comparatively well, whereas the electronics and motor vehicle industries have fared badly' (Walker, 1993: 169).

Answers to that question – both explicit and otherwise – will surface regularly in the readings which follow. One, much cited, on which you might later want to reflect, is the role of government spending in sustaining the UK at the leading edge of defence production. That, after all, may tell us much about the continuing competitive weight of British Aerospace. But it will tell us little about why ICI has retained its market power; and for that story, questions of ownership, scale of production, location of R&D, and managerial strategy might tell us more.   But in both cases, we will need to be on the lookout for current trends that might yet erode the competitiveness of UK-based manufacturing industry, even in its competitive clusters.   Three in particular seem worthy of note as we begin.

1. *The shift of manufacturing overseas*.   Karel Williams and his colleagues have recently pointed to a 'hollowing out of British manufacturing' being effected by UK-based transnational companies.   As Williams *et al*. put it in 1990, 'a sample of reports from giant companies suggests that there has been a substantial shift to overseas manufacturing over the past decade' (Williams *et al.*, 1990: 461), a shift orchestrated from *within* the UK.   If they are right, we can generalise from their sample of 25 giant UK manufacturing firms, firms heavily concentrated in categories 2, 3 and 4 of the Standard Industrial Classification.   The firms they chose were BAT, ICI, Hanson, Unilever, GEC, BAe, British Steel, BICC, Pilkington, BTR, BOC, BET, Glaxo, GKN, Hawker Siddeley, Lucas, Reed International, Bowater, T and N, Ferranti, Bunzl, DRG, Delta, BBA and Simon Engineering.   Some, like ICI and Unilever, have long had large numbers of overseas employees.   Others, like British Aerospace, have very few.   But nonetheless and overall, Williams and his colleagues felt confident they could extrapolate for manufacturing as a whole from the employment patterns of these 25.   The pattern of domestic and overseas employment of these 25 companies in the 1980s is summarised in Table 1.3.

Here is clear evidence of firms shedding labour in the UK in the recession of the early 1980s, without significantly increasing their overseas payrolls; and then, as conditions eased through the decade, increasing their overseas employment without any commensurate job creation/re-creation in the UK itself.   The overall result was a roughly matching shift in numbers – down some 330,000 in the UK, up some 200,000 overseas – and overall, a relocation of productive capacity off-shore, and a shift away from a UK focus for both employment and sales.   ICI, for example, as late as 1980 had 60% of its employees based in the UK.   By 1992 that proportion had fallen to 38%, as the company reduced its reliance on UK sales from 40% to 20% of its total output (*Guardian*, 28.4.1994).   It is the hollowing out of the UK manufacturing base of this scale and kind which led Williams and his colleagues to observe in 1990:

> From a broader point of view, offshore production aggravates our social
> and national problems by stripping out British employment and exports
> in a way which leaves behind only a rump of manufacturing activity
> which is not well placed to withstand European competition.   Worse still
> ... our case studies of giant firms suggest that part of the rump is not
> manufacturing at all, while the manufacturing that does remain is

Table 1.3   Domestic   and   overseas   employment   in   25   giant   British manufacturing firms, 1979–89 (000s)

	Total	Domestic	Domestic as % of total	Overseas	Overseas as % of total
1979	1839.8	1139.9	62.0	699.9	38.0
1983	1488.6	802.0	53.9	685.6	46.1
1985	1480.8	805.8	54.4	675.0	45.6
1989	1705.2	807.2	47.3	898.1	52.7

increasingly sheltered and/or low tech ... Our conclusion indicates that with the exception of a handful of chemical and pharmaceutical companies like Glaxo and ICI, Britain no longer has any 'national champions'. There are still signboards with familiar corporate names outside the factories on the by-passes and dual carriageways, but these boards no longer signify what they did twenty years ago. (ibid.: 472)

2. The possibility of cumulative decline. Williams and his colleagues write from a position unsympathetic to the policies of the present Conservative Government. Michael Porter, whose work was mentioned earlier, wrote from a position of a more recognisably liberal-conservative kind. He looked to Thatcherism to stem the tide of what he feared might be the 'unwinding' of his often-cited 'diamond' of interlocking conditions for successful economic growth. In his view, the UK has settled in the twentieth century in the final one of his four growth stages. It had moved through a factor-driven stage, an investment-driven one and one driven by innovation, to settle in a wealth-driven stage characterised by declining motivation, eroding human resource quality and a low rate of innovation. In such a context, the danger was real that the interlocking competitive diamond would start to unwind: that, as he put it:

Britain illustrates the self-reinforcing downward spiral of the wealth driven stage. Position lost in one industry has spread to affect others. Pressures on employment have grown. A shortage of government revenues has led to budgetary pressures that have limited spending on education, R&D, and infrastructure. Falling relative average income levels have made consumer demands less advanced except for the lingering luxury segment. (Porter, 1990: 573)

This pessimism is no monopoly of the liberal Right. Across the political spectrum we find examples of this sense of the potentially cumulative nature of economic decline – a recognition, as Perry Anderson put it, that 'the logic of the market, left to itself, necessarily tends to be cumulative rather than corrective' (Anderson, 1987: 72) – and a sense of Britain now standing on the brink of a quite cataclysmic economic fall. The fear is commonplace in the relevant academic literature that the cycle of low investment, low productivity, low competitiveness and low wages will trap the UK into a subordinate and limited position in the new international division of labour now emerging to shape the post-Cold War world. This fear is of long standing, and has been given either a demand-side or a supply-side inflection, depending on the commentator's attitude to John Maynard Keynes. This was John Eatwell's specification of the demand-side fear more than a decade ago:

> the key to solving the riddle and understanding the competitive dynamism of manufacturing is now within our grasp. High growth of demand gives productivity growth which, via price and non-price factors, gives competitive success, which in turn gives high growth of demand, which gives productivity, which gives competitiveness – and so on and so on. This is the principle of cumulative causation. The system can clearly work in reverse too. Low growth of demand gives low productivity growth, which gives competitive failure, which gives low growth of demand, which gives low productivity growth ... downhill all the way. A country which grows relatively slowly will see its relative position decline as others capture its markets at home and abroad. (Eatwell, 1982: 59–60)

3. *The balance of payments constraint.* But whether demand-side constrained by stop-go policies, or supply-side generated by inadequacies of investment, there seems to be a growing sense that the UK economy has emerged into the 1990s with its manufacturing base now too small to satisfy the levels of internal demand for manufactured goods. This was John Wells's ultimate and major critique of the Thatcher years: that, on the supply side, 'domestic output of manufactures ... can be said to be broadly stationary comparing 1973 with 1979 and 1988 – with large troughs in output registered between each of these local peaks'; while on the demand side 'domestic expenditure on manufactures was roughly 30% higher in 3Q 1988 compared to 1Q 1973' (Wells, 1989: 46). The result was an economy as far as ever from being able to reconcile internal balance (a satisfactory growth rate, full employment and price stability) with external balance, an economy indeed in which 'on the import-penetration side, manufacturing's performance during the Thatcher decade [had been] simply abysmal: the ratio of imports to total manufacturing increased by 31.2% between

1979 and 1988, reflecting a rise in manufactured imports of 98.7%' (Wells, 1992: 99–100).

The scale of the problem left for any new administration from this build-up of foreign debt is now truly massive. For 1993 'the current account deficit was £10.7 billion, so that over the last five years of recession and below-trend growth the current account deficit stands cumulatively at £69.2 billion' (*Guardian*, 4.4.1994); and foreign investment by UK-based financial institutions in the same period has taken a further £106.6 billion overseas. The UK accounts have been financed only by extensive overseas borrowing – a total inflow since 1988 of £165.8 billion. This is an economy not simply in competitive decline. It is also an economy in hock. Now is the time to explore why and how that sorry state of affairs has come to be.

Part 2

Classic views

What we term 'the classic views' have been chosen and labelled in this way because of their impact on a wide range of subsequent scholarship, and because of their capacity to speak for a significant section of the academic community in their own time and place. The writings of *Andrew Shonfield* are a case in point. References to his work are scattered through what one might be termed 'social democratic' explanations of UK economic underperformance, in the work of such writers as David Marquand, John Eatwell and Sidney Pollard. Shonfield was one of the first post-war UK academics to draw attention to the adverse effects on industrial investment of high levels of defence expenditure and capital export. He stressed also the centrality of low levels of investment in manufacturing plant and equipment to the emerging pattern of post-war economic decline. He perceived quicker than most that UK living standards were beginning to slip back in relative terms, falling behind those emerging in the rest of Western Europe as well as those already evident in the United States.

Reading him now, after a gap of more than thirty years, we sense that Shonfield located some of the key policy choices that were to cost UK manufacturing industry so dear; and that because he did, much of the subsequent work by later academics has simply taken us back to where Shonfield located the problem in the 1950s. Indeed, if you did not know when Shonfield was writing, you could be forgiven for thinking that his was a contemporary commentary on UK economic difficulties and prospects. The timelessness of his argument seems to us both a testimony to the quality of Shonfield's analysis and a measure of the intractability of the problem to which that analysis was addressed.

If Andrew Shonfield is an important point of reference for Centre-Left explanations of economic underperformance that point to weaknesses of government policy and practice in the 1950s, the writings of *Eric Hobsbawm* are equally important to those Marxist writers keen to push the sources of economic weakness back to the 1890s – back to the period when UK manufacturing industry first met international competition and new modes of industrial production. A slightly longer extract from *Industry and Empire* was reproduced in Coates and Hillard (1986). A shorter extract is included here because of the essay's continuing status and importance in the academic debate on economic decline. The 'Hobsbawm thesis' is often cited as the underlying explanation of the dwindling international competitiveness of twentieth-century UK manufacturing. It is often claimed, following Hobsbawm, that UK industrial capital did not respond to the technical and commercial requirements of 'the second industrial revolution' by remodelling its productive technologies and modes of industrial organisation. Instead it retreated from industry to finance, and from world markets to imperial ones. This process allowed the UK's place as the world's leading manufacturing nation to be captured by others. From that retreat, so the argument runs, then stemmed all the weaknesses of industrial investment, capital export and military expenditure to which Shonfield, among others, drew (and continue to draw) attention.

If Hobsbawm is the most cited historian's view that has come down to us from the 1960s, *Nicholas Kaldor*'s is the most cited of the economists. His famous inaugural lecture, delivered in Cambridge in 1966, popularised the thesis of P. J. Verdoorn on the relationship between the growth of productivity and the growth of production, and emphasised the important role of manufacturing industry as the unique source of both. On Kaldor's argument, economies grow best when manufacturing activity looms large within them; and economies are dominated by their manufacturing sectors only at an intermediate stage in their transition from early industrialisation to full economic maturity. The Kaldor argument in 1966 was that part of the slowdown in the UK's post-war economic performance was thus to be expected, and would be followed by parallel slowdowns elsewhere in Western Europe as those economies also matured.

Kaldor argued that slowdown had come to the UK earlier than to continental Europe because the UK had industrialised first and was now short of the plentiful supply of displaced agricultural labour still then fuelling the 'economic miracles' of Germany, Italy and France. His immediate policy conclusion (that the UK needed to redistribute labour back into manufacturing) enjoyed a brief period of popularity and policy-influence in the 1960s, before being effectively criticised by (amongst others) Bob Rowthorn a decade later; but his prioritising of manufacturing industry as a unique source of growth survived that critique, to remain an important element in the contemporary debate on strategies for economic regeneration. Few economic discussions of the causes of underperformance in the post-war UK proceed without at least some reference to Kaldor's inaugural address; and the bulk of it is reproduced here to make its detail available to a new generation of students and scholars.

But though influential, the Kaldor thesis was never without its critics. It never persuaded *Walter Eltis*, for example, one of the two authors of the dominant Centre-Right thesis of the 1970s (the Bacon-Eltis thesis). Bacon and Eltis agreed with Kaldor that the UK lacked 'too few producers'. They just chose not to explain that lack as the product of economic maturity, preferring to anchor it in an excess of state activity. Extracts from the Bacon-Eltis thesis were reproduced in Coates and Hillard (1986); and here, as its supplement, is part of an essay produced in a 1979 book on de-industrialisation. The underlying premise of the Bacon-Eltis thesis often proved hard to locate. It was never terribly clear whether or not it was legitimate to treat state expenditure as exhaustive of the non-market activity they wished to curtail. But in the 1979 essay this dimension of their wider argument seems much clearer: that the competitive health of an industrial economy depends ultimately on the health of that part producing goods and services for sale – on the output, that is, of the 'marketed sector'. That health is then threatened by too great a concentration of resources in the hands of state employees providing services that are distributed by mechanisms other than market exchange and paid for by taxes levied on surpluses generated by marketed production and consumption elsewhere in the economy. The UK went into economic decline, Eltis argued in 1979, because the weight of the two sectors (marketed and non-marketed) shifted adversely from the 1960s, in a political climate in which Keynesian policies and trade union power combined to erode levels of manufacturing investment and competitiveness.

Walter Eltis's arguments were one powerful critique of post-war Keynesian policies that received widespread attention in the 1970s, a critique firmly rooted in the enthusiasm of neoclassical economics for market-driven systems of resource allocation. The writings of *Corelli Barnett* provided a parallel and alternative critique. Here the roots of unease were anchored differently: in a conservative and nationalist dislike of the effects of strong trade unionism and weak industrial leadership. Barnett found the origins of both in the nature of the UK's experience of early industrialisation: with the working class forced into a ghetto of social ostracism from which they came to view technical progress as threatening to their jobs and living standards; and with industrial leaders wedded to the notion that successful business activity did not require the systematic development and application of technical education and science. The 'cult of the practical man', and a public school antipathy to industry and trade, combined to block the nineteenth-century formation of an adequate system of national education, and left twentieth-century UK industry scarred by skill shortages and status tensions at every level from the shop floor to the boardroom. Not for Barnett the quick fix of curtailed government spending. What UK industrial revival required, on his argument, was the recognition (and reversal) of habits of mind laid down over more than a century of poorly led industrial growth and world power.

There is a strong historical dimension also in the extracts included here from *Mancur Olson* and *Elbaum and Lazonick*, though in neither case are they as concerned as Barnett with ruling-class attitudes and education. Olson's general thesis – published in 1982 and then rapidly adopted by opponents of corporatism – is that complex industrial societies attract to themselves strongly-rooted private interest groups. These groups – with their capacity to collude in distributional coalitions against industrial efficiency and dynamism – are at their most potent in societies whose political boundaries and central institutions have long remained undisturbed by invasion and dictatorship. On this argument, the UK, as the most stable and least invaded of all the leading European democracies, is particularly vulnerable to the stultifying effects of special interest groups. Its economic underperformance has been the direct consequence, that is, of the corporatist universe consolidated around the post-war interventionist UK state.

Elbaum and Lazonick also see the inertia of democratic institutions at work in the UK case, but root that tendency in more economic, less political, dimensions of the UK's recent past. 'Institutional rigidity' is for them a key cause of economic underperformance; but is best explained as the intelligible consequence of past economic success. Far from time *creating* new institutions and practices which then retard growth (as Olson would have it), Elbaum and Lazonick see time *bearing* old institutions and practices down into new periods to which they are no longer appropriate. The UK's contemporary economic difficulties do not lie in corporatist additions to old structures. They lie in the presence and legacy of the old structures themselves. Elbaum and Lazonick's list of legacies is long and impressive – the structures of industrial relations, industrial organisation, education systems, financial intermediation, international trade, and state–enterprise relations – all fitting together to block the capacity of twentieth-century companies and workers to modernise the country's industrial base. And among that list of legacies and constraints they also place emphasis on the consolidation of *laissez-faire* attitudes in the political culture – cultural barriers to state invention that others in this collection also prioritise as the key to economic underperformance.

We close this part with three more recently written pieces that are particularly representative of the best of the modern debate on the UK's economic problems and international decline. The argument presented by *Sir Alec Cairncross* is a typically eclectic listing of causal forces which collectively block rates of technical innovation and diffusion – and is included partly for its eclecticism and partly for its emphasis (now very fashionable) on the importance of inventing and adopting ever more sophisticated technologies of production, distribution and management. The Cairncross preference – in the search for *the* key cause of decline – is essentially a cultural one: a lack of will to win the competitive struggle, to be found in management and workers alike. *Perry Anderson*'s choice is different. His 'figures of descent' are institutions and classes – those missing agencies of modernisation which elsewhere reinforced/replaced a weak and inert industrial bourgeoisie. Banks in Germany, the state in Japan, labour unions in Sweden and Austria – all played Anderson's modernising role, to produce decades of successful private capital accumulation and rising standards of life. But the UK lacked such modernising support – its banks were otherwise engaged, its state was too liberal and imperial, its labour unions too economistic – and its industrial performance in consequence lack-lustre and outmoded. The Cairncross piece should be read as representative of much moderate thinking on industrial performance. The Anderson piece should be read as equally indicative of the drift of much Marxist thinking in this area: and both must be seen as precursors of large sections of the more detailed analysis to which we will turn in subsequent parts of this collection.

Finally, *Bob Rowthorn and John Wells* set out to explain why employment in manufacturing industry has declined so markedly in the UK since the mid-1960s. They see that decline as in principle explicable in terms of three main sets of factors: the economy's 'maturity'; its exposure to changing patterns of trade specialisation; and national economic 'failure'. They suggest that the fall in the *share* of employment in manufacturing industry in the UK was to be expected as the economy matured and trade patterns altered; but that in the UK case the low *level* of employment (both in manufacturing and across the rest of the economy) has been associated with a general weakening of the competitive position of the manufacturing base. They distinguish between a fall in the share of manufacturing in output and employment resulting from manufacturing's strength – where productivity triggers competitiveness, and allows the fall-out of labour from manufacturing to settle easily into an expanding service sector – and one resulting from manufacturing's weakness (where factories just shut because they are uncompetitive). They call the first 'positive' de-industrialisation and the second 'negative' de-industrialisation. They note the diminished competitiveness of UK-based manufacturing; and so are obliged to treat the UK case as one of 'negative' de-industrialisation, with all this implies for lower levels of service employment and general standards of life.

CHAPTER 2

Too little production[*]

Andrew Shonfield

Why does Britain's wealth grow so much more slowly than the wealth of countries on the continent of Europe? If we start at 1952, when world economic conditions returned to something like normal after the boom-and-bust following on the outbreak of the Korean War, and measure the increase in national output that has taken place since then in Britain and in the six countries who are forming the European Common Market, we get the following picture:

	Per cent increase 1952–1956
Germany	38%
Netherlands	27%
Italy	26%
France	20%
Britain	15%
Belgium and Luxembourg	13%

Looking at these figures, one can hardly be surprised that the problem of wages and prices has proved so intractable in Britain during recent years. It is not that British wages have been going up all that much faster than wages in other countries; the crucial fact is that the output of physical goods and services to match the increase in wages has been rising much more slowly. The inevitable consequence is that British prices have been tending to rise faster than elsewhere. It is the balance between the total amount of money being spent through the shops and so on and the total volume of goods and services available for sale, which determines the price level. When the first rises more than the second, the only way to keep prices down is to pull in more imports from abroad to plug the

[*] Reproduced with permission from *British Economic Policy Since the War*, Penguin, 1958.

money–goods gap. This happens with depressing regularity in post-war Britain and results each time in a balance-of-payment crisis. The usual next step after one of these crises is a policy of restriction and investment, which imposes a check on the rate of growth of industrial output. Thus the short-term remedy aggravates the long-term problem.

If the British wage earner in the 1950s has been more demanding than wage earners in other countries – and it is true that hourly earnings in this country have gone up rather faster than on the continent of Europe – the reason is not to be sought in the exceptional greed of the British working-class character, but rather in the behaviour of the price level. Since Sir Stafford Cripps's bargaining experiment with the trade unions in 1948, when they agreed to hold the wage level stable so long as the Government held the price level, a mood of acute suspicion has settled upon British labour. The representatives of labour, who are perfectly responsible men, start with the determination, when they enter into any kind of wage bargaining, that they are 'not going to be had'. 'Being had' means that the bulk of any increase in wages – sometimes the whole – is wiped out by the substantial increase in prices. After about a decade of this experience, they naturally try to insure themselves by keeping something in hand against the likelihood of a further rise in prices. It is no use telling them that in this way they merely aggravate the problem. So far as their own particular group of workers are concerned, what matters is that they have managed for a period of a few months to get a little way ahead of the rising wave of prices.

Here is a vicious circle with a vengeance: Britain's slow rate of economic growth, which is not matched by any slowness on the part of anybody to demand a rising standard of living, causes the rise in prices; this rise carried on over a period of years results in higher and higher demands for money wages; and that in turn drives up the price level further. On the other wise the remedies which are applied, with the intention of creating a psychology of restraint through the restriction of output, tend to impose a further check on the growth of British industry.

A variety of explanations have been advanced for the failure of British economic growth to keep up with the pace of the continent of Europe since the war. It has been suggested by some people that the main cause lies in the personality defects of the British working man – on the one hand his perpetual demands for ever higher wages, and on the other his alleged unwillingness to offer an honest day's work in return. The existence of this state of mind is sometimes blamed on the trade union leadership, which occupies an unusually powerful political position in this country. An alternative view is that the trouble lies in the defects of British management: a lack of sheer professional expertise among the people who are responsible for running British industry, combined with a slowness to adopt new and useful techniques as they become available. It may be that there is something in the criticism that there is an insufficient intensity of work on the part of labour or management or both in particular firms and particular sectors of British industry. The criticism can only apply to the quality of the work, not to the quantity of hours spent at work, which are longer now than they were before the war. The average working week of adult men working in British industry is scarcely any shorter than the average in Germany, and it is about seven hours longer than in the United States. There is certainly a widespread impression that more firms tolerate slacking on the job, and more men indulge in it in this country than in the other two. But such evidence as is available comes by way of example only, and it is impossible to say whether these examples are typical of the vast majority or merely a bare minority of British industry.

As to the bargaining strength and political power of the trade unions, it is true that they are greater today than they were before the war. But if the comparison is made with contemporary unions in other countries, the differences do not appear to be very significant. The Swedish trade unions for instance are not noticeably less powerful than the British, nor are the German trade unions, to take another example, markedly more reticent about asserting their demands for ever higher wages. That is not to deny that these countries have obtained big benefits in the past from the moderation shown by their trade union leaders in the immediate post-war period. This was particularly true in Germany during the early phase of reconstruction. But it should be remembered that the British trade union leaders were not wanting in a spirit of moderation during the early post-war period, either. There has been little enough of this spirit in the 1950s. But if British workers have recently shown themselves more impatient or more greedy than workers on the continent of Europe, there is one contributory cause which should not be overlooked – their standard of living has also been rising more slowly than on the continent of Europe.

Must we then, as some writers have recently been suggesting, accept it as a fact of life in the middle of the twentieth century that Britain has become an 'undynamic society'? There is no doubt that once one starts to look around with this in view, one can find plenty of signs in contemporary Britain of a lack of dynamism. The sort of thing which catches the eye is the ferocious determination to stay put, expressed in the compacts that are made by certain groups of working men, for instance in the ship-building industry, that no member of the group will earn more than an agreed maximum sum in any week. In the conditions of today in the ship-building industry this cannot conceivably be aimed at protecting anybody from being worked out of a job. It is just an automatic gesture, derived from the past, which holds up progress. Right through the economy there are the endless demarcation lines between one job and another, dividing industry into rigid compartments, in each of which a determined effort goes on to maximise costs. And behind all this is the widespread feeling that none of it matters a damn, because whatever is done things are not going to change very much anyhow.

The British trade unions attract some of the blame for fostering this undynamic way of life. Disputes about privileges, differentials, demarcation lines between trades, opposition to any redundancy resulting from improved equipment or organisation, are not of course peculiar to Britain. But they do seem to be more effective in this country than elsewhere in putting a damper on technological initiative. That generalisation must at once be qualified by reference to those industries where labour accepts changes readily and appears to have accepted fully the conjunction of high wages and high output, with the concomitant of technical change. Steel manufacture is an outstanding instance. But unfortunately such industries are still in a minority.

The missing surplus

In spite of all this, I find the attempt to explain Britain's economic failure solely by reference to a peculiar and inherent trait of the national character not very plausible. After all, a society changes its moods. The cultural atmosphere which has just been described is not, according to the historical evidence available, a permanent feature of the island. Nor does it stick to Englishmen when they go to work abroad. Moreover, it is impossible to measure in any way the economic effects of this spiritual state; if one is personally irritated by it, one may be inclined to exaggerate the material consequences. But allowing that there is a certain lack of productive vigour more in evidence in this country than elsewhere at the moment, the cause may, I think, be found in the inhibiting psychological influence of British economic conditions for some time past.

Once one looks at the ratio of capital accumulation during the 1950s in this way, there ceases to be any mystery about our poor productive record compared with the rest of Europe. Net fixed investment as a proportion of the net national product has been consistently lower here than in any of the other industrial countries.

The tendency of Britain to grow more slowly than its competitors on the continent of Europe is no new thing. It has been in evidence ever since the beginnings of the century, and even for some years before that. At first people comforted themselves with the reflection that Britain was bound to lose some of the advantages which it had gained by being first in the field of industrialisation, as other nations began to industrialise themselves. And later on, the British failure to sustain a rapid rate of economic growth was masked by the effects of two wars and a slump. Each of the two wars caused a bigger setback on the Continent than it did here. In Britain, war actually provided the missing stimulant to investment in manufacturing industry – a most powerful stimulant in some cases where expansion had previously been held back by cautious calculations of prospective profit. After the Second World War, in particular, Britain emerged with a considerably enhanced industrial capacity in the engineering industries. After both wars German industrial production fell sharply; but the rate of advance, once the recovery began, was much more rapid than in this country. Indeed, Britain's industrial record during the years of normal peacetime prosperity that we have had in this country is consistently poor. Both in 1900–14 and again in the 1920s, in the period of prosperity before the crash in 1929, British output grew at a slower pace than that of the other industrial countries in Northern and Western Europe. But Britain managed to make up for lost time in the years of the great depression in the 1930s, when the nations on the continent of Europe found the normal outlets for their exports of manufactured goods largely blocked, and entered on a period of stagnation. It was during this period, from 1929 to 1938, that British industrial output increased by one quarter. Britain's political advantage as the centre of an empire of primary producing countries, which was used to foster the development of imperial trade at a time when world commerce was shrinking, went far to compensate for the failure of the British economy to expand at a satisfactory pace in normal times. Political successes of this kind and military victory in two wars have helped to save us from some of the worst consequences of our lack of economic vigour during the first half of the twentieth century.

The evidence as it stands seems to point to the dismal conclusion that British industry as a whole is content with a slower rate of progress than is regularly achieved by other nations ... To the question why British industry has not invested more in its plant and equipment, one simple answer is that the country as a whole did not have the necessary resources available for such investment ... The truth is, then, that British investment has been held back since the war, first because the balance of payments has been weak – our foreign exchange income has barely covered our outgoings – and secondly, because the Government has chosen to reward industrial investment as the first expendable item in an emergency. It has been constantly tempted by the idea that the balance of payments should be strengthened by a deliberate policy of denying capital goods to British industry, so that more of them would be sent abroad. There has also been the more general notion that by reducing the pressure of demand at home, on critical materials like steel and on the skilled labour absorbed in investment projects, the balance of trade would tend to improve. This would follow, because imports of materials would fall as home demand slackened, while the export industries would be relieved from the strain caused by labour and material shortages. There is little doubt that the formula works pretty well as a short-term expedient. But as a piece of first aid too frequently repeated, it suffers from the same defect as a tourniquet so tightly bound that it paralyses the limb that it is intended to save ...The analysis of the causes of the failure of British investment since the war then resolves itself mainly into the question: Why is the British balance of payments weak?

The cost of defence

The greatly enlarged defence programme, which was set in motion after the outbreak of the Korean war in 1950, effectively shackled the British economy for a couple of years. Between 1950 and 1952 the size of the defence burden that had to be carried by the economy increased by over 50 per cent. Moreover, the weight was mainly concentrated on a fairly narrow and critical sector of the economy: defence production pressed hardest on the resources of the engineering industries. Thus the demands of British industrial investment, which also fell on the engineering industries, found themselves pushed two places down in the queue, with defence orders, as well as the export orders for capital goods, way up front. In these two years, which straddled the 1951 economic crisis and the recession of 1952, the national product increased in real terms by only some 4 per cent. At the same time, the proportion of the national product taken by the defence programme rose from 6 per cent to 9–10 per cent. That meant that all but a tiny fraction of the increase in Britain's wealth over this period was absorbed by the nation's military requirements. The standard of living fell slightly and industrial investment was depressed.

Thus far we have been able to identify two factors which have helped to inhibit Britain's economic development since the war. The first is specific – the exceptionally heavy burden of military expenditure; the second more general – the fact that the whole slant of the social and political set-up in Britain is not oriented towards the task of capital accumulation.

Looking back over the decade following the war, one of the strangest aspects of British politics now appears to be the mood of insouciance in which a whole series of political decisions were taken, regardless of their effect in adding to the existing overload of economic burdens on the country. The politicians, and even more of the officials responsible, just assumed grandly that a 'way would be found' of paying for the decisions that were being taken in the interest of the nation. It was all very much like the wartime mood, extended without any sense of inappropriateness into peacetime conditions. It lasted right into the middle 1950s. The first clear signs of a change came after the Suez incident in 1956. Before this the calculation of costs tended to be the last thing which was considered in approaching an important political decision. The slogan was always: 'Of course we can afford it; it means so little, if only everyone will make the effort'.

It is when the actual content of the big rearmament programme of 1950–51 is examined more closely that the doubts begin to assert themselves with some force. One of the reasons why the burden on the British engineering industry was so heavy was the insistence of the Government on the need to manufacture itself, according to its own specifications, practically the whole range of arms and equipment required by the British services. It is, of course, natural for any great power to want to do precisely this. If it has to rely on another country for the supply of an essential piece of armament, it is no longer completely free to manoeuvre in a crisis. It has lost some part of its sovereign power.

In the mood of the early post-war period, which lasted into the 1950s, no economic considerations that anyone could have put forward would have persuaded a British Government, Labour or Conservative, to accept such a loss. It was, after all, the Labour Government which set off on the expensive business of making its own atomic bomb; and it had no qualms about hiding away the money being spent on this project in various obscure corners of the official estimates, so that there was no accountability to Parliament for the venture that had been undertaken. No one could seriously grumble at that, given the assumptions on which British policy was based; such clandestine activity was among the necessary amenities of a great power determined to keep ahead in the arms race ...

I am not suggesting that this national pride was reprehensible or stupid. It would be asking an enormous lot from any nation which had just emerged victorious from the greatest war in history to understand straightaway, and accept the fact without a struggle, that since the emergence of the two colossi, Russia and the United States, the ideal of military self-sufficiency for any lesser power had become an illusion. Certainly, it was inconceivable from the beginning that Britain would engage on an atomic war of its own. Yet the delusion of grandeur led Britain not only to manufacture the bomb independently, but also to spend huge sums of money on developing the 'V' bombers capable of delivering it on a Russian target. The only serious argument that I have heard used to justify these endeavours is that the weapons provide something to brandish at the Americans, when they are not taking sufficient notice of the British views. Having the bomb would in the last resort make it possible for Britain to commit the Americans to fighting a war which they would otherwise be reluctant to undertake. The alternative for them would be to stand by and see their most powerful ally ruined. Even if there were something to be gained in this way – which I doubt – it could hardly be enough to justify an economic policy which is in the long run suicidal for Britain.

UK investment overseas

History once again is the greatest impediment to clear thinking on the subject of British investment overseas. The words themselves have a subtly pleasing and adventurous sound. One way or another it has gone pretty deep into the folk myth that British greatness and wealth have depended on pouring out our treasure abroad, rather than hoarding it at home. And ordinary people go on believing that this kind of investment in underdeveloped countries is a most profitable form of exploitation, giving Britain economic benefits which are not open to nations that do not have access to such virgin territories. Thus has Marx triumphed. The popular attitude is a combination of shame at making such large profits out of black men and of a desire to make some more – so long as this can be done without being morally embarrassing. The instinctive reaction of most Englishmen to the thesis which I am going to put forward here – that the British economy is robbed of necessary nourishment, that its growth is stunted, as a result of this too vigorous pursuit of overseas investment – would almost certainly be to dismiss it as hopelessly eccentric.

This was also the situation in Britain during part of the nineteenth century. It is probable that even then too little was being devoted to investment in the productive equipment of British industry and too much development of resources abroad. But this development abroad did bring other important indirect benefits to Britain by lowering the cost of its imports of food and raw materials. No similar commercial principle operates nowadays. In the middle of the twentieth century it is a straight choice for Britain between home investment and foreign investment. Home investment is constantly curbed in the interests of the balance of payments. And it is the capital element in the British balance of payments, of which foreign investment is the most important, which changes a handsome surplus on current account into a deficit on our external accounts as a whole, eating away at our gold and dollar reserves and bringing with it an atmosphere of constant anxiety and crisis. At the least, this is bound to produce a mood of national niggardliness – and guilt. We find ourselves constantly compelled to put up our interest rates and restrict credit, in order to fend off would-be borrowers of sterling, or to induce nervous foreigners to keep their money here – and we succeed in inhibiting the growth of our own industries. In the end we come to feel that we can afford as a nation none of the little things that we want, and so we become ashamed of wanting them.

The central failure of post-war Britain is inadequate investment. So many of our difficulties flow from this. Because our wealth grows more slowly than the wealth of other countries, our prices rise faster; industrial relations have grown strained, and now many people have come to be positively afraid of full employment. The Government's policies in both home and external affairs are constantly restricted by penury; the balance of payments is like a raw and exposed nerve: with the first breath of adversity the economy is wracked and convulsed. It is bad for the spirit of any country to live with so little room for manoeuvre. There is a noticeable meanness of attitude in the official British approach to the arts, to public buildings, to almost any kind of cultural activity. The terror of making any kind of splash with public money eventually robs the community of major pleasures. It has been pointed out that whereas the Arts Council in this country spends altogether about £1m a year on the public patronage of drama, opera, ballet, music and touring art exhibitions, the small German province of Hesse, with a population of 4 million and not exceptionally liberal-minded in its budgeting, spends £700,000 of public money on its theatres alone. For West Germany as a whole, the expenditure of public money on the arts per head of the population, works out at about nine times as much as the corresponding figure in this country ...

It is the spiritual consequences of living in a country with a slow rate of growth which are most worrying in the long run. It is a great depressive to live in a constant atmosphere of 'make do', to exist in a place where almost any effort to do anything or to go anywhere leads you pretty soon into a bottle-neck of some kind. The way to escape from this situation is by a determined effort to get a lot richer, and to do it quickly. The first move must be to step up the rate of productive investment sharply, and then to use part of the additional wealth accruing in order to keep the volume of investment up to this higher level ...

There have been two occasions since the war which might have served as an opportunity to do precisely this. The first was the American £1,000m loan in 1946, and the second was the Marshall Plan, under which Britain received a further large sum in dollars from 1948 to 1950. If all this money had been absorbed into investment and so transformed into an addition to the country's productive capacity, the British industrial dynamic might well have been on the scale of Germany in the 1950s. But in fact – and for quite respectable reasons – the money which the Americans provided was deliberately turned to serve other ends. Britain's international obligations particularly in the sterling area, Britain's desire to free itself from independence on any form of external aid at the earliest possible moment, regardless of the level of output and growth, Britain's military obligations and the need felt to fulfil them as an absolutely independent sovereign power – all contributed to the result.

The essential truth which has to be faced is that Britain's failure to grow at an adequate pace since the war flows largely from a series of *political* decisions. It is not that these political choices were necessarily wrong – though we did see earlier that on more than one occasion, reasons of state were extended to cover some pretty narrow nationalist motives – the real complaint is that nobody bothered to count the true economic cost of international commitments which carried a traditional stamp. There was no one to remind the Government that, for example, the maintenance of our extensive overseas garrisons meant that British exports had to be boosted, to meet the foreign exchange cost, by the sale of machinery and equipment abroad, which was badly needed at home – and to ask whether it was, after all, desirable to slow down our rate of industrial growth in this way. Similarly, nobody stopped to inquire into the wisdom of the sterling area arrangement, and above all into the system of the open door for British capital going overseas, while it was being closely restricted at home. These, and many other things like them, were part of the accepted pattern of life; they were not, until recently, subjected to the test of rational query by people in the universities or by writers of books and learned articles – least of all by the politicians. Surprisingly, one is driven to the conclusion that the failure of British policy is, in large part, intellectual weakness – a failure of the spirit of inquiry.

CHAPTER 3

The beginnings of decline[*]

Eric Hobsbawm

Since the Industrial Revolution the transformation of industry has become
continuous, but every now and then the cumulative results of these changes
become so obvious that observers are tempted to talk about a 'second' industrial
revolution. The last decades of the nineteenth century were such a time. And the
break appeared all the greater, because the earlier phase of industrialism had been
unusually and visibly archaic, and because Britain, its pioneer, apparently
remained wedded to this archaic pattern, while other and newer industrial
economies did not.

The first and in the long run most profound change was in the role of science
in technology ... The second major change was less revolutionary. It simply
consisted in the systematic extension of the factory system – the systematic
organisation of mass-production by means of the planned flow of processes and
the 'scientific management' of labour; the third major change is closely connected
with the second: it consisted of the discovery that the largest potential market
was to be found in the rising incomes of the mass of the working citizens in
economically developed countries ... The last major change was the increase in
the *scale* of economic enterprise, the concentration of production and ownership,
the rise of an economy composed of a handful of great lumps of rock – trusts,
monopolies, oligopolies – rather than a large number of pebbles ... However
strongly the winds of change blew elsewhere, as soon as they crossed the Channel
to Britain they grew sluggish. In every one of the four aspects of the economy
we have just sketched, Britain fell behind her rivals; and this was all the more
striking, not to say painful, when these occupied fields which Britain had herself
been the first to plough before abandoning them. This sudden transformation of
the leading and most dynamic industrial economy into the most sluggish and
conservative, in the short space of thirty or forty years (1860–90/1900), is the
crucial question of British economic history. After the 1890s we may ask why so
little was done to restore the dynamism of the economy, and we may blame the

---

[*] Reproduced with permission from *Industry and Empire*, Weidenfeld and Nicolson, 1968.

41

generations after 1890 for not doing more, for doing the wrong things, or even for making the situation worse. But essentially these are discussions about bringing the horse back into the stable after it has gone. It went between the middle of the century and the 1890s.

The contrast between Britain and more modern industrial states is particularly striking in the new 'growth-industries', and it becomes even more marked when we compare their very feeble performance with the achievements of British industry in those branches in which the archaic structure and technique could still produce the best results. The chief of these was shipbuilding, the last and one of the most triumphant assertions of British supremacy. During the age of the traditional wooden sailing ship Britain had been a great, but by no means unchallenged, producer. Indeed her weight as a shipbuilder had been due not to her technological superiority, for the French designed better ships and the USA built much better ones; as witness the almost consistent triumphs of American sailing ships from the famous grain races of the 'clippers' to the yacht races between millionaire syndicates of our own day. Between American independence and the outbreak of the Civil War American shipbuilding expanded at a far faster rate, gained upon British shipbuilding steadily, and had by 1860 almost caught it up. British shipbuilders benefited rather because of the vast weight of Britain as a shipping and trading power and the preference of British shippers (even after the abrogation of the Navigation Acts, which protected the industry heavily) for native ships. The real triumph of the British shipyards came with the iron and steel steamship. As the rest of British industry fell behind, they drew ahead: in 1860 British tonnage had been a little larger than American, six times as large as the French, eight times as large as the German; in 1890 it was over twice as large as the American tonnage, ten times as large as the French, and still roughly eight times as large as the German.

Now none of the advantages of modern productive technique and organisation applied to ships, which were built in giant single units, of largely unstandardised materials and with a vast input of the most varied and highest manual skills. They were no more mechanised than palaces. On the other hand the advantages of specialisation in small units were immense, for they achieved, in effect, what the systematic subdivision of processes now does in giant firms, and what could certainly not then have been achieved any other way in the construction of such complex products. Moreover, they multiplied the possibilities and minimised the costs of technical innovation. A specialised marine engineering firm in a competitive market had every incentive to produce better engines, nor would the process of shipbuilding be held up because the firms specialising in ships' plumbing were not keeping pace with their own innovations. It was not until after the Second World War, when the technical advantages of integration had become much more decisive, that British shipbuilding lost its lead.

In the growth-industries of the scientific-technological type and where integration and large-scale production paid off, the story was sadly different. Britain pioneered the chemical industry and the invention of aniline dyes, though even in the 1840s already partly on the basis of German academic chemistry. But by 1913 we accounted for only eleven per cent of world output (as against thirty-four per cent for the USA, twenty-four per cent for Germany), while the Germans exported twice as much as we did and – most significant of all – supplied the British home market with ninety per cent of its synthetic dyes. And what there was of the British chemical industry rested largely on the enterprise of immigrant foreigners, such as the firm of Brunner-Mond, which later became the nucleus of Imperial Chemical Industries.

Electro-technics were, both in theory and in practice, a pioneer achievement of the British. Faraday and Clerk Maxwell laid its scientific foundations, Wheatstone (of the electric telegraph) first made it possible for the Victorian father in London to discover immediately whether or not his daughter had eloped to Boulogne with 'the tall handsome man with the dark moustache and military cloak' (to quote an illustration of the benefits of this invention in a contemporary technical handbook). Swann began to think about a carbon-filament incandescent lamp in 1845, two years before Edison was born. Yet by 1913 the output of the British electrical industry was little more than a third of the German, its exports barely half. And once again, it was the foreigners who invaded Britain. Much of the domestic industry was initiated and controlled by foreign capital – mainly American, such as Westinghouse – and when in 1905 the London underground was to be electrified and the first 'tube' constructed, the enterprise and finance were largely American ...

The saddest case was perhaps that of the iron and steel industry, for we see it losing its pre-eminence at the very moment when its role in the British economy was greatest, and its dominance in the world most unquestioned. Every major innovation in the manufacture of steel came from Britain or was developed in Britain: Bessemer's converter (1856), which first made the mass-production of steel possible, the Siemens-Martin open-hearth furnace (1867), which greatly increased productivity, and the Gilchrist-Thomas basic process (1877–8), which made it possible to use an entire range of new ores for steel manufacture. Yet, with the exception of the converter, British industry was slow to apply the new methods – Gilchrist-Thomas benefited the Germans and French far more than his countrymen – and they utterly failed to keep up with subsequent improvements. Not only did British production fall behind that of Germany and the USA in the early 1890s, but also British productivity. By 1910 the USA produced almost twice as much basic steel alone as the total steel production of Great Britain.

Why all this was so has been much debated. Clearly, the British did not adapt to new circumstances. They could have done so. There is no reason why British technical and scientific education should have remained negligible, in a period when a wealth of rich amateur scientists and privately endowed research laboratories or of practical experience in production clearly no longer compensated for the virtual absence of university education and the feebleness of formal technological training. There was no compelling reason why Britain in 1913 had only nine thousand university students compared to almost sixty thousand in Germany, or only five day students per ten thousand (in 1900) compared to almost thirteen in the USA; why Germany produced three thousand graduate engineers per year while in England and Wales only 350 graduated in *all* branches of science, technology and mathematics with first- and second-class honours, and few of these were qualified for research. There were plenty of people throughout the nineteenth century to warn the country of the dangers of its educational backwardness; there was no shortage of funds, and certainly no lack of suitable candidates for technical and higher training.

It was no doubt inevitable that British pioneer industries should lose ground relatively as the rest of the world industrialised, and that their rate of expansion should decline; but this purely statistical phenomenon need not have been accompanied by a genuine loss of impetus and efficiency. Still less was it predetermined that Britain should fail in industries in which she started with the arguable disadvantages neither of the older pioneer, nor of the late-comer, but substantially at the same time and point as the rest. There are economies whose lag can be explained by purely material weakness: they are too small, their resources too scarce, their supply of skills too meagre. Britain clearly was not one of them, except in the vague sense that any country of her size and population had, in the long run, more limited possibilities of economic development than much vaster and richer countries like the USA or the USSR; but certainly not significantly more limited possibilities than the Germany of 1870.

Britain then failed to adapt to new conditions, not because she could not, but because she did not wish to. The question is, why not?

The commonest, and probably best, economic explanation of the loss of dynamism in British industry is that it was the result ultimately of the early and long-sustained start as an industrial power. It illustrates the deficiencies of the private-enterprise mechanism in a number of ways. Pioneer industrialisation naturally took place in special conditions which could not be maintained, with methods and techniques which, however advanced and efficient at the time, could not remain the most advanced and efficient, and it created a pattern of both production and markets which would not necessarily remain the one best fitted to sustain economic growth and technical change. Yet to change from an old and obsolescent pattern to a new one was both expensive and difficult. It was expensive because it involved both the scrapping of old investments still capable of yielding good profits, and new investments of even greater initial cost; for as a general rule newer technology is more expensive technology. It was difficult because it would almost certainly require agreement to rationalise between a large number of individual firms or industries, none of which could be certain precisely where the benefit of rationalisation would go, or even whether in undertaking it they were not giving away their money to outsiders or competitors. So long as satisfactory profits were to be made in the old way, and so long as the decision to modernise had to emerge from the sum-total of decisions by individual firms, the incentive to do so would be weak. What is more, the general interest of the economy would very likely be lost sight of.

[Even] the Great Depression was, alas, not great enough to frighten British industry into really fundamental change. The reason for this was that the traditional methods of making profits had as yet not been exhausted, and provided a cheaper and more convenient alternative to modernisation – for a while. To retreat into her satellite world of formal or informal colonies, to rely on her growing power as the hub of international lending, trade and settlements, seemed all the more obvious a solution because, as it were, it presented itself. The clouds of the 1880s and early 1890s lifted, and what lay before the eye were the shining pastures of cotton exports to Asia, steam-coal exports to the world's ships, Johannesburg gold-mines, Argentine tramways and the profits of City merchant banks. In essence, what happened, therefore, was that Britain exported her immense accumulated historic advantages in the underdeveloped world, as the greatest commercial power, and as the greatest source of international loan capital; and had, in reserve, the exploitation of the 'natural protection' of the home market and if need be the 'artificial protection' of political control over a large empire. When faced with a challenge, it was easier and cheaper to retreat into an as yet unexploited part of one of these favoured zones rather than to meet competition face to face. Thus the cotton industry merely continued its traditional policy when in trouble, of escaping from Europe and North America into Asia and Africa; leaving its former markets to the exporters of British textile-machinery, which made up a quarter of all the country's rapidly increasing machinery exports. In so far as they exported, British coal flowed rapidly in the wake of the British steamship and the vast merchant fleet. Iron and steel relied on the Empire and the underdeveloped world, like cotton: by 1913 Argentina and India alone bought more British iron and steel exports than the whole of Europe, Australia alone more than twice as much as the USA. In addition, the steel industry tended – like coal – to rely increasingly on the protection of the home market.

The British economy as a whole tended to retreat from industry into trade and finance, where our services reinforced our actual and future competitors, but made very satisfactory profits. Britain's annual investments abroad began actually to *exceed* her net capital formation at home around 1870. What is more, increasingly the two became alternatives, until in the Edwardian era we see domestic investment falling almost without interruption as foreign investment rises. In the great boom (1911–13) which preceded the First World War, twice as much, or even more, was invested abroad than at home; and it has been argued – and is indeed not unlikely – that the amount of domestic capital formation in the twenty-five years before 1914, so far from being adequate for the modernisation of the British productive apparatus, was not even quite sufficient to prevent it from slightly running down.

Britain, we may say, was becoming a parasitic rather than a competitive economy, living off the remains of world monopoly, the underdeveloped world, her past accumulations of wealth and the advance of her rivals.

CHAPTER 4

The causes of slow growth[*]

Nicholas Kaldor

The purpose of my lecture is to suggest an alternative approach which seeks to explain the recorded differences in growth rates in terms of the *stage* of economic development attained by different countries rather than in the realm of personal (or rather individual) abilities or incentives. Put briefly, the contention that I intend to examine is that fast rates of economic growth are associated with the fast rate of growth of the 'secondary' sector of the economy – mainly the manufacturing sector – and that this is an attribute of an intermediate stage of economic development: it is the characteristic of the transition from 'immaturity' to 'maturity'; and that the trouble with the British economy is that it has reached a high stage of 'maturity' *earlier* than others, with the result that it has exhausted the potential for fast growth before it had attained particularly high levels of productivity or real income per head. The meaning of the term 'maturity' will, I hope, become evident in the course of this lecture; it is mainly intended to denote a state of affairs where real income per head has reached broadly the same level in the different sectors of the economy.

On this diagnosis the basic trouble with the British economy is that it suffers from 'premature maturity'. This may sound no less pessimistic a conclusion than the alternative view which attributes our failures to some basic deterioration in the national character – such as working too little, spending too much, too little initiative, vitality or incentive – but at least has the advantage that if the diagnosis were correct, and if it came to be generally accepted, steps could be taken to ameliorate the situation through instruments more powerful than mere exhortation ...

Let us then begin with the evidence. If we take the industrially advanced countries for which figures are available, we find that there is a very high correlation between the rate of growth of the gross domestic product and the rate of growth of manufacturing production, and what is more significant, we find that

---

[*] Reproduced with permission from *Causes of the Slow Rate of Economic Growth of the United Kingdom*, Cambridge University Press, 1966.

the faster the overall rate of growth, the greater is the *excess* of the rate of growth of manufacturing production over the rate of growth of the economy as a whole ...

Assuming, for the moment, that this relationship exists, is there some general hypothesis which is capable of explaining it? ... There is a possible explanation – the existence of economics of scale, or increasing returns, which causes productivity to increase in response to, or as a by-product of, the increase in total output.   That manufacturing activities are subject to the 'law of increasing returns' was of course a well-known contention of the classical economists.   One finds the origin of this doctrine in the first three chapters of the *Wealth of Nations*.   Here Adam Smith argued that the *return* per unit of labour – what we now call productivity – depends on the division of labour; on the extent of specialisation and the division of production into so many different processes, as exemplified by his famous example of pin-making.   As Smith explained, the division of labour depends on the extent of the market: the greater the market, the greater the extent to which differentiation and specialisation is carried, the higher the productivity.   Neo-classical writers, with one or two famous exceptions, like Marshall and Allyn Young, tended to ignore or to underplay this phenomenon.   As Hahn and Matthews (1964: 833) remarked in a recent article 'the reason for the neglect is no doubt the difficulty of fitting increasing returns into the prevailing framework of perfect competition and marginal productivity factor pricing'.

However, Adam Smith, like both Marshall and Allyn Young after him, emphasised the interplay of static and dynamic factors in causing returns to increase with an increase in the scale of industrial activities.   A greater division of labour is more productive, partly because it generates more skill and know-how; more expertise in turn yields more innovations and design improvements.   We cannot isolate the influence of the economies of large-scale production due to indivisibilities of various kinds, and which are in principle reversible, from such changes in technology associated with a process of expansion which are not reversible.   Learning is the product of experience – which means, as Arrow (1962) has shown, that productivity tends to grow faster, the faster output expands; it also means that the *level* of productivity is a function of cumulative output (from the beginning) rather than of the rate of production per unit of time.

In addition, as Allyn Young emphasised, increasing returns is a 'macro phenomenon' – just because so much of the economies of scale emerge as a result of increased differentiation, the emergence of new processes and new subsidiary industries, they cannot be 'discerned adequately by observing the effects of variations in the size of an individual firm or of a particular industry'.   At any one time, there are industries in which economies of scale may have ceased to be important.   They may nevertheless benefit from a general industrial expansion which, as Young said, should be 'seen as an interrelated whole'.   With the extension of the division of labour 'the representative firm, like the industry of which it is a part, loses its identity' (Young, 1928: 538–9).

This, in my view, is the basic reason for the empirical relationship between the growth of productivity and the growth of production which has recently come to be known as the 'Verdoorn Law' in recognition of P. J. Verdoorn's early investigations, published in 1949. It is a dynamic rather than a static relationship – between the rates of change of productivity and of output, rather than between the *level* of productivity and the *scale* of output – primarily because technological progress enters into it, and is not just a reflection of the economies of large-scale production.

I am not suggesting that the Verdoorn relationship applies *only* to manufacturing activities or that it applies to every manufacturing industry considered separately. But its application outside the industrial field is clearly far more limited. It certainly does not apply, on the evidence of the statistics, to agriculture and mining, where the growth of productivity has been much greater than the growth in production and where, in so far as any definite relation is shown, productivity growth and employment growth tend to be negatively related, not positively. This supports the classical contention that these are 'diminishing returns' industries: the fact that this is overlaid by technological progress or the adoption of more capital intensive methods may statistically conceal this, but it does not eliminate its significance. In some of the countries the relatively high rate of growth of productivity in agriculture is merely the passive consequence of the absorption of surplus labour in secondary and tertiary occupations, and not necessarily a reflection of true technological progress or of higher capital investment per unit of output ...

There remains the tertiary sector, services, comprising such divergent items as transport, distribution, banking and insurance, catering and hotels, laundries and hairdressers, and professional services of the most varied kind, publicly and privately provided – which together account for 40–50 per cent or more of the total output and employment of the advanced countries. Over much of this field learning by experience must clearly play a role but economies of scale are not nearly so prominent and are exhausted more quickly. In the case of activities like research or education, the Adam-Smithian principle of the advantages of specialisation and of the division of labour must operate in the same sort of way as in industrial activities. But precisely in these fields it cannot be directly reflected in the estimates of productivity, since 'output' cannot be measured independently of 'input'. In some fields in which output can be measured independently – as, for example, in transport and communications – statistical evidence shows no correlation between productivity growth and production growth. In yet others such as distribution, productivity – meaning sales per employee – tends to grow faster the faster the rise in aggregate turnover; but in this case, it is merely a reflection of the changing incidence of excess capacity generated by imperfect competition, and not of true economies of scale. In other words, productivity may rise in automatic response to the rise in consumption caused by the growth of production in the primary or secondary sectors – just as the productivity of the milkman doubles, without any technological change, when he leaves two bottles of milk outside each door instead of one bottle.

It is the rate of growth of manufacturing production (together with the ancillary activities of public utilities and construction) which is likely to exert a dominating influence on the overall rate of economic growth: partly on account of its influence on the rate of growth of productivity in the industrial sector itself, and partly also because it will tend, indirectly, to raise the rate of productivity growth in other sectors. This will happen, or may happen, both in agriculture and in the distributive trades – in the first because it induces a faster rate of absorption of surplus labour; in the second because it secures a faster increase in the through-put of goods into consumption. And of course it is true more generally that industrialisation accelerates the rate of technological change throughout the economy.

It remains to deal with the question of why it is that some countries manage to increase their rate of manufacturing production so much faster than others. The explanation, in my view, lies partly in demand factors and partly in supply factors, and both of these combine to make fast rates of growth the characteristic of an intermediate stage in economic development.

The actual course of development may at any stage be slowed down, or interrupted by supply constraints; and as I shall argue presently, it is inevitable that sooner or later the rhythm of development should be slowed down on account of them ... Such supply constraints can take one of two forms: commodities or labour. As the industrial sector expands, it absorbs growing amounts of commodities (and services) produced outside the manufacturing sector: such as food and industrial materials produced by the primary sector (agriculture and mining); manufactured goods which it does not provide itself, or not in sufficient quantities and on which it is dependent on imports – this is probably relatively more important in the earlier stages of industrialisation, but as post-war experience has shown, there is a very large scope, even among the industrially highly developed countries, for trade in manufactured goods for industrial use, both finished goods and components. Finally, industrial growth generates demand for services of numerous kinds – like banking and insurance, lawyers, accountants and so on – and is thus responsible, in part at any rate, for the fast expansion of the 'tertiary' sector. (Also, the growing use of durable consumer goods sets up a growing demand for repair and maintenance services.)

For an *individual* country – though not for the group of industrialised countries together – a commodity constraint generally takes the form of a balance of payments constraint: it arises because a particular rate of growth generates a rate of growth of imports which exceeds the rate of growth of exports. This is certainly true of countries in the early stages of industrialisation when the growth of industry, despite import-substitution, causes a substantial rise in *total* import requirements; at a stage when the industrial development adds little, if anything, to the country's export potential. But it is also suggested that it may slow down the rate of growth of industrially advanced economies; and it is a widely held view that it has been a major constraint on the post-war economic growth of Britain.

The important question is whether, *apart* from balance of payments constraints, it would have been possible to increase our manufacturing output at a faster rate. Was the growth in production mainly governed by the growth in demand for manufactured products, or was it governed by supply-constraints, which would have frustrated a higher rate of growth of output, irrespective of the growth in demand?

And here we come back to the labour situation and to Verdoorn's Law. This, as we have seen, suggests that a higher rate of growth of manufacturing output breeds higher rates of productivity growth, but not enough to obviate the need for a faster rate of growth of employment. In post-war Britain periods of faster growth in manufacturing industry invariably led to severe labour shortages which slowed down the growth of output and which continued for some time after production reached its cyclical peak – in fact, on almost every occasion, employment continued to rise after output had begun to fall. All this suggests that a higher rate of growth could not have been maintained unless more manpower had been made available to the manufacturing industry.

Indeed all historical evidence suggests that a fast rate of industrial growth has invariably been associated with a fast rate of growth of employment in both the secondary and the tertiary sectors of the economy. The main source of this labour has not been the growth of the working population, nor even immigration, but the reservoir of surplus labour, or 'disguised unemployment' on the land. In the course of industrialisation there has been a continuous transfer of labour from the countryside to the urban areas in the course of which the percentage of the labour force in agriculture diminishes in a dramatic fashion. But the *longer* this process proceeds, the *smaller* the labour force remaining, the *less* it yields in terms of manpower availabilities in the secondary and tertiary sectors. Moreover, the process of transfer is bound to come to a halt once the gap between agricultural and industrial productivity is eliminated, and thus becomes fully reflected in relative earnings. The United Kingdom, almost alone among the advanced countries, has reached the position where net output per head in agriculture is as high as in industry; though there is still a wide gap in relative wages which, I think, is mainly due to the fact that the fall in the demand for agricultural labour, owing to mechanisation, has outrun, over the last ten years, the rate of diminution in the agricultural labour force.

Britain, having started the process of industrialisation earlier than any other country, has reached 'maturity' much earlier – in the sense that it has attained a distribution of the labour force between the primary, secondary and tertiary sectors at which industry can no longer attract the labour it needs by drawing on the labour reserves of other sectors. There are disadvantages of an early start, as well as advantages – as is shown by the fact that some of the latecomers of industrialisation have attained higher levels of industrial efficiency even before they became fully industrialised.

But once it is recognised that manpower shortage is the main handicap from which we are suffering, and once our thinking becomes adjusted to this, we shall, I hope, tend to concentrate our efforts on a more rational use of manpower in *all* fields.

CHAPTER 5

Too few producers*

Walter Eltis

All economies have a sector which produces a surplus off which the rest of the economy lives. This is one of the oldest propositions in economics. It has always been understood that if the surplus is large, the economy will be able to support strong but unproductive armed forces and an extensive state establishment which meet their material needs from the extra output of agriculture, industry and commerce. If the surplus is small, the country cannot afford to employ many non-producers and if it attempts to finance them, it will push taxation to the point where agriculture, industry and commerce fail to function as they should. Their output will fall and tax revenues with it and governments will then find it increasingly difficult to finance their spending. If they push up rates of taxation as their surplus producing sectors decline, they will put these under increasing pressure and force cuts in output and employment until the conflict between the demands of government and the needs of the sector of the economy which must finance it becomes intolerable. An economic crisis then results characterised by rapid and accelerating inflation, growing unemployment, and a cessation of growth.

The surplus creating sector of economies is the market sector. This is because marketed output – output which is sold – must supply a nation's entire export needs since all exports are marketed. In addition, capital equipment is always sold to firms so all physical investment goods must come from the market sector. Finally, all the consumer goods and services which are bought privately are marketed. Hence the marketed output of industry, agriculture and services taken together must supply the total private consumption, export and investment needs of all nations.

Much marketed output is required by those who produce none. The armed forces, policemen, dustmen and pensioners all produce no marketed output. They eat and require clothing and housing and most drive cars and work in

---

* Reproduced with permission from 'How public sector growth can undermine the growth of national product', in W. Beckerman (ed.), *Slow Growth In Britain*, Oxford University Press, 1979.

buildings which have to be constructed and maintained. These are all marketed goods and they must be provided by the workers of the market sector, or obtained through international trade from the market sectors of other economies. Thus the market sector must produce marketed output in excess of its own needs to provide for all the requirements of those in the non-market sector. The market sector must therefore provide a surplus and the non-market sector lives off that surplus.

The transfer of resources from the market to the non-market sector is most efficiently achieved through the tax system. The market sector pays taxes and the non-market sector lives off the revenues obtained. Market sector employment is therefore self-financing and the ultimate source of all tax revenues, while non-market employment is tax-financed. If the budget is balanced, the aggregate taxes paid in the market sector will equal the *net* taxes required to finance the non-market sector.

The market sector includes government controlled companies which market their output as well as privately owned corporations, and government companies can finance social services from the taxes derived from their surpluses (provided they earn them) in basically the same way as privately owned companies. The vital borderline is therefore not the traditional one between the public and private sectors. Instead the vital distinction is between the self-financing companies in the *public and private* sectors which market their output, and the tax-financed non-market sector which the market sector finances through the taxes that companies and their employees pay.

Where governments finance their spending through deficits instead of taxation, the position is basically similar. Here part of the non-market sector may be financed through the voluntary savings of the market sector workers who buy government securities which allow the state to spend. Alternatively, the state finances some of the spending of the non-market sector through the printing press. The latter has the same effect as a *tax* on all cash holdings. If printing money raises prices 10 per cent, market sector workers with cash of £100 will find they can only buy real goods and services which used to be worth £90. The other £10 their cash can no longer buy can then go to soldiers, pensioners and civil servants. Ultimately therefore, the great bulk of the non-market sector is tax-financed, whether the budget is balanced or not, but the tax will be an inflation tax on cash balances rather than a more obvious method of taxation where governments have to resort to the printing press because regular taxes will not suffice to finance non-market spending.

How smooth growth to a larger non-market sector can be achieved

The fact that the market sector ultimately finances the non-market sector does not mean that it is more important to the well-being of a society. Welfare and civilisation depend on the efficiency of agriculture, industry and commerce, and equally on the effectiveness of education, health services, welfare systems, crime prevention and much more that is not bought and sold ... The fact that a growing share of resources to the non-market sector makes economic and social sense does not mean that the rule that the non-market sector must be financed from the surplus of the market sector can be broken. This rule must always be followed by any society which seeks to avoid economic breakdown. A failure to finance the non-market sector from the surplus of the market sector can only result in balance of payments collapse as efforts are made to use the resources of foreigners to provide what a population is unwilling to pay for, or physical shortages of capital as a society consumes its seed-corn in the form of extra social services, and so fails to maintain the employment creating capacity of its capital stock ...

The principal condition which must be fulfilled if a continuous transfer of resources from the market to the non-market sector of the kind illustrated is to be achieved is that the increase in taxation should be realised without damage to the underlying structure of production in the economy. What this requires is that extra taxation should be paid without damaging those economic activities which finance necessary imports and the capital investment which is indispensable to growth and long-term job creation. Taxation must therefore be paid from the surplus of the market sector and not with the economy's seed-corn. If extra taxation leads to the substitution of public for private *consumption*, there can be no damage to the underlying structure of production. Workers produce for the non-market sector what they would otherwise produce for the market sector, and the government allocates what would otherwise be distributed by market forces. As private consumption forgone pays for extra public consumption, there is no damage to the balance of payments or to investment in job creation and growth. The economy can, therefore, grow as fast, provide as many jobs, and pay for the same imports, but services are given away which would otherwise be paid for, including pension rights which would otherwise require private insurance policies.

For this transfer from private consumption to the 'social wage' to be achieved, workers must either acquiesce in the continuous increase in rates of taxation that is needed or alternatively governments must have adequate powers to ensure that workers will not pass the extra taxes on so that they fall on capital investment or the balance of payments.

It is, of course, vital if such acquiescence is to be achieved that the output of social services should rise as rapidly as expenditures upon them. If there is a preference for extra education, and taxation is raised continuously to finance it, while each generation of children is worse educated than the one before, either because the extra money is spent on administration instead of teaching, or because teachers fail to teach the technical skills which later life will require, taxpayers may not regard the extra 'social wage' as adequate compensation for private consumption forgone. In the ideal conditions assumed, it is therefore necessary that the non-market sector be as efficient as the market sector. A society will then be substituting unmarketed public services which are as efficiently produced as private goods and services for the extra private consumption it would otherwise obtain. Workers then obtain a combination of private and public goods and services which they can sensibly prefer to alternative combinations where there are fewer public goods and services. If the non-market sector is consistently less efficient, it is unlikely that combinations which take increasing fractions from this inefficient sector will be rationally preferred.

Finally, it is not enough that a continuous relative shift of resources into the non-market sector be acceptable to the average worker. Workers with above average incomes may regard the increasing 'social wage' they obtain (which will generally be no greater than the increase in the average worker's 'social wage') inadequate compensation for the above average taxes they will be expected to pay with progressive taxation. Ideally, the increasing equality involved in an ever growing non-market share will need to be acceptable to a whole community and not merely to a majority, or to workers with average or below average incomes. Dissatisfied minorities of the better off can disrupt and interrupt a smooth progression to an ever growing non-market sector.

The destabilisation of Britain

The British case is illustrated in Table 5.1. This shows that from 1964 to 1973, the last full year before the start of the world recession, non-market purchases rose 3.1 times as fast as market sector purchases. The non-market share rose a great deal more from 1973 to 1976 but this was partly due to lack of growth of market sector output because of exceptionally unfavourable trading conditions during the recession.

Table 5.1   The shift from the market to the non-market sector in Britain: 1964–73

	1964	1973	Increase
Net output per worker	100	126.6	26.6%
Purchased by the market sector per worker employed	66 (66.0%)	76.2 (60.2%)	15.5%
Purchased by the non-market sector per worker employed	34.0 (34.0%)	50.4 (39.8%)	48.2%

The period 1964–73 shown in the table was uninfluenced by such adverse factors and 1964 and 1973 are both expansion years which can safely be compared – and this period shows disproportionate non-market sector growth. Personal preferences may give priority to public services over private consumption, but it is not plausible that many will wish the public services to grow over three times as fast. The increase in taxation involved in what occurred averaged about 6 per cent in the nine years in which output per worker rose 26.6 per cent. The average worker with ordinary earnings was expected to pay the increased taxes like the rest of the community, and deductions from the average worker's pay-packet increased by 6.7 pence in the pound from 1964 to 1973, slightly more than the 5.8 per cent increase in average taxation indicated in the table.

It is reasonable to suppose that what occurred went much further than actual preferences in the community for higher public consumption. British workers wanted extra private consumption also. Many were unable to afford car ownership; many ate far less meat than they wished even before Britain joined the European Economic Community; many aspired to house ownership (55 per cent of British families live in houses they own) and house ownership was becoming increasingly expensive. Certainly more public services were desired, but it was desired that private consumption should rise rapidly also. It is probable that politicians of all British political parties appreciated this, but they made two major errors of analysis which led to the position illustrated in the table.

The first error was due to the Keynesianism that dominated British economic thought and analysis across the whole political spectrum from 1964 to 1973. There were thought to be unemployed resources in most years from 1964 to 1973, so few British politicians or civil servants or academic economists believed that extra growth of the non-market sector cost anything. On the contrary, all had been taught or themselves taught that each extra pound sterling spent by the non-market sector increased total incomes by between two and three pounds (to follow Keynes's own estimate of Lord Kahn's multiplier – the concept which taught two generations of English speaking economists that you can expand your cake and eat it faster at the same time), so the British happily allowed the non-market sector to increase at rapid rates in relation to the growth of the remainder of the economy whenever they wished to expand demand and production. It rarely occurred to those in power or their advisers that extra social spending would eventually need to be paid for. Therefore at election time, all political parties promised more expenditure on the social services and more private consumption also without ever indicating that taxation would need to rise to pay for the enlarged non-market sector. Voters never actually chose the growth imbalance which occurred. Instead they voted for more of everything many times.

The second error Britain made was that where governments actually made long-term expenditure plans, the rate of growth on which the plans were based was overestimated. The long-term rate of growth of British expenditure on the social services was consistently based on the assumption that Britain would achieve a rate of growth of final output of around 4 per cent. In reality, production grew by only 2.8 per cent a year from 1964 to 1973. An economy growing at 4 per cent could have financed the increases in social expenditures which occurred with much smaller increases in taxation, and far more growth of private consumption, than was actually achieved. It will be seen that the rapid non-market sector growth itself contributed to the slow growth of the economy which undermined the financial foundations of the social services.

Britain's third error was to fail to ensure that the non-market sector would be managed as efficiently as the market sector ... Whether for this reason, or because it was allowed to grow far faster than workers' preferences for public goods, there was a clear departure from the ideal conditions for non-market sector growth which have been outlined. Workers did not acquiesce in the increased taxation that was needed to finance the extra-rapid growth of the non-market sector, and they therefore made every effort to increase their private consumption at rates almost as fast as public consumption was growing. Private real market sector incomes grew about 1.6 per cent per annum for each worker employed from 1964 to 1973, which was a far slower rate of increase than workers had obtained in the previous decade, and continued to expect. Each individual group of workers could only increase their private consumable income at more than 1.6 per cent per annum by gaining wage increases which were larger than those that other groups of workers were obtaining or by raising wages exceptionally at the expense of profits.

Union leaders who were particularly likely to push for exceptional wage increases without inhibitions about the methods used to obtain them were therefore increasingly elected to positions of power in the labour movement, and these were often on the extreme left politically. Individual trade unions then went on to exploit each particular advantage they possessed regardless of the damage they were causing to the economy and the rest of the community. The coal miners demonstrated that the country could not function without electricity and obtained very large wage increases after long and significant strikes which set a lead for other settlements. The dockers also demonstrated their power and extracted for their members (partly in the form of high redundancy payments) a high fraction of the potential surplus value resulting from the technical advance of containerisation. Most of the unions with the opportunity to obtain exceptional wage increases by disrupting the productive process did so with the result that money wages started to rise far faster than before. There is some rate of unemployment which would have checked this inflation – monetarists call this the 'natural' rate of unemployment – but the greater militancy of the trade unions raised this critical unemployment rate. Hence successive British governments were faced with the choice of either far more inflation than before if they maintained traditional unemployment rates, or else a much higher unemployment rate to check inflation. They found both of these alternatives unacceptable and introduced a series of official 'incomes policies' in their attempts to avoid having to choose between intolerable inflation and intolerable unemployment. In these the trade unions agreed to wage restraint for two years at a time, but only in exchange for a series of concessions which included price controls that severely reduced profits.

The unions managed to raise the share of wages in two additional ways. More militant union leadership at the local level meant that much of the surplus value resulting from technical advance which previously went to profits now went to wages instead, for workers only agreed to work new plant if much higher wages were paid or they were compensated in some other way. In addition, the more militant trade union leadership that resulted from workers' frustration increased the political power of the working class in the Marxist sense with the result that a considerable amount of legislation was passed which reduced companies' property rights. Companies therefore found it more difficult to choose the employment level of a factory (since they were often obliged to continue to employ workers whom they would have preferred to declare redundant) and they could not easily obtain possession of a factory or goods in it against the wishes of the unions in their area. This meant that companies earned lower profits from a given capital stock than before.

As they also earned lower profits from the introduction of new technology, and less profit as a result of the government price controls which were frequently introduced, the share of wages rose markedly at the expense of the share of profits. In fact from 1964 to 1973 the share of profits fell by almost precisely the 5.8 per cent of output by which the non-market share rose, while the share of wages and salaries in the National Income increased. Workers were therefore able to compensate for some of the 6.7 pence in the pound increase in taxation which fell on them by squeezing the share of profits, and raising the share of wages and salaries in the National Income. Their private consumption could therefore rise almost as fast as output, while the cost of financing the rapid growth of the non-market sector fell largely on profits. The non-market sector was therefore financed, not at the expense of consumption, but to an increasing extent at the expense of investment and the balance of payments, because the profits squeeze soon led to an investment squeeze. This was especially the case in industry where union pressures were strongest and profits were squeezed most, and net industrial investment actually fell 46.2 per cent in 1964–73. In industry the link between investment and job creation is especially strong. It sometimes pays to put up buildings which provide little extra employment, but new factories always need to be manned. It will be seen that the fall in industrial investment had extremely serious consequences for the economy.

It is to be noted that if the non-market sector's share in marketed output rises as it did in Britain, while the consumption share of market sector workers does not fall correspondingly, then the share of investment and net exports (that is, exports less imports) must necessarily fall – as it did in Britain. What actually happens is partly that the accompanying profits squeeze may immediately incline companies to spend less on investment, on research and development and on product promotion in home and overseas markets – and this happened in Britain to a certain extent.   If, however, companies persist in expanding investment, despite the profits squeeze, simple arithmetic decrees that the current account of the balance of payments must then move sharply into deficit, for the share of government and workers' consumption cannot rise without a corresponding fall in the share of net *exports plus investment*.   What happens here in practice is that when output is near to its capacity limits, investment *plus* net exports are crushed between the irreducible shares of government and workers' consumption.

If investment does not give way of its own accord because profits are being squeezed, there is absolutely certain to be a large import surplus corresponding to the increased share of government and workers' consumption.   If the import surplus cannot be sustained, and this has been persistently the case in Britain, governments necessarily respond by deflating the economy which pulls job-creating investment down.   Hence when the non-market share of output rises, job-creating investment falls, either because profits are squeezed, or because of the effects of balance of payments deficits on government policies and the adverse effects these will then have on investment.   In the simplest possible terms, investment and net exports together must give way at full capacity working if the government and workers together insist on taking a larger share of marketed output.   If the current account of the balance of payments must be balanced over a period of years – and this was certainly the case in Britain – then the cost of an increase in the government share must fall in one way or another on investment. There is no other possibility.

Hence, Britain's non-market sector grew, not at the expense of the economy's consumable surplus which any society can afford, but instead at the expense of investment in job creation, the economy's seed-corn.

CHAPTER 6

The human factor and industrial decline[*]

Corelli Barnett

In the late 1940s and on into the 1950s we largely attributed our troubles to short-term or external causes – our weakness after fighting a great war, the rise in commodity prices caused by the Korean conflict and so on. At that time British leaders and the public alike comfortably assumed that we were still fundamentally a first class industrial power; that British shipbuilding, car-building, whatever, led the world; that there was nothing much we could learn from foreigners. Gradually, however, from the mid-sixties onwards, it began to dawn on the British that the fault lay not in their stars, but in themselves.

Unfortunately there is no agreement over diagnosis. There is a variety of explanations, depending upon the social or political viewpoint of the diagnoser: not enough private enterprise; not enough nationalisation; too much state planning and interference; not enough state planning and interference; the trade unions for failing economically to man new plant; management for failing to invest enough new plant; and so on. The economists and the financial pages of the newspapers concentrate on monetary and fiscal policy and the government of the day's management of the economy. There are also what might be termed the 'wooden-leg' explanations, which are constantly trotted out by patriotic apologists; explanations comforting to British sensibility. The most notable of these sees Britain as paying the penalty for having won the war, while Germany was lucky enough to be defeated. According to this popular wooden-leg story, British started the post-war era with the handicap of having virtually all her factories, shipyards and transport system intact and undamaged, whereas the fortunate Germans had had theirs smashed into dust by allied bombing or carted off as reparations by the Russians. The Germans, so the story goes on, started all over again from scratch with new plant and methods – thanks to Marshall Aid.

---

[*] Reproduced with permission from *The Human Factor and British Industrial Decline*, David Higham and Associates, 1975.

In point of fact, there is no substance in this soothing explanation. Only some 15 to 20 per cent of German industrial equipment was destroyed or damaged beyond repair in strategic bombing, while the Russians soon preferred to take the fruits of German production as reparations rather than the capital equipment itself. Moreover, Britain received 2.7 thousand million dollars in Marshall Aid, as against West Germany's 1.7 thousand million.

Leaving aside the 'wooden-leg' explanations of popular myth, the current debate on our economic ills seems to a historian to suffer from the drawback that it is too narrowly doctrinaire and partisan, and that its perspectives far too short term. Even those who correctly perceive that it is our *industrial* failings which lie at the heart of our troubles tend to regard these failings as being relatively recent phenomena, dating back to the end of the Second World War at the earliest. A historian, however, takes a very much longer and deeper view than these. Nations or national characters as they are today result from a long process of conditioning: a whole moral, social and historical environment.   For an explanation of, say, the poor labour-relations, the restrictive practices and over-manning in British industry, or the inertia and unwillingness to invest displayed by many managements, he will look at the entire pattern of Britain's very special social and industrial history over the last hundred and fifty years, if not even longer.

For the first and essential point which must be grasped by anyone concerned with our industrial shortcomings is that they are not in the least bit novel; that they are not at all simply a matter of the post-war years. A brief backward sketch will demonstrate this.

In the mid-1930s the start of rearmament forced us to take complete stock of our industrial resources, including, perhaps most important of all, skilled manpower, both technical and managerial.   For production of war purposes requires for the most part the same kind of plant and capabilities as are needed for the conquest of export markets in peacetime. What did the government find? As the Cabinet Defence Policy and Requirements Committee summed it up, 'the most serious factor in the completion of the proposed programme is the limited output of our existing resources'. The files of this Cabinet Committee provide a complete and gloomy amplification of this broad judgement.

The British steel industry, for example, was so fragmented, so old-fashioned, so limited in total output that armour-plate for new aircraft carriers and cruisers had to be ordered from Czechoslovakia. But the gravest bottleneck of all lay in highly sophisticated machine-tools for various forms of mass-production. In 1933–37 Germany enjoyed nearly 50 per cent of the world's trade in machine-tools; Britain's share was only 7 per cent. Britain therefore had to buy Swiss, German, Hungarian and American machine-tools to enable the rearmament programme to go forward. Because we had almost no clock or instrument industry the early marks of Hurricane and Spitfire had to be fitted with Swiss and American instrumentation. The Swiss provided the fuses for our shells. And so the catalogue went on.

It may, however, be argued that that was in the peculiar and unlucky conditions following the world slump; that before 1914 things were different, that we were then still 'the Workshop of the World'. As it happens, the Great War provided another and earlier audit of our industrial capability. When Britain embarked on her industrial mobilisation for war in the course of 1915, the extent of British deficiencies and dependence on foreign technology became manifest. Britain produced only half the German quantity of steel, and even then neither always of the quality nor the specialised kinds to be found in Germany. Britain possessed only a few modern mass-production industries for conversion from, say, clock-making to fuses; no modern machine-tool industry with which to equip the new factories we were forced to construct in utmost haste. 'The British machine-tool maker', wrote the Official History of the Ministry of Munitions, 'was conservative both as regards novelty in design and quantity of output.' We had come to rely for modern machine-tools on Germany and the United States.

It is therefore no wonder that in the late 1890s and early 1900s perceptive critics mounted a great 'Wake up England!' campaign in the newspapers. The articles in this campaign make depressing reading, because they make almost exactly the same comparisons between British industry and its European and American competitors as we constantly read in our newspapers and journals today – the rigidity and old-fashionedness of British management, the clinging to out-of-date products, plant and methods, the want of marketing energy and expertise, the reluctance to invest. One must note here that in this era British industry did not suffer at all from the high taxation of government 'meddling' to which it today likes to attribute its poor investment record.

If one moves back another twenty or thirty years, to the 1870s and 1880s, Britain then certainly *appears* to be genuinely 'the Workshop of the World', for in sheer volume and value of exports we comfortably exceeded every other country in the world. Yet even as early as this we had already contracted 'the English disease'. In 1884 the Royal Commission on Technical Instruction in an exhaustive analysis reported that Europeans had already passed us in the efficiency of their industrial organisation.

Indeed, if one goes even further back into Britain's Victorian heyday, to 1853, just two years after the Great Exhibition, we find Dr Lyon Playfair, in a book on *Industrial Education on the Continent*, warning that unless we altered our whole industrial outlook and methods we were bound to be overtaken by other countries. Finally, to go back two years beyond Victoria's reign even, to 1835, Richard Cobden wrote after a visit to America that 'our only chance of national prosperity lies in the timely remodelling of our system, so as to put it as nearly as possible upon and equally with the improved management of the Americans'.

Thus, far from being a relatively recent problem, our industrial incapacity dates from the very moment when British technology ceased to have world markets entirely to itself, from the very moment when other countries industrialised themselves and began to compete with us. In other words it was not some special genius for technology – as British myth has it – which gave us our early industrial lead, but various chance historical factors which caused Britain simply to be the first country into the Industrial Revolution. It was, however, only by developing such a genius – the cultivation of energy and ambition of the habits of systematic organisation, the application of science – that we could have kept up. This we have never done. Innovation and change in Britain have always come too slowly.

But why was this so? When foreign technology began to surpass our own by the 1860s, why did we not respond by surpassing *theirs* in turn? The purpose of this paper is to suggest that the answer lies in the whole nature of our early industrial experience in the second half of the eighteenth century and the first half of the nineteenth, when our very special industrial traditions and outlook were taking shape and setting hard.

In the first place, it is impossible to exaggerate the long term consequences, social and psychological, of the experience of the workforce in the industrial towns of late Georgian and early Victorian Britain under conditions of ferocious competition and uncontrolled exploitation. It was in that era, when people were flooding into the new industrial towns from the countryside and exchanging the slow, natural rhythms of the land or self-employed crafts for the mechanical pace of the factory, the cottage for the back-to-back, that the British urban working-class with its peculiar and enduring character as a culture apart, an alienated group, often embittered and hostile, was created. It was after all from study of the British working-class that Marx and Engels derived their conception of the proletariat. As E. P. Thompson writes in *The Making of the English Working Class,* 'The process of the industrialisation is necessarily painful. It must involve the erosion of traditional patterns of life. But in Britain it was unrelieved by any sense of national participation in communal effort, such as is found in countries undergoing a national revolution. Its ideology [that is, of the British industrial revolution] was that of the masters alone.'

From the very beginning therefore the machine was seen by British work people as an enemy; technical progress as the destroyer of status and independence. Yet in the same era the advance of *laissez-faire* economic doctrine led to the steady repeal of old paternalistic legislation protecting crafts, employment, status and wages. There seemed nowhere for their existence as illegal, undercover, organisation, for they were prohibited under Common Law and later under the 1800 Combination Act as 'combinations' in restraint of trade. Not until 1825 were they legalised. Other repressive legislation of the 1790s and 1800s born of fear of revolution on the French model, bore equally hardly on the emerging working-class. As a consequence of all this, in the words of E. P. Thompson, 'The workers felt that the bonds, however ideal, which bound them to the rest of the community in reciprocal obligations and duties were being snapped one after another. They were being thrust beyond the pale of the constitution' (1963: 597). By the 1830s the character of the British working-class as a nation apart, with its own values, had matured.

And Thompson sums up the enduring consequences of the bitter social and political struggles of the early nineteenth century:

> Segregated in this way, their [the working-class's] institutions acquired a peculiar toughness and resilience. Class also acquired a peculiar resonance in English life: everything from their schools to their shops, chapels to their amusements, was turned into a battleground of class ... If we have in our social life little of the tradition of égalité, yet the class-consciousness of the working man has little in it of deference. (*ibid.:* 914–15)

Here then is the explanation of why Britain is almost alone in Europe in having a 'cloth-cap' workforce instead of a bourgeois one; a cloth-cap working-class culture; here is the essential clue to Britain's unhappy industrial relations today. Yet this 'cloth-cap' working-class character, this sense of being apart, is perpetuated by management through distinctions between wage-earners and salaried staff – distinctions in terms of service, status and security of employment, and even in the provision of canteens, washrooms and so on. Indeed the state itself has very largely helped to preserve this separate working-class culture and consciousness by instituting, with the best of intentions, the council house; by creating furthermore whole homogeneous districts of council dwellings; a phenomenon without parallel in Europe; the plainest of all class badges.

Since one of the primary roles of trade-unions from the very beginning was the defence of existing crafts against extinction by improved machines, the trade-union movement, as it gained strength in the course of the nineteenth century, became an ever more potent factor making for technical conservatism in England. It was not simply the deeply branded suspicion of machines as a threat to jobs; the British trade-union also carried on the old pre-industrial traditions of the guild, revering the status and 'mystery' of crafts. This led to the endless ramification of small unions so typical of modern Britain, the demarcations, and also to a clinging to such institutions as apprenticeship as a means of industrial training – and of artificially limiting the quantity of man-power – rather than formal instruction in some system of industrial schools.

The special British experience in the first industrial revolution exercised a no less profound and long-lasting effect on the outlook and style of management. They too carried into a new age pre-industrial craft traditions of learning by experience, proceeding by rule-of-thumb and trail-and-error, and they built their businesses in similar fashion, starting small as local tradesmen or craftsmen and expanding by grace of native nous. There was therefore in British industry right from the start a tradition of the resourceful amateur, self-taught as he went along; a tradition true all the way from the boardroom to the workbench. From this arose a potent British myth which certainly survived widely until the 1930s and survives to this day in certain un-regenerate corners of industry – the myth of the practical man's thumb carried with a positive distrust of the application of intellectual study or scientific research to industrial questions; a total disdain for systematic technical training or even general education.

Unfortunately by the middle of the nineteenth century the unique nature of our initial world technological monopoly had bred a fatal complacency, arrogance even. We have come to believe, like an army after a victorious war, that we had found the formula of success, and like such an army, we clung to it with blinkered stubbornness. And that formula consisted of the individualistic competition of 'practical men' and their workforces of equally self-taught 'practical men'. Technically, psychologically and socially Britain as an industrial society stuck fast in the patterns set between 1780 and 1850 – in the primitive stage of industrialism. Yet, as men like Cobden and Playfair were pointing out by the mid-nineteenth century, our rivals had adopted a much more sophisticated approach, based on applied science and on thorough education and training at all levels. Moreover in America and Europe it was the state which provided the key piece of equipment for achieving this new professionalism – complete national education systems, primary, secondary, technical and university.

In Victorian England, however, the creation of such a system was out of the question, not only because of the 'practical men's' contempt for education and theoretical science, but even more so because of Liberal, or *laissez-faire*, economic and social doctrine. According to this doctrine, the prosperity and welfare of the nation were best promoted by leaving everything to individual initiative and the self-regulating mechanism of the market – even town-planning, medical care and national education, as well as the future efficiency of industry and agriculture. Liberal doctrine not only gave intellectual respectability to the belief in 'the practical man' and his unfettered competition with other 'practical men', it provided a new justification for a deep-seated English dislike of being organised which can be traced back to the seventeenth century and beyond. Indeed the whole thrust of English history has been against central or large-scale organisation, and *for* the individual's right to run his own life as he pleased within the framework of the law. It is what Englishmen meant by liberty; the essential distinction they perceived between English life and the life of foreigners under monarchies; it explains why they went to work in the new factories with much the same feelings as men pressed into the army or navy. The British entered the industrial era – the era of organisation, and ever more complex organisation at that – with a profound aversion to belonging to organisations, and the larger and more comprehensive the organisation the greater the aversion.

The British nation, 'in its collective and corporate character', therefore did nothing in the late nineteenth century to remedy the increasing obsolescence of British industry and its outlook either by economic or fiscal policies, or, most vital of all, by the provision of a state education system comparable to those of European countries or America. Universal state primary education only began in 1870, and then on the standard of the workhouse. As for technical education in late Victorian England, the crucial era when our rivals were overtaking us, this consisted of a scant and random collection of mostly small institutions in no way organised or related to each other as part of a national system of technical schools, or designed as part of a complete and harmonious scheme of state education. Britain lacked moreover technical higher elementary schools on the European pattern, while our part-time technical training was very greatly inferior.

It was not only that the absence of adequate national education in Britain directly affected our industrial progress; it also meant that little was being done to mitigate that proletarianisation of the British working-class resulting from the first industrial revolution. In 1884 the Royal Commission on Technical Education made the following comparison between English elementary-school children and Swiss, on visiting a Swiss school: 'We were particularly struck by the clean and tidy appearance of the boys and there was difficulty in realising that the school consisted mainly of children of the lower classes of the population'. Of Germany the same Royal commission wrote this: 'the one point in which Germany is overwhelmingly superior to England is in schools, and in the education of all classes of the people. The dense ignorance so common among workmen in England is unknown'. The contrast between European middle-management and British was no less marked. Nor were British top management and boardroom any better trained in comparison with their European opposite numbers. According to the Commons Committee of 1867–8, if top managers had arisen from the bottom, 'any knowledge of scientific principles which they may have acquired is generally the result of solitary reading, and of observations of the facts with which their pursuits have made them familiar'. Here again then is the self-taught 'practical man' still going strong. The Committee went on to add that otherwise the education of British capitalists and senior management was that of the public schools.

And here the Committee touched on another crucial and enduring factor in Britain's failure to maintain her technological dynamism after the first half of the nineteenth century – the characteristics of the British elite created by the Victorian public school, as remodelled by Dr. Arnold of Rugby and his followers. For the public school saw its purpose not as turning out well-informed and ambitious future leaders of an industrial society but Christian gentlemen with a mission of governing the lesser breeds of the Empire. The Victorian public school was the upper-class equivalent of the chapel – a potent expression of the religious revival which took place in Britain from the latter part of the eighteenth century onwards, and which has deeply influenced the whole outlook and values of the British people. The religious revival was really an expression of the Romantic Movement. It held up before men a vision of the ideal, like Pre-Raphaelite art; the morally ideal. In the course of Victoria's reign this idealistic romanticism burned deep into the British. There is of course nothing inherently incompatible between high religious idealism and the achievement of commercial and industrial success – as the examples of such families as the Rowntrees serve to demonstrate. Unfortunately such a fusion was not general. Instead, the whole bias of British upper-class education and upbringing in the nineteenth century was *away* from the realities of the industrialised world of the era, and from such topics as science and technology; more, in conscious opposition to them.

For mid-Victorians public school education consisted of the chapel, the games field and classics – Greek and Latin language and literature. When so-called 'Modern' subjects like European languages came in during the 1870s, they were regarded as refuges for the intellectually second-rate, while science even began as an out of school hours extra. Moreover, even on the so-called 'Modern' sides there was, for example, no study of modern Europe and its economic and social systems. History was all kings and queens and bishops, like a game of chess; the Industrial Revolution did not figure at all. There was little or no geography. All the cleverest boys, who read Latin and Greek, left school, as a master at Victorian Harrow admitted, knowing little or nothing of 'the two chief modern languages or the rudiments of history'. It was not until after the Great War that public school education really began to take note of the world in which their pupils were going to live and make their careers.

However, there is another aspect of the Victorian and later public school which is highly relevant to the traditionalist approach, the hidebound orthodoxy and the general pace and style of British top management until the 1940s at least. Except in the sixth form the teaching was rigid and stereotyped – great slabs of grammar and set-books to be learned by heart and recited in class. There was little room for personal curiosity or experiment. The result was that unless a boy was a brilliant classicist he soon made up his mind that intellectual study was boring and irrelevant; an attitude that could and did endure for the rest of his life, colouring his whole approach to running the family firm. In this fashion the public-school helped to reinforce the British belief in the virtues of 'the practical-man-no-fancy-theory'. Even today only 42 per cent of executives in Britain have degrees, as against 89 per cent in France and 83 per cent in the USA.

The intellectual narrowness and conformism of the public school were compounded by its compulsory orthodoxy of behaviour. British upper-class boys spent their formative years in closed and highly artificial communities where they learned by example – and the help of a cane or a five-bat – a deep respect for the established rules and for 'good form'. Organised games played an immense part in this conditioning process.

Public-school life therefore inculcated habits of mind which were in no way suited to leading an industrial nation in an age of very rapid change and innovation. The boys had been conditioned to look on the society in which they found themselves as fixed and unchanging rather than something to be analysed and criticised, and perhaps radically refashioned. Far from being encouraged to criticise, they had been taught to conform and accept: to think of a critical approach as 'bad form'. In the second place, the public school taught its boys to see leadership in terms of the prefect, or the governor-general: in other words, the conscientious routine administration of an institution as it at present existed. The very qualities Britain needed – and *needs* – in its leaders were the very qualities discouraged: that is to say, restless curiosity, driving energy and ambition, a desire to innovate. Were not these the qualities of a cad? And thirdly the public school inculcated the despising of intellectual capability in favour of 'character', as measured principally by prowess at games.

Once the post-Arnoldian public school had launched these characteristics on their way, they became self-perpetuating. Like promoted like. Like appointed like in the first place. The end product of the romantic other-worldliness and conformity of Victorian British upper class education may therefore be summarised as follows: largely ignorant and largely incurious people with a positive bias against the application of intellectual study or analysis to practical questions; intensely conservative and orthodox; remarkably out of touch with the realities of their world. Harold Macmillan – and his case is by no means unique – wrote of himself as he was when he first stood as parliamentary candidate for Stockton in 1923:

> I had no practical knowledge of the world in which I was to move. I had
> never been to Teesside or even Tyneside. Apart from Glasgow, where my
> printer cousins lived, I had scarcely been to an industrial town. I had never
> seen the great ironworks, steelworks, engineering works, shipyards, which had
> been built up on the banks of the rivers of the North of England and Scotland.
> Nor, except for the war, had I any actual experience of living among an
> industrial population.

In short, therefore, the British elite up to 1939, and perhaps much later, was brought up in dense ignorance of industrial questions, to look down on science and technology, and to aspire to a career in the professions, public service or governing the Empire. Oddly enough, to be something in the City, to manipulate money, was more respectable than going to industry; an attitude which has outlived the demise of imperial service.

This higher prestige enjoyed by the City in comparison with manufacture reflects a further important effect of the Victorian public school's emphasis on turning boys into 'gentlemen'. The sons and grandsons of the ruthless and often rough-and-ready founders of our oldest firms emerged from their public schools as gentlemen of the upper classes, with a taste for the rural life and a disdain for professionalism and 'pushfulness': those bounder-like qualities of the German and Yankee businessman. Even if they put in time at the family firm, there was too often not in them, as there was in their foreign equivalents, a restless urge to keep on improving and expanding the business – to scrap plant and bulldoze old works and sack the dead wood.

Yet the importance of the public school as a factor in Britain's industrial decline does not only lie in that it created a national elite uninterested in, or antipathetic towards, technology. It also had far-reaching social effects. For it created a caste, with public-school manners, public-school accents and public school solidarity. It was the great engine of English snobbery. Britain is therefore, doubly unique in having a 'cloth-cap' working-class and an 'old-school-tie' upper class: both sharply marked out from the indeterminate middle of society by accent, manners, internal cohesion, indeed whole style of life. The consequences of this for British industry, in terms of human relations, of co-operation and team-work, of promotion, of finding and using the best available talent, have been enormous – and baneful.

To sum up the reasons why Britain failed to display industrial dynamism once the initial wave of industrialisation was spent: whereas Britain's rivals developed by the mid-nineteenth-century not only the necessary skills for continuous technological advance, but also – and perhaps even more important – the requisite mental outlook, Britain did neither. By the end of the century British backwardness was becoming obvious enough to form the topic of newspaper campaigns instead merely of expert bodies of enquiry. Britain's industrial deficiencies were now such that they could only be repaired by a massive programme of reconstruction and capital investment; except in wartime this did not take place. To repair her deficiencies in industrial skills and reform her basic industrial outlook required a no less massive programme of education, indeed an educational revolution. This revolution did not take place.

And despite the Butler Education Act of 1944 and post-war educational reforms, such as the founding of new universities, it is possible that even today Britain has not become the equal of rivals in educating and training her populations for success as an industrial society. In 1967 the Plowden Report wrote:

Comparisons with other countries – all of them more recently industrialised than Britain but all now at a similar stage of economic development – suggest that we have not done enough to provide the educational background necessary to support an economy which needs fewer and fewer unskilled workers and increasing numbers of skilled and adaptable people.

The profound and pervasive long-term social, technical and managerial effects of our experience as the first country into the industrial revolution and of our failure until so late to create anything like an adequate education system are well summed up in the final report of the Balfour Committee on Trade and Industry in 1929. This report was founded on four years of exhaustive investigations, but was, like all previous analyses of British short-comings, virtually without effect.

The available information makes it clear that the present response of leaders of industrial and commercial enterprises to the educational efforts made to train candidates for entry into the higher grades of these organisations is much less certain and widespread than in certain foreign countries, e.g. Germany or the United States.

Although since the Great War there had been much state-aided scientific research, the results were largely neglected by industry:

> Before British industries, taken as a whole, can hope to reap from scientific research the full advantage which it appears to yield to some of their most formidable rivals, nothing less than a revolution is needed in their general outlook in science; and this change of attitude is bound to be slow and difficult, in view of our old and deeply rooted industrial traditions.

Of the effects of the special nature of British trade-unionism and working-class attitudes, the Balfour Committee observed:

> We are aware of no other country that suffers nearly so much as Great Britain from artificial and hard and fast lines of demarcation between different skilled crafts, or between workmen of difference grades of skill, and this disability is more acutely felt than ever in a period of rapid economic change, when old lines of distinction are necessarily becoming less and less consistent with the realities of productive economy.

The Balfour Committee's final judgement on boardroom and shop floor in British industry in 1929 is still, regrettable, widely applicable today, drawing attention as it does to

> the conservative habits of mind which prevent many British employers from pursuing so energetic and (as it appears to them) so ruthless a policy of scrapping old plant and replacing it by new as their competitors (say) in America or Germany, and the corresponding qualities of mind which led many workmen to cling tenaciously to obsolete trade customs and lines of demarcation and this prevents them from co-operating to the full in getting the best value out of machinery at the lowest cost.

The Balfour Committee sums up all this as 'the human factor'. It seems to the present historian that the 'human factor' – our historical legacy as an industrial power in other words – constitutes Britain's fundamental problem.   For our difficulties are not only structured onto the very texture and geographical distribution of our industrial system, but also, and perhaps even harder to eradicate, into our very minds, habits and attitudes – class and otherwise. It seems moreover to this historian that neither our politicians, nor our economists and other commentators, have grasped the profound and pervasive nature of the handicap bequeathed to us by our formative experience in the first industrial revolution, and by the inadequacies of our national education system until halfway through the present century, or the immensity and urgency of the task to be accomplished if our hundred-year-long decline is not to continue – and not merely continue, but continue to *accelerate*.

CHAPTER 7

Special interest groups and UK economic decline*

Mancur Olson

The general thesis

Implications

1. There will be no countries that attain symmetrical organisation of all groups with a common interest and thereby attain optimal outcomes through comprehensive bargaining.
2. Stable societies with unchanged boundaries tend to accumulate more collusions and organisations for collective action over time.
3. Members of 'small' groups have disproportionate organisational power for collective action, and this disproportion diminishes but does not disappear over time in stable societies.
4. On balance, special-interest organisations and collusions reduce efficiency and aggregate income in the societies in which they operate and make political life more divisive.
5. Encompassing organisations have some incentive to make the society in which they operate more prosperous, and an incentive to redistribute income to their members with as little excess burden as possible, and to cease such redistribution unless the amount redistributed is substantial in relation to the social cost of the redistribution.
6. Distributional coalitions make decisions more slowly than the individuals and firms of which they are comprised, tend to have crowded agendas and bargaining tables, and more often fix prices than quantities.
7. Distributional coalitions slow down a society's capacity to adopt new technologies and to reallocate resources in response to changing conditions, and thereby reduce the rate of economic growth.
8. Distributional coalitions, once big enough to succeed, are exclusive, and seek to limit the diversity of incomes and values of their membership.
9. The accumulation of distributional coalitions increases the complexity of regulation, the role of government, and the complexity of understandings, and changes the direction of social evolution.

---

* Reproduced with permission from *The Rise and Decline of Nations*, Yale University Press, 1982.

The application of the thesis

If the argument so far is correct, it follows that countries whose distributional coalitions have been emasculated or abolished by totalitarian government or foreign occupation should grow relatively quickly after a free and stable legal order is established. This can explain the post-war 'economic miracles' in the nations that were defeated in World War II, particularly those in Japan and West Germany ...

The logic of the argument implies that countries that have had democratic freedom of organisation without upheaval or invasion the longest will suffer the most from growth-repressing organisations and combinations. This helps to explain why Great Britain, the major nation with the longest immunity from dictatorship, invasion, and revolution, has had in this century a lower rate of growth than other large, developed democracies. Britain has precisely the powerful network of special-interest organisations that the argument developed here would lead us to expect in a country with its record of military security and democratic stability. The number and power of its trade unions need no description. The venerability and power of its professional associations is also striking. Consider the distinction between solicitors and barristers, which could not possibly have emerged in a free market innocent of professional associations or government regulations of the sort they often obtain; solicitors in Britain have a legal monopoly in assisting individuals making conveyances of real estate and barristers a monopoly of the right to serve as counsel in the more important cases. Britain also has a strong farmers' organisation and a great many trade associations. In short, with age British society has acquired so many strong organisations and collusions that it suffers from an institutional sclerosis that slows its adaptation to changing circumstances and technologies.

Admittedly, lobbying in Britain is not as blatant as in the United States, but it is pervasive and often involves discreet efforts to influence civil servants as well as ministers and other politicians. Moreover, the word *establishment* acquired its modern meaning there and, however often that word may be overused, it still suggests a substantial degree of informal organisation that could emerge only gradually in a stable society. Many of the powerful special-interest organisations in Britain are, in addition, narrow rather than encompassing. For example, in a single factory there are often many different trade unions, each with a monopoly over a different craft or category of workers, and no one union encompasses a substantial fraction of the working population of the country. Britain is also often used as an example of ungovernability. In view of the long and illustrious tradition of democracy in Britain and the renowned orderliness of the British people, this is remarkable, but it is what the theory here predicts.

This explanation of Britain's relatively slow post-war growth, unlike many other explanations, is consistent with the fact that for nearly a century, from just after the middle of the eighteenth century until nearly the middle of the nineteenth, Britain was evidently the country with the *fastest* rate of economic growth. Indeed, during their Industrial Revolution the British invented modern economic growth. This means that no explanation of Britain's relatively slow growth in recent times that revolves around some supposedly inherent or permanent feature of British character or society can possibly be correct, because it is contradicted by Britain's long period with the fastest economic growth. Any valid explanation of Britain's relatively slow growth now must also take into account the *gradual* emergence of the 'British disease'. Britain began to fall behind in relative growth rates in the last decades of the nineteenth century, and this problem has become especially notable since World War II. Most other explanations of Britain's relatively slow growth in recent times do not imply a temporal pattern that is consistent with Britain's historical experience with dramatically different relative growth rates, but the theory offered here, with its emphasis on the gradual accumulation of distributional coalitions (Implication 2), does.

There cannot be much doubt that totalitarianism, instability, and war reduced special-interest organisations in Germany, Japan, and France, and that stability and the absence of invasion allowed continued development of such organisations in the United Kingdom. My colleague Peter Murrell systematically recorded the dates of formation of those associations recorded in *Internationales Verzeichnis der Wirtschaftsverbande* (Murrell, 1983). This is, to be sure, an incomplete source, and is perhaps flawed also in other ways, but it was published in 1983 and thus cannot have been the result of any favouritism toward the present argument. Murrell found from this source that whereas 51 per cent of the associations existing in 1971 in the United Kingdom were founded before 1939, only 37 per cent of the French, 24 per cent of the West German, and 19 per cent of the Japanese associations were. Naturally, Britain also had a smaller proportion of its interest groups founded after 1949 – 29 per cent, contrasted with 45 per cent for France and 52 per cent for Germany and for Japan. Britain also has a much larger number of associations than France, Germany, or Japan, and is exceeded in this category only by the far larger United States. Of course, we ought to have indexes that weight each organisation by its strength and its membership, but I know of none.

Murrell also worked out an ingenious set of tests of the hypothesis that the special-interest groups in Britain reduced that country's rate of growth in comparison with West Germany's. If the special-interest groups were in fact causally connected with Britain's slower growth, Murrell reasoned, this should put old British industries at a particular disadvantage in comparison with their West German counterparts, whereas in new industries where there may not yet have been time enough for special-interest organisations to emerge in either country, British and West German performance should be more nearly comparable. Thus, Murrell argued, the *ratio* of the rate of growth of new British industry to old British industry should be higher than the corresponding *ratio* for West Germany. There are formidable difficulties of definition and measurement, and alternative definitions and measures had to be used. Taking all of these results together, it is clear that they support the hypothesis that new British industries did relatively better in relation to old British industries than new German industries did in relation to old German industries. In most cases the results almost certainly could not have been due to chance, that is, they were statistically significant. Moreover, Murrell found that in heavy industry, where both industrial concentration and unionisation are usually greater than in light industry, the results were strongest, which also supports the theory.

Of the many alternative explanations, most are *ad hoc*. Some economists have attributed the speed of the recoveries of the vanquished countries to the importance of human capital compared with the physical capital destroyed by bombardment, but this cannot be a sufficient explanation, since the war killed many of the youngest and best-trained adults and interrupted education and work experience for many others. Knowledge of productive techniques, however, had not been destroyed by the war, and to the extent that the defeated nations were at a lower-than-pre-war level of income and needed to replace destroyed buildings or equipment, they would tend to have an above-average growth rate. But this cannot explain why these economies grew more rapidly than others after they had reached their pre-war level of income and even after they had surpassed the British level of per capita income.

Another commonplace *ad hoc* explanation is that the British, or perhaps only those in the working classes, do not work as hard as people in other countries. Others lay the unusually rapid growth of Germany and Japan to the special industriousness of their peoples. Taken literally, this type of explanation is unquestionably unsatisfactory. The rate of economic growth is the rate of *increase* of national income, and although this logically could be due to an *increase* in the industriousness of a people, it could not, in the direct and simple way implied in the familiar argument, be explained by their normal level of effort, which is relevant instead to their *absolute* level of income. Admittedly, when the industriousness of those who innovate is considered, or when possible connections between level of effort and the amount of saving are taken into account, there could be some connection between industriousness and growth. But even if the differences in willingness to work are part of the explanation, why are those in the fast-growing countries zealous and those in the slow-growing countries lazy? And since many countries have changed relative position in the race for higher growth rates, the timing of the waves of effort also needs explaining. If industriousness is the explanation, why were the British so hard-working during the Industrial Revolution? And by this work-effort theory the Germans evidently must have been lazy in the first half of the nineteenth century when they were relatively poor, and the impoverished Japanese quite lethargic when Admiral Perry arrived.

One plausible possibility is that industriousness varies with the incentive to work to which individuals in different countries have become accustomed. These incentives, in turn, are strikingly influenced, whether for manual workers, professionals, or entrepreneurs, by the extent to which special-interest groups reduce the rewards to productive work and thus increase the relative attractiveness of leisure. The search for the causes of differences in the willingness to work, and in particular the question of why shirking should be thought to be present during Britain's period of slower-than-average growth but not when it had the fastest rate of growth, brings us to economic institutions and policies, and to the more fundamental explanation of differences in growth rates.

Some observers endeavour to explain the anomalous growth rates in terms of alleged national economic ideologies and the extent of government involvement in economic life. The 'British disease' especially is attributed to the unusually large role that the British government has allegedly played in economic life. There is certainly no difficulty in finding examples of harmful economic intervention in post-war Britain. Nonetheless, as Samuel Brittan has convincingly demonstrated in an article in the *Journal of Law and Economics* (Brittan, 1978), this explanation is unsatisfactory. First, it is by no means clear that the government's role in economic life has been significantly larger than in the average developed democracy; in the proportion of gross domestic product accounted for by government spending, the United Kingdom has been at the middle, rather than at the top, of the league, and it has been also in about the middle, at roughly the same levels as Germany and France, in the percentage of income taken in taxes and social insurance. Perhaps in certain respects of certain years the case that the British government was unusually interventionist can be sustained, but there is no escaping Brittan's second point: that the relatively slow British growth rate goes back about a hundred years, to a period when governmental economic activity was very limited (especially, we might add, in Great Britain).

Some economists have argued that when we look at the developed democracies as a group, we seem to see a negative correlation between the size of government and the rate of growth. This more general approach is much superior to the *ad hoc* style of explanation, so statistical tests along these lines must be welcomed. But the results so far are weak, showing at best only a tenuous and uncertain connection between larger governments and slower growth, with such strength as this relationship possesses due in good part to Japan, which has had both the fastest growth rate and the smallest government of the major developed democracies. A weak or moderate negative relationship between the relative role of government and the rate of growth is predicted by Implication 9.

One well-known *ad hoc* explanation of the slow British growth focuses on a class consciousness that allegedly reduces social mobility, fosters exclusive and traditionalist attitudes that discourage entrants and innovators, and maintains medieval prejudices against commercial pursuits. Since Britain had the fastest rate of growth in the world for nearly a century, we know that its slow growth now cannot be due to any *inherent* traits of the British character. There is, in fact, some evidence that at the time of the Industrial Revolution Britain did not have the reputation for class differences that it has now. It is a commonplace among economic historians of the Industrial Revolution that at that time Britain, in relation to comparable parts of the Continent, had unusual social mobility, relatively little class consciousness, and a concern in all social classes about commerce, production, and financial gain that was sometimes notorious to its neighbours:

> More than any other in Europe, probably, British society was open. Not only was income more evenly distributed than across the Channel, but the barriers to mobility were lower, the definitions of status looser ... It seems clear that British commerce of the eighteenth century was, by comparison with that of the Continent, impressively energetic, pushful, and open to innovation ... No state was more responsive to the desires of its mercantile classes ... Nowhere did entrepreneurial decisions less reflect non-rational considerations of prestige and habit ... Talent was readier to go into business, projecting, and invention ... This was a people fascinated by wealth and commerce, collectively and individually ... Business interests promoted a degree of intercourse between people of different stations and walks of life that had no parallel on the Continent. ... The flow of entrepreneurship within business was freer, the allocation of resources more responsive than in other economies. Where the traditional sacro-sanctity of occupational exclusiveness continued to prevail across the Channel ... the British cobbler would not stick to his last nor the merchant to his trade ... Far more than in Britain, continental business enterprise was a class activity, recruiting practitioners from a group limited by custom and law. In France, commercial enterprise had traditionally entailed derogation from noble status. (Landes, 1969)

It is not surprising that Napoleon once derided Britain as a 'nation of shopkeepers' and that even Adam Smith found it expedient to use this phrase in his criticism of Britain's mercantilistic policies.

The ubiquitous observations suggesting that the Continent's class structures have by now become in some respects more flexible than Britain's would hint that we should look for processes that might have broken down class barriers more rapidly on the Continent than in Great Britain, or for processes that might have raised or erected more new class barriers in Britain than on the Continent, or for both.

One reason that only remnants of the Continent's medieval structures remain today is that they are entirely out of congruity with the technology and ideas now common in the developed world. But there is another, more pertinent reason: revolution and occupation, Napoleonism and totalitarianism, have utterly demolished most feudal structures on the Continent and many of the cultural attitudes they sustained. The new families and firms that rose to wealth and power often were not successful in holding their gains; new instabilities curtailed the development of new organisations and collusions that could have protected them and their descendants against still newer entrants. To be sure, fragments of the Middle Ages and chunks of the great fortunes of the nineteenth century still remain on the Continent; but, like the castles crumbling in the countryside, they do not greatly hamper the work and opportunities of the average citizen.

The institutions of medieval Britain, and even the great family-oriented industrial and commercial enterprises of more recent centuries, are similarly out of accord with the twentieth century and have in part crumbled, too. But would they not have been pulverised far more finely if Britain had gone through anything like the French Revolution, if a dictator had destroyed its public schools, if it had suffered occupation by a foreign power or fallen prey to totalitarian regimes determined to destroy any organisations independent of the regime itself? The importance of the House of Lords, the established church, and the ancient colleges of Oxford and Cambridge has no doubt often been grossly exaggerated. But they are symbols of Britain's legacy from the pre-industrial past or (more precisely) of the unique degree to which it has been preserved. There was extraordinary turmoil until a generation or two before the Industrial Revolution (and this probably played a role in opening British society to new talent and enterprise), but since then Britain has not suffered the institutional destruction, or the forcible replacement of elites, or the decimation of social classes, that its Continental counterparts have experienced. The same stability and immunity from invasion have also made it easier for the firms and families that advanced in the Industrial Revolution and the nineteenth century to organise or collude to protect their interests.

Here [my] argument is particularly likely to be misunderstood. This is partly because the word *class* is an extraordinarily loose, emotive, and misleadingly aggregative term that has unfortunately been reified over generations of ideological debate. There are, of course, no clearly delineated and widely separated groups such as the middle class or the working class, but rather a large number of groups of diverse situations and occupations, some of which differ greatly and some of which differ slightly if at all in income and status. Even if such a differentiated grouping as the British middle class could be precisely delineated, it would be a logical error to suppose that such a large group as the British middle class could voluntarily collude to exclude others or to achieve any common interest. The theory does suggest that the unique stability of British life since the early eighteenth century must have affected social structure, social mobility, and cultural attitudes, but *not* through class conspiracies or co-ordinated action by any large class or group. The process is far subtler and must be studied at a less aggregate level.

We can see this process from a new perspective if we remember that concerted action usually requires selective incentives, that social pressure can often be an effective selective incentive, and that individuals of similar incomes and values are more likely to agree on what amount and type of collective good to purchase. Social incentives will not be very effective unless the group that values the collective good at issue interacts socially or is composed of subgroups that do. If the group does have its own social life, the desire for the companionship and esteem of colleagues and the fear of being slighted or even ostracised can at little cost provide a powerful incentive for concerted action. The organisational entrepreneurs who succeed in promoting special-interest groups, and the managers who maintain them, must therefore focus disproportionately on groups that already interact socially or that can be induced to do so. This means that these groups tend to have socially homogeneous memberships and that the organisation will have an interest in using some of its resources to preserve this homogeneity. The fact that everyone in the pertinent group gets the same amount and type of a collective good also means, as we know from the theories of fiscal equivalence and optimal segregation, that there will be less conflict (and perhaps welfare gains as well) if those who are in the same jurisdiction or organisation have similar incomes and values. The forces just mentioned, operating simultaneously in thousands of professions, crafts, clubs, and communities, would, by themselves, explain a degree of class consciousness. This in turn helps to generate cultural caution about the incursions of the entrepreneur and the fluctuating profits and status of businessmen, and also helps to preserve and expand aristocratic and feudal prejudices against commerce and industry. There is massive if unsystematic evidence of the effects of the foregoing processes, such as that in Martin Weiner's (1981) book on *English Culture and the Decline of the Industrial Spirit, 1850–1980*.

Unfortunately, the processes that have been described do not operate by themselves; they resonate with the fact that every distributional coalition must restrict entry (Implication 8). As we know, there is no way a group can obtain more than the free market price unless it can keep outsiders from taking advantage of the higher price, and organisations designed to redistribute income through lobbying have an incentive to be minimum winning coalitions. Social barriers could not exist unless there were some groups capable of concerted action that had an interest in erecting them. We can see now that the special-interest organisations or collusions seeking advantage in either the market or the polity have precisely this interest.

In addition to controlling entry, the successful coalition must, we recall, have or generate a degree of consensus about its policies. The cartelistic coalition must also limit the output or labour of its own members; it must make all the members conform to some plan for restricting the amount sold, however much this limitation and conformity might limit innovation. As time goes on, custom and habit play a larger role. The special-interest organisations use their resources to argue that what they do is what in justice ought to be done. The more often pushy entrants and non-conforming innovators are repressed, the rarer they become, and what is not customary is 'not done'.

Nothing about this process should make it work differently at different levels of income or social status. As Josiah Tucker remarked in the eighteenth century, 'All men would be monopolists if they could'. This process may, however, proceed more rapidly in the professions, where public concern about unscrupulous or incompetent practitioners provides an ideal cover for policies that would in other contexts be described as monopoly or 'greedy unionism'. The process takes place among the workers as well as the lords; some of the first craft unions were in fact organised in pubs.

There is a temptation to conclude dramatically that this involutional process has turned a nation of shopkeepers into a land of clubs and pubs. But this facile conclusion is too simple. Countervailing factors are also at work and may have greater quantitative significance. The rapid rate of scientific and technological advance in recent times has encouraged continuing reallocations of resources and brought about considerable occupational, social, and geographical mobility even in relatively sclerotic societies.

In addition, there is another aspect of the process by which social status is transmitted to descendants that is relatively independent of the present theory. Prosperous and well-educated parents usually are able through education and upbringing to provide larger legacies of human as well as tangible capital to their children than are deprived families. Although apparently the children of high-ranking families occasionally are enfeebled by undemanding and over-indulgent environments, or even neglected by parents obsessed with careers or personal concerns, there is every reason to suppose that, on average, the more successful families pass on the larger legacies of human and physical capital to their children. This presumably accounts for some of the modest correlation observed between the incomes and social positions of parents and those that their children eventually attain. The adoption of free public education and reasonably impartial scholarship systems in Britain in more recent times has disproportionately increased the amount of human capital passed on to children from poor families and thereby has tended to increase social mobility. Thus there are important aspects of social mobility that the theory offered in this book does not claim to explain and that can countervail those it does explain.

I must once again emphasise multiple causation and point out that there is no presumption that the process described in this book has brought *increasing* class consciousness, traditionalism, or antagonism to entrepreneurship. The contrary forces may overwhelm the involution even when no upheavals or invasions destroy the institutions that sustain it. The only hypothesis on this point that can reasonably be derived from the theory is that, of two societies that were in other respects equal, the one with the longer history of stability, security, and freedom of association would have more institutions that limit entry and innovation, that these institutions would encourage more social interaction and homogeneity among their members, and that what is said and done by these institutions would have at least some influence on what people in that society find customary and fitting.

CHAPTER 8

An institutional perspective*

Bernard Elbaum and William Lazonick

The British economy, once the workshop of the world, seems to have fallen victim to some century-long affliction. For lack of an adequate generic diagnosis, many observers have termed this affliction the 'British disease' (Allen, 1976). There are signs, however, that the disease may be spreading, and the recent competitive reverses of American industry in the face of Japanese and European challenges have sparked renewed interest in explanations of economic growth and decline. The Japanese success in particular has recently received most of the attention from economists and policy makers, but there is yet, we would argue, much to be learned from Britain's economic failure.

In Britain itself, the ideology directing current government policy assumes that the nation's decline has been due to the obstruction of the self-regulating market economy by trade union power and state intervention. This ideological perspective finds intellectual reinforcement in orthodox economic theory that, in both its liberal and conservative variants, views the capitalist economy as fundamentally an atomistic market economy. According to economic orthodoxy, the perfection of market competition and economic prosperity go hand in hand.

Although this proposition goes back to the time of Adam Smith, it has never been adequately supported by comparative examination of the historical experiences of capitalist economics. In particular, the issue of Britain's decline has largely been avoided by neoclassical economic historians who have been preoccupied with demonstrating that turn-of-the-century British managers 'did the best they could' by optimising subject to given constraints. Neoclassical economists who have confronted the problem of explaining national decline simply assume that the mainspring of the wealth of nations is free market competition and proceed as a matter of course to blame Britain's economic misfortunes on either market imperfections or 'non-economic' factors such as the cultural peculiarities of businessmen or workers.

---

*   Reproduced with permission from 'The decline of the British economy: an institutional perspective', *Journal of Economic History*, **44**: 567–83, 1984.

By contrast, the historical perspective presented below attributes the decline of the British economy to the rigid persistence of economic and social institutions from the nineteenth-century era of relatively atomistic competition. In such countries as the United States, Germany, and Japan, successful twentieth-century economic development has been based on mass production methods and corporate forms of managerial coordination. But in Britain adoption of these modern technological and organisational innovations was impeded by inherited socioeconomic constraints at the levels of the enterprise, industry, and society. Entrenched institutional structures – including the structures of industrial relations, industrial organisation, educational systems, financial intermediation, international trade, and state–enterprise relations – constrained the ability of individuals, groups, or corporate entities to transform the productive system.

Britain's problem was that economic decision makers, lacking the individual or collective means to alter prevailing institutional constraints, in effect took them as 'given'. In failing to confront institutional constraints, British businessmen can justifiably be accused of 'entrepreneurial failure' (Landes, 1969; Weiner, 1981). But the cause of the failure was not simply cultural conservatism, as some historians have implied. If British society was pervaded by conservative mores, it was in this respect certainly no worse off than Japan or continental European countries that were precapitalist, tradition-bound societies when Britain was the workshop of the world. The thesis of entrepreneurial failure casts no light on why Britain, the first industrial nation, should have been less successful than later industrialisers in shedding customary attitudes that encumbered economic performance.

Britain's distinctiveness derived less from the conservatism of its cultural values per se than from a matrix of rigid institutional structures that reinforced these values and obstructed individualistic as well as concerted efforts at economic renovation. In our view, the causes and consequences of such institutional rigidities remain central to understanding the long-term dynamics of economic development as well as the current crisis of the British economy.

The consequences of competitive capitalism

In the third quarter of the nineteenth century, the British economy experienced a 'long boom' that represented the culmination of the world's first industrial revolution. After three centuries of international conflict for the control of the world markets and after seven decades of intense capital investment in productive capacity, Britain emerged unchallenged in the world economy. On the basis of national domination of world markets, there was much in the way of opportunity for aspiring merchants and manufacturers. As they entered into commerce and industry, the structure of British industry became extremely competitive. By today's standards, Britain's major nineteenth-century staple industries – textiles, iron and steel, coal mining, shipbuilding, and engineering – were all composed of numerous firms with small market shares. Their industrial structures were also characterised by a high degree of vertical specialisation: distribution of intermediate and final products relied upon well-developed market mechanisms, often involving specialised merchant firms.

The managerial organisation and technology employed by nineteenth-century British firms were comparatively simple. Characteristically, firms were run by owner-proprietors or close family associates. Managerial staffs were small and methods of cost accounting and production control were crude or non-existent. The development of industrial techniques typically relied upon trial and error rather than systematic in-house research. Most enterprises were single-plant firms that specialised in particular lines of manufacture or intermediate or final products. Industries exhibited a high degree of regional concentration based upon geographical advantages as well as external economies provided by local access to skilled labour supplies, transport facilities and distribution networks, capital, and product markets.

Up to the 1870s the long-term financing for these business ventures came from country banks, personal family fortunes, and retained earnings. After the collapse of the country banks in the Great Depression of the 1870s, financial institutions had little involvement in the long-term finance of British industry. The purchasers of share capital tended instead to be individuals – among them many shopkeepers and skilled workers – who invested their savings locally. With British firms able to tap local as well as internal sources of long-term financing, there is no evidence that they were short of capital in the decades prior to World War I. The last decades of the nineteenth century also saw the extension of national banks and the development of a highly liquid national capital market. But industrial firms were reluctant to risk loss of control by issuing equity on the national market or incurring long-term debt. Financial institutions provided only short-term working capital to British industry (mainly through overdraft accounts), and as a result never developed the institutional expertise to serve the demand for long-term capital that did arise. Instead they exported most of their capital, usually in exchange for fixed-interest bonds, to finance large-scale (typically government-backed) foreign projects such as railroads. A consequence of these arrangements was the separation of provincial industrial enterprise from national financial institutions based in the City of London, a characteristic feature of the British economy well into the twentieth century.

Another outcome of British capitalism as it developed in the last half of the nineteenth century was the consolidation of job control on the part of many groups of workers in industry. During the 'long boom', individual capitalists, divided by competition, opted for collective accommodation with unions of skilled and strategically positioned workers rather than jeopardise the fortunes of their individual firms through industrial conflict while there were profits to be made. The labour movement also made important legislative gains that enhanced the ability of workers to organise unions, build up union treasuries, and stage successful strikes.

A distinguishing feature of the British labour movement was its two tiers of bargaining strength. Workplace organisations enjoyed substantial local autonomy in bargaining, backed by the leverage that national unions could exert on employers during disputes. From the fourth quarter of the nineteenth century, as intermittent but often prolonged recessions occurred and as foreign competition began to be felt by many industries, capitalists were unable to replace the job control of shop-floor union organisations by managerial control. Despite the introduction of many skill-displacing changes in technology, the power of the union organisations that had developed earlier had simply become too great. Attempts by Parliament and the judiciary to undermine the trade union movement – most notably by means of the Taff Vale decision – resulted in the emergence of a distinct political party representing the interests of labour.

The challenge of corporate capitalism

Elsewhere, from the late nineteenth century (notably in Japan, Germany, and the United States) corporate capitalism was emerging to become the dominant mode of economic organisation. Corporate capitalism was characterised by industrial oligopoly, hierarchical managerial bureaucracy, vertical integration of production and distribution, managerial control over the labour process, the integration of financial and industrial capital, and systematic research and development (Chandler, 1977).

Oligopoly, by helping to stabilise prices and market shares, facilitated long-run planning, particularly where large-scale capital investments were involved. Managerial coordination of product flows within the vertically integrated enterprise permitted the achievement of high-speed throughputs that reduced unit costs. Vertical integration of production and distribution provided the direct access to market outlets that was a precondition for the effective utilisation of mass production methods. Managerial control over the labour process in turn facilitated the introduction of new, high-throughput technologies. Integration of financial and industrial capital, along with managerial bureaucracy, made possible the geographic mobility of capital and the rapid expansion of capacity to produce for new or growing markets. Systematic research and development, particularly in such science-based industries as electrical and chemical manufacturing, provided the mainspring of technological innovation. Across countries, the degree of coordination of economic activity by the state and large financial institutions varied, with significant implications for economic performance. But the experience of successful capitalist economies in the twentieth century demonstrates the ubiquitous importance of the visible hand of corporate bureaucratic management.

In order to compete against the corporate mass production methods being developed in Germany, Japan, and the United States, British industries required transformation of their structures of industrial relations, industrial organisation, and enterprise management. Vested interests in the old structures, however, proved to be formidable (if not insurmountable) obstacles to the transition from competitive to corporate models of organisation. Lacking corporate management skills and opportunities, British industrialists clung to family control of their firms. Even where horizontal amalgamations did take place, the directors of the participating firms insisted on retaining operational autonomy. In any case, very few of these managers had the broader entrepreneurial perspectives or skills needed to develop modern corporate structures.

The British educational system hampered industry by failing to provide appropriately trained managerial and technical personnel. On the supply side, the existing system of higher education was designed almost explicitly to remove its 'aristocratic' students as far as possible from the worldly pursuit of business and applied science. On the demand side, there was comparatively little pressure to transform this system as highly competitive businesses could not afford to hire specialised technical personnel and were further reluctant to support industry-wide research institutes that would benefit competitors as much as themselves. Given the lack of interest in business and the educational establishment in fostering managerial and technical training, it is not surprising that the British state, rather passive towards industrial development in any case, took little initiative to make education more relevant to economic development.

Nor was leadership for industrial transformation forthcoming from other sectors of the British economy. The financial sector kept its distance from direct involvement in industry, preferring instead to maintain its highly liquid position by means of portfolio investment, mostly abroad. The orientation of Britain's bankers towards liquidity and protection of the value of the pound sterling was reinforced by the undisputed position of the City of London as the financial centre of the world. The concentration of banking in the City also gave rise to a relatively cohesive class of finance capitalists with much more concerted and coherent power over national policy than industrial capitalists, who were divided along enterprise, industry, and regional lines.

In the absence of a shift to corporate enterprise structure, British industrialists also had little incentive or ability to challenge the shop-floor control of trade union organisations. In the United States and Germany a critical factor in the development of high-throughput production was the ability of management to gain and maintain the right to manage the utilisation of technology. In most of Britain's staple industries, by contrast, managers had lost much of this 'right to manage', reducing their incentive to invest in costly mass production technologies on which they might not be able to achieve high enough throughputs to justify the capital outlays. During the first half of the twentieth century, British unionism was able to consolidate its positions of control at both the national and workplace levels, aided by the growing strength of the Labour Party and the emergency conditions of two world wars.

Lacking the requisite degree of control over product and input markets, British managers confronted severe obstacles in adapting their enterprise structures to take advantage of new market opportunities. As a result, in the late nineteenth and early twentieth centuries firms continued for the most part to manufacture traditional products using traditional technologies.

How these firms structured production depended very much on the prospects for selling their output. Contrary to typical textbook theory, Britain's competitive firms did not as a rule assume that the market could absorb all the output they might produce at a given price. Indeed they produced few manufactures in anticipation of demand. Almost all production was to order, much of it for sale to merchants for distribution to far-flung international markets.

In the heyday of British worldwide economic dominance, these arrangements proved advantageous to British firms. Unlike many of their international competitors, who had access only to much more confining markets, Britain's international marketing structure meant that British firms could get enough orders of similar specifications to reap economies of long production runs, and had a large enough share in expanding markets to justify investment in (what were then) up-to-date and increasingly capital-intensive plant and equipment. But the tables were turned by the spread abroad of tariff barriers and indigenous industrialisation. Because Britain had already industrialised, its domestic market for such staple commodities as textiles or steel rails had reached a point of at best moderate growth potential. Under these circumstances, British firms could not find at home a market that could match the dramatic rates of expansion of the foreign markets foreclosed to them. Indeed, given its dependence on international markets, British industry was severely constrained to keep its own domestic markets open to the products of foreign firms.

Taking advantage of their more secure and expansive domestic markets, foreign rivals, with more modern, capital-intensive technology, attained longer production runs and higher speeds of throughput than the British. By virtue of their reliance on the corporate form of organisation – in particular on vertical integration of production with distribution and more concentrated market power – Britain's rivals were better able to rationalise the structure of orders and ensure themselves the market outlets required for mass production. From secure home bases these rivals also invaded market areas and product lines where the British should have been at no comparative disadvantage.

Forced to retreat from competition with mass production methods, British firms sought refuge in higher quality and more specialised product lines where traditional craftsmanship and organisation could still command a competitive edge – in spinning higher counts of yarn and weaving finer cloth, making sheets and plates of open hearth steel, and building unique one-off ships. Unfortunately for the British, in a world of expanding markets, the specialised product of the day all too often turned out to be the mass production item of tomorrow. The arrival of mass production methods and the pace and timing of decline varied among the major staple industries, with British shipbuilding, for example, still holding a commanding competitive position as late as World War II. But all eventually met a similar fate.

Institutional rigidity

From the standpoint of the neoclassical model of competition, these developments would lead one to expect a British response to competitive pressures that would imitate the organisational and technological innovations introduced abroad. In fact, the British only adapted patchwork improvements to their existing organisational and productive structure. Facing increasingly insecure markets and lacking the market control requisite for modern mass production, the British failed to make the organisational renovations that could have allowed them to escape competitive decline.

With the massive contractions of British market shares that occurred in the 1920s and early 1930s, firms in the troubled staple industries alternated between scrambling for any markets they could get and proposals for elimination of excess capacity and concentration of productive structure. In a period of contraction the market mechanism was anything but an efficient allocation mechanism, in part because existing firms remained in operation as long as they could hope for some positive return over variable costs, their proprietors living, so to speak, off their capital. Coordinated attempts to eliminate excess capacity were confounded by numerous conflicts of interest between owner-proprietors, outside stockholders, management groups, customers, banks and other creditors, and local union organisations. In particular the involvement of the national banks in the attempts to rationalise industry was aimed more at salvaging their individual financial positions than at developing a coherent plan for industry rationalisation. In the light of the failure to achieve coordination the programs that were implemented in the interwar period were half-hearted and of limited effectiveness.

During the interwar period and beyond, the rigid work rules of British unions remained an impediment to structural reorganisation. Entrenched systems of piece-rate payment often led to higher wage earnings in more productive establishments, deterring firms from scrapping old capacity and investing in new. Union rules also limited management's freedom to alter manning levels and workloads, which in mechanical, labour-intensive industries such as textiles had particularly adverse effects on the prospective benefits of new technology. In general, management could be sure that the unions would attempt to exact a high price for cooperation with any plans for reorganisation that would upset established work and pay arrangements. On the other hand, amidst industrial decline the strong union preference for saving jobs even at low wage levels was an additional conservative influence on a generally unenterprising managerial class.

Given this institutional structure, Britain's staple industries were unable to rationalise on the basis of the profit motive. They relied too much – not too little – on the market mechanism. To be sure, there were some highly successful enterprises such as Imperial Chemical Industries and Unilever that emerged in new industries during the interwar period. But in terms of our perspective on capitalist development, these firms are the exceptions that prove the rule: success was ultimately based on control over product and input markets and the ability to transform internal managerial and production structures to maintain control. Furthermore, even the new industries were not immune to the wider institutional environment.   The slow growth of demand in new product market areas hampered the emergence of large firms and created a need for consolidation of industrial structure.   In chemicals, fabricated metals, and electrical machinery, newly amalgamated firms suffered from a dearth of appropriately trained managerial personnel and, initially, experienced serious difficulties in overcoming vested interests and in establishing effective coordination of their enterprises.   In automobile manufacturing, competitive performance was undermined after World War II by a long-established management strategy of using labour-intensive techniques that helped breed control of shop-floor activities by highly sectionalised union organisations ...

The barely visible hand

What British industry in general required was the visible hand of coordinated control, not the invisible hand of the self-regulating market. Given the absence of leadership from within private industry, increasing pressure fell upon the state to try to fill the gap. Even before World War I, calls were made for greater state intervention. By the interwar period the British state had assumed a distinctly more prominent role in industrial affairs, macroeconomic regulation, and provision of social and welfare services.

With further growth of state intervention after World War II – extending to nationalisation of industry and aggregate demand management – critics have pointed accusing fingers at the government for failing to reverse, and even for causing, relative economic decline. At various times and from various quarters the state has been blamed for undermining private-sector incentives and the natural regenerative processes of the free market economy, for absorbing resources that would have been employed more productively in manufacturing, or for failing to provide British industry with a needed environment of macroeconomic stability and a competitively valued exchange rate.

In historical perspective, however, state activism must be absolved from bearing primary responsibility for Britain's relatively poor economic performance. In the late nineteenth century, at the outset of relative decline, the most singular features of the British state were its small size and laissez-faire policies. Even in the post-World War II period, British levels of government taxes, expenditures, and employment were not particularly high by European standards. Indeed, a distinctive feature of British state policy throughout recent history has been its reluctance to break from laissez-faire traditions. It is only in the second instance that state policy is implicated in British decline, by virtue of its failure to intervene in the economy more decisively in order to take corrective measures. The consequences of this failure of state policy first became evident in the interwar period ...

The legacy of history

The British economy of the post-World War II period inherited a legacy of major industries too troubled to survive the renewed onslaught of international competition that began in the 1950s. As competitive pressure mounted, the state began to nationalise industries such as coal, steel, and automobiles that were deemed of strategic importance to the nation, and (with the exception of steel in 1951) that were in imminent danger of collapse. But nationalisation, however necessary, was by no means a sufficient response to Britain's long-run economic decline. Public ownership overcame the problem of horizontally fragmented private ownership, but not inherited problems of enterprise productive structure, managerial organisation, and union job control. Nationalised enterprises still had to confront these problems while attempting to overcome the technological leads already established by competitors.

Although the British government was called upon willy-nilly to play an increased role in industrial affairs, the basic theoretical and ideological framework guiding public policy has remained that of the self-regulating market economy. The rise of Keynesianism has led to widespread acceptance of interventionist fiscal and monetary policies but for the most part has left unchallenged the neoclassical belief in the inherent dynamism of unfettered market competition.

The monetarist policies of the Thatcher government have taken the neoclassical perspective to its extreme. Invoking laissez-faire ideology, Thatcher has attacked the power of the unions and sought revival through the severity of market discipline. But the supposition that there are forces latent in Britain's 'free market' economy that will return the nation to prosperity finds little confirmation in historical experience. The only foundation for the free-market perspective appears to be the tradition of orthodox economic theory itself.

There is considerable irony in the neoclassical focus on free market competition as the engine of economic dynamism. The focus derives from the fundamental assumption of neoclassical theory that firms are subordinate to markets. History suggests, however, that successful development in the twentieth century has been achieved by markets being made subordinate to firms. The main thrust of the perspective presented here is that the British economy failed to make a successful transition to corporate capitalism in the twentieth century precisely because of the very highly developed market organisation of the economy that had evolved when it was the first and foremost industrial nation.

By now, Britain's relative economic decline has persisted through enough ups and downs in the business cycle to indicate that its roots lie deeper than inappropriate macroeconomic policies. If contemporary economic discussion nonetheless is usually preoccupied with obtaining the right monetary and fiscal policies, it is because there has been comparatively little criticism of the microfoundations of neoclassical theory and related versions of laissez-faire ideology. Despite the prominence of mass production methods in corporate economies, conventional economic theory has failed to analyse the associated developmental process of productivity growth and technological change.

If existing institutional arrangements seriously constrained the actions of individual British industrialists and rendered impotent intervention by the state, the example of late-developing nations suggests that a purposive national programme can enjoy considerable success in adapting institutions to meet growth objectives. The task for political economy is to identify those elements of the prevailing institutional structure that will promote and those that will hinder alternative strategies of socio-economic development. The argument presented here contends that planning at the levels of the enterprise, financial institutions, and the state has become increasingly important for international competitiveness and economic growth, even within the so-called market economies. To elaborate and modify this perspective will require historical studies of the interaction of planning and market forces in economic activity and the resultant impact on performance. Thus far we have only begun to research this perspective, and to test the various hypotheses generated by it. But we view the synthesis presented here, as well as the research upon which it is based, as important foundations for understanding modern economic development.

CHAPTER 9

Britain's industrial decline[*]

Sir Alec Cairncross

What we have to explain is not a fall in the level of productivity, or even a falling-off in the rate of improvement, but a lag behind the rest of Western Europe. The lag to be explained is not in the level of productivity, although the level in Britain is now lower than in the neighbouring countries, but in the rate of improvement. Explanations that tell us only what depresses productivity and makes output per head compare unfavourably with other countries are of no relevance. We have to point to some factor that bites on the process by which productivity is made to improve year after year and can be shown to bite harder in Britain than elsewhere.

But what is it that makes productivity increase? There was a time when Sir Stafford Cripps and other Ministers appealed after 1945 for higher productivity as if there could be an instant response through extra effort.

Extra effort may, of course, produce a once-for-all gain in productivity. But unless progressively increased, it will not yield a steady rise over an extended period. There are, however, other ways in which labour attitudes impinge on the process by which productivity is improved and some of these are very material to the success of this process. Education and training, whether of management or of employees, can improve human capabilities and are exactly the kind of thing that could exercise a growing influence. Indeed, human attitudes and capabilities seem to me to be one of the two principal factors calculated to bring about a progressive improvement in productivity at a rate that experience shows to be continuous and fairly stable except when there is a major shock to the economy or a sudden change in the level of activity. The other factor is technical and organisational change; and this, more than anything else, is what underlies the secular rise in productivity and the standard of living. But if the question is why technical changes should be slower in Britain than abroad the answer comes back to human attitudes and capabilities.

---

[*] Reproduced with permission from 'Britain's industrial decline', *Royal Bank of Scotland Review*, **159**: 5–17, 1988.

Obstacles to innovation

Innovation in the sense in which I am using the term does not consist simply of new ideas and scientific breakthroughs. It is a *commercial* process in which new ideas and scientific knowledge figure as inputs. It is not invention or changes in technique as such but the *commercial* use of new ideas and techniques with a view to profit, the adoption for commercial purposes of some technical improvement in organisation, process or product. The process of discovery is only part of the story but the discovery has then to be introduced to the market place and that calls for quite different gifts and encounters quite different obstacles. A country with an outstanding record in scientific discovery may make a very poor show at using its discoveries commercially. We all know how frequently it happens that discoveries in Britain are turned to commercial advantage in some other country. The same is true of individual enterprises: those that hit on new ideas are not always successful in making a commercial success of them.

Most discoveries are made abroad. From the point of view of a single firm all discoveries other than its own are made, so to speak, abroad. Much of the process of innovation, therefore, involves import and domestication: the adaptation of a discovery to different circumstances of production and use. There has to be the ability to spot the potential of the discovery, to view it in relation to a different set of market requirements, to adapt it to the productive facilities available, and to co-ordinate all the various changes involved.

Innovation will be rapid where staffs are skilled at recognising the possibilities for change and at handling the various changes required. It will be slow where these skills are lacking or where there is inertia or active opposition to change or a failure to make proper use of new equipment and techniques, or a disposition to skim off the prospective gains as the price of acquiescence in technical or organisational change. The obstacles to innovation are obviously greater, for example, in a country flushed with victory in war and confirmed in its faith in existing institutions and practices than in one that has been defeated, devastated or occupied. Where the disturbance has been less, the chances of a re-establishment of the *status quo* are obviously greater.

There will, of course, be some innovations where the gains are so large that they proceed as rapidly in Britain as elsewhere. There is evidence that in the adoption of major inventions the British record is not appreciably different from elsewhere. But major inventions form only a small part of the steady flow of improvements in design and method by which productivity is gradually increased.

It is change and innovation that yield rising productivity and an economy seeking to improve its rate of growth has to gear itself to welcome change and facilitate innovation. It is the obstacles to innovation whether in the labour force or in management or in any other form that account for slow growth.

Since there are many such obstacles both in Britain and in other countries, it is not easy to establish which of them accounts for the lag in productivity growth.

It is impossible to identify some single factor that can by itself provide a complete explanation of Britain's relatively poor performance. Even if one could, the explanation would be unlikely to have the same force throughout the past hundred years. Moreover, an explanation that accounted convincingly for poor performance in one industry would have to be coupled with quite different explanations for others. The obstacles to innovation in the coal industry, the motor industry and nuclear power generation may differ widely. All one can hope to do is to run over some of the more plausible explanations of the divergence in performance in the more recent past and see which of them seems to hold water.

Some explanations focus on the industrial environment within which an innovator operates and point to the constraints which he cannot himself relax. These may be cultural or educational or economic. Other explanations confine themselves to the constraints within the enterprise making the innovation. These may limit the pace of innovation by dissipating the gains expected from it: through outright opposition to its introduction or failure to secure its use under optimum conditions; through higher wages to those who operate it or lower prices to the consumer or extra tax payments to the Exchequer.

The industrial environment

I need say little about cultural factors. These are always important to the pace of change. But 'cultural' is often narrowed so as to relate only to industrial leadership: a decline, as Weiner puts it, in the industrial spirit through gentrification that stifles vigorous innovation. It is hard to see how this applies to the recent past, especially as innovation has been *more* rapid in post-war years. Even on a longer view, I doubt whether 'gentrification' has been of much importance. What has mattered more are cultural influences expressing themselves in weaknesses in the educational system. On the one hand has been the English preference for learning on the job rather than first engaging in study and training; on the other, the effort to contain public expenditure, including expenditure on education, and reluctance to entrust the state with responsibility for higher education. These have combined to leave British industry inadequately educated and unable to adapt itself to rapid change. There was also at one time a neglect of science that delayed the growth of some branches of the chemical and electrical engineering industries. But how much does all that amount to in the 1980s?

There is no reason to dispute that British managements have been slow in innovating: the question is why? Their social aspirations would not seem to have been of great importance. Their lack of university education may have played a larger part in unawareness or neglect of the opportunities open to them. It may also be true that the cultural environment helped to deflect talent away from manufacturing industry. If so, this would seem nowadays to be less an outcome of the educational system, or of what Arthur Lewis calls 'humanistic snobbery', than of a sense that industry in Britain can easily turn into a dogfight best avoided by going into the professions or the City.

A cultural bias that might limit the capacity of British managements to innovate, particularly in the metal and engineering trades, which form about half the manufacturing industry of the country, is a lack of high-grade engineers. Qualified engineers in Britain lack the prestige they enjoy abroad. In contrast to other industrial countries, few of the brightest university entrants have elected to study engineering and many of those who qualify prefer not to enter industrial employment. Thus for many years the engineering profession has failed to attract men of the highest calibre (to say nothing of women). But this is not just a matter of cultural bias or appropriate training. It reflects also the value of British managements set on well-qualified engineers, and indeed on industrial training generally. So long as engineers are offered much higher salaries in the City, one can only conclude that industry does not rate their services very highly. In the same way if there is an aversion from industrial employment among graduates generally, the explanation is more likely to lie in low pay and the absence of demand than in the kind of education they have received.

One can, of course, argue that British managements were simply less competent than their foreign counterparts and there is plenty of evidence of managerial failings. One need only listen to first hand accounts of what went on between the wars, or more recently, in steel or shipbuilding or car manufacturing, to be appalled at the neglect of elementary rules of good management. My own recollections of the aircraft industry in war-time amply confirm the impression of widespread managerial shortcomings. It is not surprising if there is a lot of dead wood at the top of businesses that pass by inheritance and are in the hands of ageing proprietors, as happens with most smaller businesses – and not only in the United Kingdom. But how far does this take us? Can we be sure that the average level of business ability is lower in the United Kingdom than elsewhere? If so, we have still to explain why. We have also to explain why competition does not rid us of the less competent and enterprising managements.

Market forces and the role of competition

It is at this point that one moves over from cultural and educational to economic constraints on managerial initiative. Economists have argued that British experience demonstrates the ineffectiveness of competition in promoting industrial efficiency (especially Elbaum and Lazonick). Most British industries, it is suggested, stood in post-war years in need of extensive re-organisation into larger units, able to take a long view and enjoy modern corporate management. Instead, they remained fragmented into sub-optimal units, each competing vigorously in price but unable, because of competitive pressures, to make the profits necessary for modernisation of its equipment and adaptation of its products and processes.   One can illustrate the process from the failure of Scottish steel makers between the wars to agree on the replacement of their small and obsolete plants by a single integrated plant at Erskine Ferry.   Competition in these circumstances neither drove plants out of business nor allowed them to make the profit necessary for modernisation nor led to investment in a larger and more efficient plant making lower cost steel.   Such investment would have been too risky in face of competition from existing units.   On this showing, what British industry needs is restructuring into a few large and forward-looking units, with a management and market power to match, free to concentrate on planning for future development without the distractions of intense competition.

It is a prescription that many would endorse.   Even in Victorian times economists would have agreed that efficiency in rail transport was not likely to be promoted by multiplying the number of competing railway systems.   A single well-managed company may well prove a more successful innovator than a group of under-capitalised competitors.   Nevertheless it is hard to believe that the path to more rapid innovation in Britain lies through the swallowing up of competitors into large monopolistic units.   Experience with the nationalised industries hardly points in that direction.   In any event, large units already play as important a role in British manufacturing industry as in Germany or other industrial countries.   Whatever the workings of competition, it is not fragmentation into smaller units that distinguishes British industry; and where larger units are needed in the interests of efficiency, take-overs go at least some way to establishing them and to keeping managements on their toes.

An allied explanation of British backwardness is couched in terms of financial arrangements.   It is argued that reliance for capital on shareholders free to sell their holdings at any time obliges industry to take a short-term view and avoid innovations involving heavy capital outlay.   There is also a difficulty in raising capital for new ventures lacking an adequate track record.   Financial agencies like the investment banks of continental countries would be more likely to arrive at a reasonable assessment of risk and stick to their judgement without looking for short-term capital gains.   There is obviously some force in these considerations even if, as a matter of history, investment banks were a substitute for the kind of capital market that had come into existence in countries where the banks were able to confine themselves more narrowly to the provision of working capital. But lack of finance has rarely been a major complaint of British industry, even in periods like that before the first world war when scholars continue to assume that it must have been.   It is lack of demand for capital rather than lack of supply that has to be explained; and it is very doubtful whether lack of demand can be attributed to dependence on a host of shareholders rather than on a single backer.

There have also been wider influences at work in the international economy unfavourable to the United Kingdom.   It has been true for at least two centuries that Britain supplied a particularly wide scatter of markets throughout the world while her continental neighbours tended to concentrate to a greater extent on the markets on their doorstep.   This had two important consequences.   One was that

British exports fluctuated with the prosperity of primary producing countries overseas rather than with the prosperity of other manufacturing countries in Europe. In the post-war years this meant that British export markets expanded less rapidly than the European markets supplied by her continental neighbours, which were particularly buoyant as they recovered from the low levels of activity to which the war had reduced them. This of itself gave her competitors on the continent an advantage since productivity rises faster the more buoyant the markets supplied. In addition, the greater diversity of British markets made for a less specialised industrial structure with shorter runs and less scope for standardisation. There was less possibility, therefore, of layouts using capital intensive methods to produce to a pre-arranged design and concentrating on improvement of the design so as to reduce production costs or keep pace with market requirements. In an area like Clydeside, for example, the industrial structure shaped by market pressure was such in the late 1940s that there was virtually no experience of series production. The engineering industries, although highly diversified, were confined almost exclusively to turning out one-off jobs like ships and locomotives and had little or no familiarity with line production such as is required in the manufacture of motor-cars, aircraft, and consumer durables of all kinds.

In the post-war years therefore large sectors of British industry laboured under a double disadvantage. On the one hand, their traditional markets abroad were not particularly elastic and were thrown open progressively to competitors previously excluded by preferential tariffs and other circumstances. On the other hand, their traditional lay-outs, staffs and mentalities were ill-adapted to the requirements of an age of mass production. British industry was over-supplied with skill, under-supplied with capital, and lacking in the kind of staff needed for rapid innovation.

Labour problems

Most observers, however, would point to none of these influences on industrial productivity as the prime source of British backwardness. They would be more likely to pin on constraints within the individual enterprise, notably inadequate training both of management and of workers and bad industrial relations. The need for better labour training has been argued convincingly by S. J. Prais and its importance to the level of productivity is obvious (Prais, 1987; Prais and Steedman, 1986; Prais and Wagner, 1983, 1985). In its effects on the rate of growth in productivity, however, it is perhaps a less important factor than the confrontational atmosphere in much of British industry and it is to this that I now turn.

The obstacles to innovation are greater when managements shrink from changes likely to produce disputes or find their time (the most important single input into innovation) absorbed in trying to settle disputes; or if there is such a large price tag attached to innovation by those who are asked to give effect to it that it is robbed of profit, which oozes away trying to placate or compensate them.

Labour difficulties have been particularly marked in British industry throughout the post-war period. I should make it clear that I am not talking of strikes but of difficulties and tensions in the working day. There have been constant complaints of poor motivation of the labour force and lack of readiness to co-operate in changes of organisation, equipment and productive methods (or, put differently, bloody-mindedness and militancy). Nor are such complaints new. They were probably at their height in the years before the first world war at a time when, not surprisingly, labour productivity showed little or no improvement. Moreover, by common consent, labour relations in industry in Britain have been fundamentally different from those in our continental neighbours. We have thus an explanation of such generality and persistence that it can plausibly account for at least some of the continuing divergence between the growth of labour productivity here and abroad.

I do not suggest that labour attitudes provide the whole explanation. I have already outlined a variety of other contributory factors including the influence of managerial inertia and inadequacy. Weak and incompetent managements, moreover, make their own contribution to bad labour relations in British industry. The two things interact. If managements show inertia and weakness it is sometimes in reaction to labour militancy and strength. Even when management is competent and respected, innovation may still be held back by labour attitudes. In most other industrial countries managements feel free to decide how best to use the services of their workers; but in Britain the use to which workers' time is put is far more frequently a matter of negotiation between them and their employers.

The lack of control over activities on the shop floor in British factories originated in the low level of investment in plant, the underdevelopment of management and supervisory staff, and the general lack of direct co-ordination of the production process. Reliance came to be placed on incentive payments to maintain the pace of work rather than careful advance planning of tasks; and with this went a degree of 'labour independence' and an increase in labour bargaining power. Management economised on staff and capital but at the cost of a surrender of shop floor control ...

Conclusion

The British, I suggest, opted for slower growth. I am referring to the period before 1975, not to the slowdown since then which is quite different in origin. They did not feel the compelling need that other countries, overrun, occupied or defeated, had felt at the end of the war to give wealth-creation priority over everything else in order to survive. They continued to indulge in long-established restrictive practice and habits of confrontation, feeling no need for change. Where West German workers insisted that their employers must make adequate profits if jobs were to be secure and took a relaxed view of what profit was adequate, British workers treated profits as an incitement to wage demands. Whereas in Japan the workers literally opened the day by singing the praises of the management, British workers were alive chiefly to its errors and incompetence, real or imagined.

In the next few years what happens in the world economy will have more influence on British industry than anything done in this country. It would be rash to predict whether we are on the brink of world recovery or a fresh setback. Things may go either way. Taking a longer view, I find little reason to expect a reversal of long-established trends. With all the slack that has accumulated there is room for a sustained spurt in growth in all the industrial countries. But unless there are more fundamental changes than have yet occurred, for example in labour training and in labour relations, Britain is unlikely to show to advantage. The competitive position of British industry may weaken further and important penetration continue to gather force. In the long run as in the short, the pace of industrial recovery will be largely dictated by other countries. Fast or slow, it will leave Britain still lagging behind her neighbours and still remaining a net importer of manufactures.

CHAPTER 10

The figures of descent[*]

Perry Anderson

The fundamental origin of the decline of British capitalism lay in its initial priority. As the historical first-comer, British industrialisation arrived without deliberate design, and triumphed without comparable competitors. British manufacturing acquired its early shape unawares, from modest immediate constituents; just as it won world hegemony with no strategic plan, but simply from the spontaneous force of its own chronological lead – within the framework of an English commercial imperialism that preceded it. The easy dominance that British industry achieved in the first half of the 19th century laid down certain durable lines of development. The first country to mechanise textiles and build railways, Britain generated 'development blocs' of inter-related capital investment around them, embodied in physical technologies and spatial regions which then took on a massive historical inertia. Its enterprises started out small in size, and provincial in location; and the family firm persisted as a typical ownership pattern long afterwards. Its labour-force achieved forms of collective organisation well before any other, reflecting the decentralised company landscape and embedded in the early bloc of technologies. Once set, these structures became progressively greater handicaps in competition with later industrial economies – which started with newer fixed capital, embodied in more modern technology, larger entrepreneurial units, and less unionised work-forces. Characteristic of these followers was an element of conscious disgression from the market, inherent in their situation as they confronted an established leader that had always relied on it – the emergence of tariffs at the level of the state and cartels at the level of the firm, in Germany, the USA or France.

For the logic of the market, left to itself, necessarily tends to be *cumulative* rather than *corrective*. Its dynamic is the play of comparative advantage and disadvantage from existing or entering endowments, as these are calculated by individual entrepreneurial units. It was precisely such a play that fixed the path of

---

[*] Reproduced with permission from 'The figures of descent', *New Left Review,* **161**: 74–7, 1987.

subsequent Victorian involution itself. The sum of perfectly rational choices for particular capitals – to persist in traditional industrial sectors in which investment had already been sunk, to move into those overseas markets where competition was least, to avoid extensive reorganisation of labour processes at home, or simply to shift from profit-making altogether into rent or interest – all together determined a creeping loss of competitive capacity for British capitalism as a whole, confronted with Germany or the USA. The combined and uneven development of capital that is a product of the world market, in other words, is not amenable to correction by it. The experience of English neo-liberalism in the 1980s has in this respect merely repeated the ancestral lessons of the 1880s. The tougher labour regime brought by Thatcher's stabilisation programme was no match for those in the repressive semi-industrialised states of the Third World, bringing little benefit to Britain's manufacturers in exchange for the demand costs incurred by it; while the greater freedoms of capital have simply accelerated what Tom Nairn has called the habitual 'eversion' of British financial flows abroad. Deregulation – of labour and capital markets – could only mean still more deindustrialisation, in pre-established conditions. The laws of comparative advantage have continued to work themselves out, by their own momentum. The rectification of disadvantages requires another kind of social logic. For it to occur, a centralising force capable of regulating and counteracting the spontaneous molecular movements of the market must exist.

Patterns of regulative centralism

Since the Second World War there have been three major types of such a regulative intelligence in advanced capitalism, with a fourth subvariant. In France post-war economic reconstruction was directed by a highly trained and cohesive technocracy, closely connected to private business, but with its own independent base in the public administration of the Fourth and Fifth Republics. The stratum of *grands commis* was responsible for the modernising strategy of an interventionist state, whose planning mechanisms mobilised investment – through subsidised credits – for the deliberate and long-term project of overcoming the historic backwardness of French capitalism. The result was the creation of an industrial park of advanced, if selective technologies that allowed France to overtake the UK in national product by the mid-sixties, and to give it today a 50 per cent higher per capita income. In West Germany, on the other hand, there was no bourgeois state adapted to a similar role after Allied occupation and federalisation. There it was the banking system that performed comparable functions for the economy as a whole. Germany had always been the classical land of the investment bank, from the Wilhelmine epoch onwards – that is, of a finance capital accustomed to direct monitoring and control of the performance of industrial concerns dependent on its loans. After the Second World War this national tradition took on renewed importance, as the three big private banks came to own over a third of the equity of the country's major corporations, with commensurate representation on company boards and power over share prices, while at the same time rapidly expanding their retail functions. The resultant 'universal banks' have acted – in concert with the *Bundesbank* – as the co-ordinators of the West German 'miracle', and overseers of the export supremacy of Federal manufacturers from the sixties onwards. The even more spectacular growth of Japanese capitalism, after yet greater physical devastation and defeat, has for its part been based on a combination of the French and German patterns. For in Japan a purposefully interventionist state, with a masterful bureaucracy, has worked in tandem with the cluster of powerful banks that constitute the strategic core of the *keiretsu*, the great Japanese multi-industrial groupings, to lend a uniquely centralist cast to the national economy. High rates of corporate investment, for long-range returns, are orchestrated by abundant low-cost credit from these banks, covered in their turn by the Bank of Japan. Through this dual system, public planning and private accounting can interlock effectively across the commanding heights of industry, giving Japan its unrivalled capacity for rapid and flexible reconversions in response to changing conditions of international competition in different product lines.

These cases of a supra-market logic have each in their own way exemplified the two typical agencies distinguished by Gerschenkron in his account of the motor forces of late-comer industrialisation in 19th-century Europe – first industrial banks, then the state. They can be regarded as 20th-century versions of the same imperative – the need for a qualitatively superior quota of central orchestration if economic handicaps are to be reversed rather than aggregated, on the world market. The contemporary epoch has also seen, however, a third model of this kind of agency, of more recent formulation. In Sweden or Austria – small countries occupying marginal, and potentially precarious, niches in the world economy – labour has played an institutional role comparable to that of bureaucracy or banking elsewhere. There, stable social-democratic hegemony in the political order, based on mass trade-union and party organisation, has been translated into sustained economic steerage towards competitive industrial branches, capable of assuring long-term employment in favourable social conditions. The key to this variant is a highly unified and disciplined labour movement, capable not only of winning repeated electoral victories but also of centralising wage-bargaining on a national scale; willing not only to respect the rules of capital accumulation but actively to enforce and promote them, in exchange for the benefits of economic growth and social security. Swedish labour market policy and Austrian concertation, each deliberately geared to export performance, have been the expression of working-classes at once self-confident and self-limiting, habituated equally to the occupancy of offices of state and to the permanency of bourgeois society outside them.

Britain's singularity

The singularity of Britain has been to lack any of these three possible correctors, once the process of decline became manifest. Not that their equivalents in the UK have been weak, or negligible. On the contrary, it is an irony that they have all of them been exceptionally strong in their own terms. But in each case, it was the wrong kind of strength – one which disabled rather than fitted them for a historical rectification of the plight of British capitalism. The UK state has long been uniquely formidable as a constitutional structure for securing the active consent of the population to the political order; it is now equipped with the most experienced and professional apparatus for the exercise of coercion in any domestic emergency as well. No other major Western society of this century has been so stable and secure, civically and ideologically, as the one over which Westminster and Whitehall preside. But the British state, constructed to contain social conflict at home and police an empire abroad, has proved impotent to redress economic decline. The night-watchman acquired traits of the welfare officer, but never of the engineer. Sustained and structural intervention in the economy was the one task for which its organic liberalism was entirely ill suited. Similarly Britain has always possessed the most powerful financial sector of any imperialist economy in this century, or the last. Its bankers and brokers have amassed outsized fortune and influence within the constellation of English capital as a whole. From the epoch of the arrival of modern industry to that of the onset of its departure, the weight of the City in national development has not had a proportionate equivalent in any other country. Yet precisely the success of the peculiar British form of financial and mercantile capital on a world state has prevented it from acting as the central nervous system of corporate manufacturing at home. The profits of global intermediation have so eclipsed those of industrial supervision that the actual effect of City institutions has been the very opposite of that of the classical investment banks – not co-ordinating and reconstructive, but centrifugal and unbalancing.

Finally, the labour movement too has its own claims to some international precedence. Working-class organisation in the sphere of production is not only the oldest in the world, but also still among the least tamed or tractable. There have been labour movements which have achieved more impressive levels of unionisation and superior electoral records – above all in Scandinavia or Austria. There have been others which have demonstrated greater revolutionary ambition and political insurgency – above all in the Latin countries. But the British labour movement has been marked by a combination of traits that set it apart from either – a pervasive and deep-rooted union implantation, unlike its Mediterranean counterparts, with a traditional lack of central authority and obdurate resistance to rationalisation of the factors of production, unlike its Nordic equivalents. It was this configuration which blocked any prospect of a Swedish or Austrian path in the post-war UK. The alloy of class ambition and accommodation that characterised the successful reformism of Central and Northern Europe was missing – indeed, inverted in the specifically British mixture of demission and recalcitrance. Hence the complete failure of social-democracy in Britain to acquit any of the tasks of bourgeois modernisation whose urgency it eventually came to proclaim. Trade-union powers were not sublimated into a successful tripartism in the service of re-industrialisation, but harassed in vain attempts to break the springs of shop floor solidarities. The result was that just as Britain possessed a state inured to colonial military intervention yet incapable of consistent economic intervention at home, and a world capital of finance without true finance capital, so it had a corporate working-class that never generated an operative corporatism. In each case, on the contrary, the particular strength of the forces in presence was not merely displaced but actually counterproductive for the recovery of the first industrial nation. The imperial traditions of the state led to the sub-contracted rearmament and overseas commitments that dissipated a post-war export lead; the global transactions of the City diverted potential investments abroad; the localised unruliness of labour discouraged a general reconversion of production processes. The *fainéant* industrial bourgeois of modern British history found no understudies for their role. The other actors compounded rather than compensated for their abdication from the scene.

The predicament of British capitalism, confronted with deepening decline and short of any credible corrective against it, can be seen in a yet clearer relief by one furthe comparison. Its patron is today before a not dissimilar situation. The United States has been the other great loser in the race for higher-than-average productivity, during the boom and into the slump. Its rates of increase of output per labourer have been persistently lower than those of any other country since the mid-sixties, save the UK itself. The basic historical reason for that slowdown must be sought in the American triumph in the Second World War itself, which made the USA the world's premier power. The colossal growth of the US war economy, and the post-war prosperity that succeeded it, which laid down the grid of the major part of the country's stock of fixed capital, created a set of development blocs that would ultimately prove as fateful for subsequent accumulation as the mid-Victorian proved to be for English capitalism; while at the same time, world imperial commitments further narrowed the domestic path of growth, by their diversion of research and investment into military technologies. America's defeated rivals, by contrast, started their cycles of post-war accumulation a decisive period later, after far-reaching dislocation and destruction of their pre-war or war-time industrial landscapes; nor were they burdened with the same military wastage.

Once overall US dominance began to falter, as the American share of world manufacturing trade dropped steadily under the impact of their competition, Washington was faced with much the same historical issues as London. For American capitalism also lacks any of the proven mechanisms for checking or reversing the laws of uneven development, once the play of comparative advantages turns against it. The Federal State is still less equipped, by tradition or vocation, for purposive re-industrialisation than its unitary British opposite.

The banking system, technically debarred from fusing investment with clearing functions or retailing across state lines since the Depression, is poorly positioned for central steerage roles, which it effectively lost before the First World War. The labour movement is politically vestigial. In these circumstances, coherent remedies or reactions to relative economic decline are likely to prove very difficult. The great difference between the two Anglo-Saxon cases, of course, is not just their timing but the still towering force of large industrial capital in the USA, to which Britain has never possessed any equivalent. Its logic, however, is that of the world market rather than the national economy. For all the local advantages of their sun-belt internal frontier, the reality is that the largest and most advanced manufacturing corporations of the United States are even more thoroughly multinational than those of the UK in their location and direction. Their anchorage in domestic supply or demand is progressively loosening. An ever greater extra-territoriality lies ahead of them.

Britain, then, not only witnesses the probable early beginnings in America of something like a vaster repetition of the same historical process it has undergone, in the absence of the same gyroscopes it has lacked, but also perhaps the signs of its ultimate generalisation throughout the advanced capitalist world. For the radical internationalisation of the forces of production – not to speak of circulation – that defines the spearhead forms of capital in the final years of the 20th century promises to render all national correctors, whatever their efficacy to date, increasingly tenuous in the future. In that sense, no bourgeois society – not even the last great classically national economy, Japan – will be immune to the unpredictable tides and tempests of an uneven development whose elements are acquiring a well-nigh meteorological velocity around the world, across all frontiers. The British crisis has no solution in sight; and perhaps the time in which one was possible, as a national recovery, has passed. At the zenith of English capitalism, Marx declared that his portrait of it in *Capital* held a mirror of the future to the rest of the world. Now towards its nadir, the superscription may lead once again: *De te fabula narratur*.

CHAPTER 11

De-industrialisation in the UK: three theses*

Bob Rowthorn and John Wells

Whether one considers relative shares or absolute numbers the decline in industrial employment in the UK has been spectacular. What accounts for it? Why did this decline begin so much earlier in the UK than in most other countries and why has it been so great? ... We can identify three potential explanations for what has happened.

The Maturity Thesis

The first thesis locates Britain's own historical experience within a more general theory of economic development and structural change. ... [We know that] economic development is accompanied by an almost continuous rise in the share of services in total employment ... [and that the] impact of this on industrial employment depends on the stage of development that an economy has reached. In the early and intermediate stages of development, services grow at the expense of agriculture and their share in total employment rises, whilst that of agriculture falls. Meanwhile, the share of industrial employment generally rises. However, at a later stage of development, once an economy has reached 'maturity', the situation is quite different. In such an economy, only a small fraction of the labour force is employed in agriculture and any major increase in the share of services in total employment must be at the expense of industry, whose share must fall. This, in a nutshell, is the Maturity Thesis. It explains why, in a mature economy, the share of industry in total employment falls in the course of time ...

The Maturity Thesis is primarily about employment shares and not absolute numbers. The absolute number of people employed in the industrial sector

---

* Reproduced with permission from *Deindustrialization and Foreign Trade*, Cambridge University Press, 1987.

depends on the behaviour of total employment. Where total employment is growing rapidly, the relative share of industry may fall a considerable amount without there being any reduction at all in the absolute number of people employed in this sector. On the other hand, where total employment is increasing slowly, any major reduction in the relative share of industry will be accompanied by an absolute fall in industrial employment. The second point concerns economic performance. The Maturity Thesis asserts that, at a certain stage in development, the share of industry in total employment will start to fall. In a successful mature economy this fall in industry's share of employment will be accompanied by a rapid growth in output and labour productivity in the industrial sector. The growth in service employment will be enough to provide work for virtually all who require it, including people displaced from the industrial sector through automation and other labour-saving measures. ... We use the term 'positive de-industrialisation' to describe the kind of dynamic change in employment structure which occurs in a successful mature economy. In an unsuccessful mature economy, a similar shift in employment structure occurs, but the mechanism is different. In such an economy, industry is in a state of crisis, industrial output is rising very slowly or even falling, and industrial employment may be falling absolutely. Although service employment may be increasing, it is not doing so fast enough to prevent a considerable rise in unemployment. ... We use the term 'negative de-industrialisation' to describe this kind of shift in the structure of employment. Thus, in a mature economy, no matter how good or bad is the performance of the industrial sector, the share of industry in total employment will normally fall in the course of time. Depending on what happens to total employment, this fall in the share of industry may or may not be accompanied by an absolute fall in industrial employment. This, at least, is the claim made by the Maturity Thesis.

The Specialisation Thesis

A second potential explanation for the decline in manufacturing employment in the UK is concerned with foreign trade, with the huge changes which have occurred in the structure of UK trade over the past thirty years ... By the time post-war recovery was complete, Britain had once again become a highly specialised 'workshop' economy, importing vast amounts of food and raw materials, as well as oil, in return for manufactured exports. This can be seen from the balance of payments figures. In 1950–2, the surplus on UK manufacturing trade averaged 10.5% of GDP whilst, on non-manufacturing trade, the average deficit was 13.3% of GDP. These are truly remarkable figures, which have never been equalled, before or since, in British history. The reasons for such a remarkable situation are briefly as follows. On the non-manufacturing side, global scarcities in the aftermath of the Second World War had forced up to unprecedented levels the real cost of items which Britain had always imported in bulk, such as food and raw materials. Moreover, Britain's previously massive income from service activities, such as shipping and the City of London, had fallen, whilst receipts from coal exports, which had earlier been enormous, had almost vanished. This combination of inflated import prices and reduced earnings from service and coal exports explains why the deficit in non-manufacturing trade was so large in the early 1950s. To cover this deficit, the UK had no alternative but to export manufactured goods. Her profits from overseas investment had been greatly reduced by the enforced war-time sale of assets in the US and elsewhere, and the scope for overseas borrowing was limited. So, to finance her huge deficit on non-manufacturing trade, the UK required a surplus of almost equal magnitude in her manufacturing trade. This surplus was achieved through a vigorous combination of industrial protection and export promotion.

The early 1950s mark the high point of the UK's role as a 'workshop' economy. Since then, the picture has been transformed beyond recognition. In non-manufacturing trade, the old deficit has disappeared completely, to be replaced by a small surplus averaging 1% of GDP in 1981–83. Meanwhile, in manufacturing trade the opposite has occurred, and the old surplus has been replaced by a small deficit. This transformation is often seen as a symptom of Britain's industrial decline and of the failure of her manufacturing sector to compete successfully in international markets. However, ... such an interpretation is unfounded. Certainly, the performance of manufacturing industry has been very poor during the past thirty years, but this is not a major factor explaining why there has been such a dramatic transformation in the structure of UK trade. The cause of this transformation lies mainly in events largely unrelated to the country's industrial performance. Since the early 1950s, there has been a whole stream of autonomous developments whose cumulative impact on Britain's trade structure and pattern of specialisation has been enormous. It is these autonomous developments which explain why Britain is no longer a workshop economy, why she no longer has a large deficit on her trade in non-manufactures or a large surplus on her manufacturing trade.

Since the early 1950s, imports of food and raw materials have become much cheaper in real terms; increased domestic food production has reduced the need for food imports; new methods of production and a changing composition of output have reduced the need for imported raw materials; service exports in such areas as civil aviation, consultancy and finance have risen; finally, the discovery of North Sea oil has turned Britain into a major oil producer. Between them, these developments explain why the UK's balance of trade in non-manufactures has improved so dramatically since the early 1950s. They also explain why the balance of trade in manufactures has deteriorated so dramatically over this period. In the early 1950s, the UK was a 'workshop' economy because she had to be. To finance the huge deficit in non-manufacturing trade, the country required a huge surplus in manufacturing trade. There was simply no other way to remain solvent. Nowadays, however, the situation is quite different.

The UK no longer has a huge deficit in non-manufacturing trade and, as a result, she no longer requires a huge surplus in her trade in manufactures. The UK is no longer a massive net exporter of manufactures, because she no longer needs to be, and her poor industrial performance has only a marginal bearing on the matter. The dramatic decline in the UK's manufacturing surplus during the past thirty years is not primarily a symptom of industrial failure but is mainly a response to developments elsewhere in the economy. Autonomous developments in non-manufacturing trade have led to a new pattern of specialisation, a new role for the UK in the world economy, of which the loss of her formerly huge manufacturing surplus is but one expression ...

Here, then, is a potential explanation for what has happened to manufacturing employment in the UK over the past thirty years. In the early 1950s, the UK was a highly specialised manufacturing exporter, perhaps the most extreme example of a workshop economy the world has ever seen. This, in itself, helps to explain why such a large fraction of her labour force was employed in manufacturing industry. Since those days, because of developments in non-manufacturing trade, the British economy has become much less specialised. The country no longer requires such a large surplus in manufacturing trade and, as a result, no longer needs to employ anything like such a large fraction of her labour force in manufacturing. Moreover, no other country has experienced such a massive transformation in its foreign trade structure during the past thirty years. No other country, not even Austria or Norway, has experienced such a vast improvement in its non-manufacturing balance over the period, nor such a deterioration in its manufacturing balance. This may help to explain why the decline in manufacturing employment has been so much greater in the UK than in most other countries.

The Failure Thesis

So far we have considered two explanations for the decline of manufacturing employment in the UK ... There is, however, a third possible explanation – the 'Failure Thesis'. As its name suggests, this thesis sees the decline in manufacturing employment as a symptom of economic failure: the growing failure of manufacturing industry to compete internationally or to produce the level of output required for a prosperous and fully employed economy. The Failure Thesis can be summarised in the following set of propositions:

(1)   The UK's economic record in the realm of incomes and employment has been poor;

(2)   This is largely due to the weak performance of UK manufacturing industry;

(3)   If the performance of UK manufacturing industry had been much stronger, UK manufacturing output would have been much greater;

(4)   This would have stimulated the non-manufacturing side of the economy and led to the creation of more employment in services and other non-manufacturing activities;

(5)   Finally, if UK manufacturing output had been higher, neither the absolute number of people employed in manufacturing, nor this sector's share in total employment, would have fallen anything like as fast as they have done.

Many of these propositions are quite uncontroversial and are universally accepted by economists of all persuasions. Even so, let us examine them briefly.

Consider the question of Britain's economic record. Here the evidence of failure is overwhelming. By international standards, real per capita income has risen slowly in the UK, particularly since 1973. Moreover, growth in GDP since 1973 has been entirely the result of North Sea oil production; indeed, between 1973 and 1983, non-oil GDP actually fell by 2%. The cumulative effect of slow growth on the UK's position in the international hierarchy can be seen ... In 1953, the UK was amongst the half dozen richest countries in the world. By 1983, of all the advanced capitalist countries, she was amongst the poorest. In the realm of employment, the UK's record is equally dismal. In the 1950s, there was almost full employment in the UK, and the bulk of her population had never enjoyed greater economic security. However, by 1984, well over three million people were out of work and, of all the advanced capitalist countries, only Belgium and the Netherlands had a greater fraction of their labour force without employment. Not since the 1930s have so many British people faced such a bleak and insecure future.

So much for economic welfare. What about the role of manufacturing industry in all of this? Here again the evidence is overwhelming. By international standards, the performance of British manufacturing industry has been very poor, especially since the oil crisis of 1973. Prior to 1973, British manufacturing output and productivity rose quite fast compared with the country's previous historical experience. However, in many other countries they rose even faster. As a result, despite moderately fast industrial growth, Britain was overtaken by many of her foreign rivals during this period and, by the time the world crisis broke at the end of 1973, she was no longer a first-rank industrial power. Thus, up to 1973, the decline of British manufacturing was relative rather than absolute. Since then, however, industrial decline has become absolute and manufacturing output is now lower than it was in 1973. Meanwhile, manufacturing output has continued to rise in other countries, albeit irregularly. Between 1973 and 1982, manufacturing output fell by 18% in the UK, whilst in the six major OECD countries it rose by 15% on average ...

The weakness of manufacturing industry is certainly the main reason why the UK has become a relatively poor country and why per capita incomes in the UK are now the lowest in Northern Europe. It also helps to explain why the unemployment rate is so high.

Consider what it would mean if Britain's manufacturing industry were much stronger and more competitive than it is at present, having more equipment, using more advanced methods of production and producing a wider range and higher quality of output. For a start, manufacturing output would obviously be much greater. Part of this additional output would go directly to meet domestic requirements, and part would be exported to pay for imports from foreign countries. Some of these additional imports would be non-manufactures, such as raw materials and services, but there would also be a large increase in manufactured imports. Taking account of additional supplies from both domestic industry and foreign producers, the total amount of manufactured goods available for use in the UK would be much greater than it is at present. Since the production and distribution of manufactured goods involves a wide range of complementary activities, output would be greater in areas such as construction, mining, consulting, transport and retail distribution. Moreover, real incomes would be higher and, consequently, consumers' expenditure of almost every kind would be greater, as would public expenditure on items such as health and education. Thus, with a stronger manufacturing sector, there would be more output in almost every sector of the economy.

What about employment? Would it also be greater? In answering this question, we must distinguish between employment in the economy as a whole and employment in particular industries or sectors. Taking the economy as a whole, total employment would certainly be much higher than it is now, if Britain's manufacturing industry were much stronger and had performed much better over the past thirty years. The weakness of manufacturing industry has been largely responsible for the inflation and balance of payments problems which have plagued the UK for many years. In the face of these problems, successive governments, Tory and Labour alike, have imposed deflationary measures which both reduce employment in the short term and inhibit its longer-term growth. If manufacturing industry had performed better, there would have been less need for such measures. Inflationary pressures would have been weaker, because more output would have been available to meet the rival claims of workers, employers and the state; meanwhile, the balance of payments would have been stronger, because British industry would have been more competitive in home and overseas markets. Thus, governments could have pursued more expansionary policies without jeopardising their targets for inflation and the balance of payments; as a result, the overall level of employment would have been much higher. How would this increase in total employment have been distributed between one sector of the economy and another? In particular, how would employment in the manufacturing sector itself have been affected, and what would have happened to the share of manufacturing in total employment? ...

As we have just argued, if manufacturing industry had performed much better over the past thirty years, then total employment in the UK would by now be much greater than it is. Given such a large addition to total employment, we can assume that almost every major sector of the economy, including manufacturing itself, would have gained extra jobs: either new jobs would have been created or old jobs saved. As a result, more people would now be employed in construction, in the services and, of course, in manufacturing itself. Thus, employment would be greater than it now is, in both manufacturing and non-manufacturing alike. However, this still leaves open several possibilities. Suppose the stronger performance in manufacturing industry had been accompanied by a large increase in labour productivity; in this case, relatively few additional jobs would have been created in the manufacturing sector itself, despite the large increase in manufacturing output, and most of the additional employment would have been in non-manufacturing, especially services. In this case, the *share* of manufacturing in total employment would have fallen as fast or even faster over the past thirty years than it has done. Conversely, suppose a stronger performance in manufacturing industry had been accompanied by only a modest increase in labour productivity – an unlikely, but logically conceivable combination. In this case, many of the additional jobs would have been in the manufacturing sector itself. As a result, the *share* of manufacturing in total employment would be much greater than it is now and over the past thirty years this share would have fallen much less than it has done. Both these scenarios are logically conceivable and, on a priori grounds alone, there is no way of choosing between them.

All we can say with complete certainty is that if the UK's manufacturing sector had been much stronger, then manufacturing output would have been much higher. It is also likely that more people would now be employed in this sector than at present ...

The three theses: a quantitative assessment

Table 11.1 shows what has happened to UK manufacturing employment since 1950, both in absolute terms and as a share of total employment. In this table, changes in manufacturing employment during selected periods are broken down into a number of distinct components. There are three major components, which correspond to the three theses listed above. There is also a catch-all term which measures the effect of miscellaneous factors ... The individual components shown in Table 11.1 are defined as follows:

(1) *The Net Failure Effect.* This measures the *net* impact of poor economic performance on manufacturing employment. By definition, it is equal to the actual change in manufacturing employment during a given period minus the change which would have occurred during the same period (for whatever reason), if UK industry had performed better and the economy had grown more rapidly ...

(2) *Unavoidable job losses: The Maturity Effect.* This effect indicates the extent to which the fall in manufacturing employment during a given period was inevitable simply because the UK economy was already relatively mature at the beginning of the period concerned ... Note that much of the fall in manufacturing

employment – ascribed here to the maturity effect – was, in practice, the result of layoffs, factory closures and the like. In a proximate sense, therefore, most of the fall in employment under this heading was the result of poor industrial performance.

Table 11.1 Analysis of manufacturing employment since 1950

(a) Change in relative share of manufacturing in total employment (percentage points)

	1950–83	1955–83	1966–83
Net failure effect	1.3	1.9	1.4
Maturity effect	-5.5	-7.6	-8.5
Specialisation effect	-6.9	-4.8	-3.1
Effect of miscellaneous factors	1.0	-0.8	0.1
Total (= actual change)	-10.1	-11.3	-10.1

(b) Change in manufacturing employment (thousands)

Net failure effect	-373	-253	-312
Maturity effect	-193	-929	-1830
Specialisation effect	-1825	-1344	-859
Effect of miscellaneous factors	525	47	114
Total (= actual change)	-1866	-2479	-2887

However, these jobs would still have been lost even if UK manufacturing industry had performed better, though the causal mechanism would have been different. With a more dynamic and successful manufacturing industry, the jobs in question would have been eliminated through automation and other labour-saving measures. Thus, given the stage of development reached by the UK economy, the loss of manufacturing jobs indicated by the maturity effect was inevitable. The only question was, how would this loss come about? In practice, it came about through factory closures and the like. In a more dynamic economy, it would have come about through automation and similar measures.

(3)   *The Specialisation Effect.* This indicates the extent to which autonomous changes in the structure of UK foreign trade have affected manufacturing employment ... Note that this effect measures the purely 'structural' impact of

foreign trade on manufacturing employment. In evaluating this impact, total output and employment in the economy as a whole are taken as given, and any macro-economic effects resulting from changing trade specialisation are ignored. Note also that the 'specialisation effect', as measured in Table 11.1, is 'performance adjusted', i.e. the figures embody a correction to eliminate the effect of slow economic growth on the structure of UK trade.

(4)   *The Effect of Miscellaneous Factors.* This is a catch-all item which takes into account a variety of factors, such as errors in specification, random disturbances and interaction effects.

After this preamble, let us now examine Table 11.1. As can be seen, three time periods are shown: 1950–83, 1955–83 and 1966–83. The justification for choosing these periods is as follows: 1950 was the year in which the UK economy achieved its largest-ever trade surplus in manufactures (as a percentage of GDP); 1955 was the year in which the share of manufacturing in total employment reached an all-time peak; whilst the absolute number of people employed in the manufacturing sector reached its all-time peak in 1966. Looking at the numbers shown in Table 11.1, perhaps the most striking feature is the minor importance of the *net* failure effect. Depending on the time period concerned, this effect accounts for between one-tenth and one-sixth of the absolute fall in manufacturing employment. Moreover, in the case of relative shares, this effect is actually positive and hence accounts for none of the fall in manufacturing's share in total employment.

From the table, it is clear that virtually all of the decline in manufacturing employment, both absolute and relative, is accounted for by two components: the maturity effect and the specialisation effect. It is also clear that the relative importance of these two effects depends on the time period concerned. Over the entire period 1950–83, taken as a whole, the specialisation effect is the most important: it accounts for most of the absolute fall in manufacturing employment and over half of the fall in this sector's share in total employment. However, if a later starting-point is chosen, the picture is rather different. As the starting-point moves closer to the present, the maturity effect becomes increasingly important, until eventually it supplants the specialisation effect as the major component. For example, over the period 1966–83, manufacturing employment fell by 2.9 million. Of this fall, the maturity effect accounts for around 1.8 million and the specialisation effect for around 900 thousand.

From the figures shown in Table 11.1, the following points emerge concerning the three theses. The Failure Thesis explains very little of the absolute or relative decline in manufacturing employment. Most of this decline is explained by the other two theses we have considered: the Maturity Thesis, which stresses that Britain was already on the brink of economic maturity in the 1950s, and the Specialisation Thesis, which stresses the huge changes that have occurred in the UK's pattern of trade specialisation since 1950. Given the stage of development already reached by the British economy in 1950 and the changes in trade specialisation which have taken place since then, manufacturing employment was bound to fall dramatically over the coming decades no matter how good or bad the performance of UK manufacturing industry. This is the first and most important point.

Our second point is concerned with the relative importance of the maturity effect and changing trade specialisation in explaining what has happened to manufacturing employment. Over the entire period 1950–83, changes in trade specialisation have been the major factor. They account for most of the absolute decline in manufacturing employment over the period as a whole, as well as for most of the decline in manufacturing's share in total employment. However, if we take a more recent starting-point, the picture is more complex. In 1950, the UK economy was approaching maturity but had not yet reached it. By the 1960s, the economy was fully mature and, for this reason alone, the share of manufacturing in total employment was bound to fall by a considerable amount in the coming years. Moreover, given the underlying trends in labour supply, this fall in manufacturing's relative share would inevitably be accompanied by a considerable fall in the absolute number of people employed in the manufacturing sector. The extent of this unavoidable fall is indicated by the maturity effect in Table 11.1. According to the figures shown, manufacturing employment was destined to fall by at least 1.8 million between 1966 and 1983, simply because the UK was already a fully mature economy at the beginning of the period in 1966. This fall would have occurred even if there had been no changes in trade specialisation during these years and even if UK manufacturing industry had been more dynamic and output had grown more rapidly. Of the 2.9 million manufacturing jobs lost between 1966 and 1983, approximately 60% were bound to go simply because the economy was already mature in 1966, and another 30% were eliminated by changes in the pattern of trade specialisation (North Sea oil, greater food self-sufficiency, etc.). The remaining 10% represent the jobs that were lost as a result of poor economic performance and would have been saved if UK manufacturing industry had been more dynamic and the economy had grown more rapidly.

Conclusion

The main conclusions of this chapter are as follows. The post-war decline in manufacturing employment in Britain has been an example of 'negative de-industrialisation' (resulting from poor industrial performance), compounded by the effect of changes in trade specialisation. However, almost as many manufacturing jobs would have been lost and manufacturing's share would have fallen even further if industrial performance had been more successful. If this had happened, Britain would, instead, have been an example of 'positive de-industrialisation'. Thus, a large reduction in manufacturing employment was unavoidable in post-war Britain, since the country was already on the verge of economic maturity in 1950. Manufacturing employment was bound to decline over the coming decades, no matter how good or bad the performance of British industry. Thus, in the last analysis, the number of manufacturing jobs lost as a result of industrial failure was relatively small. The fact is, in a 'mature' economy, the behaviour of manufacturing employment is not always a good indicator of industrial performance. In such an economy, a dynamic manufacturing sector may be shedding labour yet, at the same time, contributing indirectly to the creation of employment elsewhere in the economy as steady increases in industrial production lay the material foundations for a prosperous and expanding service sector.

Part 3

Labour and training

In our 1986 reader the role of trade unions in Britain's relative economic decline constituted the major issue of contemporary interest. In the wake of a concerted government effort to restrict the ability of unions to bargain collectively – as well as the strategic victory in the miners' dispute – this was the time when Britain was in the midst of what was described as a productivity miracle. The connection between rapid productivity growth and the unions' restricted freedom was viewed by some commentators as the key to the 'miracle'; and, in government circles at least, the 'taming' of the unions is still seen as the enduring contribution of the Thatcher regime. Come the next General Election, the spectre of the 'winter of discontent' will be dutifully paraded before the British populace as a reminder of 'the bad old days when the unions ran the country'. Even at the height of the anti-union hysteria, we were sanguine about the prospect for sustained recovery arising from simply attacking workers' rights. In retrospect, our caution was justified, as the miracle dissolved into the longest recession in British economic history. Although the present government continues to play the union card, such as in its opposition to the Social Chapter, there is now a growing awareness that, far from being too powerful, trade unions may now be too weak to prevent Britain's slide into a low-wage, low-skill sweatshop economy.

It is around such issues that *Peter Nolan* addresses his review of the relationship between trade unions and productivity. He argues that the 'negative' view of trade unions is strongly conditioned by an uncritical acceptance of the prescriptions of orthodox economic theory. In the ideal world of 'perfect competition' trade unions are assumed *by definition* to be counter-productive by interfering with the market mechanism which ensures the most efficient allocation of resources. Unions are dismissed simply as monopoly sellers of labour acting as an impediment to the achievement of technical efficiency. Also, through their political impact unions lead to damaging effects on the economy as a whole. As Nolan points out, not only is the abstract world of neoclassical economics far removed from the reality of Britain in the 1990s, but also it has a static vision of the economic process. Economic orthodoxy cannot comprehend the sources of economic change and the role of institutions, such as trade unions, in the developmental process.

Nolan then examines alternative perspectives which contextualise trade union activity within a social setting and, not surprisingly, such approaches lead to profoundly different conclusions to the conventional wisdom. He draws on German and American research to present the hypothesis that, far from being 'blockages' to the productive process, trade unions can provide a positive spur to management to upgrade their design, production and marketing strategies. For example, unionised firms are potentially more productive because they are forced to use inputs more efficiently in the face of competition from non-unionised firms which can employ a low wage production strategy. Reviewing recent empirical work in the UK Nolan argues that unions do not necessarily reduce productivity and, in this light, the productivity 'breakthrough' of the 1980s is subject to critical scrutiny. Nolan contends that it is the relative *weakness* of trade unions in the UK that has prevented them from closing off low wage, labour intensive routes to profitability. This situation was made worse in the 1980s and served merely to consolidate an industrial structure which militates against the upgrading of the UK economy. In the long-run, therefore, it will be increasingly difficult for British firms to compete in the expanding market for high research intensive, high technology products.

With the emergence of recession at the end of the 1980s, even those commentators sympathetic to Thatcherite policy in the industrial relations arena began to qualify their assessment of what had been achieved. In particular the long-term neglect of training provision received growing attention when it was realised that the productivity breakthrough was not being sustained. *D. Finegold and D. Soskice,* in a very influential contribution to the debate on underperformance, locate the failure of Britain to educate and train its workforce relative to its international competitors as both a product and cause of Britain's poor relative performance. The failure has trapped the economy in what they describe as a low-skills equilibrium. They use the term 'equilibrium' to denote the existence of a self-reinforcing network of institutions which taken together militate against the upgrading of skill levels. Their analysis of the interdependent nature of the problem means that changes in one aspect – say the operation of the education system itself – is unlikely to have much impact without concomitant shifts in the other institutional variables seen by Finegold and Soskice as contributing to the failure of training as a whole. (In a broader sense, the drift of their analysis implies that all mono-causal explanations of underperformance are unsatisfactory, that identifying one factor as *the* cause of relative decline may be convenient for conviction politicians but is unlikely to solve the problem.) Finegold and Soskice outline the shortcomings in the various political-economic institutions – the organisation of industry, firms and the work process, financial markets and the state and political structure – which together have contributed to the creation of enterprises with poorly trained managers and workforces possessing low levels of skill.

In a more critical vein *Tony Cutler* examines the way in which the training issue came to occupy the same prominence in the late 1980s as 'the labour problem' had a decade earlier. He traces the transition from the worker being viewed as villain to that of a victim and compares the social scientific justifications used to justify each categorisation. This extract complements the Nolan piece by reviewing the methods used in the 1960s and 1970s to 'prove' that trade unions were deleterious to economic health. Cutler builds on the work of Theo Nichols who, in *The British Worker Question* (1986), demonstrated effectively that the methods employed by the majority of researchers on trade unions were seriously flawed. Cutler recapitulates Nichols' critique of the studies relating to the 'British labour problem' which exposed, amongst other things, bias in the respondents used, the dubious basis of the labour productivity figures and problems of comparative data. Nichols concluded that the hypothesis that the British worker is 'to blame' for lower productivity is not scrutinised but legitimised. Most important, the determinants of productivity are analysed in 'factoral' terms which excludes 'non-production' contributions to overall productivity.

Cutler then examines the literature devoted to analysing 'the training problem' and discovers striking parallels between the methodologies applied in the research on labour productivity and those employed in judging the impact of vocational training (or the lack of it) on economic performance. In particular, the entire drift of the training problem debate is based on the 'productively virtuous enterprise', without which the findings of the research are rendered tenuous. Finally Cutler asks why calls for the expansion of vocational training have become the *sine qua non* improving economic performance. He finds the answer in the shift away from 'traditional' policies of intervention, such as regional aid and demand management, towards policies aimed at addressing individual components of 'market failure'.

CHAPTER 12

Trade unions and productivity*

Peter Nolan

Trade unions have featured prominently in explanations of Britain's relative industrial decline. For at least a century, indeed ever since manufacturing industry in Britain first began to falter under international competition, unions and their members have been accused of damaging productivity, increasing labour costs and destroying jobs. So entrenched had such claims become by 1979 that the new Conservative government under Mrs Thatcher had little difficulty in mobilising popular support for a sustained offensive against the unions. The erosion of their 'power and privileges', her government proclaimed, was a necessary precondition for industrial renewal in Britain. According to Hayek, one of Thatcher's key advisers at that time, unions were 'the prime source of unemployment' and the 'main reason for the decline of the British economy in general' (Hayek, 1980).

The purpose of this paper is to scrutinise the case against unions, and to see whether it rests on systematic argument and evidence or mere prejudice. Had this exercise been conducted at the time Hayek issued his diagnosis, it would have been difficult for two reasons to resist the conclusion that unions were a convenient scapegoat. First, in the 1960s and 1970s – the years in which union power allegedly became intolerable – very few studies sought systematically to unravel their economic effects. Second, those that were undertaken and widely cited at the time (Caves, 1980; Pratten, 1976) contained serious flaws which rendered their key conclusions unsafe (see Nichols, 1986). But now, according to one commentator, the position is different: a spate of new empirical studies has made it 'possible to spell out with confidence the influence that unions have on the performance of companies, the economy and on individual welfare'. Among other things, unions 'lower labour productivity and raise the pay of their members relative to comparable non-union members' (Metcalf, 1989b).

---

* An earlier version of this paper was presented as the Shirley Lerner Memorial Lecture to the Manchester Industrial Relations Society in 1992.

This review focuses on the union–productivity link, and has four main parts. The first places the recent research in its wider context, the second situates it in respect of competing theoretical perspectives, including recent American controversies, and the third evaluates the weight and quality of the new empirical findings. In the concluding section the analysis is broadened out to consider the consequences of diminishing union membership and influence for the structure, performance and future prospects of the British economy.

The context

The rekindling of academic interest in unions' economic effects ironically coincided with a dramatic decline in their aggregate membership and political influence and the reassertion of managerial prerogative in the workplace. It also took place against the backdrop of major shifts and upheavals in the economy and political map of Britain. During Mrs Thatcher's first administration, unemployment rose by a factor of three, bankruptcies were legion and manufacturing output fell by 20 per cent between 1979 and 1981. Yet by the start of her second administration in 1983 the economy was beginning to revive, albeit from a very low base and with whole industries decimated. Five years of growth followed as manufacturing output (but not employment) climbed back to its 1979 level. Industrial productivity and company profitability soared (for reasons discussed below), and service sector output and employment grew very rapidly. Ministers began to talk about an economic 'miracle' and traced its origins to the effects of Thatcher's radical policy agenda.

Four key elements of this agenda are relevant in this context. First, a stylised version of 'monetarism', stressing the virtues of state minimalism and unfettered markets, replaced the policy objectives of previous administrations. The control of inflation thus superceded employment as the primary macroeconomic objective. Second, the Government set about dismantling the tripartite structures which had given unions limited access to the corridors of power in the 1960s and 1970s. Third, a complex set of legislative reforms were introduced, roughly on a two year cycle, with the clear aim of eroding the social power of trade unions and increasing managerial control of industrial relations. Fourth, labour markets were deregulated and employers exhorted to free themselves of the allegedly rigid, collective structures of employment regulation which had arisen before 1979.

Independent economic assessments of Thatcher's policies were initially positive, and gave substance to the Government's view that there had been an economic 'miracle'. The post-1983 spurt in manufacturing labour productivity in particular was cited as powerful evidence of a supply side breakthrough (Muellbauer, 1986; Maynard, 1988; Crafts, 1988). By the end of the decade, however, most economists were far less bullish as the legacy of under-investment in the first half of the decade – in new plant, equipment, and labour force skills – became more evident. Crafts, for example, provided a more qualified assessment of her governments' achievements, stressing in particular their neglect of training and technology provision (Crafts, 1991).

By contrast, in the key policy area of industrial relations, the Government continued to attract the unqualified support of most economists. Crafts, again reflecting the dominant perspective, claimed that Thatcher's 'get tough' approach to the unions had yielded significant benefits for the economy, which may prove enduring 'if the bargaining power of workers over manning levels remains weak' (Crafts, 1991). Metcalf, similarly, linked the measured performance gains in labour productivity to the restoration of management authority in the workplace. He contrasted the effects of Thatcher's anti-union policies in the 1980s with the pluralist strategy of the 1960s and 1970s, and concluded that whereas the latter had failed to kickstart the economy and promote growth, Thatcher's policies 'seem to have done the trick' (Metcalf, 1989a).

These arguments are examined in detail below. First, however, it is important to investigate why most economists, consciously or otherwise, support the principle of management 'prerogative' in the workplace, and why they instinctively link unionism with problems of economic inefficiency.

Perspectives

1) Economic orthodoxy

Strictly speaking neoclassical economic theory, at least in its more refined forms, has little or nothing to say about the functions, processes and 'prerogatives' of management. As any student of the subject would explain, it is the market mechanism which governs the selection and deployment of factor services in production. Managers are mere ciphers, prisoners of underlying market and technological forces. In practice, however, most economists tend to deviate from this highly abstract view, which after all amounts to a denial of one of the most salient institutions of modern capitalism. Relying more on pragmatic judgement than the underlying theory, they would typically argue that the management hierarchies and authority structures which characterise modern organisations developed as an efficient response to prevailing deficiencies in the utilisation of information, technology and productive resources. By interposing themselves between the market and the direct producers, the new managerial cadres apparently succeeded in raising the yield from given inputs and thereby created an income for themselves.

Unions are treated far less generously. Regarded as monopoly sellers of labour, they are accused of distorting otherwise efficient market mechanisms; of producing technical inefficiencies in production; and of pursuing narrow, sectional gains in the political arena at the expense of the common good. Each charge is discussed in turn.

First, it is argued that union wage demands in excess of prevailing competitive rates will destroy both jobs and output. By exploiting their monopoly position in the labour market unions may well succeed in securing higher rewards for their members, but the consequence will be reduced job opportunities as employers substitute alternative inputs (e.g., physical capital) for the now relatively expensive unionised labour. Correspondingly, output will fall as firms take steps to bring their inflated costs in line with given revenues. Initially confined to unionised establishments, these effects will be amplified as the displaced unionised workers are gradually re-employed at lower wages in relatively labour intensive, low productivity jobs in non-unionised firms.

Second, unions are identified as a major obstacle to technical efficiency in production. Seeing the work process as a predetermined technical relationship between inputs and outputs, neoclassical theorists regard the imposition of union based job controls over work allocation, effort levels and training as a severe impediment to productivity and future profitable investment. Interruptions to production through strikes and other 'hostile' practices (work to rules, overtime bans, etc.) are cited as further evidence of unions' deleterious effects.

Third, it is suggested that unions may inflict further damage by seeking to influence the character and scope of government economic policy for the benefit of their members. Neoclassical theory advances a very limited view of the legitimate role of government, effectively restricting it to the tasks of controlling the money supply, safeguarding the law of contract, and limiting the distortions from externalities and natural monopoly. From this point of departure, it follows that if governments acquiesce to unions, or other organised sectional interest groups, the economy's allocative and productive properties will be severely damaged.

Like the treatment of management in orthodox theory, the above propositions about unions should be treated with considerable caution. For they are derived from a model of the economy which is highly abstract, ahistorical, and preoccupied with static, allocative questions. It is helpful to elaborate these points.

The method of neoclassical theory construction involves, in the first instance, the elaboration of the allocative and distributive properties of a perfectly competitive economy. Prominent institutional features of the modern capitalist economy, including firms and unions, are ruthlessly excised. Then, by taking the individual as the basic unit of analysis, and assuming away all transactions costs, the theory is able to demonstrate the existence of an equilibrium price vector which allows all mutually beneficial trading opportunities to be fully exploited. In their dual role as producers and consumers, 'transactors' freely interact in exchange, with the purpose of maximising present and future consumption, given prevailing resource, market and technological constraints.

Exponents of this approach, of course, readily concede that the model is merely an 'ideal type', a device to better understand the workings of the real economy. Yet in practice, the real economy is judged against the properties of the model rather than the other way round. This can clearly be seen in the case of unions, and other key institutions, which are inserted into the analysis as 'imperfections', in other words as unwelcome sources of variance from the 'first best' world of perfect competition. And having been defined thus, and deemed corrosive of economic welfare, it is but a short step to the argument that they should be rooted out to facilitate a movement towards the 'first best' world of perfect competition. Such indeed is the fate prescribed for unions.

Yet not only is this conclusion predetermined at the outset by the assumptions of the model, it is also generated without consideration of the dynamic properties of the system. What are the sources of economic change, and what role do historically forged institutions like unions play in the developmental process? Dynamic issues of this kind were central to the studies of the classical political economists, like Smith, Ricardo and Marx, but they are almost totally eclipsed in the contemporary debate. The idea that interest conflicts may be a powerful force for economic change is simply not considered.

Nor, moreover, is there any serious attempt to comprehend the root causes of interest conflicts in production and exchange. Evidence that such tensions predated the formation of unions, indeed that they helped spur the growth of worker combinations, is swept aside in a relentless effort to ascribe to unions the blame for strikes, wages struggle and associated industrial relations difficulties. This is perhaps the most striking illustration of the theory's neglect of history. To concede that conflicts may be deeply rooted in the wage labour system would expose the folly of directing exclusive attention to its institutional manifestations through unions and other agencies. Yet the fact is that countless empirical studies have found that conflict in employment is rife, regardless of union presence. (The classic study is Mathewson, 1931.)

2) Alternative views

Although neoclassical theory enjoys a hegemonic position within Western countries not all researchers subscribe to the above propositions about unions. Studies, from a variety of theoretical positions (institutionalist, radical, Marxist), have rejected the method and substantive conclusions of the neoclassical approach. Thus instead of wrenching unions from context and treating them as an exogenous determinant of productivity, the best work has sought to recontextualise their social practices and view them as one element in a complex parallelogram of market, technological and institutional forces determining outcomes in production. Issues of power and conflict are allowed to surface, as are detailed questions about the social purpose and dynamic effects of rules, hierarchies and other institutional constraints. Streeck's influential analysis of the West German manufacturing system – what he refers to as 'diversified quality production' – is a striking example (Streeck, 1985; 1991).

Inverting the logic of neoclassical theory, he argues that the high quality, high value added production system, which accounts for West Germany's competitive advantage in manufactures, emerged precisely because of the *existence* of powerful and binding 'institutional constraints'. Especially important was the presence of strong workplace based trade unions with the organisational capacities to force companies to pursue a strategy of continuous modernisation and improvement. Other vital ingredients listed by Streeck include: a system of 'rigid' wage determination, which forced employers to 'adapt their product range to non price competitive product markets capable of sustaining a high wage level'; a legally enforceable system of employment protection that promotes internal flexibilities and a commitment to invest in training and retraining; and 'a set of binding rules' compelling employers to consult with their employees 'and seek their consent above and beyond what many or most would on their own find expedient' (1985: 22–3; 1991: 52–3).

Streeck's achievement is to break decisively with the conventional wisdom, which would instinctively condemn the above system of rules and constraints as a fetter on economic efficiency. He argues, by contrast, that their net effect has been to produce 'a virtuous circle of upmarket industrial restructuring' (1991: 54). By blocking 'quick-fix' solutions, and by blocking low wage routes to profitability, this framework of rules and institutions has 'forced, induced and enabled' managements to embark on more demanding design, production and marketing strategies.

Detailed empirical studies of Britain's industrial history demonstrate the force of the above analysis, and expose a similarly dense and complex interplay of social, economic and technological relationships in production. Crucially, for the present argument, what emerges from these studies is a far richer understanding of the ways in which the pattern of industrial restructuring and the outcomes of production are shaped by shifting structures of power and the politics of co-operation, conflict and compliance in the workplace.

Consider the case of the Lancashire cotton spinning industry, which experienced rapid decline in the last quarter of the nineteenth century in the face of the superior competitive challenge from American producers located in the New England district. Lazonick, in a series of studies (but see in particular Lazonick, 1981), has shown that whereas American cotton textile companies were spurred by a configuration of tight labour markets, high wages and industrial concentration to innovate and produce with the latest 'ring spinning' machines, Lancashire cotton firms struck compromises with the accommodating mule spinners craft union to increase work effort and lower unit costs on existing machines. The deal effectively sealed the long term fate of the British industry.

According to Lazonick, efforts by the skilled textile workers to maintain their relatively privileged position in the hierarchical division of labour led them to agree to an intensification in the pace of work, as well as a reduction in the quality and hence cost of inputs. Yet by making existing machines more cost effective in the short run, the mule spinners removed the incentive and pressure on employers to innovate.

In the British coal industry, three decades later, colliery owners achieved a decisive victory over the highly fragmented Federated Miners Union of Great Britain. The conflict, which culminated in the General Strike of 1926, had been precipitated by wage cuts and work intensification as ailing colliery companies sought to cut costs in order to compete in international markets with coal producers from Germany and elsewhere.

Fine *et al.* (1985) have noted that with the union in disarray, and with the threat of increased foreign competition, the colliery owners had both the power and the incentive to modernise methods of production. Instead, they opted to take advantage of their situation by further degrading wages and working conditions. Productivity and profitability levels were thus lifted in the short run through pay cuts and enforced extensions in the working day, while investment in new methods and machinery stagnated. By 1938, as a result, mechanised coal cutting accounted for only 55 per cent of output in Britain, as compared with 97 per cent in Germany, 98 per cent in Belgium and 88 per cent in France (Fine *et al.*, 1985). And by 1945 the industry had become moribund.

Both industries powerfully illustrate how, in the absence of robust pressure from unions, management sought short term, quick-fix solutions to boost the productivity and profitability of their industries. And both studies confound common-sense views about the universal desirability of worker co-operation or compliance in production. In textiles, investment in new methods was postponed not out of fear of resistance from a hostile union, but because the dominant craft union co-operated with management in raising the short term competitiveness of existing methods. In the coal mines, a defeated and demoralised labour force was unable to prevent opportunistic colliery owners from raising profits and productivity while eschewing investment in the new mechanised mining techniques commonly deployed elsewhere.

3) American controversies

The above arguments have yet to make any significant impression on mainstream thinking, yet by contrast the recent research of American economists at Harvard University – which claims that unions may be good for productivity – has succeeded in stirring quite a debate. What is striking about the Harvard research is that while it reproduces some of the crucial insights of the detailed case studies discussed above, it stops short of wholesale rejection of mainstream theory.

Essentially the Harvard economists, notably Freeman and Medoff (1979; 1984), have attempted to augment the basic theory. Their argument, in brief, is that unions have 'two faces': in addition to the monopoly face, uniquely stressed by the orthodoxy, unions have a more positive face associated with 'collective voice'. Invoking Hirschman's distinction between 'exit' and 'voice' behaviour (see Hirschman, 1970), Freeman and Medoff note that unions give voice to workers' aspirations and grievances, and thus help to improve communications, raise morale and motivation, and reduce quit rates. In non-unionised settings, by contrast, voice is difficult to achieve and so disputes and grievances fester.

In addition, the Harvard economists argue that unions may spur innovation and the diffusion of 'best' management practice, by blocking low wage, labour intensive routes to profitability. Referred to as the union 'shock' effect, this argument parallels Streeck's analysis of the dynamic consequences of institutional 'rigidities', including strong union organisations, in West Germany. Noting that the labour contract is incompletely specified, the Harvard economists stress that productivity outcomes are indeterminate: they are the result of a dynamic social process which may or may not be conducive to high productivity. Unionised firms, however, have a strong incentive 'to extract more output from a given amount of inputs' – in other words utilise inputs more efficiently – because they must compete with non-unionised firms which have recourse to low wage production strategies.

These arguments have been tested against the empirical evidence for the United States, at enterprise, industry, and national levels, as well as for different time periods, and the results on balance suggest that unionised firms are more productive. Especially noteworthy is Clark's time series study of the impact of unionism on management practice and labour productivity in six cement plants, which moved from non-union to unionised status between 1953 and 1976. He found, after allowing for other possible determinants, a positive union productivity effect of around 6 to 8 per cent. Interviews with union officials and management revealed that the gains derived from a union 'shock' effect, which prompted 'extensive changes in management personnel and procedures' and 'a more business like approach to labour relations' (Clark, 1980).

Results such as Clark's have not been warmly received by the mainstream, and criticism has been directed at the empirical methods and conceptual framework which produced them. Indeed some writers have been moved to question the integrity of the researchers themselves. Thus Reder (1985), commenting on Freeman and Medoff (1984), claimed that the book was an 'anti anti-union text' which had proved influential because the authors are willing 'to provide easy answers to hard questions'. More prosaically, Addison (1985) dismissed the theory of collective voice as 'a conspicuous failure'. Space precludes a detailed discussion of this debate, but the following points are pertinent in this context.

First, whatever its shortcomings, the Harvard research has sought to empirically scrutinise the 'collective voice' hypothesis. The orthodox view of unionism, by contrast, is a product of deductive reasoning, the central conclusions of which are determined at the outset by the properties of the hypothetical, idealised world of perfect competition. Before the appearance of the Harvard studies, only one notable attempt had been made to quantify the welfare losses due to unionism, and the study in question (Rees, 1963) relied heavily on informed 'guesstimates' and can scarcely be judged a model of methodological rigour. Second, the Harvard economists do not claim that unions are always good for productivity: much will depend on how employers react to them, and on the character and the strategies of the unions themselves. The force of this latter argument has been illustrated by the historical evidence for two of Britain's staple industries and will be further discussed below in the context of recent developments in the British economy.

British evidence

Have British trade unions impeded cost cutting changes in production, as proponents of orthodox economic analysis claim? Or are they more usefully viewed as a potential force for economic dynamism, among other things by blocking low wage, labour intensive routes to profitability? What does the recent research evidence reveal?

The idea that Thatcher's policies in the early 1980s may have engendered a productivity breakthrough was first mooted by Muellbauer (1986). Although he was unable to specify the precise nature of the connections his investigation pointed to a trend shift in total factor productivity (TFP) after the third quarter of 1980. According to Muellbauer, TFP averaged 2.76 per cent annually between 1980 and 1985 as compared to 0.62 per cent between 1973 and 1979. Because, as noted above, TFP is estimated as a *residual* it is open to a number of possible interpretations. The one that was seized upon, by Maynard (1988) among others, was that the Thatcher Government's tougher approach to the unions had allowed previously unexploited gains in efficiency to be realised.

Metcalf echoed this perspective in his wide-ranging review of the changing character of post-war British industrial relations (Metcalf, 1989a). Thatcher's policies – anti-union legislation, the freeing of market forces, and the permissive stance towards high unemployment – had effected a profound change in work-place behaviour and practices. Workers had been disciplined by the 'fear' of unemployment and plant closures, and were no longer in a position to resist change. In the exceptionally brutal conditions of the early 1980s management had seized the initiative and subordinated their employees to harsher work routines which demanded higher levels of work effort and productivity.

While these arguments were in line with the available evidence – for example the reported rise in the Percentage Utilisation of Labour (PUL) index (Bennett and Smith Gavine, 1988) – far more controversial was his claim that Thatcher's policies were succeeding. Comparing their effects with the pluralist reform strategy of the 1960s and 1970s, Metcalf concluded that, whereas the latter had failed to yield any significant productivity improvements, Thatcher's policies 'seem to have done the trick' (1989a: 27). In a similar vein Crafts claimed that Thatcher's 'get tough' approach to the unions had yielded significant benefits for the economy, which might endure 'if the bargaining power of workers over manning levels remains weak' (Crafts, 1991). Others, for example Nolan (1989a) and Nolan and Marginson (1990), took issue with Metcalf's interpretation of the evidence and suggested that Thatcher's reforms might be promoting short term gains at the expense of the more fundamental structural reforms, including investment in plant, people and technology, urgently required to re-invigorate the economy.

In a separate review of the evidence, Metcalf reported that there was little support for the 'Harvard' proposition that unions are good for productivity (Metcalf, 1989b). On the contrary: the weight of the evidence suggested that 'union presence is associated with lower labour productivity'. Is this conclusion borne out by the most recent evidence?

Nickell *et al.* (1989) and Wadhwani (1990) looked at the impact of unions on rates of productivity growth. Using data culled from the accounts of 124 manufacturing companies between 1972 and 1986, they were able to track changes in productivity during the second half of the 1970s (a period of relative union 'strength') and the first half of the 1980s (a period of union 'weakness'). Wadhwani found that unions in the 1970s, and the 'pro-union' legislation of that period, did not discourage investment or inhibit productivity growth; while both studies noted that unionised firms in the first half of the 1980s experienced faster productivity growth than their non-unionised counterparts.

These results are consistent with different interpretations. It is possible that unionisation was positively correlated with faster productivity growth in the first half of the 1980s, not because of unionisation *per se* but because of other forces acting within and without the companies in question. It is also possible, as the authors note, that the faster rates of growth were the product of the removal of obstacles to work re-organisation. Yet the interpretation which Wadhwani and Nickell *et al.* stress is that 'there is no simple association between unionism and productivity growth' ... 'Contrary to what is alleged, unions do not consistently reduce productivity growth' (Nickell *et al.*, 1989: 21 and 29). Wadhwani is even more emphatic: 'there is no evidence here for the view that unions reduce productivity growth' (1990: 382).

Machin and Wadhwani (1991) reported a 'positive association between unionism and organisational change' for the period 1981–84. Organisational change is defined as 'substantial changes in work organisation or work practices not involving new plant, machinery or equipment'. Their study focused on 721 private sector establishments of which 27.2 per cent had experienced some form of organisational change. Machin and Wadhwani interpreted their results in two ways. On the one hand, the higher incidence of change in unionised establishments may have reflected the removal of restrictions on managerial discretion. On the other hand, it is possible that union voice effects, by improving communications in the workplace, may have encouraged organisational change. Noting that there is evidence for both explanations the authors 'incline towards the view that *both* the above channels combine to give us a positive association between unionism and organisational change' (1991: 852).

Unfortunately Machin and Wadhwani are unable to tell us why unions are associated with positive voice effects in some establishments and damaging restrictive practices in others. Presumably, as the Harvard economists have argued, the effect of unionism in any given situation will reflect the character of management–labour relations. Attempts to rip unions from that wider context and attribute to them sole responsibility for particular organisational change outcomes may thus be ill-advised.

Three further points are relevant in this context. First, the WIRS data used by the authors is solely based on the qualitative responses of management; hence what is being reported is management's perceptions of the change process. Second, it seems surprising that the overwhelming majority of establishments (over 70 per cent) reported no organisational change in this period. What does this reveal about the effects of Thatcher's policies which were supposed to be cutting through entrenched restrictions? Finally, it would have been helpful to know something about the incidence of change in non-union firms. Evidence of widespread changes in non-unionised firms would, of course, challenge the motivating assumption of this study that output restrictions are more pervasive in unionised organisations.

The final study of note, by Gregg, Machin and Metcalf (1993), develops the theme that the harsher environment of the 1980s led managers to reassert their authority, among other things by repudiating union membership agreements. This change of approach, we are told, represented a clear 'signal' to employees to work harder. Recalling a theme of Metcalf's earlier work, the authors claim that the higher productivity levels observed in the 1980s stemmed from the removal of restrictive practices in unionised firms. Their evidence, which is derived from a regression analysis of company accounts and the data on changing union status generated by Gregg and Yates's earlier postal survey (Gregg and Yates, 1991), relates to 328 companies, the majority of which were in manufacturing.

In common with much of the recent work on this issue, this study unfortunately tells us nothing about productivity dynamics and the effects of Thatcher's policies in the expanding non-unionised sector. Unionised firms are said to have out-performed non-unionised firms between 1985 and 1989, and there is further evidence that the process of union derecognition gave a further fillip to productivity. But why was the performance of non-unionised firms inferior? Presumably the authors would argue that the growth of productivity will be higher in unionised firms because there is more scope for improvement. But that was also the implication of the results of the earlier studies for the first half of the decade. In short, we are asked to accept that throughout the entire duration of Thatcherism non-union firms performed less well on average than their unionised counterparts. When coupled with the finding that some 70 per cent of firms reported no organisational change in the early 1980s (Machin and Wadhwani, 1991), might that not suggest that the harsh winds of competition unleashed by Thatcher failed to promote up-grading, except in unionised firms where perhaps the Harvard positive voice and shock effects were at work?

Trade unions and the British economy in the 1990s

The academic evidence notwithstanding, the fact is that since 1979 four Conservative governments have sought to shift the balance of power in Britain's industries and restore the 'prerogative' of management by waging an offensive against trade unions. Space precludes a detailed discussion of the various steps taken by the Government and (some) employers to restore management authority in the workplace (for which see Evans, *et al.*, 1992). Here the focus is on the economic consequences of diminishing trade union presence and influence in the workplace. Are employees working more flexibly and productively, and have employers developed more systematic and efficient labour utilisation policies?

As far as productivity is concerned, many economic analysts took the view that there was a 'breakthrough' in performance in the 1980s – a step increase in productivity growth rates and levels as measured by total factor productivity or the cruder labour productivity figures. The argument was that a combination of policies – tax reductions, privatisation, labour market deregulation and, crucially, industrial relations reforms – had unleashed a new spirit of enterprise at all levels in industry. The corollary was greatly improved efficiency and productivity. Aided by the authoritative statements of Muellbauer, Crafts and others, this view had become dominant by the mid-1980s.

It was clear at the time that the measured gains in manufacturing productivity were in part the product of the large scale redundancies, which took place even after output had bottomed out. The gains were seen to be indicative of a general increase in work effort, and a movement by firms and industries towards the production frontier as outmoded and entrenched working practices were progressively rooted out by an increasingly confident and assertive management (Muellbauer, 1986; Crafts, 1988; Metcalf, 1989a).

Sceptics warned that the observable improvements would prove short lived, in so far as they derived from increased labour effort and work intensity and were the product of a specific set of exceptionally brutal conditions (Nolan, 1989a; 1989b). The idea was generally dismissed and confidence in the strength of the economy continued to grow. Warnings that vital investment – in plant, machinery, and workforce skills – was being neglected were not heeded, nor was the argument that the offensive against trade unions may actually be making matters worse, by enabling management to make short term gains in productivity and profit at the expense of more fundamental structural reforms. Particularly relevant was the relationship between profit and investment. Comparative data for the leading industrial countries between 1979 and 1988 reveal that manufacturing companies in Britain enjoyed relatively high profit levels in the Thatcher years, yet investment was low.

In the event there was a major reappraisal of industrial performance in the 1980s. The cosy consensus, which stifled serious debate for so long in the 1980s, began to break up as the economy lurched into its second crisis in a decade. Yet, it is still true that unions are widely held to have been a damaging influence and that their present position of relative weakness is a bonus for industry. In short, the idea that unions may be a force for dynamic efficiency remains highly unpopular. Is it relevant to an assessment of the recent history of British industry?

The argument in brief is that unions in Britain have been unable to close off low wage, labour intensive routes to profitability. Contrary to what is usually claimed, they have failed to limit management 'prerogative' sufficiently to promote the conditions in which a high wage, high productivity virtuous circle might have emerged. However paradoxical this argument may seem to orthodox economists and supporters of the conventional wisdom, the fact is that both the historical and contemporary evidence reviewed above highlight the hazards of a social, political and economic structure which gives management more or less unlimited rights to organise their capital so as to best take advantage of a cheap and disposable workforce.

Since the early 1960s Britain has been a relatively low labour cost country (Nolan, 1989a). This situation has encouraged the proliferation of investment in labour intensive, low value added work – much of this coming from American and increasingly now from Japanese multinationals – which has entrenched a low productivity structure in manufacturing.

In the 1980s, the Government took the view that the attraction of ever greater quantities of foreign direct investment was vital for the regeneration of manufacturing industry. And to serve this end, it was deemed essential to maintain British workers' status, within the advanced capitalist countries, as a relatively cheap and disposable labour force. New efforts were thus made to contain wage costs and the other social charges on labour (e.g. National Insurance payments), while increasing labour flexibility, or more accurately its disposability. Hence much of the individual and collective employment rights established over the previous decades were swept aside (Evans *et al.*, 1992).

Few informed commentators would deny that labour in Britain is now more disposable, and also relatively cheap by international standards, as a result of the Government's actions. But is it more flexible? Relevant to this question is the highly influential model of the 'flexible firm', popularised by Atkinson (1984). The phenomenon of labour market segmentation – the progressive compartmentalisation of the labour force into 'good' and 'bad' jobs – was already deeply entrenched in Britain prior to 1979. But Atkinson claimed it took new forms in the 1980s and was underpinned by a new dynamic, with employers allegedly pursuing more systematic labour force differentiation strategies in pursuit of cost savings and flexibility gains. The result was a new duality comprising privileged 'core' workers on the one hand, and a larger mass of 'peripheral' employees on the other.

Core workers, according to Atkinson, tend to be employed full-time, and enjoy relatively high status because they possess scarce skills. Included in the core labour force are managerial and professional staff, technicians, and an apparently growing number of 'multi-skilled' employees who work flexibly with the latest micro-electronic computerised production systems. Peripheral workers, by contrast, have fewer specific skills and can be more easily replaced at short notice, thereby affording employers greater 'numerical' and 'financial' flexibility. Atkinson presented his model as a description of emergent trends in some organisations. What does the empirical record show?

First the evidence contradicts the idea that employers are adopting more systematic human resource management policies. Hakim (1990), on the basis of the 1987 Employers' Labour Utilisation Survey, concluded that a minority of employers (35 per cent) claimed to be pursuing a coherent employment strategy. Out of the total of 877 employers surveyed, only 11 per cent said that they sought to compartmentalise their employees into core and periphery segments. The majority admitted to having an 'opportunistic' approach to human resource management issues. Subsequent studies by Hunter and MacInnes (1992) and McGregor and Sproull (1992) found similar evidence of pragmatic opportunism.

Second, recent evidence on the changing character of tasks and skills in manufacturing – the main focus of Atkinson's model of the flexible firm – also points against the emergence of a polyvalent, flexible workforce. Cross (1988), for example, revealed that despite widespread reports of changing working practices throughout industry multi-skilling is rare. He surveyed the working practices of 236 major manufacturing sites and found that while there had been some erosion of traditional boundaries between production and maintenance work, there had been no comparable progress in the breaking down of divisions among craft workers. Engineering and electrical work remained distinct activities undertaken by different craft groups.

More broadly the case study and survey evidence shows that work patterns have not been revolutionised by advanced, micro-electronic technologies. Summarising the evidence, Elger (1990) suggests that change has been uneven and piecemeal; most studies report that technical changes have been assimilated into pre-existing patterns of occupational segregation (Steedman and Wagner, 1987; 1989). Furthermore, by international standards the diffusion of new technologies and new work patterns has been slow. Only 16 per cent of manual workers in manufacturing worked directly on processes utilising micro-electronics in 1987. Elsewhere, in office work and the banks, for example, automation has advanced swiftly, but in other areas of clerical work the pace of change has been slow. Elger concludes that greater flexibility at work in Britain has been dominated by labour intensification and the horizontal enlargement of tasks, rather than skill deepening.

In short, the concerted offensive against labour in the 1980s appears to have reinforced the already powerful obstacles to the emergence of a high wage, highly skilled and productive workforce. The Government's efforts to consolidate British labour's low cost status have done little to persuade firms, particularly multinationals, to break with the past and site their most advanced manufacturing systems in Britain. The absence in the past of powerful incentives for firms to invest in modern plant and equipment and workforce skills in Britain has helped consolidate a pattern of international specialisation which militates against the upgrading of domestic industry. And, as countless studies have shown (e.g., Finegold and Soskice, 1988; Porter, 1990; Knell, 1993), the absence of a suitably qualified labour force is now a powerful *disincentive* to modernise.

Conclusions

Two main conclusions emerge from the above discussion. First, the research on unions and productivity for Britain does not demonstrate a clear, unambiguous negative link. If anything it points in the opposite direction: that is against the commonplace idea that unions lower the level and growth rate of productivity. Yet the available evidence remains too impressionistic, and too limited by a conceptual framework which separates unions from the other dynamic factors which bear on productivity outcomes, to be reliable. More conceptual refinement, and more attention to the dynamic effects of institutions, is urgently needed to enhance our understanding of the complex role of unions in contemporary capitalist economies.

Second, it has been argued that a decade or so of hostility towards trade unions has done little to reverse the deep seated weakness of industry in Britain. There has been no sustainable improvement in the productivity, efficiency or competitiveness of Britain's economy, and industrial structure has continued to develop in a direction which will make it more, not less, difficult to participate in the expanding markets for high research intensive, high technology products. Hence, the prospect for industrial renewal in Britain looks remote at present. In the medium term it looks likely that the Government's cheap labour policies will dominate the competitive strategies of firms and industries located in Britain.

CHAPTER 13

The failure of training in Britain[*]

David Finegold and David Soskice

We will argue that Britain's failure to educate and train its workforce to the same levels as its international competitors has been both a product and a cause of the nation's poor relative economic performance: a product, because the ET (education and training) system evolved to meet the needs of the world's first industrialised economy, whose large, mass-production manufacturing sector required only a small number of skilled workers and university graduates; and a cause, because the absence of a well educated and trained workforce has made it difficult for industry to respond to new economic conditions.

The best way to visualise this argument is to see Britain as trapped in a low-skills equilibrium, in which the majority of enterprises staffed by poorly trained managers and workers produce low-quality goods and services. The term 'equilibrium' is used to connote a self-reinforcing network of societal and state institutions which interact to stifle the demand for improvements in skill levels. This set of political-economic institutions will be shown to include: the organisation of industry, firms and the work process, the industrial relations system, financial markets, the state and political structure, as well as the operation of the ET system. A change in any one of these factors without corresponding shifts in the other institutional variables may result in only small long-term shifts in the equilibrium position. For example, a company which decides to recruit better-educated workers and then invest more funds in training them will not realise the full potential of that investment if it does not make parallel changes in the style and quality of management, work design, promotion structures and the way it implements new technologies. The same logic applies on a national scale to a state which invests in improving its ET system, while ignoring the surrounding industrial structure ...

* Reproduced with permission from 'The failure of training in Britain: analysis and prescription', *Oxford Review of Economic Policy*, **4**: 21–53, 1988.

Britain's failure to train

Comparative education and training statistics are even less reliable than cross-national studies in economics; there are few generally agreed statistical categories, wide variation in the quality of ET provision and qualifications, and a notable lack of data on training within companies. Despite these caveats, there is a consensus in the growing body of comparative ET research that Britain provides significantly poorer ET for its workforce than its major international competitors ...

The baseline comparison for ET effectiveness begins with how students in different countries perform during compulsory schooling. Prais and Wagner (1983) compared mathematics test results of West German and English secondary schools and found that the level of attainment of the lower half of German pupils was higher than the average level of attainment in England, while Lynn (1988: 6) reviewed thirteen-year-olds' scores on international mathematics achievement tests from the early 1980s and found that 'approximately 79 per cent of Japanese children obtained a higher score than the average English child'. The results are equally disturbing in the sciences, where English fourteen year-olds scored lower than their peers in all seventeen countries in a recent study (Postlethwaite, 1988).

This education shortfall is compounded by the fact that England is the only one of the world's major industrial nations in which a majority of students leave full-time education or training at the age of sixteen. The contrast is particularly striking with the US, Canada and Sweden and Japan, where more than 85 per cent of sixteen year-olds remain in full-time education. In Germany, Austria and Switzerland, similar proportions are either in full-time education or in highly structured three- or four-year apprenticeships. Britain has done little to improve its relative position. It was, for example, the only member of the OECD to experience a decline in the participation rate of the sixteen–nineteen age group in the latter half of the 1970s (OECD, 1985: 17). Although staying-on rates have improved in the 1980s – due to falling rolls and falling job prospects – Britain's relative position in the OECD rankings has not.

The combination of poor performance during the compulsory schooling years and a high percentage of students leaving school at sixteen has meant that the average English worker enters employment with a relatively low level of qualifications.

Workers' lack of initial qualifications is not compensated for by increased employer-based training; on the contrary, British firms offer a lower quality and quantity of training than their counterparts on the Continent. A joint MSC/NEDO study (1984: 90) found that employers in Germany were spending approximately three times more on training than their British rivals, while Prais and Steedman's analysis (1986) of comparable construction firms in France and Britain revealed that French workers' training was more extensive and less firm-specific. Overall, British firms have been estimated to be devoting 0.15 per cent of turnover to training compared with 1–2 per cent in Japan, France and West Germany (Anderson, 1987: 69). And, neither individuals nor the Government have compensated for employers' lack of investment in adult training ...

Britain's relative failure to educate and train its workforce has contributed to its poor economic growth record in the post-war period ...

Why has Britain failed to train?

Economists' normal diagnosis of the undersupply of training is that it is a public good or free rider problem: firms do not invest in sufficient training because it is cheaper for them to hire already skilled workers than to train their own and risk them being poached by other companies. While the public good explanation may account for the general tendency to underinvest in training, it does not explain the significant variations between countries' levels of training, nor does it address the key public policy question: Given the market's inability to provide enough skilled workers, why hasn't the British Government taken corrective action? To answer this question we will look first at why political parties were long reluctant to intervene in the ET field, and then, at the two major obstacles which policy-makers faced when they did push for ET change: a state apparatus ill-equipped for centrally-led reform and a complex web of institutional constraints which kept Britain in a low-skills equilibrium.

Political parties

Through most of the post-war period, the use of ET to improve economic performance failed to emerge on the political agenda, as a consensus formed among the two major parties on the merits of gradually expanding educational provision and leaving training to industry. Underlying this consensus was an economy producing full employment and sustained growth, which covered any deficiencies in the ET system. The broad consensus, however, masked significant differences in the reasons for the parties' positions. For Labour, vocational and technical education were seen as incompatible with the drive for comprehensive schooling, while the Party's heavy dependence on trade unions for financial and electoral support prevented any attempts to infringe on union control over training within industry. In the case of the Conservatives, preserving the grammar school track was the main educational priority, while intervening in the training sphere would have violated their belief in the free market. An exception to the principle of non-intervention came during the war, when the Coalition Government responded to the manpower crisis by erecting makeshift centres that trained more than 500,000 people. When the war ended, however, these training centres were dismantled.

The state structure

One of the main factors which hindered politicians from taking a more active ET role was the weakness of the central bureaucracy in both the education and training fields. On the training side, it was not until the creation of the Manpower Services Commission (MSC) in 1973 that the state developed the capacity for implementing an active labour market policy. The staff of the primary economic policy-making body, the Treasury, 'had virtually no familiarity with, or direct concern for, the progress of British industry' (Hall, 1986: 62) and none of the other departments (Environment, Trade and Industry, Employment or Education and Science) assumed clear responsibility for overseeing training. There was, for example, a dearth of accurate labour market statistics, which made projections of future skill requirements a virtual impossibility (Reid, 1980: 30). Even if the state had come up with the bureaucratic capability to develop a coherent training policy, it lacked the capacity to implement it. Wilensky and Turner (1987: 62–3) compared the state structure and corporatist bargaining arrangements of eight major industrialised nations and ranked the UK last in its ability to execute manpower policy.

While responsibility over education policy in the central state was more clearly defined, resting with the Department of Education and Science (DES), the historical decentralisation of power within the educational world made it impossible for the DES to exercise effective control. Those groups responsible for delivering education, local authorities, were able to block reforms they opposed, such as vocationalism. The lack of central control was particularly apparent in the further education sector, an area accorded low priority by the DES until the 1970s.

The main obstacle to ET reform, however, was not the weakness of the central state, which could be remedied given the right external circumstances and sufficient political will, but the interlocking network of societal institutions which will be explored in the following sections, beginning with the structure, or lack of it, for technical and vocational education and entry-level training.

The ET system

Technical and work-related subjects have long suffered from a second-class status in relation to academic courses in the British education system ...

The responsibility for vocational education and training (VET) fell by default to the further education (FE) sector. The 1944 Education Act attempted to provide a statutory basis for this provision, declaring that county colleges should be set up in each LEA to offer compulsory day-release schemes for fifteen–eighteen year-olds in employment. The money was never provided to build these colleges, however, with the result that 'a jungle' of different FE institutions, courses and qualifications developed. There were three main paths through this 'jungle': the academic sixth form, the technical courses certified by independent bodies, such as City & Guilds, BTEC or the RSA, and 'the new sixth form' or 'young stayers on', who remain in full-time education without committing to an A-level or specific training course. A host of factors curtailed the numbers pursuing the intermediate route: the relatively few careers requiring these qualifications, the lack of maintenance support for FE students and the high status of the academic sixth, which was reinforced by the almost total exclusion of technical students from higher education.

The majority of individuals left education for jobs which offered no formal training. Those who did receive training were almost exclusively in apprenticeships. The shortcomings of many of these old-style training programmes, which trained 240,000 school-leavers in 1964, were well known: age and gender barriers to entry, qualifications based on time served (up to seven years) rather than a national standard of proficiency and no guarantee of off-the-job training. The equation of apprenticeships with training also had the effect of stifling training for positions below skilled level and for older employees whose skills had become redundant or needed updating.

In the early 1960s the combination of declining industrial competitiveness, a dramatic expansion in the number of school-leavers, growing evidence of skill shortages and 'poaching' prompted the Government to attempt to reform apprenticeships and other forms of training. The route the state chose was one of corporatist compromise and minimal intervention, erecting a network of training boards (ITBs) in the major industries staffed by union, employer and government representatives (Industrial Training Act, 1964). The ITBs' main means of overcoming the free-rider problem was the levy/grant system, which placed a training tax on all the companies within an industry and then distributed the funds to those firms that were training to an acceptable standard, defined by each board.

The boards created a fairer apportionment of training costs and raised awareness of skills shortages, but they failed to raise substantially the overall training level because they did not challenge the short-term perspective of most companies. The state contributed to new funds for training and each board assessed only its industry's training needs, taking as given the existing firm organisation, industrial relations system and management practices and thus perpetuating the low-skill equilibrium. Despite the Engineering ITB's pioneering work in developing new, more flexible training courses, craft apprenticeships remained the main supply of skilled labour until Mrs Thatcher came to power in 1979.

Industrial/firm structure

Industry Type. One of the main reasons that British industry has failed to update its training programmes is the concentration of the country's firms in those product markets which have the lowest skill requirements, goods manufactured with continuous, rather than batch or unit production processes. An analysis of international trade in the 1970s by NEDO found that the UK performed better than average in 'standardised, price-sensitive products' and below average in 'the skill and innovation-intensive products' (Greenhalgh, 1988: 15).   New and Myers' 1986 study of two hundred and forty large export-oriented plants confirmed that only a minority of these firms had experimented with the most advanced technologies and that management's future plans were focused on traditional, mass-production market segments.

Training has also been adversely affected by the long-term shift in British employment from manufacturing to low-skill, low-quality services. Manufacturing now accounts for less than one-third of British employment and its share of the labour market has been declining.   The largest growth in employment is in the part-time service sector where jobs typically require and offer little or no training.   The concentration of British service providers on the low-skill end of the labour market was highlighted in a recent study of the tourist industry (Gapper, 1987).

While the type of goods or services which a company produces sets limits on the skills required, it does not determine the necessary level of training.   Recent international comparisons of firms in similar product markets have revealed significant variations in training provision depending on how a company is organised and the way in which this organisational structure shapes the implementation of new technologies.   In the retail trade, for instance, 75 per cent of German employees have at least an apprenticeship qualification compared with just 2 per cent in the UK.   In the British case, the many, integrally-related components of firms' organisational structures and practices have combined to discourage training ...

Management.   Linking all of the elements of firm organisation is the role of management in determining training levels.   The poor preparation of British managers, resulting from a dearth of technical HE or management schools and a focus on accounting rather than production, is often cited as a reason for the lack of priority attached to training in Britain.   A recent survey of over 2,500 British firms found that less than half made any provision at all for management training (Anderson, 1987: 68).   In those firms which do train, managers tend to treat training as an operating expense to be pared during economic downturns and fail to incorporate manpower planning into the firm's overall competitive strategy. For managers interested in career advancement, the training department is generally seen as a low-status option.   And for poorly qualified line managers, training may be perceived as a threat to their authority rather than a means of improving productivity.   It is important, however, to distinguish between bad managers, and able ones who are forced into decisions by the institutional structure in which they are operating ...

The short-term perspective of most British managers is reinforced by the pressure to maximise immediate profits and shareholder value.   The historical separation of financial and industrial capital has made it harder for British firms to invest in training, with its deferred benefits, than their West German or Japanese competitors, particularly since the City has neglected training in its analysis of companies' performance. Without access to large industry-oriented investment banks, British firms have been forced to finance more investment from retained profits than companies in the other G5 nations.

Industrial relations

Just as the operation of financial markets has discouraged training efforts, so too the structure, traditions, and common practices of British industrial relations have undermined attempts to improve the skills of the work force. The problem must be analysed at two levels: a) the inability of the central union and employer organisations to combine with government to form a co-ordinated national training policy; and b) the historical neglect of training in the collective bargaining process.

CHAPTER 14

Vocational training and British economic performance[*]

Tony Cutler

Commentaries on the post-war British economy have a certain changeless character. It would be overstating the case to say that they involve a discussion of perennial crisis but it is, with a few brief and illusory exceptions, true to say that this is a discourse on failure. What does seem to change is the diagnosis of failure. This article is concerned with two influential attempts to explain why we have failed ...

It is also concerned with the role of social scientific investigation in these diagnoses of failure. Our discussion will be concerned not just with the provenance of these two diagnoses but, also, with how social scientific investigation has related to them.

From the British labour problem to the British training problem

Our first characterisation of the reasons for British economic failure is best designated the 'British Labour Problem'. Here the source of the British economic problem is seen to lie in the obstructive and conservative character of manual workers in British industry.

Laments concerning the inadequacies of the British worker relative to foreign counterparts go back a long way (Nichols, 1986: 4–6) but the British Labour Problem had its time. As Nichols puts it, 'talk of the problem of the British worker had operated like constant background music but, by the late 1970s, the volume was turned up, the theme was inescapable' (Nichols, 1986: xi). To be more precise the 1970s was the central *discursive* time of the British Labour Problem. A number of influential studies were published which purported to

---

[*] Reproduced with permission from 'Vocational training and British economic performance: a further instalment of the British labour problem?', *Work, Employment and Society*, **6**: 161–83, 1992.

show that concern over working practices in British industry was not just the stuff of anecdote. On the contrary, sober social scientific work appeared to demonstrate that British labour practices were a central reason for Britain falling behind her major competitors economically.

However, the British Labour Problem also had its political moment, and that came later, in the 1980s. Conservative governments 'tackled' the labour problem. The British worker had to be 'disciplined' and the trade unions, the institutional support for bad working practices, 'curbed'. Thus, a plethora of legislative measures restricted the powers of trade unions and narrowed the scope of individual employment rights ... For a time in the 1980s these measures and, in the case of unemployment, the omissions were seen as having 'done the trick'. The dominant refrain in economic commentary was a celebration of the 'British economic miracle'. However, the subsequent years of trade crisis and recession have shown that this was not a new economic dawn for the UK. This leads to our second diagnosis; in this case the time frame moves forward a decade both discursively and politically. This new prognosis, with its associated remedy, is the perceived weakness of vocational training.

In the case of the British Labour Problem much of the essential critical work has already been undertaken in a work of great forensic rigour and elegance, Nichols' *The British Worker Question*. It is important to recapitulate Nichols' critical analysis of the key social scientific texts underpinning the British Labour Problem since, as we shall see later, the same problems recur in the literature on vocational training.

The second part of *The British Worker Question* concentrates, in particular, on the two influential studies, Pratten's (1976) book on *Labour Productivity Differentials Within International Companies* and the Central Policy Review Staff's *The Future of the British Car Industry* (1975). Pratten's work investigated labour productivity differences in the *same* multi-national companies; operations in different countries were examined and the study involved three sets of paired comparisons: UK–North America, UK–Germany and UK–France. This study was in the form of a social survey where respondents were asked to indicate both the extent of labour productivity differences in the companies concerned and the reasons for them. The CPRS study was narrow in scope, being concerned specifically with the motor industry. In this case the model was that of a 'controlled experiment' where the aim was to isolate the effects of variations in labour practices by controlling for other factors, such as differences in capital equipment. In both cases the studies produced 'headline' conclusions which indicted the British worker. For example, Pratten found that roughly 50% of the lower British productivity in the UK–Germany comparison was due to factors such as strikes, restrictive practices and manning levels; while CPRS concluded that '*productivity ... in British car assembly* plants is considerably lower than in continental plants. It takes almost twice as many man-hours to assemble similar cars using the same or comparable plant in Britain as it does on the continent' (CPRS, 1975: 79, emphasis in the original).

However, Nichols shows that both these studies were flawed in both conception and execution. There were marked biases in the respondents used. In Pratten's study while 119 operations were covered only 5 trade unionists were interviewed. Thus sources of information and interpretation were virtually exclusively management. The basis of labour productivity figures were often questionable. For example, one of the three observations cited as indicating the effects of British overmanning in the CPRS study did not involve a comparison between plants at all but contrasted UK manning levels with a hypothetical 'competitive level' calculated by industrial engineers. There was no evidence that comparisons were representative of overall performance since they related to process comparisons rather than completed product comparisons. Comparisons did not always involve identical equipment but the fact that differences in equipment were *not* a significant cause of productivity differences was simply asserted rather than demonstrated. Finally, there were biases in the treatment of factors which appear to reflect an *a priori* commitment to a particular conclusion. Thus elaborate methodological arguments were used to justify the conclusion that differences in capital equipment were not a cause of labour productivity differences while the equally difficult issues connected with attributing a causal role to labour practices were brushed aside.

Nichols concluded that the key social scientific texts on the British Labour Problem reproduced the *a priori* at the level of *conclusions,* the prejudice that, to a large extent, it was the British worker who was 'to blame' is not scrutinised but legitimised. However, there is another important sense in which the *a priori* is reproduced. Both Pratten and the CPRS look at the question of the determinants of labour productivity in 'factoral' terms. In Pratten's case it is a question of allocating causation between and within 'economic' and 'behavioural' factors. The former included length of production runs and differences in plant and equipment, the latter strikes, restrictive practices and manning levels. In the CPRS case it is a question of seeking to determine the respective roles of capital equipment and labour practices. However, it is important to ask on what terrain such 'factors' operate. Here what is striking is the dominance of an abstracted 'production' location. The CPRS report discusses a whole series of potential determinants of labour productivity. Some of these, e.g. the character of capital equipment, labour practices and so on, are located within production processes, others are not. The report pointed to weaknesses in the character of the model range of the British producers and to the fact that British Leyland's distribution network was much smaller than its principal continental European competitors. Such features could have obvious connections to labour productivity since poor sales could be reflected in limitations on factory throughput. In such cases a slow work pace could be a response to *de facto* low output targets. In fact the report *does* make the connection between such product and marketing deficiencies and sales. What, however, is not done is to make the *further connection to labour productivity.* Anyone who reads the report will find that, when it comes to explaining low productivity, insofar as the figures can be relied on, we are in the hypostatised world of production – non-production factors simply do not figure.

Now, then, we have a basis for our comparison. The British Labour Problem operated within an *a priori* with two central features: the pre-supposition that labour practices were a central cause of lower levels of labour productivity and that other potential causes were not, was re-inscribed in conclusions via mechanisms such as the use of questionable measures and inadequate controls. However, equally and correlatively, the determinants of productivity differences were sought in an abstracted world of production: *the world of these studies is not a world of capitalist enterprises, it is a world of factors interacting at the level of production.*

Exemplary contemporary social science?

How does the British Labour Problem relate to this contemporary development, the British Training Problem? To examine this issue it is necessary to look at the nature of the research undertaken by the National Institute of Economic and Social Research (NIESR). The studies may be divided into two separate groups: on one hand, there are studies which are essentially concerned with estimating differences in the extent of vocational training in different economic sectors; the comparisons here are between the UK and either France or Germany. These articles *do* contain some discussion on the relationship between the differences in the extent of vocational training and the comparative economic performance of the sectors in the countries concerned. However, they do not involve any systematic investigations at plant or establishment level. The primary function of the articles concerned is to estimate the numbers obtaining given vocational qualifications in a particular year, the total 'stock' of individuals with such qualifications in the workforce and the comparability of the qualifications concerned.

There is also a second set of studies. In these detailed investigations were made of a sample of firms in Britain and Germany and they were used as a means of attempting to determine the impact of vocational training levels on labour productivity in the firms concerned. Even a cursory reading of these studies reveals a first basic similarity between them and the Pratten book and the CPRS report: vocational training is looked at as a *factor* which may or may not have an impact on a chosen measure of economic efficiency. In particular, vocational training is seen as contributing to the input of 'human capital' to production processes. This factorial approach is clear in characterisations of the whole research project. Thus, for example, Steedman and Wagner (1987: 84) tell us that 'the overall object of the National Institute's research project in the field is to examine the relative contribution of physical and human capital to productivity'.

As the object of the studies is to isolate the respective roles of 'human' and 'physical' capital the firm-based cases attempt to follow (like the CPRS) the 'controlled experiment' model. To this end the firms analysed were 'matched samples' from Britain and Germany where a similar range of firm sizes were taken in both countries. However, before attempting to examine in detail whether 'controlled experiment' conditions *were* met it is worth making a point on the scope of the studies themselves. The 'matched sample' studies consist of studies of 4 sectors, 3 in manufacturing, the production of basic metal-working products such as valves and springs (Daly *et al.*, 1985); kitchen furniture (Steedman and Wagner, 1987); and women's 'outerwear' – coats, raincoats, jackets, dresses, etc. (Steedman and Wagner, 1989); and one in services, hotels (Prais and Wagner, 1989). The canonic status of the National Institute texts has meant that they have been cited as evidence on the *general* issue of the relationship between vocational training and comparative economic performance. However, not only are a very limited number of sectors covered but relatively simple products are selected for study which do not involve lengthy and complex transformations.

Given the fact that the NIESR project followed the 'controlled experiment' model there are, necessarily, methodological similarities with the CPRS study. Most notably, if the object is to separate out the respective roles of 'physical' and 'human' capital then the impact of differences in the character of equipment used must be controlled for. However, given the fact that the NIESR research is concerned not with the impact of labour practices, but with the impact of vocational training it involves two issues which are quite specific to training.

Quantity and quality of training

It must be possible to show that differences in the extent of vocational training apply. This is, of course, not simply a matter of comparing the proportions of a workforce with a given vocational qualification. In the absence of international qualifications it is necessary to establish the relative 'level' of each qualification. Thus, for example, it is perfectly possible that a larger percentage of the workforce in one country hold a particular vocational qualification than in another but that the standard of attainment is lower in the former country. If qualifications are used as an index of workforce training level in such a case it would be indeterminate which workforce was 'better trained'.

It is also important not just to look at *whether* training has an effect on work performance but also the possible mechanisms involved. For example, vocational training *could* be significant because of its effects on *overall* skill levels within the work force. Alternatively, the effects may be achieved via the training of particular 'key' workers (e.g. maintenance personnel, supervisors). This is particularly significant in the context of arguments on national training policy. For example, *if* the effects of training operate via imparting technical skills to 'key' personnel then a programme aimed at raising *overall* skill levels could have no significant effects on work performance.

A controlled experiment?

In this part of the argument the objective is to examine how far the NIESR studies live up to the standards which they set themselves: to carry out a controlled experiment on the relationship between vocational training and economic performance.

If, *faute de mieux*, the NIESR conclusions on comparability are accepted, the studies consistently show larger proportions of the workforce with (comparable) vocational qualifications in France and Germany as against the UK. For example, in mechanical trades, adjusting for the number employed in the occupations concerned, in 1984 three times as many employees obtained a vocational qualification in France compared to the UK (Steedman, 1988: 58); there was also a major difference in the numbers obtaining supervisory qualifications: in 1985 roughly six times as many workers passed the major German supervisory qualification as the principal UK qualification and the evidence presented indicates that the German was substantially more demanding (Prais and Wagner, 1988: 35). At least at the level of (comparable) vocational qualifications the German and French workforce is 'better trained' than the British.

If levels of training are different what of the 'outcome' measures used in the study? Here a number of important difficulties arise. In the kitchen furniture study the productivity comparison is not in terms of completed products per person but rather the output of a particular *process* in the overall production sequence, the production of basic panels for the carcass of the kitchen cabinet (Steedman and Wagner, 1987: 87). Similarly, the study on metal-working involves a combination of comparisons in terms of products and processes: 'depending on how the production process was laid out, and how records were kept, we sometimes took only an important single part of the production sequence, in others a series of operations, and yet in others the total number of completed products' (Daly *et al.*, 1985: 51). This raises a basic problem. Where figures are used which relate to particular *processes* there is no guarantee that results are representative of overall output per person at the level of the enterprise as a whole.

However, of perhaps even more central relevance is the extent to which the effects of the 'key' factors, human and physical capital, are distinguished. The NIESR studies *do* discover differences in the percentage of employees generally, and in the sample firms, with vocational qualifications (of comparable quality), with a much larger percentage of the German workforce with vocational qualifications. Consequently, any argument for the effects of such 'human capital' differences would be strengthened if the firms concerned exhibited significant labour productivity differences *and* similarities in the capital equipment used.

However, in fact this was not the case. In the study of metal-working while the age of the equipment used was broadly comparable there were very marked differences in the type of equipment used: 15 out of 16 German firms visited were using numerically controlled machines as against 7 out of 16 UK firms (Daly *et al.*, 1985: 53–4). It is true that the authors discount the significance of these differences in equipment used, 'although there was a relative lack of *NC* machinery in the British plants in our sample, *in our judgement* the greater part of the productivity gap came from other sources' (Daly *et al.*, 1985: 59; my emphasis); this is more a question of an *ex cathedra* statement than a demonstration.

The lack of comparability of capital equipment used is even more striking in the case of the kitchen furniture study; 'in Germany even in small firms (20 employees) highly sophisticated – usually computer numerically controlled (CNC) – woodworking machinery was installed', whereas 'in Britain, on the other hand, fully linked machine lines with automatic feed and automatic off load were hardly to be seen in the plants we visited' (Steedman and Wagner, 1987: 87–8). Furthermore, this difference in capital equipment is, in fact, accorded a crucial role in accounting for the observed labour productivity differences. As has already been indicated, the productivity comparison in kitchen furniture related to a specific part of the product, the production of the panels for the carcass of the kitchen cabinet. In the process concerned labour productivity in the German sample was, on average, 2.3 times that attained in the UK sample. *Prima facie* this could appear surprising. German enterprises were producing a more varied product mix which was customised to the specific requirements of purchasers. In contrast, UK firms usually produced standardised 'flat packs' which were sold via DIY outlets. However, when Steedman and Wagner attempt to account for the combination of greater product variety and higher labour productivity in the German enterprises they make a direct reference to the effects of differences in the equipment used: 'The use of CNC drills and edge banders which could be re-set quickly by feeding the appropriate codes to the controlling device however offset [the] disadvantages' (Steedman and Wagner, 1987: 88). The disadvantages concerned related to the greater variety in the German product involving more re-setting of equipment.

So, in two of the three matched sample studies of manufacturing there is no comparability of the physical capital used by the firms concerned and in the kitchen furniture study *differences* in such capital equipment are attributed a significant role in accounting for the labour productivity differential.

Equally, if there are major practical problems in distinguishing the relative effects of human and physical capital in the Institute studies there are parallel problems with respect to the question of 'training *en masse*' versus 'targeted training'. The researchers come down firmly in favour of the virtues of 'training *en masse*'.

Yet, again, such assumptions cannot be sustained by reference to evidence from the Institute's research. For example, a consistent finding of all three studies of manufacturing was that differences in German and UK labour productivity in the matched samples were associated with high levels of machine breakdown, exacerbated by delays in repairing equipment in the British case while such problems were virtually absent from the German plants studied. However, it is by no means clear from the studies that, insofar as such differences can be attributed to vocational training, the British deficiency lay in an inadequate supply of skilled labour *per se* or inadequate training of 'key' employees or both. For instance, the metal-working study shows that a common feature of the German plants was a period of planned maintenance when both machinery was cleaned and various simple problems rectified before they developed into serious faults. The setting aside of such a period was, clearly, a supervisory decision and this arguably *may* have related to the technical competence of supervisors. Equally, the effectiveness of the planned maintenance period may have rested on the competence of the German direct labour employed, or a combination of both. The support for a policy of training in depth clearly rests on distinguishing these effects, yet another article which is part of the overall Institute project admits the considerable difficulty of making such distinctions: 'it needs to be emphasised ... that one can usually observe *only the consequences, as a whole of the work of a 'team' of operatives, foremen and higher levels of management ... it is not always easy to detect to what extent greater skills at one level rather than another are important*' (Prais and Wagner, 1988: 38; my emphasis). So, here we have a crucial parallel with the CPRS report. The ideal in both cases is the controlled experiment but the practice diverges: varied measures of labour productivity whose representative character is unclear; differences in capital equipment; indeterminacy on the mechanisms by which training is deemed to work.

The terrain of the argument

What then of the terrain in which factors operate? In discussing this issue I want to bracket two questions together, that of the terrain and the role, implicitly, ascribed to enterprise management.

Again, like the discourse on the British Labour Problem we are not situated in a world of capitalist enterprises, we are dealing with an abstracted sphere of production. In the matched sample studies in manufacturing, as in the CPRS study, determinants of production practice lying outside the sphere of production are referred to but they are not analysed. For example, in the study of kitchen furniture it is pointed out that an important influence on the decision of management in the British firms *not* to use CNC equipment is the requirements of British retailers for deliveries at short notice (Steedman and Wagner, 1987: 88). However, in general, as in the labour problem, the effect of non-production determinants is ignored.

This failure to deal with enterprises rather than abstracted spheres of production also has a telling effect on the role played by management in these studies. The article on the vocational training of supervisors is titled: 'Productivity and Management', but the 'management' concerned is, in fact, just the first-line supervision. Management above this level is barely glimpsed but an implied role *is* in fact ascribed to British enterprise management. It is implicitly seen as a *victim* of the absence of sufficient vocational training. In the study on clothing British manufacturers are said to be using expensive computerised grading equipment, 'even though German production was more suited to such equipment' because 'lack of skills and the need to obtain more accurate results [were] ... the main reasons for installing such equipment'. Equally, supervisors' time was seen as being absorbed in teaching low-skilled machinists (Steedman and Wagner, 1989: 45, 49). A similar note is struck in the article on vocational training of mechanical and electrical craftsmen in Britain and France. In this article it is suggested that a necessary adjustment to technical change in manufacturing is the formation of 'teams' of skilled manual workers with 'an overlapping range of ... skills'. French firms were argued to have moved much further in this direction than UK companies. However, 'British firms are undoubtedly aware of the need to move in the same direction' (Steedman, 1988: 67). What, then, was stopping them? Steedman singles out three factors: two of these take us back to the familiar terrain of the British Labour Problem, 'although some progress has been made in moving away from rigid job demarcation, real flexibility – whereby one worker could tackle a wide range of tasks as required – had not yet been agreed between unions and management' (*ibid.*). Further, 'the problems of introducing highly qualified team leaders on to the shop floor at an appropriate level of pay and seniority had not been resolved, and it was thought likely that suitably qualified employees in firms subject to such restrictions would leave for better pay in firms less subject to traditional working practices' (*ibid.*).

Two key points need to be made about these arguments: as in the cases analysed by Nichols what is not clear is whose version of events we are getting here. Secondly, it is important to bear in mind that this article is *not* a matched sample study, its main object was to look at the numbers of employees in mechanical and electrical trades in the two countries who have vocational qualifications. Equally, what is implicit here is that French manufacturers are obtaining efficiency advantages via 'team working'. However, no evidence whatsoever is presented on this score, we do not know that 'team working' is more effective, we are simply supposed to take this on trust.

However, if all this has obvious echoes of the 'bloody minded worker' the last reason for the failure to adopt team working raises more general issues concerning the role ascribed to enterprise management: 'the very low skill levels prevailing among those employed in production ... means that the reorganisation of production to use new technology fully could not be carried through without very lengthy and expensive re-training' (*ibid.*). This point is not developed further but it is, at least, consistent with the 'market failure' arguments which function as a justification for state intervention with respect to vocational training. Thus, in such cases if employers expended the substantial resources required to train the individuals concerned then their inability to prevent the staff concerned being 'poached' would nullify the gain to the enterprise of such investment. Naturally, the corollary of such arguments is that state intervention would raise training levels above such a 'sub-optimal' base and hence improve manufacturing efficiency.

The assumption of a productively virtuous enterprise

However, to accept such arguments it is also necessary to accept a particular model of the enterprise, that manufacturing is 'undertaken by a management dedicated to the operation of one going concern: bought in physical inputs of resources, labour and capital are combined so that the firm realises profit through the manufacture of a product which has use value for the consumer' (Williams *et al.*, 1990: 458*)* ... It is not hard to see that if such a conception of the productively virtuous enterprise is used then it is essentially consistent with the NIESR arguments on vocational training. The object of the enterprise is assumed to be to sell manufactured goods in a competitive market and such is the source of enterprise profit.   Consequently, if development of a key input would substantially improve the enterprise's manufacturing performance it would, equally, aid the aim of increasing profit. A failure to improve the standard of 'human capital' thus invites the conclusion that this is a case of 'market failure'. Consequently, for the NIESR model to work the national economy concerned, in this case the UK, must consist of manufacturing enterprises corresponding to this model. In the NIESR arguments this is implicitly assumed. How valid is such an assumption?

A key point to be made here is that there is no logical link between the fact that an enterprise is classified as engaging principally in manufacturing activities and the model of the manufacturing enterprise pre-supposed in the NIESR studies. Such a conception is one which assumes a trajectory of organic growth via sale of manufactured products to (satisfied) consumers. Yet this is, of course, not the single road to profit for a manufacturing enterprise: diversification into non-manufacturing activities can generate a significant source of profit and a manufacturing enterprise can effectively treat its subsidiaries as so many financial assets. In such cases the pursuit of profit is radically disengaged from organic growth in manufacturing. The NIESR studies related to arguments for training policy in the UK. If manufacturing activity can be, to a large extent, divorced from the pursuit of organic growth, how far is this the case in the UK?

To begin to look at this issue we need to refer again to the article by Williams *et al.*   They discuss what they term 'The Hollowing Out of British Manufacturing', a process not just of manufacturing decline but also of a reaction to decline in the calculation of enterprise management ... [Their] picture is hardly one of manufacturing enterprises in search of organic growth and generating demands for skilled labour which, in the context of market failure, has to be supplied via state organised programmes. It is hard to see how plentiful supplies of skilled labour could have anything to offer to such enterprises.   Trained workers are likely to be amongst those made redundant as the plant is closed down by an organisation in retreat from production or treating its manufacturing establishments as assets to be traded.

Conclusion

If there are so many doubts concerning the validity of the findings of this research, why has it proved so popular with politicians and journalists, who have seen the expansion of vocational training as a *sine qua non* of improving economic performance?

The attraction of the expansion of vocational training as a policy instrument is not a peculiarly British phenomenon. On the contrary, it is a policy tool, which has, in recent years, been consistently promoted at a European level.

The single market programme adopted by the EC in 1985 involved two 'tracks': on the one hand there was the market based programme where 'non tariff barriers' such as protectionist public procurement policies and state subsidies to loss making industries were to be abolished. On the other hand, there was to be 'Social Europe' which involved not only a floor of employment rights across the EC but also a planned extension of expenditure in the sphere of regional policy via the regional and social funds of the Community. What is particularly crucial here is the rationale for the choice of areas of expenditure. The privileged policy instruments were infrastructural investment and, yes, vocational training.

What was central to other approaches was the right and obligation of the state to intervene to directly influence or control the distribution of output. Such policies are *not* part of the agenda of current EC regional policy because it has been developed within a context where intervention *against* the market is to be precluded. Thus, for example, the kinds of instruments which characterise the older regional policy were themselves 'non-tariff' barriers. Training is congenial precisely because it fits neatly into a model where the less affluent regions must pull themselves up by their bootstraps. Such an instrument is not intervention against the market but rather 'enables the market to work more effectively' (Cutler *et al.*, 1989; Chapter 3; 1991).

The popularity of training is a policy also relates to general political developments in Europe in the 1980s. Faced with the ideological and political onslaught of right wing economic doctrines Social Democratic parties in Europe have moved to the right. Consequently, the critique of market mechanisms has virtually disappeared from their economic programmes. This, particularly in circumstances like those currently operating in the UK, where the Conservatives are in the process of moving to the centre, has created something of an identity crisis. It is thus hardly surprising that policies to expand vocational training have been embraced so readily. In this sphere it becomes possible to chatter about 'market failure' but, equally, to make it clear that one is impeccably respectable and that such 'market failure' is only applicable to quite determinate and limited areas.

In this respect the theoretical weaknesses which exclude the kinds of questions confronted by Williams *et al.* on the hollowing out of British manufacturing are politically convenient. To confront this issue would be to face, in a new form, a classic problem: a situation of contradiction between the conditions of enterprise success on the one hand and social and economic welfare on the other. Yet this is not on the current agenda of European Social Democracy and training is a much safer way of 'differentiating the political product'.

Part 4

Culture and education

As a number of the earlier extracts have already demonstrated, it is hard to discuss the origins of UK economic underperformance without at some point raising the question of culture. Attitudes, ideas, values and preferences seem to distinguish one national economic system from another, and to play some hard-to-establish role in the shaping of economic activity. A whole literature abounds in this area of decline studies, a literature keen to establish the peculiarities of the English here, and to locate both the social causes and the economic consequences of English cultural particularism.

In the first volume of our series of readers, we reproduced an extract from the 1981 essay by Martin Weiner on *the loss of the industrial spirit*. Weiner's work remains an important point of reference for all the cultural debate on economic underperformance in the post-war UK, though the detail of the Weiner argument has now received some very severe academic rebuttals (some of which are included in this section). But before we do, it is important to introduce material from two of the finest review articles on the whole cultural issue, by Mathieson and Bernbaum, and by Warwick.

The *Mathieson and Bernbaum* extract takes us back to an issue already touched on by Barnett, and by Finegold and Soskice: supposed deficiencies in the quality and content of UK education as a cause of dwindling industrial competitiveness. Mathieson and Bernbaum demonstrate for just how long, and in just how consistent a way, dominant institutions within the English education system have neglected subjects, skills and attitudes vital to economic success: prioritising arts subjects over science ones, neglecting technology, and sustaining attitudes of indifference (even hostility) to industry and commerce. Mathieson and Bernbaum tie the character and content of the English curriculum to the dominance within it of the public schools and the traditional universities, and out through them to wider questions of culture and class with which many analysts of UK economic underperformance have also been concerned.

One such analyst is *Paul Warwick*. Warwick too offers a culturally-based explanation of twentieth century industrial decline, but does so without dropping back on the stereotypical (and crude) thesis of the aristocratic embrace. Warwick's industrial owning class is not subverted from its historic purpose and function by the pursuit of land, title and status.   Rather it is aristocratic capriciousness which he sees as historically tamed and reset – in the first half of the nineteenth century – by its confrontation with a self-confident industrially-based middle class morality. In the Warwick scenario, aristocracies and industrial bourgeoisies are then transformed together – towards the end of the century – by their joint immersion in the culture of Empire.   Industrial dynamism was lost, according to Warwick, in the late nineteenth century acquisition of 'an imperial mentality', and the legacies of empire remain with us to this day – as a cultural barrier to a much needed social and economic renewal.

But we have to be careful with all – or most – of this. The writings of cultural historians tap dimensions of contemporary reality that many of us can recognise in ourselves, and have a *prima facie* credibility that is quite beguiling. But we have to ask who is being beguiled here. Is it a case of manufacturing industry in decline being ensnared into a culture of empire; or is it a matter of the academic industry of decline being seduced into the empire of culture? The case for this second possibility has also to be examined; and that is why it is important to read the work of *W. D. Rubinstein* with considerable care. Time and again, Rubinstein has established that British culture is, and has been, certainly no more antagonistic to business than cultures elsewhere in the advanced capitalist world, and in many cases distinctly less antagonistic. British culture, after all, contains Adam Smith and Herbert Spencer. German culture has Nietzsche and Brecht. It is Rubinstein's contention that a careful examination of the historical record reveals that English industrial capitalists remained more resistant to social climbing, and more enthusiastic for investment and profits, than the stereotypical culturalist explanation can allow. He notes the peculiarities of cultural variation here, concedes them a role, wonders about the direction of causality, and insists that – in this area of the debate – the jury must still be out. And in doing all that, he points us to more structural explanations of economic underperformance, of a kind we will examine later in this volume.

CHAPTER 15

The British disease: a British tradition[*]

Margaret Mathieson and Gerald Bernbaum

This article will argue that many of the critics of contemporary British education are only repeating long standing anxieties about its nature and organisation. For over the last hundred years there have been intermittent periods of critical analysis which have drawn attention to the greater success of other nations' educational institutions in producing pupils and students who are well prepared to meet commercial, industrial and scientific needs. Additionally it will argue that the relative failure of earlier critics to introduce effective reforms cannot be ignored. Their failure stands as a monument to the outstanding success of the British education system in embodying and perpetuating the values of British society's dominant elites. It should serve to instruct contemporary critics and reformers who ignore those standing, deep rooted structural features of British society which have been responsible for the development of the educational system. Too many past reforming efforts have failed because the educational system has been viewed as a discrete unit, whose personnel act independently of other institutional arrangements in society and are supposedly uninfluenced by the values of its elites. Our purpose is not to criticise the present drive for reform. It is to place it in a context which treats the current prescriptions and recommendations as themselves problematic, and as being at risk precisely because the level of analysis from which they begin is inadequate. A more complex, and historically aware, analysis might, perhaps, enable a somewhat different view to be taken of recent concerns and recommendations and hence of their likelihood of success where so many others have previously failed ...

Central to our argument is that an arts based, Christian notion of gentlemanliness, which excludes, and even opposes science, technology and commerce, dominated high status educational institutions in the nineteenth century. This literary, Christian notion both reflected and consolidated the values

* Reproduced with permission from 'The British Disease: a British tradition', *British Journal of Educational Studies*, **26**: 126–66, 1988.

of Victorian society, which conferred the highest status upon the ownership of land and the style and manners associated with gentlemanly distance from the daily labours on that land and from what were regarded as the sordid features of industrialisation and urbanisation. Special emphasis will be placed upon this antipathetic response to science and technology which was, and continues to be, represented in the values embodied both in an arts based curriculum and in the relationship of the education system to other parts of society ...

Education and the economy

The composition and values of British elites, the role of the church, the restricted nature of British liberalism, particularly as it has been affected by the notion of gentlemanliness, the ethos of the public schools, as well as the role allocated to the mass, or popular education in state schools and modern universities, must all be seen as contributory factors in an investigation of Britain's economic performance relative to that of the rest of the world. The last decade has seen the appearance of a variety of scholarly commentaries on this performance. These books, taken together, emphasise the diversity of explanations and the range of conceptual tools needed to come to grips with the current economic position. They stand in marked contrast to the hortatory, unproblematic assertions which, as has been indicated, characterise those who blame the schools and universities for this country's problems and weaknesses. Those who have looked at Britain's performance since the Second World War draw attention to a number of serious deficiencies in this country's production processes. Whilst the points they make in some cases appear to be unrelated to education, we shall suggest, in our historical analysis, that they cannot, in fact, be separated from the values held by dominant elites which our educational institutions have traditionally embodied and continue to uphold ...

What unites all investigators of Britain's economic plight, whichever particular perspective they adopt, is an agreement that management and the managers of British industry have contributed to the decline of that industry. They comment upon two particular but inter-related features; firstly the failure of British industry to attract the brightest and best of each generation, and secondly the lack of sensitivity, imagination and technical expertise amongst those who eventually take up leadership roles in British industry. This perspective, we suggest, should not be seen as one which is merely to be regretted. It should be seen, rather, as an important illustration of the nature of elite education in industrial Britain. It was Martin Weiner who was the first, in a scholarly and sustained fashion, to draw attention to the disjunction between the workaday world of industry and that offered in the elite institutions of the Victorian pattern. In his words, these 'reflected and propagated an anti-industrial bias'. He refers to an Oxford science don in the first decade of this century who observed that this university had 'always ostentatiously held itself aloof from manufacturers and commerce'.

Weiner reminds us that Sir Ernest Barker, himself a scholar of very humble origin, could nevertheless deplore what he perceived as the advent of courses in universities related to industrial needs. Barker feared lest universities degenerated into 'handy' institutions providing 'even the world of business with recruits'. According to Barker, the ancient universities had a special duty to defend the 'stronghold of pure learning' and 'long time values against the demands of material progress' (quoted in Weiner, 1981: 132–3). As recently as 1958 a vice-chancellor, quoted by Weiner, observed with telling adjectival contempt that 'the crude engineer, the mere technologist are tolerated in universities because the state and industry are willing to finance them, tolerated but not assimilated'. It is easy to multiply such sentiments. Roderick and Stephens (1982) make similar points, whilst Pollard observes, towards the end of his analysis of British economic failure, that 'among the permissive causes affecting the British economy adversely is the frequently discussed weakness in applied science and engineering. The low status of these subjects has its roots in history ... [It] implies a preference for "gentlemanly" arts subjects in the training of entrepreneurs.' Pollard goes on to argue that 'the essence of the British problem lies in the inability of the engineering profession to reach in any numbers the highest echelons of power in private industry as well as in government' (Pollard, 1982: 160).

The nineteenth century: religion and literature

It is to the unique characteristics of British society and its emergent educational institutions during the nineteenth century that we now address ourselves. Central to our discussion is the religious, arts based intellectual concept of gentlemanliness which developed in response to anxieties about perceived threats to the quality of society consequent upon industrialisation and urbanisation. This concept controlled elite educational institutions in the nineteenth century and continues to dominate British society and education today ...

Victorian headmasters' enthusiasm for the moral virtues, which they believed to be realisable through Christianity, the study of the Classics and the corporate life of the school, derived partly from the values associated with the style and manners of the country's great landowners. Land ownership, and the responsible exercise of authority, came to represent, like the splendid houses and landscaped estates, both the physical and spiritual separation from the squalid sources of their owners' wealth. The encouragement which Classical studies was believed to give to pupils' spiritual refinement was perceived to be essential if, like the best and most responsible country gentlemen, these pupils were to resist the potentially brutalising pressures of industrialisation and urbanisation.

Their faith in the value of an arts based Christian education, originates, to a large degree, also in the Romantic protest, in England, against the scientific, materialistic temper of the Enlightenment. It represented the response of

Coleridge, especially, and the Victorian educators whom he influenced, to the disintegrative forces of their period: the French Revolution; Non-Conformity; philosophic radicalism; industrialisation; urbanisation; the popular press; commercialism; utilitarian education of the labouring classes ...

Coleridge's efforts to reaffirm notions of order and unity during a period of political, spiritual and cultural fragmentation were very influential, first upon nineteenth century conservative theorists and later upon those who carried the literary tradition and literary creative values into twentieth century education ... Part of our argument is that it is the success of Victorian liberals' crusade against science, under the banner of literature, which goes far towards explaining the apparent 'failure' of today's schools and universities. It needs to be fully recognised that Coleridge's concept of the clerisy, an educated, literary elite with the special responsibility to diffuse the virtues associated with religion and literary culture throughout society, penetrated the writings of Thomas and Matthew Arnold and extends through liberal theorists in England to F. R. Leavis and to contemporary supporters of literature and the arts. Coleridge's views underpinned their convictions about the superiority of literature, the artistic imagination and religion over science and technology in the education system, most particularly in the education of the nation's elite. The way in which these views have been carried forward into this century has been of great importance in all the debates about the nature of the school curriculum and about the kind of provision which should be made available in teacher training establishments ...

It is a major part of our concern to demonstrate how the shared gentlemanly values of aristocratic landowners, Victorian headmasters, and educational theorists who advocated the supremacy of the literary curriculum succeeded in establishing a dominant literary elite in English society. The potency of their success will become evident in ... the contrasting fates of the two major challenges made to it, firstly by science and technology and secondly by progressive, child centred education. Proponents of scientific and technical education failed to bring about significant and lasting changes at any level of education. Supporters of progressive child centred education, however, from Edmond Holmes, through Sir Percy Nunn, to David Holbrook, achieved a remarkable degree of success in converting the Inspectorate to their views, even though it was not until the nineteen sixties that these were given serious consideration. A major factor in their success, in contrast with those attempting seriously to introduce science and technology into education, was the progressive educators' belief in the educational and spiritual value of the arts ...

The continuity of the Coleridgean tradition well into this century has been, we argue, a major influence upon both the public schools and the nature of state education as it developed in the elementary schools and the secondary schools which were gradually provided through rates and taxes. Definitions of education persisted which emphasised Christianity in its religious mode and high morality in its secular mode. For the mass of children, discipline and good behaviour became the dominant themes. For a few, intellectual achievement could be emphasised, but only of a kind which seemingly allowed entry into a latter day clerisy, through the Classics and literature. Even the penetration of progressive educational ideas after the First World War, and their revival in the nineteen sixties, did little to alter those basic conditions. For progressive education itself became defined in terms of the spirit and the imagination. Whichever way one turns, therefore, technical, scientific and vocational education occupy inferior positions. The buttress to all this was, of course, the maintenance of the gentlemanly ideal.

The Romantic protest against the Enlightenment in England has, therefore, resulted in persistent conservatism in this country's educators, traditionalists and progressives alike. No serious challenge has succeeded in displacing official faith in an arts based curriculum believed to be creative of pupils' superior moral health and a cohesive sense of community ... We are not, of course, pretending that there were not alternative perspectives on the school curriculum and the nature of education. From the end of the nineteenth century there was always a minority who drew attention to the superior technical and vocational education of Britain's major economic competitors. They were, however, persistently unsuccessful in challenging the dominant rhetoric and practices.

CHAPTER 16

Did Britain change?*

Paul Warwick

The debate over the causes of the economic decline in Britain has been vigorous, protracted, fascinating, and without sign of resolution. Although some areas of broad agreement do exist, other matters of historical fact that might seem amenable to consensus, such as the approximate time at which the British economy ceased to perform well, have elicited intense controversy. Economic, political, educational and attitudinal explanations continue to vie with one another for acceptance in the market-place of academic opinion and views differ accordingly on what the decline ultimately consisted of and how it might be reversed. What is clear is that the most general consensus is a negative one; it holds that the causal factors favoured among the general public and the world of popular journalism – the burdens of the welfare state, the recalcitrance of the trade unions, the high rates of taxation, the low levels of domestic investment – are erroneous or inadequate in themselves. But from this point, the paths to truth are multitudinous and diverse ...

At the roots of this diversity, it seems to me, lie three fundamental issues. The first is the aforementioned issue of timing. Can the economic decline of Britain be treated essentially as a post-second world war phenomenon, or do its origins more properly lie in events that occurred much earlier, say in the latter part of the nineteenth century? Those who place causal emphasis on the errors of government policy tend to favour the short-term options, while the longer view clearly necessitates a search for more profound and pervasive defects. In general these have been of two sorts, which raises the second issue: did the British economy begin its decline because of a withering away of the 'industrial spirit' or some kindred cultural or attitudinal deficiencies in late Victorian Britain, or can a purely economic explanation, such as the nature of profitable business or investment opportunities in that era, alone or primarily account for it? Finally, and at a more fundamental level of causation suggested mainly by Marxist

---

* Reproduced with permission from 'Did Britain change?: an inquiry into the causes of national decline', *Journal of Contemporary History*, **20**: 99–133, 1985.

scholars, are the sources of decline traceable to the persistence of a pre-industrial mercantile ethos and social structure unsuited to modern industrial capitalism, or, on the contrary, is the root cause a fundamental change in the nature of British society during the nineteenth century that rendered it quite unlike the aggressive, open, and mercantile society of the eighteenth century? In short, did Britain change at some crucial point, or fail to do so when it needed to, and thereby engender its own decline?

The issues are listed in an order of logical priority, but it is not the order in which they have been taken up or the order of importance they have been allotted in the literature. Without doubt, the second issue – whether the decline, assumed to be long-term, was caused by attitudinal or economic factors – has provoked the most enduring and extensive scholarly attention. In a sense this is regrettable, for the interpretation one gives to the first issue – which itself is by no means as straightforward as it might seem – profoundly conditions the manner and extent to which one credits the alternative explanations offered in the second. This chapter will attempt to rectify this imbalance by giving more consideration to the timing issue than to the other, but the answers suggested by discussion of both issues ultimately point to one basic conclusion: it is neither the first nor the second but the third, least debated issue which holds the key to the entire matter.

Let us begin with the loss of Britain's mid-nineteenth century economic supremacy. There is little dispute that Britain's industrial and commercial domination had been considerably eroded by the first decade of the twentieth century. Between 1870 and 1914, British industrial production was increasing at an annual rate half that of her principal rivals, the United States and Germany. Growth rates for industrial productivity, which declined from an average of 1.2 per cent per annum in the 1870s to just 0.25 per cent between 1890 and 1914, trailed those in Germany and the US by even greater margins. The increasing trade imbalance after 1870 rendered the nation ever more dependent upon earnings from City of London financial services, shipping, and foreign investments, as export growth also lagged behind that of her principal competitors. Britain's share of the world market in manufactured goods fell dramatically from 41.4 per cent to 32.5 per cent in the two decades between 1880 and 1899. Britain, which led the world in iron and steel production up to the 1890s, was producing not much more than one half as much as the US in 1910. In the newer chemical and electrical industries, her relative position was far worse. Overall, Britain had fallen from first place among industrial powers to third, as first the US and then Germany caught up and overtook her ...

To some extent, it was inevitable that British industrial supremacy should suffer with the rise of the new industrial powers protected by tariff barriers. It is not immediately clear, however, that the industrialisation of these other nations needed to have resulted in Britain being left behind. Previous capital investment in plant and equipment in Britain may have inhibited the conversion to more productive methods and machinery but, as Hobsbawm (1968: 162) notes, this cannot explain the lack of success in industries in which Britain was not an early leader. Moreover, a mature industrial nation possesses advantages in terms of accumulated technical expertise and financial resources which can more than offset any potential disadvantage in being the pioneer. The 'climactic' thesis, which posits a disjuncture between the point at which it was no longer possible to generate further productivity increases in established industries through the spread of existing technology, on the one hand, and the full emergence of the new chemical, electrical and motor industries of the 'second industrial revolution' on the other, does not in itself explain why British industry was relatively slow in moving into those industries. Great success at one level of technology does not necessarily induce tardiness in developing and adopting the next level, as the Japanese are busy demonstrating today ...

Those who would argue for an economic explanation for Britain's relative loss of economic position must, therefore, provide something more. For many, that added ingredient is the suggestion that British industry's loss of innovating and expanding thrust in those years can be related to the increasing orientation of economic activity towards financial services and capital exportation rather than industrial production as such. According to Rosecrance (1979: 215–17), an international economic empire can be maintained either through a strong surplus in merchandise trade or through a surplus in 'invisibles' such as shipping, insurance and financial services. Britain 'chose' the latter route, which had the advantage, at least initially, of providing her trading partners with the income through merchandising surpluses with Britain to enable them to purchase her manufactured goods and financial services, and afforded Britain the luxury of presiding over a world system of exchange that was in rough equilibrium. In the late nineteenth century, the rising industrial prowess of Germany and the US, far from threatening Britain's economic security, led to a mutually beneficial triangular trade pattern in which Britain ran a visible trade deficit (mainly due to imports of advanced industrial products) with Germany and the US, who found it increasingly necessary to import raw materials from the less developed world, including the British Empire, itself a prime importer of British manufactures. Britain provided the finance and shipping, as well as the international currency for this trade pattern and, in addition, eagerly invested her earnings in underdeveloped countries and colonies, thereby generating an added source of income for herself and tying those markets to her exports ...

However much industrial leadership had been ceded to Germany and the US in this period, Britain's overall economic performance remained respectable. 'As her industry sagged', notes Hobsbawm (1968: 151), 'her finance triumphed, her services as shipper, trader, and intermediary in the world's system of payments became more indispensable.' Moreover, even for those 'sagging' industries, it still remained possible to make reasonable profits in the old ways by exploiting the less developed markets. From a strict business point of view, it made sense to persist in so doing, for it 'provided a cheaper and more convenient alternative to modernisation – for a while' (*ibid.*: 191). Thus Britain continued to rely heavily on the staple export industries of iron and steel, coal and textiles long after

Germany had risen to industrial prominence on the strength of her chemical and electrical industries and the US had revolutionised transportation on land and in the air by means of the internal combustion engine. Regrettably, the future belonged to these newer industries, and Britain's success as a provider of financial and other services could not substitute for the relative decline in living standards that industrial backwardness ultimately entailed ...

This interpretation of Britain's industrial decline is defended by Hobsbawm with the comment that economic explanations of economic phenomena, where available, should be preferred to sociological ones. This perspective has not been universally welcomed, however. Weiner, for one, emphatically rejects it with a dismissive: 'The question of the causes of British economic decline remains beyond the grasp of the economists' (1981: 170). In its stead, Weiner proposes the thesis that the decline is rooted in the existence of 'a cultural *cordon sanitaire* encircling the forces of economic development – technology, industry, and commerce' (*ibid.*: 1). The theme is, of course, neither original nor unexplored. Most authorities, even Hobsbawm, admit that one can find ample evidence of the existence of attitudes among the middle and upper classes of that era that slighted the process of material enrichment. But, for Weiner, these values amounted to a pervasive culture that was both non-industrial and anti-industrial. It was non-industrial in the sense that it tended to uphold the outlook and lifestyle of the leisured gentleman, rather than that of the rugged entrepreneur, as worthy of emulation by the Victorian middle classes. Education or training was disparaged to the extent that it appeared to have any practical or vocational relevance, and science and technology, with their connotations of narrowness and utility, yielded under the impact of public-school and university reforms to the broader, humanistic formation of the student schooled in the classics. It was anti-industrial in the sense that it reflected an unease over the course that industrialism had taken and glorified occupational pursuits to the extent that they took one away from industrial and even materialistic concerns. The life of the countryside, the 'England is a garden' myth, was held up as a counter-ideal to the industrial squalor and the grey, monotonous, de-humanising city life of this, the most urbanised and industrialised of societies. In contra-distinction to a simple-minded Marxian view of nineteenth-century Britain as a society where the industrial entrepreneur ruled supreme, industrialists were held in exceptionally low esteem and exhibited less self-confidence and pride in their activities than one would have expected from a supposedly dominant economic class. For themselves or for their children, they dreamed of escape from involvement with industry as soon as the accumulation of wealth and the acceptance of their social superiors made it practicable to do so. In the meantime, stability rather than risk, effortless survival rather than fevered, ambition-soaked activity, being the right sort of person rather than doing the exceptional thing, were valued. 'By modelling themselves – in varying proportions – upon civil servants, professional men, and men of landed leisure, industrialists found acceptance at the upper reaches of British society.

Thus, the famous 'Establishment' and its consensus was created (Weiner, 1981: 159), and economic deadline begun ...

It is possible that the willingness of the business class to concern itself with technological innovation, its preference for the tried and true methods, may have been an indirect inheritance of the first industrial revolution, which had been created largely by 'practical men' lacking in formal scientific training. Certainly, the historical fact that the industrial revolution had not been based on new scientific breakthroughs provided a justification for the resistance of both unions and managers to the self-conscious application to industry of scientific research and the new 'scientific management' techniques that emerged in the late nineteenth century. In Barnett's view, 'The cult of the "practical man" led to a positive distrust of the application of intellectual study or scientific research to industrial problems' (1972: 94). Allen (1976) sees this as the root cause of Britain's economic decline.

The reluctance to espouse the means necessary to innovate successfully in industrialism's second revolution reflected more, however, than just a preference for the classical education of the gentleman or the feeling that the mystique of the practical man would continue to prove its value in industry. At a more fundamental level, it has been suggested that a distaste for change in general may have been involved. The emergent culture of the 'Establishment' in Nairn's view, had (and still has) as its main-spring the 'alert containment of novelty' (Nairn, 1979: 239). There was a belief that industry did not need to be encouraged but rather controlled. As Perkin (1972: 443) points out, this was the underlying intent of the introduction of limited liability in 1862, and factory and other acts designed to limit industrial abuses and business malpractices proliferated after mid-century. Prosperity seemed assured, providing that things could be kept as they were. Defensiveness rather than adaptability became the central characteristic of economic activity; by 1914, notes Barnett (1972: 89) the industrial system presented a 'positively medieval picture of complicated private and corporate customs and privileges hardened by time into absolute rights legalistically defended'. Meanwhile there were the fruits of the first industrial revolution to be enjoyed:

> The area of great opportunity for new men lay in catering to the needs of a long-enriched business class freed of the habit and custom of abstinence, of a labour force enjoying for the first time an income above the minimum of decency, of a growing rentier class reposing on the returns from home and overseas investments. (Landes, 1969: 339)

Complacency, amateurism, the desire to enjoy the returns of past economic success blended with loftier aspirations. The elite education institutions – the public schools and Oxbridge – aimed to inculcate in their charges the 'Roman imperial values' of stability, order, and justice, qualities Barnett feels were better suited to the officers of an empire than to the managers of industrial concerns. There was, accordingly, 'a tendency somewhat to deprecate the aim of maximising profits' (Coleman, 1973: 114). It is not surprising, in this light, that business in Britain could have been effectively 'colonised' by government, in particular by the permanent Civil Service. 'Public interest is their peculiar property, goes naturally with the job, but it does not go naturally with business – indeed the rugged entrepreneur is almost by definition barred from suffusion by it' (Nettl, 1965: 37). The result was the adoption by the socially inferior business community of civil service procedures and orientations characterised above all by restraint, moderation, consensus, and concern for the public interest that even today act to inhibit aggressive, innovative entrepreneurship ...

There can be little doubt of the existence and perhaps even the prevalence of this complex of anti-entrepreneurial attitudes in late-nineteenth-century Britain as there is of the fact that industry on the whole was profitable in that era. But which factor – the economic conjuncture or the cultural value system – was the one that led to decline? Many observers have pointed out that Victorian gentlemen were just as content to make money as anyone else; could it really be that they simply backed the wrong horses for perfectly sensible reasons, just as Germans backed the right horses for what Landes (1969: 354) concluded were 'wrong, or more exactly, irrelevant reasons'? If, on the other hand, one wishes to credit the attitudinal explanation, one has to wonder why a nation which had pioneered the agricultural and industrial revolutions and been a commercial forerunner for centuries should have come to adopt in the nineteenth century, at the very culmination of its economic success, a cultural complex so obviously disdainful of that achievement and inimical to its furtherance? It is hardly satisfactory to conclude that both the cultural and the economic factors existed simultaneously by some sort of unfortunate coincidence ...

Yet it is difficult to deny that some validity does pertain to both types of explanation. Was Britain in decline before 1914? Cliometricians have been able to produce models that generate both answers, but what is clear is that Britain had found itself in an economic situation in which profits and prosperity were possible without major changes in industrial methods or massive transfer of resources to the emergent industries that were to command the economic future of the developed world. It is just as clear that resistance to the kind of active and enthusiastic industrial involvement that the second industrial revolution would have required of the British middle classes suited them perfectly well, and enabled them to ignore the cries of alarm for the future. Ultimately, an unease over the coincidence of factors remains, however, and provokes the search for some perspective that can unite them under the umbrella of a more general and comprehensive explanation ...

In the pursuit of that, let us begin with British society in its eighteenth-century or pre-industrial incarnation. The defining characteristic of that society, if one is to believe Perkin (1972: 17) is that it was 'an open aristocracy based on property and patronage'. As such, it was like no other in Europe. Its nobility possessed no legal privileges or exemptions of consequence to distinguish it from the rest of society. Apart from the very few families of peerage, its ranks were open to anyone wealthy enough to purchase an estate. Its openness extended in both directions: younger sons of the nobility, deprived by primogeniture of the possibility of inheriting part of the family estate or even a title, might enter middle-class occupations, including commerce, without fear of derogation of status. Although the number who actually did go into business was probably small, the example was all-important: according to Landes (1969: 68) it 'sanctioned pecuniary rationality as a way of life'. Because the aristocracy and the gentry chose to see to the maintenance and enhancement of their wealth above all else, social barriers were far less inviolate than on the continent. Arthur Young could marvel at the English lord who thought nothing of dining with his tenant farmers, but Dr Johnson's famous remark about the completeness of London life reflected, as Carswell observes, the same approbation of a pervasive sociability that cut across status lines ...

The spirit of the time was, indeed, mercantile. In Namier's view, 'every country and every age has dominant terms, which seem to obsess men's thoughts. Those of eighteenth-century England were property, contract, trade, and profits' (Namier, 1975: 23). To a certain extent, the possibility of emulating and eventually joining the ranks of the country gentlemen inspired the frenzy for material gain, as it did everywhere in Europe, with the significant reservation that achievement of gentle status in England did not oblige one to dis-invest from commerce. But this was not true in every case. According to Perkin (1972: 72) religious dissent was a manifestation of hostility to the landed aristocracy, and its praise of hard work and ambition reflected a desire to win out at the 'game of getting rich' ...

Hostility to the aristocratic ideal received important intellectual support as the century wore on. Among the great political economists of the late eighteenth century and early nineteenth century, Ricardo stands out for his attacks on land-owners as parasites who did not merit the wealth and position they held in society; the theme was, however, a common one among political economists. In utilitarianism, too, can be seen important strands of this sentiment, for it became axiomatic that it was the hard-working, frugal, middle-class capitalist, creating, accumulating and re-investing his profits, rather than the idle, spendthrift aristocrat who contributed most to the betterment of society in general ...

The industrial revolution stimulated the fascination felt at all levels of society with the process of material enrichment. In the early nineteenth century, Britain did not lack that 'acute, even irrational, joy in technical progress as such, which we think of as characteristically American'. Bentham and J. S. Mill promoted the idea that education should be scientific and useful to society, a sentiment shared by the business class in general, and technical education was made widely available to the lower orders through a variety of publications as well as technical and proprietary schools and colleges. At home, middle-class women diligently studied books on political economy, and Samuel Smiles became the leading exponent of a popular 'self-help' literature which proclaimed that material prosperity would be the reward to those willing to embrace the virtues of thrift, self-discipline, and hard work.

How different all this seems from late Victorian Britain. If eighteenth-century Britain was an aristocratic society absorbed with materialistic values, Victorian Britain seemed to become, increasingly, a bourgeois society dedicated to the task of eradicating all traces of pecuniary concerns from its inner consciousness and outer aspect. Business constituted for middle-class Victorians, not the means to prosperity or even the manner of demonstrating moral righteousness, but a way of providing for the life-style of the leisured gentleman. This concept, however, bore very little resemblance to the reality of eighteenth-century landed life: the 'bullying squire', with his rather philistine approach to book-learning and his disdain of religion, had yielded to the ideal of the Christian gentleman with his sound moral education based on scripture and the classics of antiquity, and his disdain of functional training or acquisitive pursuit ...

This new version of the gentlemanly ideal did not, of course, just emerge; it was devised and propagated to great effect in the nineteenth century. The reformed Victorian public schools and universities were instrumental in this regard. They helped to mould a single governing class, identifiable by a shared set of values and perspectives, whose concerns and manners contrasted sharply with the traditional English character and who set a fundamentally different tone to the whole of British society. As Perkin (1972: 280) succinctly puts it, 'between 1780 and 1850 the English ceased to be one of the most aggressive, brutal, rowdy, outspoken, riotous, cruel, and bloodthirsty nations in the world and became one of the most inhibited, polite, orderly, tender-minded, prudish and hypocritical'.

Bertrand Russell once suggested that the concept of the gentleman was devised by the aristocracy as a means of keeping the middle class in order; alternatively, one might argue that the concept was a middle-class invention, receiving its impetus from the religious revival of the early nineteenth century and the romantic movement, but reflecting as well, perhaps, the 'traditional puritanism of the English middle ranks' (Perkin, 1972: 281). In the face of the middle-class moral and material onslaught, it was the aristocracy which had to adapt in order to survive. In fact, it not only adapted by relinquishing total control of the levers of power and culling out the grosser elements of its traditional comportment, but by opening its ranks as never before to the more 'acceptable' of the bourgeoisie, even as it divested itself of its open and voracious pursuit of profit. The welcoming embrace of this more respectable aristocracy was extremely difficult to resist, and what emerged in the late nineteenth century, most observers agree, was a plutocracy no longer hostile to landed wealth, no longer aggressively entrepreneurial, no longer obsessed with the business of making money (although quite happy to spend it).

Another curious inversion of the eighteenth-century pattern took place at this time. Britain not only democratised its parliamentary institutions; its rulers increasingly concerned themselves with the welfare and the fate of the working classes. But at the same time, the channels of communication between levels of the social hierarchy closed. The country estates and West End drawing-rooms of the aristocracy were opened to the magnates of City finance and commerce, but that other bourgeoisie, the northern industrial, was for the most part left out. More importantly, the redesigned educational system of the Victorians seemed deliberately constructed to create class barriers and inhibit mobility across them. The public schools, which traditionally had exercised an important function in educating poor but gifted local boys, instead took on the function of blending the prosperous middle class and gentry into a common mould that poor boys, no matter how successful they might eventually become, could never share. Although state education was expanded (at the primary level mostly), 'the whole aim was to segregate the classes so as not to educate the lower above their station or embarrass the higher with lower company' (Perkin, 1969: 301). The society which had amazed foreigners with its openness and fluidity in the eighteenth century had become a society renowned for its invidious class distinctions and hostilities by the twentieth. If the price for creating this new society was the loss of technological and industrial leadership to Germany and the US, it was, apparently, a price influential Victorians thought was worth paying ...

What caused the transformation? Unquestionably, the moral climate of Britain had been revolutionised, but the nature of the new ethos, as propagated in the public schools, suggests that something more than the serious attention to Christian (Anglican) virtues was involved. By the 1880s, loyalty, team spirit, submission, conformism, patriotism, and 'manliness' had become the common fare of public schools, increasingly dominated by a profusion of *rules*, codes, privileges, customs and traditions. None of this has much to do with sound academic or moral formation; some of it is positively hostile to intellectual inquiry. Clearly, the aim was elsewhere. But where? Barnett (1972: 27) makes the point well: 'the school playing-field was seen as a preparation for the battles of an ever-widening empire'.

The British, in essence, had acquired an imperial mentality, and in their reformed public schools were undertaking to transmit to the offspring of their middle and upper classes the skills and values deemed appropriate for imperial governors, or 'Head Prefects of the World' in Rae's felicitous phrase. In sharp contrast to previous periods of imperial expansion, the motive for acquiring this empire was not, in the first instance, commercial. To Victorians, it would have been preferable to enjoy the benefits of trade and foreign investment without the burdens of formal control, and when that control did come, it was more likely to have been either provoked by the challenge posed by the expansion of other empires, or necessitated by strategic consideration (especially concerning the route to India), or brought about by individuals acting on their own initiative in the territories in question. But acquisition of a huge empire, however effected, did have its impact on the British: 'Some of them it gave jobs to, or honours, or their authority, or a mythology, or a sense of purpose or a feeling of pride and superiority' (Porter, 1975: 199), and having created these needs, the continuance of the empire was required in order to satisfy them. For a generation and a class that aspired to worthier goals than those which preoccupied their eighteenth century forefathers, empire provided a suitably uplifting vision. The fact that their education equipped them for little else contributed no small part to this sentiment. But it was easy to take a nobler view: 'It seemed a marvel: so many millions, scattered so wide, ruled over by such a mere handful of Britons' (Porter, 1975: 201). Surely, it was felt, the efforts of the nation's best-educated sons, those from its 'finest' families *should* be directed towards this awesome responsibility rather than towards the menial task of material production, which had always succeeded on its own and which, in any case, would certainly benefit from the trade and investment opportunities that empire created.

The argument of this chapter, then, is that the nature of British society experienced a fundamental change in the nineteenth century. But the change in question was not simply the familiar transformation from a traditional, rural society into a modern, urban and industrial one. Rather, the change consisted of the erection in Britain of a type of society, the territorial imperium, with its associated hierarchical and ascriptive status system, which had existed elsewhere in Europe in its basic outlines, but which had hitherto distinguished England by its absence. By the late nineteenth century, the signs of this change were abundant: economically, the turning-away, whenever possible, from entrepreneurial activity, the reliance on safe overseas investments, and the preference for small family firms rather than dynamic, expanding enterprises; socially, the connection between social status and remoteness from 'trade', the importance of class distinctions made obvious through cultured differences in education and access, the prestige associated with public (especially imperial) service, and the proliferation of honours, military orders, and titles; culturally, the re-making of the gentlemanly ideal and the revival of Catholic and high Anglican religious thought; politically, the domination of democracy through the myth of government by those born to rule and the rise of an enormously popular cult of monarchy.

Despite the very considerable changes that have taken place in the last hundred years, much of the ethos of this society remains in present-day Britain. It can be seen in Civil Service recruitments and university graduate occupational preference patterns and in engineering-school enrolment figures; it forms the basis for the Conservative Party's continuing appeal (if no longer its stated programme); and it assures British television of a large audience for melodramas with upper-class Victorian or Edwardian settings. Nonetheless, Britain is changing today, and rather rapidly at that. The old pattern has lost much of its vitality and its validity, and doubtless will continue to do so. The question for the future is, can Britain ever change enough through peaceful means to catch up with nations which have successfully institutionalised change as an essential aspect of contemporary life?

CHAPTER 17

Cultural explanations of decline: how true?*

W. D. Rubinstein

It now seems extremely difficult to argue for the primacy of cultural factors in Britain's apparent economic decline as opposed to purely economic or simply fortuitous factors, though, clearly, there is more than enough substance to the thesis to warrant a very close examination. The cultural thesis fails, in my view, to devote sufficient attention to the peculiarities of the British economy or to deep-seated trends which began before 1870; it is not fully consistent with the actual chronology of change or, in some crucial aspects, with the true nature of British entrepreneurship; and it fails to present a persuasive nexus to account for the transmission of cultural values into economic behaviour and performance. Nevertheless, in a qualified form cultural factors may well be important in accounting for the type of society which Britain has become ...

Is British culture anti-capitalist and anti-business? Perhaps, indeed, it is, but the absolutely central point must be made that every cultural system in the world is anti-capitalist and anti-business. Indeed, it is probably no exaggeration to say that all of Western high culture in its ideological substance over the past 150 years has *consisted* of attacks upon capitalism, and the liberalism with which it is strongly associated, from the perspective of the extreme right, the extreme left, or from a generalized anti-urban, anti-technological standpoint. On any comparative basis – and here we come once again to this central matter of comparison – British culture has been markedly less strident in its condemnation of capitalism than virtually any other Western culture, probably because doctrinaire and self-conscious ideology of any standpoint has been so much rarer and less extreme than in most other countries. There is absolutely nothing in British culture, for instance, to set beside the cosmic anti-bourgeois sarcasm and distilled hatred and loathing of a Brecht or any other Marxist writer on the left or a Nietzsche or any

*   Reproduced with permission from 'Cultural explanations of Britain's economic decline', in B. Collins and K. Robbins (eds), *British Culture and Economic Decline*, Weidenfeld and Nicolson, 1990.

other proponent of proto-fascist 'cultural despair' on the right so common in Germany. Even in the United States, the homeland of capitalism rampant, the writers and intellectuals who lived contemporaneously with America's industrialization, like Emerson, Thoreau, and Melville, notably ignored it; many of their successors from Henry Adams through Hemingway and T. S. Eliot, left America to escape it; those who remained behind regularly attacked it, from left-wing writers like Theodore Dreiser and Upton Sinclair to right-wing anti-urbanist writers like William Faulkner; not one, or hardly any one, embraced it, although most personally profited mightily from the American reading public's apparent taste for self-flagellation. If the milk and water equivalents of Brecht, Nietzsche, and Henry Adams who are seen as comprising the British equivalent of this tradition, from Matthew Arnold to Dean Inge, so essentially affected British entrepreneurship, how is it that American and German culture failed to be so affected? I know little of Japanese culture, but what little I do know suggests that it was and is even more ostensibly radically anti-capitalist than its Western equivalents.

Patently, too, the notion that British culture was pervasively anti-capitalist ignores those cultural and quasi-cultural figures who are not anti-capitalist – more numerous, in all likelihood, than in most Western countries – who explicitly defended capitalism from Adam Smith, Macaulay, and, obviously, Samuel Smiles and his many imitators, to philosophers like Herbert Spencer. At least as importantly, it ignores the arguably more significant tradition which emphasized rationality and science as the primary desiderata of evolving society, a tradition which in my view animated such important intellectual movements as Utilitarianism and Fabianism; plainly, too, an emphasis on science, technology, and rationality was close to the centre of the ideology connoted by what we commonly term 'the Victorian middle classes' ...

In my view, the closer one carefully examines the evidence and the links in the argument, the more doubts one must have about the cogency of the thesis. Take, for example, the nexus or lack of nexus between the transmission of cultural values and entrepreneurial performance: just how was Britain's anti-business ethics transmitted into a haemorrhage of talent from business life and into a notably poor entrepreneurial performance? The major nexus which is so often postulated is, of course, the public school system, wherein the sons of successful middle-class businessmen absorbed the gentrified values of the older elite, pursued social status and the standing of the gentleman at the expense of their old entrepreneurial drive, and created the celebrated intergenerational haemorrhage of talent away from business life. Professor Weiner (1981: 20) has given us an epitome of this process:

> The public schools gradually relaxed their entrance barriers. Boys from commercial and industrial families, however, were admitted only if they disavowed their backgrounds and their class. However many businessmen's

sons entered, few future businessmen emerged from these schools, and those who did were 'civilized'; that is, detached from the single-minded pursuit of production and profit.

As plausible and frequently encountered as this critique doubtless is, the best evidence now available is that it is only partially true at the very best.   Before turning to my own evidence, I should note that the only source given as a citation in support of this statement in Professor Weiner's book is Bishop and Wilkinson's (1967) book on *Winchester and the Public School Elite*, 'passim'. On examining Bishop and Wilkinson's book however – a book I have frequently used and cited in my own research – I am regrettably unable to find a shred of evidence which supports the statement I have just quoted.   The only relevant evidence on this matter in Bishop and Wilkinson is a comparison of the author's Chapter 4, Table 5 (pp. 104–8), which outlines the occupants of 8,187 fathers of Wykehamists educated between 1820 and 1922, with Chapter 2, Table 10 (pp. 64–9), which similarly outlines the occupations of the 7,105 Wykehamists educated in this period for whom occupational evidence could be traced in the Winchester Alumni Books. A comparison of these two tables reveals that 11.1 per cent of the Wykehamists' fathers were businessmen, while 16.4 per cent of the Wykehamists themselves were businessmen – in other words, precisely the opposite of the point made by Professor Weiner.   (In fact, since only the Winchester Alumni Books have been used as a source by Bishop and Wilkinson, the actual total of both businessmen fathers and sons was likely to be somewhat higher, since many entries either give no information as to occupation or only limited information.)   As it happens, I have recently conducted quite extensive research into just this matter with the aim of studying in a very detailed way the occupations, probate valuations, and much other information from samples of 60–100 entrants at eight leading public schools, entering in 1840, 1870 and 1895–1900, going beyond the school alumni books with comprehensive use made of birth, marriage, and death certificates, probate data, and the like.   The results of this larger study are, seemingly, extremely similar to those of Bishop and Wilkinson.   Most public school-educated sons entered, broadly speaking, the same types of occupational fields as their fathers – the sons of professionals generally became professionals, the sons of businessmen became businessmen. Even when there was a drift away from business life in the second generation, it is nothing like the massive shift implied by Professor Weiner's remarks ...

There is certainly little or nothing in the available evidence which permits us to say that the public school *ethos* led its products away from business life. Why is there such a widespread notion that it did?   Among many other reasons, I strongly suspect that there is a pervasive demographic illusion involved, wherein the third, fourth, fifth, and sixth sons of businessmen, superfluous to the continuing needs of their family firms, often left the business sector for the professions; towards the later part of the nineteenth century, they may well have been compensated for by the superfluous sons of landowners and professionals who moved the other way.

In the more recent past and down to the present, given the decline, presumably to the vanishing point, of the older type of landed gentry, clubland *rentier* wastrel, and *pukka sahib* administrator of Empire, it is only to be expected that many more public school graduates would enter business life or professions closely related to business life. One study of *The English Public Schools* by James McConnell, published only in 1985, noted a survey of 2,035 old Etonians who left between 1967 and 1977 which showed that 450 were 'in accountancy, stock broking, insurance, or some form of banking', while over 100 other occupations were noted. Observers of elite education in Britain have for some decades noted the profound changes, in the direction of modern-looking, technological and utilitarian training, which have recently occurred in the syllabuses of the public schools. According to McConnell's recent survey, to take some fairly random examples, 'Marlborough: until 1983 Engineering attracted the biggest number of Marlboroughs going on to degree courses, but in that year Business Studies took the lead ... Turning to Cheltenham, when Cheltenham outgrew its strongly military identity and the ideal of the Empire became outmoded, no new inspiration was found. From 1932 until the late seventies [Cheltenham] steadily fell behind other Great Schools. The past six years have been a period of ... renewal and fresh direction ... A new thrust has been in Electronics ... the new Electronics lab is probably the most advanced in the UK'. At Rugby, 'in the last 30 years the number of students doing Science has risen from 10.6 per cent to 26 per cent', and so on at every major school.

None of this will be news in any sense to Britain's left-wing sociologists and social historians of elites. As everyone will know, it is a stock-in-trade of their critique of British society and its economic development over the past century that Britain's elite economic positions such as the chairmanships of the major corporations, have been overwhelmingly dominated by a small, closed circle of men from well-to-do backgrounds educated at public school and Oxbridge. This common perception is seemingly supported by objective evidence. In Stanworth and Giddens' (1974) study of 495 leading company chairmen holding their position between 1900 and 1970, the percentage educated at what the authors term a public school rose from an already high 58 per cent among those born in 1840–59 to 74 per cent among those born in 1900–19. Among those born between 1840 and 1879 – in other words, holding office between about 1890 and 1945 – nearly two-thirds were educated at one of the eight Clarendon Schools and about 45 per cent at Eton and Harrow alone. Even a brief comparative perusal of the entries in the *Dictionary of Business Biography* will make clear the striking change, from backgrounds of small family firm and apprenticeship, to backgrounds of public school and university, which has overtaken Britain's business leadership over the past century or so. Certainly public school education had few adverse effects upon these business leaders.

The second point to be made about the empirical evidence is this. Commonly the movement away from business life across the generation is depicted as the search for status, and, normally, the acquisition of status in Britain is seen, equally commonly, as entailing the purchase of land as an absolute prerequisite to achieving gentry status. Yet those recent historians who have studied the empirical evidence concerning the purchase of land on a large scale by businessmen, like the Stones and myself, have found, remarkably, no evidence whatever for the large-scale purchase of land by businessmen. In 1884, at the time of the compilation of the official *Return of Owners of Land* by Parliament, much less than 20 per cent of all land by landowners with 3,000 or more acres was owned by post-1780 businessmen, and only a minority of very wealthy businessmen, even those leaving £500,000 or more, owned so much as 3,000 acres. Moreover, most of those who purchased very large landed estates, like the Rothschilds or Lord Overstone, were multi-millionaires who still retained vast investments in their business firms and securities. Even if these wealthy businessmen did purchase very small estates, or a country address and a gentry *mien*, the point is that the vast bulk of their assets remained in business investments or securities and were *not* transferred into the land, contrary to the widely held myth. Indeed, Professor Stone has recently suggested that land purchase of this kind may well have been far more common on the continent than in Britain. Quite conceivably too, the percentage of all successful businessmen purchasing land in quantity declined markedly from the pre-industrial period. I find the behaviour of these wealthy businessmen quite inconsistent with the popular image of a status-seeking, ever more gentrified class.

Yet another point of dispute is the matter of profits and profitability. In the quotation from Professor Weiner given above, there was also the suggestion that second-generation businessmen were no longer dedicated 'to the single-minded pursuit of profit and production'. This is an interesting point; quite conceivably, second- and third-generation businessmen may as a rule have headed companies which were less profitable than those built up by the founder; but possibly they didn't. Against those whose profit rates declined must be set, presumably, all first-generation bankrupts and ne'er-do-wells, while it would be exceedingly difficult to attribute a decline in profitability to entrepreneurial inability alone, as opposed, say, to the effects of untimely depressions or to changing market conditions. Most business millionaires, if this is any test, were actually the sons of moderately successful businessmen – fathers who improved upon the family fortune, like Lord Leverhulme, whose father was a moderately successful soap maker who left £75,000. It depends what one means by a public school, but a fair share of these were public school-educated, it would seem, although quite possibly there is an important negative connection here which I will discuss shortly.

Although it appears that the difficulties in compiling an overall index and the overall share of profits in company net output has prevented a broad historical index prior to the Second World War, there have been several detailed and reliable studies of the overall amount of business profits in the British economy in this century. The overall amount of profits among firms where this could be measured varied directly with general economic conditions, peaking, during the inter-war period in the 1919 boom, in the late 1920s, and declining by roughly 40 per cent during the 1920–22 and 1930–33 depressions. There is no evidence of any general, secular decline or any abandonment of profit-seeking by British entrepreneurs: quite the reverse. Indeed, the whole thrust of wage-cutting during the inter-war period (and before, obviously), was to increase profits. In the first post-Second World War years for which figures exist for the share of profits in company net output (profits and wages paid), for 1950–54, this stood, according to two Marxist economists, at 25.2 per cent, which hardly sounds like an abandonment of the profit motive (Glyn and Sutcliffe, 1972). Indeed, the point of this Marxist critique, and many others from a similar perspective, is that the extraordinarily high rates of profits in British industry were 'squeezed' by rising labour costs and international competitiveness from the 1960s on, which may have led directly to Britain's present unsatisfactory economic circumstances. This also happened in other Western countries, like America. The restoration of profitability by many Western governments during the 1980s may, indeed, be the most important long-term contribution by monetarist governments to the long-term health of Western economies in the post-Keynesian period. A final point is that since 1850 profit-making may have been too easy rather than too hard for Britain's businesses: presumably, most critics of Britain's economic decline would have preferred that investors or entrepreneurs have deferred the making of super-profits in, say, Malayan rubber plantations or property development in order to invest in long-term growth areas involving initially vast commitments of technology and capital.

Does all this mean that the cultural thesis would be rejected *in toto*? I do not believe this. It seems to me unarguable that there are distinct national cultures and that they heavily influence economic performance in demonstrable ways ... I would like here briefly to point to three or four such specific areas.

First, although the public schools may well not have been responsible for a large-scale intergenerational movement of businessmen's sons away from business life, nevertheless there is evidence from the probate records that the sons remaining in business (or transferring to it from other sectors) were in the main markedly poorer than their fathers. There are innumerable *caveats* to accepting this at face value, such as the fact that many of these sons, from the 1895/1900 public school cohorts, died in very recent decades, when levels of estate duty avoidance were much higher; that large numbers were killed in the World Wars; that families with many siblings would have had to divide their father's legacy into smaller portions, and so on. Nor is this conclusion, if true, in any way inconsistent with the fact that a minority of such sons were wealthier than their fathers and better entrepreneurs. Nevertheless, the *quality* of entrepreneurship, at least as judged by wealth accumulation, may have declined across the generations. Whether this was due to anything peculiarly British, or was or is common to all capitalist societies following the first generation of entrepreneurs, must in my view be examined objectively.

Secondly, some *types* of business life might well have been virtually immune to entrepreneurial failure of this kind: in particular of course, the City of London, the most upmarket, establishmentarian, gentrified realm of all – and the wealthiest – which nevertheless never 'failed' in the sense so frequently claimed of British industry, and whose dynasties have never withdrawn from business life. Why this is so would probably repay as much careful study by proponents of the cultural thesis as their obsession with Britain's industrial and manufacturing failure.

Thirdly, this: proponents of the cultural thesis frequently talk of the aim of British entrepreneurial activity as status attainment and gentrification, for example by the acquisition of landed estates. In my view this misrepresents the essential motivation of the modern British middle classes, which is not the attainment of status, but the attainment of *security* – two values which, though superficially resembling each other, are quite different. If the attainment of security rather than the attainment of status be seen as the overarching goal of much of the middle classes, including its businessmen, I believe that much which is seemingly puzzling and contradictory in the behaviour of the middle classes will become much clearer. Recent scholarship appears to provide evidence to the attractiveness of *secure* stocks and securities as consistently the most attractive to the British investor from the mid-Victorian period at least, the popularity of secure stocks and other investments was unquestionably reinforced by the increasing importance of trustee investment – for family trusts, probate income, charitable and educational institutions, and so on – that was especially important in a country with as much 'old money' as Britain.

Finally, the suggestion is that British culture has influenced the British economy. It should be equally clear that the British economy given *its* peculiarities, constraints, and evolution, has profoundly influenced British culture and cultural values. The stronger claim of causality runs this way rather than its reverse.

Part 5

Capital

In this part of the collection, we are still firmly on the terrain of the historians, but now the economic rather than the cultural ones. We begin with two extracts emphasising the degree to which twentieth century economic success depended on organisational structures and practices which were qualitatively different from those vital to the UK's initial industrial dominance in the mid-Victorian period. The nineteenth century take-off of the first industrial nation did not require sophisticated forms of corporate structure and enterprise management. Small-scale family-based entrepreneurial activity normally sufficed. Not so by the end of the century, when the emergence of large-scale corporate organisations enabled firms to *manage* markets rather than merely *respond* to them. *William Lazonick* makes the general case (in the first extract here); and *Alfred Chandler* (in the second) provides some of the detailed evidence on which this new orthodoxy of analysis has been built. It is an orthodoxy which we met earlier in the Elbaum and Lazonick thesis on 'institutional rigidities' – rigidities which locked UK manufacturing industry in the outmoded forms of what Lazonick here calls 'proprietary capitalism' and Chandler labels 'personal capitalism'. The failure of the UK manufacturing sector in the twentieth century was not, on this argument, ultimately a cultural failure. It was an organisational one. It was not a failure imposed on manufacturing industry from without – by values, teachers, governments or unions. It was a failure created from within, through a conservative inability to restructure managerial systems and practices in ways which could fully exploit the new technical and marketing possibilities of the Second Industrial Revolution.

It is this orthodoxy which is then reviewed so perceptively by *M. W. Kirby*. The extract from the Kirby essay carries the 'Chandler thesis' down to the modern day, tracing its applicability to a range of UK industries (cotton, iron and steel, shipbuilding and motor vehicle assembly). But while conceding its applicability in those cases, Kirby warns against the dangers of over-generalising the organisational variable. The UK economy has grown through the years of institutional rigidity – suggesting that organisational conservatism was at best a retardant rather than a negator of industrial change. Nor does organisational conservatism seem to apply throughout UK industry – certainly not to the services, retailing and oil sectors which have continued to flourish. And with this in mind, Kirby seeks to balance Elbaum and Lazonick's concentration on organisational variables and supply-side rigidities by re-asserting the importance of other factors: not least market pressures, levels of consumer demand, and the inappropriateness of Chandler's ideal multi-divisional managerial structure to all kinds of industries and products.

The extracts from work by Fine and Harris, Zysman and Radice then pull our attention away from the management of capital to the spheres in which it is located, and to the changing global terrain on which it can now be accumulated. The biggest issue at stake in this part of the debate on economic underperformance is the significance or otherwise of divisions of location and interest between different sectors of capital: finance against industry, multinational against local. The simplest proposition here has traditionally been that UK industry suffered in the twentieth century from a systematic neglect of its needs by local financial institutions, a neglect with no equivalence elsewhere in the advanced capitalist world. That simple proposition is rarely now presented unadorned: and three forms of its adornment are represented here.

The *Fine and Harris* argument is that financial institutions have blocked the capacity of UK-based manufacturing industry to turn to the state for strategic guidance and investment, while failing themselves to fulfill that role and need. The *Zysman* thesis is that such a blockage is in no way surprising, but reflects the highly specialised and fragmented nature of financial institutions, and the sophisticated stock and bond markets, which have long surrounded industrial activity in the United Kingdom. Zysman sees London-based financial institutions as competitors with the UK state as potential modernisers of the economy's manufacturing base, yet as financial institutions whose history, fragmentation and experience leaves them singularly ill-equipped for this task. And *Radice* questions the contemporary validity of the industry/finance distinction itself – pointing to the way in which industrial (as well as financial) capital in the UK has now gone global, leaving the UK in pursuit of higher returns elsewhere. The work of Fine and Harris, and that of Zysman, stand congruent with the writings of Perry Anderson, cited earlier, on the absence of adequate modernising agencies supporting UK-based industrial production. Radice's essay takes us further still, to the arguments on the 'hollowing out' of that manufacturing base by large-scale industrial capital itself.

CHAPTER 18

Lessons of history[*]

William Lazonick

Economic dominance, once attained, does not last forever. With the culmination of the post-war Japanese 'miracle' over the past two decades, US industrialists, politicians, and academics have begun to learn this lesson of history. Indeed, it is a lesson that the British had learned before World War II. Yet there is scarcely a consensus concerning the means to restore the industrial competitiveness of once-dominant economies such as Britain and the United States, in large part because there are deep disagreements concerning the sources of Japanese success and the causes of national economic decline.

The conventional wisdom has it that the erosion of national competitiveness is simply the result of a maladjustment of market forces that can be corrected by changes in relative wages, exchange rates, and the elimination of unfair trade practices. The economies of Britain and the United States are, after all, 'market economies'. Let the market work to equilibrate supply and demand and 'get prices right'.

So mainstream Anglo-American economists tell us. But the history of modern capitalism tells a different story – one that challenges beliefs that letting the market work will either generate industrial success or reverse competitive decline. Since the late nineteenth century, the most successful capitalist economies have moved away from market coordination toward the planned coordination of their productive activities. The movement to planned coordination has not occurred solely, or even primarily, at the level of the state, but at the level of the business organisation. Far from economic prosperity requiring a 'perfection' of the market mechanism, the experience of the twentieth century has shown that the wealth of different nations has become increasingly dependent on the planned coordination that takes place within business organisations.

---

[*] Reproduced with permission from *Business Organisation and the Myth of the Market Economy*, Cambridge University Press, 1993.

There was a time and place when market coordination sufficed in international economic competition. The time was the late nineteenth century, the place was Britain, the world's first industrial nation. The institutional basis for market coordination was the proprietary firm – an enterprise owned and managed by family members or a closed partnership for their own benefit. Constrained by limited managerial and financial resources, the proprietary firm tended to be a single-plant operation that specialised in a narrow range of activities. It therefore had to rely extensively on market relations to supply its various inputs as well as to distribute its products. The state maintained internal law and order, undertook essential welfare programmes, provided elementary education, and ensured the defence of the realm. But in the coordination of economic activity, industry was left to react to the unregulated forces of supply and demand.

By the 1870s market-coordinated proprietary capitalism had made Britain the 'workshop of the world'. In 1870 labour productivity was higher in Britain than in the United States – 14 per cent higher by one estimate. In the early 1880s Britain had more than 40 per cent of world manufactured exports and the United States only 6 per cent.

The following decades, however, saw a reversal in the relative productivity levels of the two nations and dramatic changes in their export market shares. US productivity had caught up to the British level by 1890, if not before, and on the eve of World War I was at least 20 per cent greater. From the 1890s the British share of manufactured exports steadily eroded while the US share steadily increased, until by 1929 Britain exported 24 per cent of the world's manufactures and the United States 22 per cent. Britain remained an advanced industrial economy in the twentieth century, but continually lost ground not only to the United States but also to nations such as Germany and Japan.

Proprietary capitalism

Enterprise management was important to the success of the pioneering factories in the early stages of the British Industrial Revolution. Yet as the nineteenth century progressed, firms came to rely more on the external environment than on internal planning and coordination to ensure access to the productive resources required to generate (what were by the standards of the time) high-quality products at low unit costs. The most important external resource that became available to British manufacturing firms in the nineteenth century was an ample supply of highly skilled and well-disciplined labour. Senior workers – who eventually came to be known collectively as the 'aristocracy of labour' – not only provided their own skills to the building and operation of machinery but also recruited junior workers whom they trained and supervised on the shop floor. As reflected in the widespread use of piece-rate payments to senior workers, however, the employment relation between capitalist and worker was basically a market relation: pay in proportion to output produced.

Capitalists' reliance on skilled labour to organise work and reproduce the labour force had the advantage of low fixed costs not only for individual firms but also for the British economy as a whole. The progress of the British Industrial Revolution did not rely to any significant extent on state-supported or industry-supported education. The reproduction of an abundant and skilled labour force, effected as it was by worker-run, on-the-job training, required little, if any, expense to either employers or the state. Eager to gain entry into the aristocracy of labour, younger workers were motivated to work hard by the prospect of promotion. The older workers, generally protected by union bargains that assured them shares of daily or weekly revenues, were themselves not averse to long and steady labour. In addition, the skilled workers' intimate practical knowledge of production methods meant that, as by-products of shop-floor experience, they were able to keep imperfect machinery running steadily and contribute to minor technological improvements.

The reproduction and expansion of a labour force with particular industrial skills was a community-based phenomenon. As older workers trained younger workers, supplies of specialised labour expanded in certain localities during the nineteenth century. Given an industrialist's choice of business (itself typically a function of his own specialised training in a particular locality), he would tend to invest where labour with the necessary specialised skills was in relatively abundant supply. As a consequence, particular industries became increasingly concentrated in particular regions of Britain during the nineteenth century. The regional concentration of specific British industries meant that employers had access not only to large supplies of labour with the requisite skills, but also to communication and distribution networks that supplied a regional industry with its basic inputs, enabled work in progress to flow through its vertically specialised branches, and market its output. As the extent of the market for a regionally concentrated industry expanded, all the firms in the industry experienced external economies as the fixed costs of infrastructural investments in communications and distribution networks were spread over a larger industry output.

The growth of a regionally concentrated industry facilitated the vertical specialisation of constituent firms in a narrow range of activities, these firms relying on other firms both to supply them with the necessary inputs and to purchase their outputs for resale downstream. The tendency toward vertical specialisation was self-reinforcing because the growing availability of suppliers and buyers for intermediate products made it all the more easy for new firms to set up as specialists. Hence, the growth of a regionally concentrated industry was characterised more by the entry of new firms than by the growth of existing firms. Vertically specialised industries became horizontally fragmented industries.

The evolution of industry structures characterised by regional concentration, vertical specialisation, and horizontal fragmentation as well as employers' ongoing reliance on skilled labour to organise work on the shop floor diminished the need for business firms to invest in the development of managerial structures and organisational capabilities. The lack of managerial organisation in turn reinforced the tendency for industrial structures to be fragmented and specialised. Limited in their managerial capabilities, proprietary firms tended to confine themselves to single-plant operations, thus facilitating the entry of new firms into vertical specialities, and hence increasing the extent of horizontal as well as vertical fragmentation of industrial sectors.

The result was the rise during the nineteenth century of a market coordinated industrial economy. By reducing the managerial as well as financial resources necessary to run a business, the vertically specialised and horizontally fragmented structure of industry permitted capitalist families to avoid the separation of capital ownership from managerial control; their firms remained proprietary. Market coordination and proprietary capitalism – both expressions of the dominance of individualism in the coordination of economic activity – went hand in hand.

Relying more on markets than managers to co-ordinate industrial activity, and hence more on external than internal economies to cut costs over time, British industry gained international competitive advantage. It was the institutions of market-coordinated proprietary capitalism, including heavy reliance on a self-reproducing supply of skilled labour to co-ordinate as well as execute work, that permitted British manufacturing to dominate world markets in the late nineteenth century. Britain's rise to industrial dominance occurred without significant investments in managerial structures that could develop firm-specific organisational capabilities. If the coordination of industrial activity by markets could ever lay claim to generating superior industrial performance, it was in Britain in the late nineteenth century.

The limits of proprietary capitalism

The case of Britain shows how the institutions of proprietary capitalism that had formed the basis of British dominance could be formidable obstacles to institutional transformation and become central to the problem of long-run economic decline. The sources of the institutional rigidities facing British capitalism in the twentieth century were the vested interests and limited abilities of those who participated in, and contributed to, the nation's prior success. Yet the impediments to institutional change far outlived the generation of individuals who had been involved with the organisations and technologies that had secured the economic domination of Britain in the third quarter of the nineteenth century. Even new industries and new movements for institutional change succumbed to overwhelming incentives to achieve their objectives by relying on existing productive resources and social institutions rather than undertaking the massive and concentrated investments to generate technologies with more productive potential and organisations with more capability to plan and co-ordinate.

Put simply, the origins of twentieth-century institutional rigidity in Britain can be found in the nature of industry and enterprise structures that characterised Britain's rise to economic power. On the one hand, the horizontal and vertical fragmentation of firms – itself a consequence of the reliance of British industrialists on external economies, including the ready availability of large supplies of skilled labour in certain localities – made it unnecessary to develop managerial structures that could generate economies internal to the enterprise. In the staple industries – iron and steel, shipbuilding, mechanical engineering, and textiles – that had brought Britain to economic supremacy, more organisational capability resided in craft control on the shop floor than in the underdeveloped managerial structures.

Insofar as British craft workers continued to cooperate with their employers in the twentieth century, it was typically by squeezing as much productivity as possible out of the *existing* technologies (often by failing, within limits, to maintain the quality of the product), driving their shop floor assistants as well as themselves to supply more effort, and, as it became necessary in order to retain their jobs, accepting lower wages. Immobile because of their highly specialised skills, both workers and employers had the incentive to ensure the survival of the firms through which they gained their livelihoods. Many British firms in the staple industries were able to survive for decades by living off the plant, equipment, and infrastructures accumulated in the heyday of proprietary capitalism.

In some industries (mechanical engineering in particular), employers tried to use their collective power to break craft control over the organisation of work and the determination of remuneration. Even when employers rolled back prior union gains, however, craft control was not eliminated, in large part because proprietary capitalists had no organisational alternative to put in its place. What is more, even in *new* machine-based industries such as automobile manufacture, in which the craft unions were not already ensconced, craft-like organisation of production emerged in the first decades of the twentieth century as the automobile manufacturers tended to rely on craft workers to plan and co-ordinate the flow of work on the shop floor.

Reliance on shop-floor workers to perform what we would consider to be managerial functions continued during the interwar period, even in firms such as Austin and Morris that were becoming dominant mass producers in the British market. In the 1940s and 1950s, under conditions of tight labour markets combined with the limited opportunities for firms that relied on labour-intensive technologies to generate new sources of productivity, these workers took advantage of the shop-floor organisational responsibilities that had been delegated to them to form strong specialised craft unions. The result was that by the 1960s one could find scores of separate craft agreements in place at any time in any one automobile plant, thereby placing severe constraints on the planned coordination of the specialised division of labour.

Yet the British automobile industry remained viable in international competition until the 1960s because of its low fixed costs (including the almost complete neglect of R&D) as well as the acceptance of relatively low returns by workers, managers, and owners. The 1960s and 1970s revealed, however, that like the staple industries of the nineteenth century, the British automobile industry had reached the technical and social limits of the utilisation of its resources. Facing the continued development of the Continental producers as well as the rise of the Japanese automobile manufactures, the economic viability of the British industry could no longer be sustained.

The development of organisational capability was somewhat different in the science-based industries of the Second Industrial Revolution – chemicals, rubber, electrical equipment and appliances – in which it was impossible to enter into competition on the basis of technological capabilities inherited from the past. Largely through the efforts of dedicated and aggressive entrepreneurs (typically, although not always, owners as well as managers) who either developed new technologies or controlled foreign patents, a number of British firms such as Lever Brothers, Pilkington Brothers, Dunlop, Courtaulds, Crosfield's, Nobel's, and Brunner Mond were able to become serious competitors in the late nineteenth and early twentieth centuries.

Nevertheless, after the turn of the century, the largest British enterprises were not only much smaller than the largest US enterprises, but also much more under the control of family ownership. The British practice of passing on managerial control of the firm to family members from generation to generation, regardless of relevant career credentials, stifled the growth of the enterprise and the development of organisational capability. The family firm often adopted a nonexpansionary strategy in order to avoid becoming dependent on outside creditors or shareholders who might threaten loss of control or to avoid becoming reliant on, and potentially subservient to, a bureaucracy of technical specialists and middle managers.

During the interwar period, an increasingly common route to growth for British firms was amalgamation. But this type of enterprise growth was the result of a strictly adaptive response that represented attempts by competitive firms to combine to control product prices rather than rationalise operations. Such amalgamations tended to leave previous family owners with their autonomy intact within the amalgamated structures.

The persistence of family control meant that at the higher managerial levels recruitment was from within a fairly closed circle. The heads of the most successful firms, themselves typically of middle-class origin, sought to have their sons educated at the elite public schools and at Oxford and Cambridge – institutions that remained firmly under the control of the aristocracy of landowners and financiers who had little use for industry or technology. When the largest enterprises recruited potential top managers from outside the family, an Oxbridge education was the most highly preferred credential. As a result, and in contrast to the dramatic transformation of the US system of higher education early in the century, there was little pressure on the British educational system to offer technical and managerial training to the future captains of industry until the 1960s and 1970s, when the British finally began to take cognisance of their long-term relative decline.

The ultimate impact of the pursuit of aristocratic status by industrialists was to legitimise and reinforce the closed circle of managerial succession by constituting higher management as a separate social class within the enterprise. The relatively closed ranks at the higher management levels in effect segmented general management from technical specialists and lower-level line managers. As British companies grew in size in the inter-war period, organisational segmentation between top management and the rest of the employees became the norm and remained characteristic of British managerial structures even into the 1960s and 1970s. Again, we see a sharp contrast with the United States. Although US managerial personnel were an elite relative to white-collar and blue-collar workers, higher education and internal promotion policies integrated specialists and lower-level managers into this elite rather than excluding them, as was the case in Britain.

Throughout the twentieth century, organisational segmentation *has* been present in the United States, but it divides shop-floor and clerical workers from professional, managerial, and technical workers, with educational credentials serving as means of allocating people to hierarchical segments and legitimising the segmentation. As a general rule, however, US *managerial* structures have been characterised by organisational integration. Conversely, in terms of training and promotion in British industrial hierarchies, highly trained technical specialists tended to be more closely integrated with shop-floor workers below than with general managers above. Within what we have come to think of as the corporate managerial structure, organisational segmentation remained widespread in Britain well into the second half of the twentieth century, this segmentation between top management and enterprise employees thwarting the development of organisational capability in British industrial enterprises.

CHAPTER 19

The continuing commitment to personal capitalism in British industry*

Alfred Chandler

In my earlier study, *The Visible Hand*, I investigated the coming of managerial capital by examining the evolution of several types of modern business enterprises in a single country, the United States. Here I examine the beginnings and growth of managerial capitalism globally, focusing on the history of its basic institution, the modern *industrial* enterprise, in the world's three leading industrial nations.

Of all the new forms of managerial enterprise, the modern industrial enterprise played the most fundamental role in the transformation of Western economies. They had been rural, agrarian, and commercial; they became industrial and urban. That transformation, in turn, brought the most rapid economic growth in the history of mankind. At the centre of the transformation were the United States, Great Britain, and Germany, which accounted for just over two-thirds of the world's industrial output in 1870. Before the coming of the depression of the 1930s they still provided just under two-thirds. And the speed with which the output of the United States and Germany surpassed Great Britain, the world's first industrial nation, was striking ...

As a result of the regularity, increased volume, and greater speed of the flows of goods and materials made possible by the new transportation and communication systems, new and improved processes of production developed that for the first time in history enjoyed substantial economies of scale and scope. Large manufacturing works applying the new technologies could produce at lower unit costs than could the smaller works.

In order to benefit from the cost advantages of these new, high-volume technologies of production, entrepreneurs had to make three sets of interrelated investments. The first was an investment in production facilities large enough to

---

* Reproduced with permission from *Scale and Scope:The dynamics of industrial capitalism*, Harvard University Press, 1990.

exploit a technology's potential economies of scale or scope. The second was an investment in a national and international marketing and distributing network, so that the volume of sales might keep pace with the new volume of production. Finally, to benefit fully from these two kinds of investment the entrepreneurs also had to invest in management: they had to recruit and train managers not only to administer the enlarged facilities and increased personnel in both production and distribution, but also to monitor and co-ordinate those two basic functional activities and to plan and allocate resources for future production and distribution. It was this three-pronged investment in production, distribution, and management that brought the modern industrial enterprise into being.

The first entrepreneurs to create such enterprises acquired powerful competitive advantages. Their industries quickly became oligopolistic, that is, dominated by a smaller number of first movers. These firms, along with the few challengers that subsequently entered the industry, no longer competed primarily on the basis of price. Instead they competed for market share and profits through functional and strategic effectiveness. They did so *functionally* by improving their product, their processes of production, their marketing, their purchasing, and their labour relations, and *strategically* by moving into growing markets more rapidly, and out of declining ones more quickly and effectively, than did their competitors ...

There were many more such enterprises in the United States than in either Britain or Germany. As early as World War I the new institution dominated the core industries in the United States. The founders of the new enterprises had made extensive investments in new and improved processes of production, had assembled the essential marketing networks, recruited the salaried teams, and developed the organisational capabilities that assured them places as long-term leaders in their industries. By World War I nearly all of these enterprises were being administered by teams of full-time, experienced, largely salaried managers. And since these firms competed for market share and profits at home and abroad, it can be said that the industries had come to be operated through a system of *competitive managerial* capitalism.

The British experience ... was different because in Britain the commitment to *personal* capitalism continued. The failure of British entrepreneurs to make the investments, recruit the managers, and develop the organisational capabilities needed in order to obtain and retain market share in many of the new industries often meant that they lost their markets not only abroad but at home. As a result of this continuing commitment to personal management, Britain became a late industrialiser in many of the new industries of the Second Industrial Revolution. These British industries only became competitive with those of the United States and Germany after modern industrial firms were belatedly created. Even then they remained handicapped in national and international markets because of their late start ...

Underlying differences

In Britain the large industrial firms clustered in a small number of significant industries, as they did in the United States and Germany. Indeed, they clustered in even fewer industries. In 1919, 177 (88.5%) of the top 200 operated in seven industrial groups – food, textiles, chemicals, metals, and the three machinery groups. Statistical data compiled by Leslie Hannah on Britain's 100 largest firms show that these leaders already produced a substantial share of total manufacturing output. The 100 largest accounted for 21% in 1924, 26% in 1930, and 23% in 1935, slightly less than the leading 100 in the United States, where the figures were 24% for 1929 and 25% for 1935 ...

Even though the large industrial firms in Britain clustered in much the same broad categories as did those in the United States, within the categories they were concentrated in quite different subdivisions. A much larger proportion of the British enterprises produced consumer, not industrial, goods. Many more were in long-established industries, such as brewing, textiles, publishing and printing, shipbuilding, and the older branches of the chemical and machinery industries. Far fewer were in the new, technologically advanced, growth industries. Indeed, until after World War I the largest enterprises in Britain in oil, electrical equipment, and light machinery were subsidiaries of American or German enterprises ...

Although British entrepreneurs responded with alacrity to the opportunities in distribution that appeared when the new railroad, telegraph, steamship, and cable systems were being completed, they reacted much more hesitantly to those offered by the revolution in production techniques that was engendered by the new transportation and communications networks. In those industries where British entrepreneurs did make the three interrelated investments that created the modern industrial enterprise, these enterprises and industries were able to compete successfully in international markets. But – and this calls for repetition and emphasis – in the new industries of the Second Industrial Revolution, British entrepreneurs too often failed to make an investment in production large enough to utilise fully the economies of scale and scope, to build a product-specific marketing and distribution network, and to recruit a team of salaried managers. And when they did, they made smaller investments and made them in a more evolutionary manner. So they continued to rely on older forms of industrial enterprise – firms that were personally managed, usually family-managed. In many of these new industries substantial tripartite investments were, indeed, made in Britain; but foreign, not British, enterprises made the investments. Foreign firms reaped the profits and developed the product-specific organisational capabilities. The failure of British entrepreneurs and enterprises to build such capabilities – in terms of both facilities and skills – continued to handicap these British industries and the British economy for decades ...

To summarise, in the industries in Britain where owners made the investments in production and distribution that were needed to exploit new technologies, and where they recruited even relatively small managerial hierarchies, their enterprises competed effectively in global oligopolies. Because the domestic market was smaller and because global markets were limited by cartel agreements, these managerial hierarchies remained less extensive than those of American firms, making it easier to retain family control at the top. But if British entrepreneurs failed to move quickly into a new technology, to recruit the necessary management teams, and to make a substantial investment in distribution, marketing, and purchasing organisations, they were unable to compete abroad or to have significant influence in global cartels, or even to retain their home markets.

Accounting for entrepreneurial failure

Why, then, did British entrepreneurs, the heirs of the First Industrial Revolution, exploit to such a limited extent the opportunities of the new technologies of the Second Revolution?   The answer to this historical question is enormously complex ...

The nation's small geographical size, its lack of raw materials, its still profitable industries – those created before the advent of the railroad and telegraph – and its extraordinarily rich consumer markets provided incentives to invest resources (facilities and personnel) in consumer industries, particularly branded, packaged products and mass retailing, and in the older producer-goods industries of the First Industrial Revolution. With these continuing opportunities for profit, investments large enough to exploit the full potential of economies of scale and scope of the new industries – steel, electrolytically produced copper and aluminium, light machinery, electrical and other heavy machinery, and chemicals – may have appeared less attractive.

In some cases the failure of British entrepreneurs to make the investments and create the organisation essential to compete at home and in the new industries was quite understandable. In steel, British entrepreneurs may have been paying the price of having been pioneers before the opportunities to fully exploit the new technology appeared. Their relatively small initial investment in new production technologies, their reliance on commercial intermediaries, and their personal management – all these reflected the presence of a market still too small to exploit fully the economies of scale. When American and European markets for rails, structures, tubes, and other steel products took off in the 1880s, American and German producers had a far greater incentive to make investments that would fully utilise the cost advantages of the new technologies. They were closer geographically and also culturally to these markets. Once they had made such investments and acquired first-mover advantages, their British competitors had little choice but to turn their production to meeting the still sizeable demand of the domestic British market, and particularly of its rapidly growing shipbuilding industry.

Understandable, too, was the British failure in machinery. In the mass production of light machinery American first movers had developed, before the turn of the century, such effective competitive capabilities in both production and distribution that they remained unchallenged until well after world War II. So, too, German manufacturers who had initially exploited economies of scope to build heavy machinery for the many new and growth industries easily maintained their competitive advantages.

On the other hand, in chemicals, electrical equipment, and copper, British (and French) entrepreneurs had almost the same opportunities as the Americans and Germans. In dyes and pharmaceuticals British entrepreneurs had even greater opportunities and incentives than German industrialists to create new enterprises. In electrical equipment, British inventors were as innovative and British markets as potentially lucrative as any in the world. In copper, the owners and operators of the Rio Tinto Company and the three leading processors had an even better opportunity to dominate European markets than the Mertons who established Metallgesellschaft.

In those three industries the availability of capital in Britain was hardly a constraint; London was the largest and most sophisticated capital market in the world. The more successful British companies had no difficulty in raising funds there. Germany and American first movers financed their subsidiaries in London. Nor, of course, was the availability of trained labour a constraint. The workers in the factories of these foreign subsidiaries were British.

Whatever the exact reasons for such entrepreneurial failure were, two points are clear. First, entrepreneurial failure in the new industries can be precisely defined. It was the failure to make the three-pronged investment in production, distribution, and management essential to exploit economies of scale and scope. Second, the time period in which that investment could have been made was short. Once first movers from other nations had entered the British market, often supplementing their marketing organisations by direct investment in production, the window of opportunity was closed.

And once closed, that window was difficult to reopen. One reason was that continuing, cumulative innovation within an industry usually occurred within established enterprises. Thus when British steel makers attempted to modernise their industry in the interwar years, they had to rely wholly on American techniques and methods. Likewise, in chemicals – organic, electrical, agricultural – research and development had remained concentrated in Germany and the United States, at least until after World War I. In electrical equipment the innovation and commercialisation of products and processes continued in Berlin, Schenectady, and Pittsburgh. Moreover, what was true of innovations in production was also true of those in distribution and marketing. Here British challengers had to compete both at home and abroad against established firms with national and international sales organisations whose experienced managers understood the many and changing needs of their customers.

Even in those industries where British entrepreneurs made the necessary three-pronged investment, they recruited fewer salaried managers and placed a smaller number of them on the governing boards of their enterprises than American and German industrialists did.   In those industries British industrialists appear in general to have had a distrust or dislike of losing personal control over enterprises they had either created or inherited.   Throughout the late nineteenth century British entrepreneurs continued to view their businesses in personal rather than organisational terms, as family estates to be nurtured and passed on to heirs ...

The ways of personal management lasted much longer in large industrial enterprises in Great Britain than in the United States ... In Britain, sons and other relatives of the founders usually took over control of the enterprise.   In some cases they selected board members from their managerial ranks, but even as late as World War II this remained the exception rather than the rule.   In the United States nepotism had a pejorative connotation.   In Britain it was an accepted way of life ... In all but a handful of even the largest companies the owners preferred to recruit lower and middle managers from personnel with long on-the-job training within the company and to select top management from their own families or from those of their close associates.   As a result, the educational infrastructure so essential to sustaining modern industry appeared much later in Britain than in the United States and Germany.

The continuance of management by a small number of gentlemen and players had the least impact on the performance of large enterprises in industries where the exploitation of scale economies did not call for technologically sophisticated processes of production or for specialised marketing and distribution skills or organisations.   In branded, packaged foods and consumer chemicals, marketing required little more than placing advertising through specialised agencies, calling on distributors and retailers, and co-ordinating flows to see that deliveries arrived on time.   Younger generations of gentlemen might easily learn to administer the marketers, as well as the engineers and accountants, under their command.

But where high-volume production and distribution required extensive investment in complex, product-specific production and distribution facilities and the creation of product-specific technical and managerial skills, personal management constrained the growth of enterprises and the industries in which they operated.   Even where British entrepreneurs in the new industries did make the investments in manufacturing, marketing, and management that were needed to compete effectively at home and abroad, their preference for personal management slowed the development of the functional and administrative skills necessary to maintain market share and to grow by exploiting competitive capabilities.   Their enterprises moved overseas more hesitantly and less successfully than those of many of their foreign competitors.   They also moved more slowly and less systematically than did German and American companies into industries where economies of scope provided them a competitive advantage.

The economic costs of the commitment to personal management were high. In the new industries the period before the window of opportunity closed was brief. In many cases the time between the initial commercialising of a new product or process and the coming of the three-pronged investment that determined the players in an industry was little more than a decade. Because British entrepreneurs hesitated, Americans and Germans made the investments that permitted them to dominate British as well as international markets. They did so in copper and other non-ferrous metals; in abrasives and tin containers; in organic chemicals and electrochemicals; in light mass-produced office, sewing, and agricultural machinery and automobiles; in light industrial machines from elevators to printing presses; in electrical equipment that powered the new factories and provided light and transportation to the world's growing cities; and in the heavy machinery used to produce the unprecedented volume of goods in both old and new industries ... By World War I the British had become 'late industrialisers' (to use Alexander Gerschenkron's widely applied term) in the new industries that were the dynamos driving the growth of industrial capitalism after the 1880s ...

Implications of the British experience

[The collective] history of branded, packaged products – industries in which British enterprises continued to be the most successful – reflects the larger British experience from the 1880s until World War II. The ability to continue to compete in soap and meat packing required the creation of an organisational structure and the development of organisational capabilities comparable to those of foreign competitors. Where the challenges in the British market were less direct – as was the case in whiskey, beer, cigarettes, chocolate, biscuits, preserves, sugar, confectionery, and other branded food products – enterprises managed in a personal manner were able to remain profitable at home and even to develop businesses abroad. They could do so, however, only in markets where they were not directly challenged by modern industrial enterprises of other countries. Nor did they expand overseas on the scale of the managerial American food and consumer-chemical companies, or even on the scale of the pre-1914 Lever Brothers, the enterprise which had the largest managerial staff in these industries.

These British producers of branded, packaged products did not expand by aggressively moving into related product lines. They did not use their distribution capabilities to take on new products in the manner of their American counterparts. British firms rarely merged in the manner of General Mills and General Foods to make use of complementary facilities and skills. Moreover, these British firms did not invest in research that might have developed products using the same raw materials and production processes. Whereas Procter & Gamble developed Crisco and other cooking oils before World War I, Lever

Brothers moved into margarine only under pressure from the government during the war. In the interwar years it remained far behind Procter & Gamble and Henkel in the development of detergents and other non-soap cleansers. Lever's diversification into trawlers and fish shops resulted from the unplanned, personal decisions of William Lever. Nor did the British food, soap, and paint companies diversify into chemicals and other non-food products in the manner of American firms. On the other hand, the few firms that did make important investments in research, such as ICI, Burroughs Wellcome, and Dunlop, did begin to develop a broader line of products. They remained the exceptions, however. Therefore the American pattern of large firms competing in several different industries through different sets of companies began to be seen in Britain only after World War II.

The continuing failure to make such investments and to recruit and train the necessary managerial staffs may reflect differences between the basic goals of British and American enterprises, or, more properly, between enterprises managed personally or by families and those administered by salaried managers. In American managerial firms the basic goals appear to have been long-term profit and growth. Growth ensured increased assets for large investors, including founding families. Growth also ensured long-term income and long-term tenure for managers and, in many cases, for workers. In Britain the goal for family firms appears to have been to provide a steady flow of cash to owners – owners who were also managers. On the other hand, the published histories of ICI, Unilever, and British Petroleum indicate that for the relatively few British managerial firms the goal became, as it was for such American companies, long-term growth of assets financed through retained earnings ...

All of these characteristics help to account for the failure of many British firms to maintain up-to-date facilities and to reinvest in product and process development. They also help to account for the failure of those companies to sharpen product-specific managerial and technical skills in the functional departments, as well as the capabilities of monitoring, planning, and resource allocation in the top corporate office. The failure to develop such organisational abilities, in turn, explains at least partially the inability of enterprises and the industries in which they operated to compete for market share abroad and even at home, or to move into more profitable related industries. Attempts by firms to maintain market power solely through the use of patents, advertising, cartel arrangements, and mergers were doomed to failure once they were challenged by enterprises that had made investments and developed capabilities. British entrepreneurs had the patents. They had access to advertising agencies. They had created enforceable cartels in the form of holding companies. They had much closer ties with and access to British financial institutions, government bureaux, and Parliament than did American and German competitors producing and selling in British markets. In a number of basic industries they enjoyed every source of market power against these competitors, except the capability to compete. Thus British entrepreneurs lost out in many of the most dynamic new industries of the Second Industrial Revolution.

On the other hand, those few entrepreneurs who did make the investment in new production machinery and product-specific marketing personnel and facilities and who also recruited managerial teams – as they did in glass, explosives, rayon, rubber, and soap – became effective competitors at home and took their place in the rising global oligopolies. Of even more significance, British enterprises that became successful later challengers to first movers in existing oligopolies did so by making comparable investments, as they did in petroleum, metal containers, steel tubes, motorcycles, cables, radios, in selected industrial chemicals (particularly after the formation of ICI), and in meat packing. They also did so, but to a lesser extent, in automobiles and electrical equipment; there they remained less effective challengers because the founding entrepreneurs recruited fewer middle managers, because they continued to manage personally from the top, and because they invested less in research. In both industries the development of new products and processes continued to be carried on primarily in the United States and Germany.

The industries in which entrepreneurs did make the three-pronged investment and did develop organisational capabilities had relatively little need to seek the assistance of financial institutions and government bureaux. In these industries banks rarely played any significant role. Except for oil, the initial investment came from the founding families and local sources. In oil the government gave financial support to Anglo-Persian in response to an immediate military need for its product. Nevertheless, the government's part in making both short-term operating decisions and long-term strategic decisions at Anglo-Persian remained minimal. In the more fragmented industries, such as textiles and steel, the role of government officials and bankers was far more significant. There, however, the privileged access to outside support provided little help in maintaining the profits and performance of the enterprises or their industries, precisely because the industrial enterprises had failed to create competitive capabilities. Indeed, in steel this access was a positive deterrent to overall productivity and growth because some firms used such connections to prevent others from making the investment and developing the skills needed to become competitive.

The general failure to develop organisational capabilities weakened British industry and with it the British economy. In the first place, the failure to consolidate industry-wide federations into modern industrial enterprises, as Robert Barlow did in metal containers and McGowan and Mond did in chemicals, meant the lack of effective enterprises to rationalise industries by investing in state-of-the-art facilities and developing the skills essential to exploit the economies of scale and scope. Second, when British entrepreneurs did succeed in creating such enterprises in their industries, the success of those industries in international competition depended on the extent to which only one or two such firms had developed their facilities and skills. In oil, rubber, and metal containers the dominant enterprises did continue to improve products and processes and to compete effectively both functionally and strategically in the international marketplace. But in other industries, where the desire for family control and income delayed the development of such capabilities – as was the case in rayon and in glass until the mid-1930s – the British industry fell behind.   Even in electrical equipment and automobiles, British enterprises remained very dependent on the United States for the development of new processes of production and, to a lesser extent, of new products.   Finally, the failure to develop competitive capabilities resulted in high economic and social costs in terms of rate of return on investment and of employment.   On the whole, British industries benefited far less from technological innovation than those of the United States and Germany in the years before World War II and those of Japan after that war.

In sum, the collective histories of British enterprises demonstrate the essential need to create and maintain competitive capabilities in order to assure continuing profitability and productivity in an industry.

CHAPTER 20

Institutional rigidities and economic decline: reflections on the British experience[*]

M. W. Kirby

The growth-inhibiting effects of entrenched institutions have certainly attracted attention in the historiography of Britain's economic malaise, never more so, perhaps, than in Olson's (1982) classic study of economic growth and decline in mature industrial economies.   It is one thing, however, to highlight the phenomenon of 'institutional sclerosis' as part of a generalised hypothesis: it is quite another to advance a coherent analysis based upon detailed accounts of economic performance.   But now, as a result of the work of Elbaum and Lazonick (1986), in collaboration with a team of American and British historians, there exists a sequence of industrial and institutional case studies which collectively stands as a major contribution to our understanding of the process of relative economic decline ...

Never before have institutional impediments to economic progress been subject to such widespread comment and analysis. The purpose of this paper is to examine the validity of the new institutional approach as an explanation of Britain's relative economic decline in the twentieth century ...

The Elbaum-Lazonick thesis offers a predominantly American perspective on the British economy since it uses Chandler's (1977) model of the visible hand, in which the institutions of competitive capitalism were replaced by large-scale corporate enterprise.   The latter is characterised by 'industrial oligopoly, hierarchical managerial bureaucracy, vertical integration of production and distribution, managerial control over the labour process, and the integration of financial and industrial capital' (Elbaum and Lazonick, 1986: 4).   It was the progressive erosion of the self-regulating market system which underpinned the successful development of the American, German, and Japanese economies after

---

[*]   Reproduced with permission from 'Institutional rigidities and economic decline: reflections on the British experience', *Economic History Review*, 637–48, 1992.

1900. It was Britain's failure up to 1960 to emulate this experience in any significant degree which largely accounts for the country's industrial retardation. The visible hand of market coordination facilitated the introduction of high-throughput mass production techniques in industry, while UK businessmen remained committed to disintegrated market structures. They preferred the 'invisible hand' of competition as the arbiter of resource allocation. The resulting atomistic economic organisation was well entrenched by the end of the nineteenth century. Although it had been consistent with international competitive advantage in the pre-1890 phases of industrialisation, Britain's fragmented capitalism cast a long shadow forward by preempting long-term technological and organisational innovation both at the industry-wide level and within the individual firm.

Thus, the Elbaum-Lazonick view of British industry rests on four readily identifiable propositions. First, firms are highly competitive, exercising little market power. Secondly, average firm size is small compared with overseas practice. Thirdly, vertical integration is notable for its absence in that the different stages of production are linked not by managerial hierarchies, but by markets. And finally, control over shopfloor organisation and the introduction of new technology is exercised by highly unionised groups of workers. The industries chosen for study – cotton textiles, iron and steel, shipbuilding, and motor vehicles – provide striking illustrations of the growth-inhibiting effects of these characteristic features of Britain's industrial economy.

Lazonick's (1986) survey of the cotton industry lays great stress on the highly competitive and vertically disintegrated organisational structure in the nineteenth century which conspired with powerfully entrenched labour unions to prevent internal restructuring, technical re-equipment, and the development of modern managerial stills after 1919. Elbaum (1986: 67, 70) demonstrates that the steel industry was subject to a similar set of constraints by the end of the nineteenth century. In this case the adverse effects of 'a heritage of small unintegrated producing units' and a union of steel smelters whose behaviour approximated to that of a 'discriminating monopolist' placed major impediments in the way of productivity growth. The result was a loss of international competitiveness and mounting import penetration of the domestic market. The structure of the iron and steel industry, like that of so many other manufacturing sectors in the UK, was dominated by family firms determined to retain their independence and dependent upon the vagaries of internal recruitment to sustain managerial standards. It is true that in the difficult trading conditions of the interwar period the baleful effects of diffuse family-based control were widely recognised, but as Tolliday points out, the necessary large-scale amalgamations and investment in best practice techniques were obstructed by a profusion of conflicting interests locked in to short-term strategies for immediate survival (Tolliday, 1986). Governments and the Bank of England as external agencies had the necessary coercive power to impose restructuring but they shrank from doing so for reasons of financial and political expediency. Thus, when the industry received tariff protection under the Import Duties Act of 1932 iron and steel manufacturers were able to circumvent official pressures for fundamental reorganisation ...

A similar pattern of organisational inertia was to emerge in the shipbuilding industry. Down to 1914 the international competitiveness of British shipyards was overwhelming and the industry continued to dominate the world market until the mid-1950s. Thereafter, decline was precipitate. Historically the British industry's comparative advantage had rested on the skill and organisation of the workforce in producing a specialised bespoke product. But following the innovation of large, standardised vessels in which capital intensive techniques could be employed with advantage, a new premium was placed on the achievement of dynamic economies of scale arising from product standardisation and hierarchical management in the Chandlerian fashion. In these circumstances the inherited structure of the industry – its fragmentation and extreme competitiveness – precluded the creation of large, multi-yard, and specialist firms. Once again, it was the independent family firm which stood in the way of integration. The few mergers that took place in the 1950s were between adjacent companies 'and were instigated to meet the technical requirements of building larger vessels, rather than any broader vision of the industry's needs' (Lorenz and Wilkinson, 1986: 123). As a case study of competitive decline the experience of the shipbuilding industry underlines a critical deficiency in the generalisations of the 'entrepreneurial failure' school. As Lorenz and Wilkinson (*ibid.*: 127–8) point out, the fact that the onset of decline in shipbuilding long post-dates that of cotton and of iron and steel casts doubt on the universality of general cultural values, unless analysis proceeds on the unrealistic assumption that 'such values strike in different places at different times'.

Every industry has its own economic and institutional context and this must be borne in mind when evaluating the quality of entrepreneurship. These points take on added force when applied to the motor vehicle industry. Rather than emulate US practice, British manufacturers from the outset rejected the high throughput and capital intensive production techniques pioneered by the Ford Motor Company. Profits were maintained at acceptable levels, however, by offsetting low productivity on the shop floor by the payment of low wages. By the end of the interwar period the piece-work system was the norm in the industry, permitting labour to exercise some control over the pace of work. After 1945 the legacy of these developments was to serve the industry ill at a time of full employment and mounting foreign competition from the mid-1960s. The latter encouraged the adoption of capital intensive production methods, but in a labour market subject to enhanced union power. Thus, the efficiency gains of new work methods were offset by higher wages and overmanning. When management began to move towards 'a Ford-style direct control strategy' after the mid-1960s it was confronted by a set of institutional constraints which proved extremely difficult to overcome, and which paved the way for the industry's progressive market collapse in the 1970s and early 1980s.

As an explanation of industrial decline the Elbaum-Lazonick thesis is persuasive and credible. It certainly offers a more satisfactory explanation of Britain's economic problems than do the advocates of entrepreneurial failure. Each industrial case study demonstrates that British businessmen performed as well as could be expected given the obstacles to enhanced competitiveness imposed by existing institutions. It can, of course, be argued from a Schumpeterian perspective that entrepreneurial failure was present to the extent that businessmen accepted inherited constraints as given and reacted passively, rather than innovatively, in confronting these constraints. But in endorsing this view Elbaum and Lazonick point out that failure in the Schumpeterian sense cannot be ascribed to the cultural conservatism that lies at the heart of the entrepreneurial failure thesis: 'If twentieth century British society was pervaded by conservative mores, it was in this respect no worse off than Japan or continental European countries that were pre-capitalist, tradition-bound societies when Britain was the workshop of the world' (Elbaum and Lazonick, 1986: 2). Rather, Britain's decline was underpinned by established institutional constraints that reinforced conservatism and preempted both individualistic and collective efforts either to remove them or to mitigate their growth-inhibiting effects.

Elbaum and Lazonick and their associate authors can be congratulated for presenting a sequence of case studies which are both intrinsically interesting, and together help to reinforce their general thesis. That said, problems arise on several counts if their institutional approach is to be deployed as an all-embracing explanation of Britain's economic decline. First, it must be noted that economic growth in the UK was sustained throughout the period covered by the thesis: decline has only been relative. Certainly, the post-1920 decades, when a pervasive institutional legacy of atomistic markets was supposedly exerting increasing downward pressure on the growth rate, were not marked by deteriorating economic performance (Feinstein, 1988). This suggests that institutional structures, rather than presenting absolute or insurmountable barriers to economic growth, have acted more as a retarding influence. Furthermore, even if the Elbaum-Lazonick thesis presents a convincing explanation of decline in its own terms, it is nevertheless based on a limited number of industrial case studies. Institutional impediments to growth may have loomed large in cotton textiles, iron and steel, shipbuilding, and motor vehicles, but as everyone familiar with the historiography of decline is aware, the historic and current performance of British business is not marked by persistent failure, especially when the focus of critical attention is broadened to include such activities as financial services, retailing, and oil.

This point has been stressed by Coleman (1987, 1988) both in a review of the Elbaum-Lazonick thesis and in his recent survey of failings and achievements in British industry. After surveying the performance of a number of leading business organisations Coleman (1988: 8–9) concluded that a recurrent theme in their history was 'an attitude of mind antipathetic to building change into the system'. It was, in effect, a modified conservatism which, while permitting change, drew strength from the existing 'culture of the firm', itself derived from the internal perception of the history, distant or very recent, of the enterprise. Yet as Coleman is at pains to point out, when market signals indicated that change was the necessary price for survival in a competitive economic system, it was implemented, usually with vigour and determination. This is exemplified by such episodes as the Beeching revolution on the railways, the reorganisation of W. H. Smith in the 1960s and 1970s, the managerial revolution in Courtaulds after the late 1950s, the successive reorganisations of Pilkingtons and the electricity supply industry over an extended period from the 1930s to the 1980s, and the revitalisation of managerial structures and attitudes within ICI during the last two decades. It may well be that reorganisation was unduly delayed in relation to the onset of failing profits in a number of instances. Coleman's analysis, however, demonstrates that there can be no easy assumption of binding institutional constraints applicable to the business sector as a whole. Even within the sectors chosen for study by Elbaum and Lazonick, historic performance at the level of the individual firm was not one of unrelieved gloom. Thus, in shipbuilding it is possible to point to an outstanding record of technical excellence at Harland and Wolff together with successive phases of more or less radical managerial reorganisation through to the late 1960s. Similarly, in iron and steel the firm of Colvilles underwent a major technical and organisational metamorphosis in the 1930s, registering significant productivity gains and establishing 'an increasingly centralised, functionally departmentalised structure' (Payne, 1979: 246). This may have fallen short of the 'Harvard Business School-approved diversification strategy and mature multidivisional structure', but as the most recent historian of Colvilles has concluded, it is arguable that by 1939 the firm 'possessed one of the most efficient managements in the British steel industry' (Hannah, 1976: 197).

Examples such as these fit uneasily into the Elbaum and Lazonick analytical frameworks. If some firms proved capable of challenging successfully a given set of constraints they were clearly not as insurmountable as Elbaum and Lazonick would claim. The same point has been developed further by Dintenfass (1988) in his reappraisal of entrepreneurial performance in the interwar coal industry, a sector which is not analysed by Elbaum and Lazonick but which might be expected to have exhibited the symptoms of institutional rigidity in an extreme form. It was, after all, an industry subject to rampant individualism, reflecting the ubiquitous presence of the family firm or partnership and where, in the 1920s at least, the structure of district wage rates was governed by a binding national agreement. But as Dintenfass points out, on the basis of a painstaking analysis of individual colliery enterprises in Yorkshire and Northumberland, it was possible for medium sized family based concerns to overcome institutional constraints and to achieve consistently good rates of return as a result of 'efficient production, astute marketing and profitable working'. If some firms in particular coalfields were able to surmount institutional barriers to growth by judicious investment in machine mining techniques, and reduce non-labour costs by enhancing the pre-sale quality of the product, why did other colliery enterprises fail to follow suit?

To pose this question brings the entrepreneurial failure thesis back into play almost by default.

The coal industry also raises the critical issue of the general applicability of advanced corporate structures to British industry. As Dintenfass observes, coalmining was a relatively simple business which provided infertile ground for continuous process and assembly line technologies. The raw material requirements were limited and the distribution of the final product did not depend on the availability of highly specialised marketing services. In these circumstances the gains from radical managerial innovation could well have been marginal. It is salutary to remember that, contrary to the impression given in earlier work, Chandler did not advocate the wholesale adoption of 'M-form' structures. They were particularly inappropriate for the manufacturers of semi-finished products dependent on a small number of large industrial consumers. This certainly applies to the iron and steel industry, not least in the US itself where, as Hannah has noted, the steelmakers opted for large functional departments rather than the 'M-form' precisely because their marketing processes were comparatively simple. In Britain the United Steel Companies 'established centralised control over its subsidiaries in the 1920s, with strong central functional departments handling administration, purchasing and sales'. A centralised programme of works rationalisation was introduced together with budgetary control, leaving local boards of management with 'power only over production and works management'. As Hannah concludes: 'Multidivisional organisation was neither created nor required' (Hannah, 1976: 197). In textiles the Lancashire Cotton Corporation, formed in 1929 as the vehicle for a multifirm merger among coarse yarn manufacturers, encountered severe managerial problems as a result of the attempt to introduce a divisional structure. Following the resignation of the managing director responsible 'a centralised, functionally departmentalised management structure was adopted, a structure which was almost certainly more appropriate to an undiversified company selling a standardised semi-finished product like cotton yarn to a limited range of industrial consumers' (Hannah, *ibid.*). Such examples certainly give pause for thought in accepting the universal applicability of multidivisional organisation.

A further related cause for unease is the assumption, writ large in the Elbaum and Lazonick thesis, that the visible hand of managerial hierarchies is always superior to the market in allocating resources. But to quote again from Hannah's pertinent discussion, 'the market remains an important discipline on managers whose beliefs in the power of their own visible hands are sometimes found to be exaggerated' (Hannah, 1983: 172). In the textile depression of the 1970s it was the medium size vertically integrated firms which performed best, while Courtaulds suffered due to a market strategy which rendered it especially vulnerable to import competition. Even a firm such as ICI, which began to move towards multidivisional organisation from its inception in 1926, could not escape the adverse financial consequences of an inappropriate investment decision for the manufacture of nitrogenous fertilisers at Billingham. The same firm was also slow to appreciate the importance of plastics in the 1930s partly as a result of vested interests located within existing divisions.

Elbaum and Lazonick are undoubtedly correct in emphasising the adverse consequences of atomistic structures for the competitive advantage of a number of British industries. The resulting forfeit of technical and managerial economies and limited commitment to in-house research and development have been discussed at length in the literature on twentieth-century industrial development in Britain (see Ackrill, 1988). But as Crafts and Broadberry have argued in their analysis of Anglo-American productivity differences in the 1930s and 1940s, undue emphasis should not be placed on differences in corporate structure to explain Britain's lagging performance (Broadberry and Crafts, 1990). There are several stages to their argument. In the first instance the interwar period in general and the 1930s in particular were marked by a weakening of competitive pressures in the face of the spread of collusion and cartel formation. In 1919, 500 trade associations were in existence, a figure which had reached 2,500 by 1943 when up to 60 per cent of manufacturing output may have been subject to restrictive agreements. The dangers inherent in these developments were acknowledged in the 1944 *Employment policy* white paper when it drew attention to the possibility that aggregate demand management might be thwarted by the pricing policies of collusive organisations. Although poor productivity performance was not an inevitable outcome of cartelisation there is sufficient evidence in the reports of the Monopolies and Restrictive Practices Commission in the 1950s to suggest that cartels underwrote inefficiency by preventing the exit of high cost producers in sectors such as cotton spinning, blast furnaces, steel making, and electric lamps. To the extent that '[productivity] performance was poor where cartels comprised of family owned firms immune from hostile take-overs' (Broadberry and Fremdling, 1990: 416) there is an apparent convergence of views between Crafts and Broadberry and Elbaum and Lazonick. It is also the case, as Hannah (1976: 199) has emphasised, that a considerable proportion of merger activity in the UK before 1939 led to the adoption of loose holding company structures which permitted a continuing role for small scale family firms:

Companies like AEI, Hawker Siddeley, GKN, Liebigs, Cadbury-Fry, Stewarts and Lloyds, Tube Investments and Reckitt and Colman appear to have been little more than loose confederations of subsidiaries, and it may reasonably be doubted whether such a structure can have achieved many of the potential economies of large scale. Suspicion is inevitably aroused that they were a form of cartel – albeit a strong and permanent cartel – which could achieve many of the private benefits of monopoly power whilst forgoing the social benefits which strategic and organisational innovation were more likely to generate.

But it is equally valid to argue that insofar as the UK productivity lag rested primarily on insufficiencies in the use of factors of production, emphasis on corporate structures should give way to 'the competitive environment as a key determinant of conduct' with a particular focus on the reasons for the tardy disappearance of high cost producers. In the latter context the absence of hostile takeover bids in British business until the 1950s, the quasi-rents to be earned from existing plant and equipment in declining industries, and trends in government industrial policy in the 1930s are clearly relevant factors. Their relative contributions to productivity lag have yet to be ascertained, but it seems reasonable to assume that the suppression of competition via collusion would loom large in any general analysis of 'barriers to exit' (Broadberry and Crafts, 1990: 287–8). In this respect Crafts and Broadberry's analysis conforms to the main thrust of Olson's thesis of institutional sclerosis. The latter places 'distributional coalitions' at the centre of growth retarding influences and indicates that faster economic growth is dependent upon 'freer trade and fewer impediments to the free movement of factors of production'. Olson's approach thus differs profoundly from that of Elbaum and Lazonick. Far from markets being an institutional rigidity in themselves, according to Olson, they are the potential solvents of such rigidities if only the rent seeking coalitions producing market imperfections can be removed. It is also important to note that when British firms did attempt to achieve scale economies through mergers the results were often meagre. In the post-1950 period there were, of course, successes, represented at one end of the spectrum in the early history of Lord Weinstock's GEC. There were, however, equally spectacular failures, notably British Leyland which, despite the receipt of major public subventions, experienced progressive market collapse almost from its inception in 1967. UK mergers undoubtedly contributed towards enhanced market power and higher managerial salaries but, as Meeks (1977) has shown, the performance of merged firms in the period 1954–72 was consistent on average with reduced profits and productivity. Efficiency gains, moreover, tended to be small with even GEC achieving productivity improvements only in the 15–25 per cent range. What this suggests is that 'at the very least, the Chandler school pays insufficient attention to the conduct rather than the structure of industry'.

Even in those cases where multidivisional structures were adopted (often on the basis of advice from North American management consultants) the results in terms of enhanced productivity performance were disappointing. By 1970, 72 per cent of the top 100 UK companies had adopted the Chandler 'M-form', far ahead of the 40 per cent in Germany. Yet by that date German labour productivity in manufacturing exceeded the UK level by 30 per cent having been more than 30 per cent below it in 1950. Econometric testing has shown that 'M-form' structures did have a positive effect on industrial productivity but with increases confined to the range between 15 and 20 per cent (Steer and Cable, 1978). What seems incontrovertible is that British firms proceeding towards 'multidivisionalisation' failed to adopt the full range of managerial practices which had come to be the norm in US enterprise. A key deficiency was the lack of uniform and effective accounting procedures both within and between divisions, and, in the case of holding companies adopting multidivisional structures, a tendency to insert a cosmetic layer of management falling far short of fundamental reform. The net result was that British multidivisional firms were less profitable than their American counterparts operating in similar product markets. In this light, therefore, it is a gross assumption that the early and widespread adoption of advanced American-style corporate structures would have produced a more dynamic economy in the context of global competition ...

The cumulative effect of these reservations is to highlight the fact that the Elbaum and Lazonick thesis offers a predominantly *supply-side* explanation of Britain's economic decline. Yet there is a long sequence of studies which has drawn specific attention to the role of demand-side forces in retarding the introduction of mass production technology and large-scale corporate enterprise. The contrast has invariably been drawn with the USA in the latter half of the nineteenth century when the internal market was growing rapidly on the basis of homogeneous consumer tastes leading to standardised patterns of consumption. In Britain, class distinctions were more finely drawn with the result that there continued to be a demand for 'aristocratic goods of high individual quality'. Product differentiation helped to 'divide and sectionalise the market' thereby raising obstacles to 'innovations that depend for their success on large-scale output and consumption' (Frankel, 1957: 74). These general points have been endorsed by Chandler himself when he notes that in the later nineteenth century the distribution of income was less skewed in the USA than in Britain. The comparative newness of the market also meant that 'institutional arrangements had less time to become rigid and that the established middle men were less entrenched'. More fundamentally, rapid market expansion and relatively uniform tastes

> provided the incentive to create the modern integrated centrally administered industrial enterprise in the United States in the years after 1880. The opportunity to exploit the economies of a high volume throughput was an underlying reason for building nation-wide sales, purchasing and raw materials departments and for creating a managerial hierarchy to co-ordinate the high-speed flow of materials through the process of production and distribution from the supplier of raw materials to the ultimate customer. (Chandler, 1976: 47)

This is not to suggest that the nature of market demand provides a more complete explanation of the reasons for organisational backwardness in British industry than supply-side constraints. In motor vehicles, for example, it might be thought that in comparison with the USA the relatively restricted size and rate of growth of the British market until the 1930s severely limited the opportunities for technical standardisation and plant modernisation.   But even those economic historians sympathetic to the argument that market structure did play a role in retarding the industry's progress have conceded that severe supply-side deficiencies were present, in particular a continuing obsession with the technical product rather than with techniques of production, and resistance to company mergers.   Nevertheless, there is a good case for claiming that in downgrading the importance of demand-side factors the Elbaum-Lazonick thesis can only provide an incomplete explanation of Britain's recent economic history.

CHAPTER 21

The role of the City[*]

Ben Fine and Laurence Harris

The special problems of British industry, symptomised by de-industrialisation and the weakness of new technology, have to be seen in the context of industry's relation to financial capital as well as its relation to labour. The special position of the British state, making it non-progressive for industrial capital operating in this country, is often explained by its connections with and orientation to the City of London. The left and liberals have, throughout this century, frequently argued that one particular section of capital, the financial interest, has prevented the state from stimulating and furthering industrial growth while at the same time financial capital itself has not filled the gap and has failed industry. That view is undoubtedly correct in a general sense, but many of the arguments and evidence that are brought in its support are wrong. To understand why the relation between state and industry has been so problematic, and why British industry has fared so much worse than elsewhere, a careful assessment of the role and character of the City is crucial.

There are two main planks to the, by now, orthodox left-wing analysis of the City. First, the financial bourgeoisie has formed an alliance with other fractions of the ruling class which ensures the state furthers their interests at the expense of industrial capital. One influential line in Marxist history is the thesis that the old landed classes formed an alliance with the financial bourgeoisie to retain state power in the early stages of capitalism and this alliance has shaped British history ever since. Another version of the alliance thesis emphasises the City's links with imperialism and the overseas investment and trade sections of British capital; it argues that the two have constituted an 'overseas lobby' which, particularly in this century, has influenced the state in pursuit of its interests at the expense of British industry. The second plank is that the City has failed industry by failing to supply the finance required to ensure growth and modernisation. The argument is that the City has directed funds toward 'unproductive' uses, thereby creating a

[*] Reproduced with permission from *The Peculiarities of the British Economy*, Lawrence and Wishart, 1985.

shortage of industrial finance, and the finance it has put into industry has been short-term instead of the long-term investment capital that was needed to finance innovation.

Each of the strands in the orthodox left-wing assessment of the City's role is flawed, although they both touch upon important elements of reality. There has not been a permanent alliance between finance and land or finance and internationalised capital squeezing industrial capital at home. And industry has not been, in the modern period, starved of finance for growth and modernisation. The City *has* blocked the development of state policies which are progressive for industrial capital, and it *has* itself failed to stimulate industrial growth, but the source of these vices is more complex than the orthodox line supposes.

The activities of the City fall into two categories, trading and financing, but each has money and monetary assets as its object. Trading in bonds and shares (as stockbrokers do), in foreign exchange (banks and foreign exchange dealers), in insurance risks (Lloyd's brokers) and similar financial categories is at the heart of the City's business; the ups and downs of 'the market' – whether it be the stock market, the foreign exchange market or another – dominate the City. And integrally linked to this trading is the City's other function, providing finance. Borrowing and lending, whether to industry, to other finance houses, to individuals or to states is what marks the City off, for trading alone would not distinguish it from other merchants. In the provision of finance, five types of City institutions predominate: banks, building societies, insurance companies, pension funds and investment- and unit-trusts. The differences between types of trading and financing make it surprising that there could ever be a unified City 'interest', a policy voiced and pursued on behalf of the City as a whole. Yet there have been such policies and the City's interests have been pursued with a clarity that industry has never matched: while the organisations of industrial capital have been chronically fragmented and unable to provide industrial leadership throughout this century, the overall interests of the City have been articulated and struggled for under the leadership of the Bank of England. The unity of the City at this level, despite the diversity and special interests of the institutions within it, results from there being one feature common to all its activities, the making of money out of money.

Profiting from dealing in money, and from borrowing and lending it, defines the City's character. It is the basis of its economic and political power and is at the root of its connection with the state; it explains the manner in which the financial system blocks the state from an active involvement in industry while eschewing any active involvement itself.

The drive toward making money out of money has given rise to a division of functions between the City on the one hand and industry on the other in providing the finance for industrial accumulation. The predominant source of funds for industrial investment has been industry itself; in comparison to other countries British industry has relied to an unusually large extent upon self-financing. In this century the banks have until recently concentrated their loans to industry on short-term financing and, to the extent that insurance companies, pension funds and trusts have related to industry, they have largely invested in stock market securities rather than lending directly to industry. This division of functions has not starved industry of funds but, on the contrary, has secured industry's financial needs in a way that has suited industrial management as well as the City.

The result has been twofold. Industry has not needed to turn to the state for finance (except in particular circumstances which, *in extremis,* have accompanied nationalisation) and there has therefore rarely been a liaison through which the state achieved the ability or need to intervene in management and stimulate accumulation. And the financial institutions themselves have not had to intervene in management; their arm's-length relationship has enabled them to concentrate on reaping profits from money while avoiding involvement with production. The bankers' maxim has been 'We leave industrial management to the people who know about it' and, when it comes to such things as innovation, investment, and the organisation of production, the state has been so uninvolved in industrial finance that even under the most interventionist governments it, too, has left management to the managers.

Origins of the problem

The division of functions with industry looking after much of its own finance, the financial institutions satisfying industry's residual needs and otherwise concentrating on making money without industrial involvement, and the state being excluded from intervention, has not been paralleled in all advanced capitalist economies. Germany, for example, has been well known since the end of the last century for the degree of involvement of its banks in both the financing and direction of industry. There are three reasons for this division having arisen so strongly in its particular form in Britain: the strength of markets and trading in the City, the size of the state's debt, and the City's international position. Other factors such as the particular character of the concentration and centralisation of banking have worked within the framework of these three.

Markets and trading have always had a major role to play in the City. The stock market for trading in bonds and shares is the oldest stock market and the London markets for trading in other financial assets (including contracts for commodities) have been better developed than in any other country at least since the end of the eighteenth century. One implication, which Ingham (1984) has emphasised, has been the strength of a specifically merchant-based interest (distinct from a financing interest) in the City's political formation. Another, which is our concern here, is that financiers have escaped the necessity of being involved in the industry they finance.

Always inherent in money and finance under capitalism is a tendency toward maximum flexibility; financial capital always seeks to be independent of constraints and the banks and financiers that control it seek to obtain maximum profit with maximum liquidity. Investment in industry is always a threat to that, for if an industry runs into difficulties – if, for example, its profitable production is threatened by labour militancy – the financier can be locked in. In Britain, however, the strength, size and resilience of the financial market has meant that when industry does issue bonds or shares to finance investment, the lenders lend while not immobilising their capital. They have been able to buy bonds and shares in the knowledge that they can sell them on the market. Avoiding being locked in also means that lenders avoid having to become involved in the management of the firms. By contrast, when Germany's nineteenth-century industrialisation required finance there were not the same well-developed markets to provide liquidity and permit the great flexibility that is financial capital's essence. In consequence, financiers there were necessarily involved in a long-term commitment to the firms they financed; in those circumstances finance could only develop on the basis of a strongly interventionist role. Financiers had to intervene in the industries they financed, they had to have an ownership and managerial stake to supervise their investment for there was little room for selling out on the market if the going started to get tough.

Another reason why the strength of markets and trading was so important in the development of British finance is that banks developed an orientation toward providing the short-term financial needs of trade, rather than the long-term committed money needed for industrial growth. But the banks' concentration on overdraft financing (which is characterised as short-term) in the twentieth century owes much to their own special history ...

State debt is the second element that has shaped the City, moving it in different directions from other countries' financial systems. The City turns its face toward the British state just as sun-worshipping civilisations turned theirs toward the golden orb, for lending to the state is more vital to it than lending to industry. Again, the tendency of all finance and money to seek maximum flexibility and liquidity is what gives this factor special importance. Financiers can obtain the greatest flexibility if profits can be made on assets which are not tied up in the business of industry and commerce; the greater the distance from the operation of productive capital the more ideal is financial capital. The interest and redemption value of state debt is backed by the state's power of taxation and, as long as the state itself is stable, is therefore guaranteed in a way that money owed directly by private firms could not be. Lending to the state ranks higher than industrial finance in the calculations of bankers, and financiers everywhere operate in state loans to a high degree.

But the City has, historically, had a stronger orientation toward financing the British state than bankers elsewhere have towards their respective governments. It is symbolic that the founding of the Bank of England in 1694 was a device for securing a state loan. The growth of the state's outstanding debt to the present has accelerated strongly in particular periods; the Second World War and the immediate post-war years generated an expansion that has had the greatest influence on the character of the 'long boom' and de-industrialisation. The

British state financed its great war spending by several means: forced loans from India, other parts of the Empire and other sterling-using Third World countries; lend-lease from the USA; sales of overseas investments (forced upon Britain by American interests); taxation; compulsory loans to the state by ordinary people; and the raising of credit from the City. By the end of the war the City held a mass of government bonds and bills. The post-war nationalisation of coal, railways and other industries increased the volume, for the owners were recompensed with newly-issued government bonds. Thus, whereas the financial system in the United States had low stocks of American government bonds (especially medium and long-term) until late in the 1950s, the City was able to operate and deal in a flourishing market in British government bonds while Japanese, West German, and French bankers were involved in the post-war reconstruction of industry.

The predominance of state debt in the City's operations significantly affected its relations with industry. Critics of state spending and socialist programmes argue that state borrowing starves private industry of funds and 'crowds out' its investment financing. There is no evidence that the City's orientation toward the state has had that effect; its importance is that it has enabled the City to carry forward its basic tendency, the distancing itself from involvement in the management and operation of industrial capital. State bonds yield secure profits with the maximum flexibility for they are traded with ease, and their volume and variety in London means that financiers can hold exactly the types they want. Because the City has historically made money from the British state on such terms, their lending to industry, too, has been on terms which give the greatest flexibility and, hence, the least involvement in industry's problems. In the abstract, the City could have reacted differently; the state's debt could have been a secure cushion on the basis of which the City's lending to industry could have been more involved, risky and less arm's-length than otherwise. But, given financial capital's basic tendency toward the greatest flexibility and independence, London's financiers used the availability of such terms on state bonds to impose the same terms on lending to industry; if industrial finance had required involvement in management, money had an alternative bolt-hole. The readiness with which the owners of mines, railways and other industries (except the most highly profitable such as steel) took state bonds for their industrial shares in the post-war nationalisations graphically illustrates the point.

City policies and ideology on state financing, however, have been two-edged and, as a result, have constructed and conformed with the exceptional role of financial capital in Britain. On the one hand, the City has welcomed and thrived on state borrowing because of the flexibility and independence from industrial capital this has given it. On the other, it has fought against the deficit spending that reformist governments would need to carry out in order to plan a rational restructuring of industrial capital. Thus the City has contributed toward blocking coherent state intervention in industry while at the same time itself being oriented toward state financing and avoiding involvement in industrial problems.

International orientation.   The third aspect of financial capital in Britain, enabling it to follow the basic tendency of distancing itself from industrial capital in such a way that the role of finance in Britain has been quite different from elsewhere, is its international character. Finance everywhere seeks a world stage to minimise the risks that would arise if its profits stemmed from a narrow or purely local base, but the City has sought and achieved that international role in unique ways.

For much of the nineteenth century, London's bankers and financiers dominated international finance and the latter dominated their business; for example, international finance was the backbone of the London stock market for decades. To some extent this resulted from and reflected the world leadership of Britain's industry, but the City's international importance has continued throughout this century even though Britain's industrial leadership did not.

The conditions the British state secured for financial capital underpinned its modern international role. From the late nineteenth century to the 1960s the Empire was the political framework within which the City's international role developed, maintaining its world predominance despite the relative decline of British industry. In this it marked a new stage in its independence from industry; the City's position as the centre of the investment flows and monetary mechanisms of the Empire and the Sterling Area, which, from the 1930s, was constructed around it, enabled the City to maintain a wider world role around this core.

The political arrangements that maintained the Empire and Sterling Area were the basis; the key to the system was that other countries' foreign exchange reserves were kept in sterling while state intervention to regulate exchange rates gave the stability this needed. When that broke down, the City, particularly London's banks, maintained their international lead with the aid of the state in different ways. From the 1960s the basis of the City's international role switched; instead of its centrality to the Sterling Area and Empire, the City's leading role in Eurodollar operations, multilateral borrowing and lending, became the basis of its world role. The reason London rather than, say, New York became the centre of this new international credit system was that whereas United States banks were hedged round with restrictions and regulations, London banks were, as a matter of policy, less regulated than those in any other advanced capitalist country. In borrowing and re-lending foreign currencies, which was the essence of the new international system, the City had succeeded in ensuring that neither Tory nor Labour governments imposed restrictions.

Thus, the British financial system has consistently had a uniquely favourable framework for its international business and for carrying through the aim which financial capital everywhere seeks to achieve, deriving its profits from world-wide operations rather than tying them to a local basis in national industry. The City is predominantly international in the sense that, because it has taken full advantage of these opportunities, its whole business, including its financing of British industry, is marked by its international business. It is not that the City's overseas lending has starved industry of funds, but that its orientation toward the flexibility and independence from industry that its world role gave it meant that the industrial financing it did do had to be on a similar arm's-length basis giving finance the maximum independence. Financial capital in France, Germany, Japan and other countries was not able to achieve such great independence.   By comparison its outlets were restricted to industry in those nations, and bankers and financiers had to minimise their risks by involving themselves in the direction and rationalisation of industry rather than distancing themselves from it.

The importance of international business to London's bankers is indicated by their share in it. London accounted for 27 per cent of all international bank loans outstanding in September 1982, whereas its nearest rival, the US, accounted for only 14.5 per cent (and only 9.3 per cent in 1980). Looking more directly at the significance of foreign business to UK banks, their international loans accounted for 75 per cent of their total lending in 1982.

It is significant that this represents the international business of banks operating in London rather than British owned banks. At the start of the 1980s there were some 400 branches and subsidiaries of foreign banks in London, accounting for a substantial proportion of the City's foreign business and they had made significant inroads into the domestic business of London's banks, especially the United States banks.   The strength of foreign-owned banks in London is a measure of the extent to which the City, or financial capital in Britain, is internationalised.

Through its orientation toward markets, toward state credit, and toward international operations, financial capital in Britain has achieved an independence from industrial capital that financiers everywhere seek but rarely achieve as successfully as London's have over the years. As a result, the British financial system has not become involved with industry and has not acted as an external rationalising and disciplining force in the way it has elsewhere. But at the same time it has had a blocking role, preventing the state from playing such a role in its place.

CHAPTER 22

Markets and growth[*]

John Zysman

[My] central proposition is that in advanced industrial countries the structure of the domestic financial systems helped shape the politics of industrial change in the post-war years. Financial systems influence both the leadership that state bureaucracies can exercise in the industrial economy and the nature of the conflicts about which goals governments should pursue ...

The argument

There are three distinct types of financial systems, each of which has different consequences for the political ties between banks, industry, and finance, as well as different implications for the process by which industrial change occurs. The three types are: (1) a system based on capital markets with resources allocated by prices established in competitive markets, (2) a credit-based system with critical prices administered by government, and (3) a credit-based system dominated by financial institutions. To distinguish between these three systems we focus on the process by which savings are transformed into investments and then allocated among competing users. Our emphasis is on the structural arrangements – the relations between the several markets and institutions through which funds flow – which shape this process in each country ...

[In the British case] the organisation of both the financial system and the state's economic administration – constructed in years when Britain was an industrial pioneer with a pre-eminent position in international markets – limited government's ability to intervene systematically and purposefully in industry affairs to promote industrial redevelopment. The government's struggle to build and reform institutions that would serve interventionist purposes opened up conflicts about the distribution of gains from growth and about the place of

---

[*] Reproduced with permission from *Governments, Markets and Growth*, Basil Blackwell, 1983.

businessmen, bureaucrats, union leaders, and financiers in the governance of the economy. In part as a consequence, the seemingly technical question of how to promote industry became a political struggle within the elite over who would govern the process. The broader battle about whether and how to conduct a promotional policy to reverse industrial decline shattered an underlying consensus about the need to give new priority to industrial growth. The will to modernise the economy was therefore dissipated in a struggle about who would gain and who would lose from development. The financial system enters the story as a source of constraints on state action and as a source of political conflict when the government attempted to lift those constraints ...

The financial system

The British financial system grew up financing commerce and eventually became the self-governing centre of the international monetary system. No system of long-term finance to promote industrial growth was established, because as Alexander Gerschenkron has contended, none was needed in this first and unique case of industrialisation. The result was a certain distance, a lack of direct involvement, between industry and finance on the one hand, and a lack of detailed government involvement in the affairs of finance and in the allocation of industrial credit on the other. Thus, when an interventionist policy thrust re-emerged at the end of the 1950s, the financial system offered a few natural handholds to those trying to implement an industrial policy.

The question here is what structural features produced this outcome – the distance and lack of involvement between finance, industry, and government. We must distinguish structural features – characteristic rules, procedures, and roles of the different institutions that are forced by the organisation of the financial markets – from procedures that stem from the attitudes of bankers about 'appropriate' behaviour. Of course, individual attitudes about how to behave are entangled in the structure of choices, but the emphasis here is on the pattern of choices created by institutional and market arrangements. Let us first consider the relations between finance and industry.

The British financial system evokes the image of a complex and competitive market. Large numbers of investors and savers meet in the marketplace, where no small group of institutions can dominate. London's position as a leading financial centre has been based on the multiplicity and specialisation of the financial intermediaries operating there. Several of the markets, particularly the retail banking market, are in effect oligopolies. Yet in Britain, power in one financial market, such as bank lending, does not translate into power in other markets, such as the security or money markets. The result is that businesses seeking funds do not face a single set of capital suppliers who can exert power in their affairs. This situation contrasts sharply with the French system, in which lending relationships and bank stockholdings tend to establish enduring institutional ties between finance and industry. The British financial system can be characterised by its arm's-length relations, in which investors are buying financial assets for their portfolios.

Several characteristics reveal the nature of the British system. First, the securities markets and investing institutions are at the heart of the system and are vastly more important than they are in France. One measure of the relative importance of the securities markets is the ratio of domestic securities to the Gross Domestic Product (GDP). Table 22.1 illustrates the contrast in 1975. The securities markets, once the domain of individual investors, are increasingly dominated by pension funds, insurance companies, and unit trusts. Between 1963 and 1980 the portion of securities held by individuals dropped from 54 to 37 per cent, and by the year 2000 institutions are expected to expand their holdings to between 70 and 85 per cent of the value of United Kingdom equities. A few institutions holding major corporate stocks suddenly find themselves with the influence to affect both company policies and the resolution of industrial crises. British non-bank financial institutions nevertheless differ in major respects from the French *banques d'affaires* and the German general all-purpose banks, which also have large equity holdings. The newly powerful British institutions are accustomed to making arm's-length judgements about future stock prices; they do not have the expertise or inclination to become industrial counsellors or advisers. So long as power in the form of equity is diffused among a restricted set of large financial institutions, no one institution will be dominant in any single company. Collectively they have power, and in most instances they must act collectively in order to exercise that power. The power of large institutions and banks in the British market thus remains more fragmented than it is on the Continent, although the changes now taking place may one day permit closer ties between finance and industry. The importance of these institutions can be seen in Table 22.2.

Table 22.1 Securities markets in France and the United Kingdom, end 1975

Country	Bonds as percent of GDP	Equities as percent of GDP
United Kingdom	43	41
France	16	11

Source: Figures taken from Appendixes 1A to 9A of Dimitri Vittas, ed., *Banking Systems Abroad* (London, Inter-Bank Research Organisation, 1978).

Table 22.2 Share of investing institutions in liabilities and claims with the non-financial sector, end 1975 (per cent)

Country	Liabilities	Claims
Germany	20.0	13.0
France	11.3	9.3
Italy	6.9	2.6
Japan	16.0	15.0
United States	32.3	31.2
United Kingdom	39.5	24.4

Note: Liabilities represent deposits; claims indicate loans.

Source: Dimitri Vittas, ed., *Banking Systems Abroad* (London, Inter-Bank Research Organisation, 1978), p. 25.

Despite concentration in the securities markets, the dominant investors in the securities markets do not control access to those markets, nor do they make loans. Conversely, the commercial banks do not invest the securities markets. Corporate access to these markets is arranged by brokers, such as the merchant banks. Buyers of securities, arrangers of access to securities, and lenders represent three distinct groups. To oversimplify, savings institutions (such as insurance company pension funds) and investment companies, as well as individuals, buy securities. Merchant banks arrange the offerings and commercial banks lend the money for short-term needs. Financial institutions specialise in specific market activities.

Close relations between banks and firms are based on either long-term loans or share holdings. Neither of these mechanisms ties British commercial banks to their clients. They are not substantial investors in corporate equity. When lending to companies, they have traditionally taken narrower and more short-term views of their clients than have their counterparts in other advanced countries. The short-term view permits these banks to function without a detailed understanding of company situations or an ongoing concern with industrial management. The British banking system was never organised to finance industrial development and the old preference for short-term, arm's-length lending continues. In the 1950s the president of the Institute of Bankers, who was also the vice-chairman of one of the major banks, contended that long-term lending was not the proper business of banks; their proper function was short-term lending. Despite an expansion of medium-term lending by British banks, only 15 to 20 per cent of their loans to industry are term loans – that is, extended for more than one year. In Germany and France, the figures are closer to 60 per cent. Happily the differences are dramatic, because problems of definition and measurement mean that precise numbers are of dubious usefulness. One difficulty in making such comparisons is that many British short-term loans really amount to a renewable facility that creates long-term loans at short-term rates. These overdraft facilities may well provide medium-term money, but they maintain the more limited type of bank–company relations called for by short-term loans. The banks have provided term loans during periods of industrial crisis in the 1970s, but this policy was not part of their longer-term strategy and certainly was not a central characteristic of British industrial finance in the years we are considering. In all such studies, however, the numbers follow a consistent direction that suggests a bias toward short-term financing and away from longer-term industrial finance.

A short-term bias in company loans is sometimes justified by the banks' need to be prudent in assuring a proper balance between short-term and long-term funds. The British banks, however, have not made any attempt to raise long-term money in the bond market, as a strategy of medium-term industrial finance would require. Larger British companies themselves have direct access to the bond market for long-term debt finance. Smaller firms are generally agreed to lack reliable sources of medium-term capital and plausibly could benefit from innovative financing arrangements. Comparative studies show that German banks borrow money in the bond market which they then lend to companies, and that French banks lend on to industry on the basis of short-term deposits. The reason is not that German and French bankers are smarter and better risk-takers than British bankers, but that the structure of the financial systems constrains banks differently in each of the three countries.

The financial structure of British companies is also a measure of the nature of bank lending. British firms have not been heavily dependent on long-term debt that would allow outside financial influence in their affairs. They have turned to bank credit during crises, both in the aftermath of the first oil price hikes and more recently during a deepening recession, but these cases and others like them are viewed as exceptions. Financial gearing is a measure of the ratio of equity to debt in non-financial companies. The ratio suggests dependence on outside debt finance but does not distinguish dependence on bank loans, which is an institutional relation, from bond indebtedness, which is not. Again, precise numbers prove little because so much in the ratios turns on accounting practice, which varies between countries. Such ratios have historically been lower in Britain than on the European continent or in Japan, however. The national ratio of internal funding and equity to fixed investment suggests the same thing. British companies finance expansion from savings and the sale of equity, not from credit. In fact, German, Japanese, and French firms invest more than they save from profits and get the rest of their funds from borrowing.

With an elaborate stock and bond market available for long-term financing in England, a prima facie case can be made that British bank lending ought to limit itself to short-term needs. The proper comparison for testing the notion that British banks have a peculiarly short-term bias is the banking system in the United States, whose structure is closer to that of the British system. In the United

States the multiple functions to finance have been divided into separate institutions, which are co-ordinated by markets rather than combined into single institutions and co-ordinated by administrators. The New York commercial banks – the centre of American banking activity – make 23 per cent of their loans to business in the form of term advances; if the figures are meaningful, they suggest a marginally higher level of long-term lending in the United States than in Britain. The American and British cases together suggest that in an economy with a strong securities market the level of term lending by banks to non-financial firms will be lower than it is in countries that have weak securities markets. This suggests that the British relation between finance and industry is the product of a type of financial system, and that British banking attitudes, though more conservative and less innovative than American views, derive from that structure.

What matters here is that the traditional British banking view and the structure on which it rests affect the way the bank deals with its clients, putting distance between finance and industry. The British Treasury argued this position in hearings before the Committee to Review the Functioning of Financial Institutions headed by Harold Wilson in 1977:

> The government has the impression that in the UK, there has been a tendency for financial institutions to maintain an arm's-length relationship with clients to a greater extent than in other countries. It can be argued that they would be better placed to meet industry's needs for capital effectively if their relations were closer and their understanding greater ... More generally, neither the institutions nor banks have sought on any scale to stimulate management performance by intervening in the companies' affairs, given the need for expertise and management time which would be involved. (Wilson Committee Hearings, 1978: 58–9)

When making medium- or long-term loans, banks must assess a company's overall competitive position in its industry, looking beyond its short-term ability to repay a loan. Long-term loans are not self-liquidating, that is, they do not depend on the farmer's repaying the costs of planting when his crop goes to market or on an importer's repaying his borrowing as he sells off the stock he has purchased. The Association of American Banks in London also testified before the Wilson Committee. It made a distinction between a liquidation approach and the going-concern approach. And while acknowledging that all banks use some elements of both approaches to evaluate the creditworthiness of borrowers, the committee concluded that the 'former is the traditional basis of overdraft lending in UK clearing banks while the latter is the method preferred by the American banks, who lend mainly on a term basis'. The contrast made by the American banks is certainly self-serving, but it underlines the nature of British banking.

In sum, the distinction between long- and short-term lending is of great importance to the relations between finance and industry. Long-term loans must be repaid from future profits and therefore, as a minimum, the bank must make an assessment of the company's competitive future. Short-term loans can simply be secured against existing company assets. Long-term lending, to caricature the issue, is a matter for investment banks; short-term lending against secured assets is a matter for the pawnbroker. Different financial structures reflecting distinct origins may resolve similar problems in unique ways. The emphasis on short-term lending is not necessarily an economic flaw in the British financial system, but it does have political consequences. If companies are not dependent on outside funding, the financial system has no levers with which to influence them. The British financial system has evolved rapidly in the last two decades, but the changes have not altered the compartmentalisation of financial and industrial worlds. The banking system has been an oligopoly and concentration in the purely British banking community increased. Mergers decreased the number of major British banks from eleven to four. At the same time, the American banks operating in England have grown to rival their British hosts in size and importance. Their rapid expansion was initially made in order to follow American companies abroad and to escape American regulation. Though the American banks have not sought to establish a chain of branches competing for deposits but have competed only for a portion of business, their banking practices have inevitably begun to seep into British banks. A change in banking and money supply regulations in 1971 also encouraged bank competition, further modernising the traditional British practices.

Another way of capturing the essence of the British system, and of identifying the kinds of reforms which would be necessary if the government were to use financial institutions or the financial system to help conduct industrial interventions, is to look at the banks themselves. The British merchant banks, to choose one example, have their homologues in the continental *banques d'affaires* and the American investment banks. All three types are turned toward the long-term problems of companies, but their differences represent three different national relationships between industry and finance. The British merchant banks are at their core banks to finance commerce; they emerged in the last century as a place where for a fee a bill of exchange could be guaranteed and thus used to provide operating funds to a company. The American investment banks have traditionally provided advice and assistance to companies looking for money rather than supplying the required funds themselves. The French *banques d'affaires*, by contrast, are industrial banks concerned with the business of industrial companies; they take even more direct interests in firms by underwriting in their own names (or that of others for whom they act) a part of the capital issues of industrial companies.

Let us imagine three concentric circles. In the first circle are the American investment banks, which perform the two functions shared by all long-term banks: giving advice and assistance in placing surplus corporate funds and in obtaining additional funds when necessary; and structuring the overall financial position of a company and advising it in its negotiations with other companies, for example during mergers or take-over.   American investment banks are forbidden by law to engage in commercial bank credit operations, whereas important tasks such as raising capital for the private sector by equity issues are reserved to them.   In the second circle are the British merchant banks, which are investment banks that also have a certain limited capacity to lend money and take deposits.   Their depositors are for the most part large companies and a few wealthy individuals, in contrast to the mixture of large and small clients that deal with the commercial banks.   This limited clientele means, however, that the merchant banks have a smaller amount of money to lend from their own deposits than do the commercial banks.   Consequently they must finance credit operations with funds drawn from more expensive wholesale markets (such as domestic money markets and internal markets like the Eurocurrency market) – markets that are also available to their larger competitors.   This situation places the merchant banks at a competitive disadvantage.   In the third circle we find the *banques d'affaires*, a merchant bank that also manages an industrial portfolio.   This merging of the activities of a bank and a holding company gives it a captive clientele for its services and a captive source of deposits.   But the activities of holding company and merchant bank are more closely tied together than that.   A *banque d'affaires* is a bank that, in light of the restructuring of the national economy or the international economy, uses together its varied instruments that range from its own credits and the issues of stocks or bonds to actually take a share in the capital in the companies.   Investing its own funds is seen as an act of confidence that can attract more outside money.   During periods of crisis this can permit the bank to reorganise companies without a liquidation of assets.   This is not to say that the banks directly manage companies, but rather that they supervise company interests and help guide them.   These banks become directly involved in industrial reorganisation.   The former president of one such bank remarked that: '*To change the structure* [of companies and industry], *it is necessary oftentimes to enter into the structures*'.

The contrast between the *banques d'affaires* and the merchant banks is evident: 'It is a characteristic of most merchant banks, especially British ones, that they flourish without much intervention in management and with no real machinery for investigating the performance of firms' (Foster, 1971: 164). Obviously, the differences in the three types of financial systems are embedded in the process of industrialisation.   The *banque d'affaires* is the clear counterpart of the 'player' or developmental state, whereas the merchant bank and the investment bank reflect a situation in which government has an arm's-length relation to the economy.   Since the securities market and retained earnings are thought to provide long-term money and the banks are considered the proper source of short-term funding, industry and finance are left to occupy independent spheres.

Having sketched the nature of relations between finance and industry in Britain, let us examine the relation between the British government and the financial system. To begin with, the British government does not control channels of borrowing and lending which would facilitate the selective manipulation of credit allocation by the political executive. Handles available in other countries, particularly the parapublic banking institutions that are important in France, simply do not exist in England. The public sector collects a very small percentage of the national savings; the recently established postal savings system, for example, represents less than one-tenth of 1 per cent of national savings. More important, such public institutions are rivals to the highly developed private banking system. Indeed, such institutions as Finance Corporation for Industry, Industrial and Commercial Finance Company, and Equity Capital for Industry were established as the Bank of England's response to outside pressure and were intended to preclude more extensive government intervention. The FCI and ICFC were formed in 1945 and the ECI was established in 1975. These financial institutions (FCI, ICFC, and ECI) are in fact collectively owned by the private financial institutions and the Bank of England. The National Loans Board, which administers lending to nationalised companies, is an administrative rather than decision-making body. The limited significance of these long-term credit institutions is indicated by their share in the claims and liabilities of financial institutions with the non-finance sector.

When the British government does intervene in the financial markets, it generally acts through reserve requirements or open market operations, both of which preserve the market character of the system. That is, it affects the volume of bank lending either by imposing requirements on reserves the banks must hold or by buying or selling government issues in the market. These sales increase or decrease the liquidity in the system. The central bank announces the direction it expects interest rates to move and in anticipation other financial institutions act on those announcements. It is the Bank of England's ability to affect market conditions in ways that will move prices (interest rates) in the directions it chooses which gives those announcements such force. When the bank does act, it does so through the discount market, which consists of a set of institutions specialised in buying, selling, and holding Treasury and commercial bills. These banks mobilise short-term funds that would otherwise stand unused and make them available to the government and to other banks. The discount market helps keep the banking system and the government as a whole in balance; it also acts as a buffer between the Bank of England and the commercial banks. Commercial banks buy and sell in the money market, dealing with the discount houses which in turn deal directly with the central bank.

Since 1971 the British have moved even further toward pure market mechanisms, attempting to discard the limited quantitative restrictions on bank lending imposed in the 1960s. The 1971 Competition and Credit Control Act was a forceful move toward arm's-length management of the system. Importantly, quantitative controls were never viewed as a central component of the system tied to government-imposed prices, but were considered an unfortunate deviation from market principles.

Many of the arrangements in the British system of monetary management result from an emphasis on managing the government debt, which was the fundamental task of the central bank from the end of the war until late in the 1970s. The *Radcliffe Report* of 1959 (the major government review of the financial system) considered debt management to be the bank's fundamental task. This view implied that controlling the structure of interest rates was the central object of policy, since interest rates dictated the cost of debt. The *Radcliffe Report* was very explicit: 'The authorities ... have to regard the structure of interest rates *rather than the supply of money* as the centrepiece of the monetary mechanism. This does not mean that the supply of money is unimportant, but that its control is incidental to interest rate policy' (italics mine) (Radcliffe, 1959). This emphasis meant, as Catherine Hill argues, that aggregate demand management was dominated by fiscal policy, because monetary policy was linked to financing public debt (Hill, 1982). *Government could not effectively manipulate interest rates for industrial development because it was already manipulating them for purposes of financing the debt.* Jacques Melitz (1980) raises this practice to a principle, contending that in those countries with massive government debt, such as the United States and Britain, the problem of financing this debt becomes the focus of government financial intervention. Recent Thatcherite reforms and an emphasis on government policy simply reaffirm the arm's-length principles. The money-supply aggregate becomes the dependent variable and interest rates are simply a result of market demand for money. Government debt management remains the crucial constraint.

Despite the market organisation of government intervention, a series of qualitative interventions has taken place in the form of Bank of England directives about the proper composition of lending. Two aspects of these qualitative controls are important to us. First, 'the directives do not specify a curtailment of the business of any particular bank or any particular customer, but only the whole of a class of business. A directive to [a bank] to restrict lending to Imperial Chemical Industries would be considered most improper' (Anthony, 1979: 12). There is a 'great reluctance to interfere in the business relationship between individual customers' (*ibid.*: 5). In other words, these interventions do not approach those of the French or Japanese in terms of administrative control or specificity. Second, while some of the directives to maintain lending to industry were linked to exemptions from ceilings on lending, most were aimed at restricting consumer spending. These qualitative restrictions are enforced more by moral suasion than by direct administration. In fact, they amount to nothing more than an *ad hoc* resolution of temporary conflicts between interest-rate policy and particular economic needs. They are not envisioned as a means of conducting industry policy or organising the financial markets.

The government executive's place in the financial system can be understood by looking at the Bank of England itself. The bank's existing responsibilities in that traditional system create both a technical and a political barrier against its being transformed into an instrument of government industrial intervention.

First, the bank has been responsible for managing Britain's international monetary position. At one time, of course, that role made it the central regulator of the international monetary system and a defender of the role of sterling as a reserve currency in international trade. The bank advocated maintaining a high value for sterling in terms of gold and supported the domestic economic policies that this position implied. Much has been written about how this stance led to over-valued British goods in international markets and provoked a series of domestic restrictions that took the heart out of any boom. The collapse of sterling's value and the emergence of the Eurocurrency markets have relieved that particular tension between domestic and international goals. By dealing in everyone else's currency, London has been able to remain a pre-eminent financial entrepôt, although the rise of the Eurocurrency system has made the British economy more vulnerable to outside events. The earnings from the City of London's financial dealings are a significant contribution to the balance of payments, and maintaining the financial community as a service export sector is a legitimate and important concern of the government. Although a combination of interventionist regulation in the domestic market and a less restrictive and less formal management of international financial operations might be technically possible, such a schizophrenic position would certainly be hard to sustain. The old tension between foreign and domestic financial concerns, expressed once in the fight over exchange rates, re-creates itself as a tension over regulation in London markets. Moreover, there is a clear institutional bent toward the international and away from the domestic. Until recently the Bank of England had no industry policy group charged to consider the problems and needs of industry and to administer policies explicitly aimed at satisfying those needs. Such institutional biases can be changed, but not easily or immediately.

Second, the Bank of England sees some conflict between its fundamental responsibilities in managing the money supply and any role it might play in rediscounting bank lending to industry, either to encourage long-term loans or to influence the direction of financial flows ... The problem could be managed, but at the price of controls more formal than either the bank or the system has been accustomed to. Management of the monetary aggregates – interest rates or money supply – dominates the bank's thinking.

Finally, and perhaps most important, the Bank of England has been a spokesman and a lobbyist for banking interests with the central government bureaucracy at the same time that it has been the government's central regulator. This role has deep roots in British history. In fact, whereas the elaborate financial markets originally emerged more to finance government than to finance industry or commerce, the Bank of England was one of the sites for the fight between the political capitalism of the Stuarts and the market capitalism of the Puritans. The bank has worked to insulate financial institutions from central government control, which in practice has meant augmenting its own influence in promoting projects of its own as alternatives to government propositions. Although since its nationalisation the bank is formally subordinate to the Treasury, there is a kind of arm's-length arrangement between them. Indeed, the bank has distinguished between its own business and matters in which it serves as agent of the Treasury. Its own affairs include fixing the bank rate and managing the money market and the exchange markets – responsibilities that, Samuel Brittan argues, are the best predictor of the bank's actual behaviour.

The important result is that Whitehall officials – the central bureaucracy – are not intimately acquainted with the financial sector leaders or with the operations of those financial markets. Indeed, the Bank of England's insulation of the financial sector from the government is directly tied to Whitehall's ignorance and separation. An expansion of government-directed lending, particularly if the direction were set in Whitehall and implemented by the banks, would involve the Bank of England in a politically determined industrial strategy – a profound reversal of its historical role. Particularly since it has not developed expertise in the area of industrial policy, its own autonomy would be undermined. The bank does not lend itself easily to service as an instrument of government policy for industry.

CHAPTER 23

Britain in the world economy: national decline, capitalist success?*

Hugo Radice

> The important point is that British capital saw the whole world, not merely Britain or even the Empire, as its field of operation. It still does. (Barratt Brown, 1988: 36)

I   Introduction

The 'British decline' has been going on for a very long time now – for some writers, since the mid-nineteenth century. Always a relative decline in most respects, after 1945 it took the form of a markedly slower rate of economic growth than that of most other advanced capitalist countries. In the global context of the post-war boom, the decline was attributed variously to bad economic management, to institutional features of the labour and capital markets or of the state, to attributes of British education and culture, to the class system, and to the unavoidable legacy of imperial rule. Whatever the reason, the analysis of decline centred on the problem of lack of international competitiveness, rooted in low and slowly-growing industrial investment and productivity. This led, in the familiar Keynesian argument, to a recurring constraint on growth set by the balance of payments.

---

*   This chapter is revised and updated from a paper originally presented at a conference on Instability and Change in the International Economy in Stephentown, NY, in May 1988. I am grateful to Monthly Review Press for permission to reprint material from the published version (Radice, 1989). I am grateful to Michael Barratt Brown, Ben Fine and Colin Leys for their helpful comments. For reasons of space, statistics in the text have not been referenced. Current figures are taken from current editions of the UK Central Statistical Office publications *Economic Trends, Monthly Digest of Statistics* and *UK Balance of Payments Pink Book*. Historical data are drawn mostly from Barratt Brown (1970), Blackaby (1979) and Rowthorn and Wells (1987).

By the late 1970s, the problem of relative decline had been redefined as one of de-industrialisation (Singh, 1977; Blackaby, 1979), and two very different solutions were being propounded. The first Thatcher government saw the answer in freeing British capitalism from the stifling embrace of an overweening state and the obdurate obstructionism of the trade unions. They pushed through trade union and labour market reforms that had been proposed but never enforced by the Wilson and Heath governments in the decade from 1965 to 1975; they followed more rigorously the monetarist policies initiated under Chancellor Healey in 1976; and they embarked on a radical programme of privatisation and deregulation. The result was, they claimed, the 'productivity miracle' of the mid to late 1980s. For Thatcherism, the problem of de-industrialisation was side-stepped, since free market dogma does not permit the privileging of any particular sector such as manufacturing: given the right fiscal, legal and social climate, the market mechanism would ensure that resources were optimally employed according to consumer choice, factor endowments and the law of comparative advantage.

On the left (and in parts of the centre and right too), the diagnosis of de-industrialisation has remained central to this day. The main thrust of policy in the Labour Party has shifted, from the old faith in state interventionism through public ownership and an active industrial policy, to the new faith in 'supply-side' intervention in education, training and R & D, and in industrial and financial 're-regulation'. One strand in the left critique has, however, retained its hold: namely, that important factors in de-industrialisation have been the persistently high levels of outward foreign investment by UK capitalists, and the economic and political dominance of the City. Finance that is not invested abroad is available only on a short-term basis and at a high cost in accordance with the City's interests, thus deterring investment in innovation and long-term restructuring.

This argument can be traced back for a century at least. The rentier character of pre-1914 British capitalism is clear: in 1913, net property income from abroad covered 25% of the country's total import requirements. For J. A. Hobson, this dependence lay at the root of the politics of colonial imperialism. Later, J. M. Keynes repeatedly stressed the dangers that uncontrolled international capital flows posed for domestic economic stability and policy effectiveness (Radice, 1988). After 1945, however, few commentators placed much emphasis on international capital flows in explaining relative decline, except as a minor aspect of the balance of payments constraint. This was for the very good reason that for 25 years or so from the departure of sterling from the gold standard in 1931, British capitalism was characterised by a degree of introversion unparalleled in its history, and the City's powers were greatly reduced by very low interest rates, the partial loss of convertibility and tight monetary controls. In the 1950s, the UK was virtually self-sufficient in manufactures, and the stock of outward foreign investment had fallen to a historic low. The apparent triumph of Keynesianism and the achievements of the post-war Labour and Conservative governments showed that national reconstruction was possible, and that active economic management could guide the national economy to full employment and price stability. Investment abroad was no longer an issue, and the City appeared to have been tamed.

In this light, the continual if precarious recovery of the UK's overseas investment position in the 1960s and 1970s, and London's role in global finance, was readily seen by the left as a potential threat. If the UK financed long-term investments abroad by drawing in short-term capital inflows, then we could easily be 'held to ransom' by the 'gnomes of Zurich'. Furthermore, in the payments crisis of 1966–67, all the old arguments were marshalled by the City against devaluation. And despite the conclusion of the Reddaway Report (Reddaway, 1968) that foreign direct investments benefited the UK balance of payments, it was easy to argue, as our relative industrial decline became steeper, that more investment abroad meant less at home.

After 1979, these fears seemed fully realised as the government pressed on from the lifting of exchange controls to the privatisation bonanza and financial deregulation. The financial sector expanded very rapidly, and foreign investment soared. Merchant banks helped UK firms to acquire capacity abroad through takeover, especially in the USA, while the pension funds poured into foreign securities in the pursuit of portfolio diversification and currency hedging. In the late 1980s, UK capital joined wholeheartedly in the global expansion of international capital flows, from direct investments in booming East Asia to the remote and volatile markets in financial derivatives.

Surely, then, any alternative to Thatcherism should be firmly based on a programme of national 're-industrialisation', including the full subordination of the City to the need for productive investment, and a reintroduction of controls on capital exports? I shall argue in this paper that any alternative must be based on a full understanding of how thoroughly global UK capitalism has become, and what that implies. British capital *as a whole* has played and continues to play a leading role in the restructuring of *world* capitalism. In this context, de-industrialisation has not in itself been a sign of weakness of British capital. At the same time, the City and British industry, while still being antagonistic 'fractions' of British capital, have nevertheless become thoroughly integrated in a form of finance capital and share a common global horizon. There is no longer a viable 'national capitalism', based on an alliance between national capital, labour and the state, waiting to be freed from the dominance of financiers and foreign investors. As a consequence, a *national* alternative of reform and re-industrialisation is not a feasible option, except under conditions of radical social change.

The argument is developed by examining first recent trends in the balance of payments, and especially foreign capital flows; then the relation between de-industrialisation and foreign direct investment; and lastly the relations between the City and industry.

II   UK trade and capital flows

Our reappraisal begins by asserting that UK capitalism is thoroughly global, and that its condition cannot be understood except in the context of changes in the world economy. In developing a critical analysis of decline, we start from the changes in the nature of capitalism as a world-wide system, and in the role of British capital within that system. As Spence (1985) puts it, there has been a strong tendency on the British left to view Britain as a 'victim' of these changes – imposed on, as it were, by outside forces and their treacherous allies (notably in the City). Instead, he argues,

> There is a danger of forgetting something which is central to any
> understanding of British history over the past 150 years, a home-truth which
> may be painful but must be faced. Britain is an imperialist power. The very
> structure of British capital is founded upon its imperialist status. Britain is, in
> fact, the second most important imperialist power in the world, after the USA.
> Any analysis of this country's economic crisis, and of the options facing the
> working-class movement, must start from this obvious, but apparently easily-
> forgotten fact. (Spence, 1985: 117)

Among the changes in the global system of capitalism to be taken into account are: the slowdown in the global rate of capital accumulation; the emergence of new centres of capitalist industrialisation; the global integration of financial markets; the spreading and deepening of multinational corporations as agencies for the global restructuring of productive capital; the growth of a global industrial reserve army; the decomposition of traditional industrial working classes throughout the advanced capitalist world; the transformation of the Keynesian international economic organisations into enforcers of pre-Keynesian domestic economic policies; and the growth of debt peonage in Latin America, Africa and Eastern Europe in particular. Because of the crucial role of British capital and the British state in the global system of imperialism, these trends all necessarily help to determine the course of capitalist development in Britain: they are not merely 'additional factors to be taken into account'.

What trends, then, are visible from the UK's recent balance of payments statistics? Until the devaluation of the pound in 1967, the UK's post-war external accounts followed a rather stable pattern. The visible trade account tended to be slightly in deficit; this was not usually offset by a sufficient surplus on invisible trade; and both long- and short-term capital flows were also slightly negative. The overall balance of payments was usually in deficit, and the trend deficit was growing. During this period, the UK's competitive trade performance in manufacturing appeared to be steadily deteriorating: the UK's share of world manufacturing exports declined from 25.5% in 1950 to 10.8% in 1970, and many studies showed a high UK income-elasticity of demand for imports, along with a low world income-elasticity of demand for UK exports. As for the invisibles account, here the consistent surplus on private services trade was reduced by a significant deficit on the government account, attributed mostly to the continuing cost of maintaining military forces abroad. Meanwhile, the net outflow of long-term capital remained at a historically-low level of 0.5 to 1% of GDP: portfolio investment abroad was restricted by exchange controls to reinvestment of profits earned abroad, while direct investment by UK companies was offset by foreign (mainly US) direct investment in the UK.

Although the devaluation of 1967 led to a considerable improvement in the UK's current account, this was swamped in the 1970s as a whole by other dramatic changes. After 1972 the floating pound sank downward, and the rise in oil prices contributed to a visible trade deficit that averaged nearly £3b from 1972 to 1978, i.e. 2–3% of GDP. The long-term capital account deficit grew only slightly, with rising outward investment offset by the inflow of capital for North Sea oil development. However, in 1976 the Labour government was forced by the mounting payments deficit to call in the IMF, and impose the austerity programme which was a major factor in their electoral defeat of 1979.

By then, however, North Sea oil was coming on stream, and this, coupled with the economic policies of the Thatcher government, transformed the UK's external accounts in the 1980s. Under the impact of oil revenues and deflation, the pound appreciated by about 25% between 1979 and 1981, but it subsequently fell steadily to reach only half its 1980 value by 1993. From 1980 to 1985 the current account averaged a surplus of £3.6b at current prices, or 1.4% of GDP. After 1985 the current balance deteriorated dramatically, reaching –£22.5b or –4.2% of GDP in 1989; with renewed recession the deficit narrowed to –1.4% of GDP in 1992.

On the capital account, the complete abolition of remaining exchange controls in October 1979 ensured that the subsequent current account surplus fed a rapidly rising capital outflow. The balance on the long-term capital account averaged –£2.3b in 1979–80, –£7.9b in 1981–83 and –£13.9b in 1984–86; but in 1987, the balance changed dramatically to +£18b, and thereafter the picture has been one of large fluctuations, especially in portfolio flows (Table 23.1). However, the most striking and certainly least-recognised feature is the rapid growth in inward direct investment, which rose to over £18.5b in both 1989 and 1990 and exceeded outward direct investment in 1990–92 by some £9b in total. At the same time, the dramatic expansion, or rather renewal, of the City as a world financial centre saw a huge rise in short-term capital flows in both directions, with a surplus helping to finance the long-term capital deficit as the current account deficit soared after 1987. No doubt the consistent policy of maintaining high interest rates, even as the UK's inflation fell back in comparison to other countries, encouraged the inflow of short-term funds. In consequence, however, net overseas assets fell as a proportion of GDP from a peak of 23.4% in 1986 – when we were second only to Japan as a net creditor country – to only 2% in 1992.

Table 23.1 Long-term capital transactions, 1979–92, £b (annual averages and six years 1987–92)

	Direct investment			Portfolio investment			Total
	Outward	Inward	Balance	Outward	Inward	Balance	Balance
1979–80	−5.4	3.7	−1.7	−2.1	1.5	−0.6	−2.3
1981–83	−5.2	3.1	−2.1	−6.5	0.6	−5.8	−7.9
1984–86	−8.7	3.4	−5.3	−16.3	7.7	−8.6	−13.9
1987–92	−15.1	13.0	−2.1	−20.2	17.1	−3.2	−5.2
1987	−19.1	9.4	−9.7	5.4	22.2	27.7	18.0
1988	−20.9	12.0	−8.9	−11.2	16.5	5.3	−3.5
1989	−21.5	18.6	−2.9	−36.3	16.1	−20.2	−23.2
1990	−10.5	18.5	8.0	−16.5	7.7	−8.7	−0.8
1991	−8.8	9.0	0.2	−29.2	19.2	−10.0	−9.8
1992	−9.4	10.3	0.9	−33.4	20.5	−12.9	−12.0

Source: CSO, *Economic Trends Annual Supplement,* 1994, Table 1.18.

So far I have been dealing with aggregate capital flows. Turning to their geographical distribution, Table 23.2 shows the geographical distribution of the stock of outward direct investment, measured by the year-end value of net assets held overseas. The proportion located in North America rose from 25% in 1978 to 35% in 1981, and peaked at 47% in 1989. The share of Western Europe over the same period first fell back, before recovering to 30% in 1991 in the run-up to the European Union's Single Market Agreement.[1] Meanwhile, the pattern of inward investment in Table 23.3 shows the North American share of net assets still at 62% in 1981, but then declining to 50% in 1987 and 43% in 1991, little more than the total for Western Europe. Substantial Australian and Japanese investments account for the rising share of other developed countries. Unfortunately, data are not available on the geographical distribution of portfolio investments; it is however highly likely that the bulk of these are to and from North America, given that EC stock markets are relatively undeveloped.

Concluding this review, the UK in the 1990s is an extremely open economy, with high levels of both trade and capital flows. Despite massive current account deficits in recent years, large outflows of long-term capital have been sustained by inflows of capital, both long- and short-term.

Table 23.2 Shares of outward FDI: % of total net assets (book value)

	Western Europe	North America	Other developed	Rest of world
1978	31.4	25.1	23.0	20.4
1981	23.2	34.7	20.4	21.8
1984	24.0	42.1	15.6	18.3
1987	28.2	42.6	12.0	17.1
1991	30.1	42.7	10.3	16.9

Table 23.3 Shares of inward FDI: % of total net assets (book value)

	Western Europe	North America	Other developed	Rest of world
1978	29.7	64.0	4.5	1.8
1981	26.5	61.8	7.1	4.7
1984	37.1	53.6	4.2	4.9
1987	36.0	49.6	9.4	5.0
1991	40.6	43.1	12.8	3.4

Source: CSO, *MO4 Census of Overseas Assets,* 1987; *Overseas Direct Investment,* 1991; CSO *Bulletin,* 28/93.

III   De-industrialisation and foreign direct investment

The extent of UK de-industrialisation is usually assessed by the comparative performance of the UK in global manufacturing: the relative growth of manufacturing productivity, the balance of manufacturing trade, the UK's share of world manufacturing production and exports, and its degree of import penetration. On criteria such as these, there is wide agreement on the disastrous comparative performance of UK manufacturing industry over the long term. However, before examining the arguments linking poor performance to foreign direct investment, it is worth noting the two alternative theses on de-industrialisation which do not necessarily imply poor performance, the 'maturity thesis' and the 'specialisation thesis' (Rowthorn and Wells, 1987).

The maturity thesis argues that a reduction in the share of manufacturing in employment may be an indication of successful economic performance, if it is the result of relatively fast industrial productivity growth which reduces labour demand in the manufacturing sector (*ibid.*: 213).[2] The agent of relative de-industrialisation could thus be the success, not the failure, of manufacturing. However, in the UK case it is clearly hard to argue that manufacturing productivity growth was fast, at least before the mid-1980s. The specialisation thesis, on the other hand, is more substantive. Rowthorn and Wells argue that the UK's decline in manufacturing employment may have arisen because of more or less exogenous changes in the UK's foreign trade. Thus, in 1950–52, the UK surplus on trade in manufactures averaged 10.5% of GDP, while her deficit on trade in non-manufactures (food, beverages, tobacco, basic materials, fuel and non-government services) was 13.3% (*ibid.*: 218); by 1981–83, however, the balance of trade in non-manufactures had shifted dramatically to a *surplus* – equivalent to about 1% of GDP. This they attribute mainly to a massive growth in domestic food production, reductions in raw materials use, and North Sea oil – with non-government services (including financial services) playing only a modest role. The result is that the UK no longer needs a huge surplus in its manufacturing trade.

Rowthorn and Wells do not, however, conclude that Britain's manufacturing performance was after all satisfactory. If a surplus on manufacturing trade is no longer required, that says little about the *absolute* level of manufacturing output and employment. Thus in relation to the 1980s experience, the burgeoning North Sea revenues – worth some £10b by 1985 before the collapse in oil prices – could have been spent on £10b of manufactured imports for immediate consumption, with, *ceteris paribus*, no change in the absolute level of manufacturing output or employment; but alternatively, and particularly in the context of a programme of reflation and rising investment in industry, they could have been spent on £10b of capital and intermediate goods, with rising consumption met to a much greater extent from domestic sources, and an overall rise in manufacturing output and employment. In practice, the foreign currency benefits of North Sea oil were used largely for increased consumption and for the funding of capital outflows.

Regardless of the actual outcome, the 'specialisation thesis' stresses the important point that the level of manufacturing output must be judged in relation to the balance of payments, as in Singh's (1977: 128) well-known definition of de-industrialisation.

Accepting that manufacturing performance has been poor, in what ways could foreign direct investment be responsible? The first common argument focuses on *outward* FDI: that the high international mobility of British industrial capital has enabled it to participate fully in the changing international division of labour, by effectively shifting production abroad from the UK in order to escape from the crisis of UK manufacturing. The argument is a two-stage one. First, the general crisis of accumulation in the advanced capitalist countries since the late 1960s has 'globalised' capitalist manufacturing in a 'new international division of labour'. Following the analysis of Frobel *et al.* (1980), this leads to a relocation of relatively labour-intensive sectors or production activities, which are moved to low-wage production sites, while capital-, technology- and management-intensive sectors and activities are located in the advanced capitalist countries; the process as a whole being very much under the control of advanced-country MNCs through their control of technology and final markets. Secondly, the UK is seen as coming off particularly badly in this process for several reasons: a relatively poor quality, low skill labour force is unsuited to the location of high-level productive activities in the UK; it has a relatively large share of the type of traditional industry most vulnerable to relocation; and it has a disproportionate share of the world's MNC-controlled production.

A good example of this analysis is provided by Cowling (1986), and many sectoral and regional case studies have backed it up (e.g. Gaffikin and Nickson, 1984). The typical conclusion is that UK multinationals have taken the easy way out – and the most profitable, at least in the short run – by moving production abroad rather than investing in improving productivity at home. On the other hand, other writers such as Reddaway (1968) and especially Shepherd *et al.* (1985) argue that exports are not normally fully substitutable for production abroad because many markets require proximity to customers for technical reasons or to avoid tariff or non-tariff barriers. Direct investment may be far more effective as a means of extending, or even holding on to foreign markets. Indeed, successful production abroad *supports* exports from the UK by providing a market for UK-sourced inputs and a distribution network for the firm's other products.

However, although this may be partly to do with the inherent nature of many industrial products and markets (e.g. customers demanding 'just-in-time' supplies), it does not square with the apparent ability of Japanese and German firms to continue relying much more on exports. This suggests three underlying reasons for the relative growth of overseas production by UK firms. First, the faster growth of other economies (at least until the mid-1980s) means that those UK firms which are already firmly implanted in foreign markets, by whatever means, are bound on average to experience faster growth in their overseas sales. Secondly, the poor performance of UK-based industry cumulates into significant 'locational disadvantage' for the UK – including the perception (if not the reality) of high labour costs. And thirdly, the *already high* internationalisation of UK manufacturing makes it much easier for UK firms to choose overseas production over exporting.

The second main argument deployed on the left has concerned *inward* foreign direct investment. In the 1970s and early 1980s, the low level of inward FDI, as compared to outward, simply reinforced the previous argument concerning the 'vicious circle' of manufacturing decline and locational disadvantage: if UK firms did not want to invest in the UK, then nor would foreign firms. As inward investment recovered through the decade, however, a new thesis emerged focusing on the *quality* rather than the quantity of inward FDI. Especially by comparison with the main continental economies, the UK offered a low-skill, low-cost manufacturing labour force, and a relatively deregulated environment in which industrial relations problems had been cured. In a more complex version of the new international division of labour, the UK could therefore be an ideal site for low-value-added activities aimed at the European market as a whole, in particular 'screwdriver' assembly work. This fits in with the long-standing view of many analysts that UK manufacturing has been characterised, in comparison with leading capitalist countries, by low quality, low prices, and especially low research-intensity (see e.g. Saunders, 1978; Pratten, 1976; Pavitt, 1980 and Daly *et al.*, 1985).

An important body of recent research supports this view at the regional and sectoral levels. Turok (1993), for example, argues that local linkages might have been expected to 'embed' foreign electronics firms in Scotland and contribute to the emergence of a high-value-added indigenous industry. However, these linkages are limited to capacity or labour sub-contracting, or to bulky non-electronics parts, and correspond more closely to a simple 'dependent' model of supply rather than a 'developmental' model. Love (1989) reviews evidence on the consequences of external acquisition on suppliers to the acquired firms, and while he finds little evidence of the wholesale substitution or downgrading of local supplies, he does find a reduction in the supply especially of services, a narrowing of management functions, and some loss of R & D capacity. Young and Hood (1992) examine the role of foreign TNCs in the UK machine tool industry, and find that the most dynamic segment, offering customised 'factory of the future' systems, have the highest levels of imported components and are likely to locate their own production in the richest customer markets. Lastly, Phelps (1993) reviews a wide range of theory and evidence on the evolving spatial division of labour: while theories of flexible production and new industrial districts imply that branch plants might become more locally-embedded, 'where corporate technical divisions of labour are more complex, devolvement of decision-making and processes of externalisation and localised linkage formation may be that much weaker' (Phelps, 1993: 89). Such views certainly appear to support the view that the recent recovery of inward FDI does not mean an end to de-industrialisation: instead, de-industrialisation is redefined in qualitative terms, in particular with regard to the level of value-added and the dependence on a 'value chain' controlled and dominated from abroad.

The two arguments developed thus far can clearly be combined into a dynamic analysis of relative national decline. UK TNCs invest abroad in order to embed themselves into more profitable, rapidly-growing or technologically-sophisticated markets; while foreign TNCs simultaneously invest in the UK as a low-cost base for low-level production stages aimed at supplying European markets. This has been reinforced in some accounts by the observation that inward FDI is increasingly directed towards less technology-intensive sectors (e.g. Young *et al.*, 1988: 71–3). However, the available statistics on this use broad sectoral categories and take no account of wide differences within sectors such as electrical engineering or the motor industry.[3] It seems more realistic to expect that the quantity and quality of FDI in both directions will vary greatly, not only by sector, but also by firm. Thus the pharmaceutical industry is widely regarded as a UK success story, in which high levels of both outward and inward FDI are associated with a high concentration of high value-added R & D activity (*ibid.*: 76–7). At the same time, the rapid growth of FDI globally in recent years is widely seen as being accompanied by more global corporate strategies and structures: this suggests that the 'level' of a particular plant in terms of value-added may depend as much on 'corporate comparative advantage' as on national comparative advantage.

To conclude, the view that high FDI levels have promoted the decline of UK manufacturing is convincing if formulated as a dynamic process, but it requires qualification. First, UK manufacturing has become highly differentiated, with islands of global competitiveness and high value-added within a broad picture of decline. I have argued elsewhere that it has been subject in addition to a process of vertical disintegration, in the sense of the links between manufacturers and their suppliers of capital goods and technology: the main evidence for this is the growth in import penetration in such goods and the growth in the purchase of foreign licences. In this view the UK no longer has a *national* manufacturing capability on which industrial regeneration could be based across a range of key dynamic sectors. Secondly, the fact that the UK has continued to be a major source of FDI, and that UK TNCs have maintained their position among the world's top firms, emphasises that while *UK-located industry* has declined, *UK-based capital* has been comparatively successful in global competition.

Before we can look at the policy implications of the role of foreign direct investment in industrial decline, we must examine the other main element in the traditional left critique, namely the role of the City.

IV   The role of the City

The rapid rise in capital exports after 1979 raised the possibility that British capital is seeking to return to the position of international rentier which it held before 1914. In aggregate terms, this is hardly likely. In 1913, net property income from abroad covered fully 25% of total import requirements and about 9% of net national income: in 1986, the peak recent year for net overseas assets, the net inflow of interest, profits and dividends at £4.6b only covered some 6% of visible imports and under 2% of net national income. Since 1986, net overseas assets have slumped to a mere 1.9% of GDP, although they are now rising again as a result of the depreciation of sterling. Nevertheless, given the apparent 'export of jobs' by MNCs, the very low level of industrial capital formation in Britain, and the outward flood of portfolio investment, it is not surprising that attention has focused on the relation between industrial capital and financial capital.

The traditional left argument on this is as follows. Historically, UK financial capital in the form of 'the City' has developed as a network of capitalist interests oriented towards world markets for commodities and for money. The precocious development of manufacturing industry in Britain assured industrial capitalists of very high profits, so that their accumulation was largely self-financed, drawing at most on the mobilisation of regional savings for short-term finance through the provincial banking system. This meant that London-based merchant and banking capital played virtually no direct role in industrial accumulation; instead, it functioned as commercial and banking capital in worldwide trade and investment. Throughout the decline of the last hundred years, the internationally-oriented City has thwarted efforts at industrial renaissance, partly by refusing to supply capital for domestic investment, and partly by successfully controlling government economic policies to ensure that its sectional interests were favoured (notably a high value of the pound and minimal controls on capital flows). This, in essence, is the position reformulated by Ingham (1984) and taken up in *New Left Review* by Leys (1985, 1986) and Perry Anderson (1987), with a critical reply by Barratt Brown (1988). Recently, attention has focused more on the overall relation between finance and industry, with the widespread critique of the 'short-termism' of the City, i.e. its unwillingness to supply long-term risk capital (Goodhart and

Grant, 1988); this is connected with the propensity for hostile take-overs among UK companies and the dominance of external owners in their corporate governance.

There is little doubt on two points: that the City of London is a highly open global financial centre, and that it plays a very powerful role in the determination of economic policy, particularly by its influence via the Bank of England on the Treasury. On the first point, from the emergence of the Eurodollar market in the 1960s through to the abolition of exchange controls in 1979 and the 'Big Bang' of deregulation in 1987, London has flourished as a centre for global finance (Bank of England, 1989; Toporowski, 1989; and Coakley and Harris, 1992). The internationalisation and securitisation of lending in recent years has reinforced London's overall position in the issuing and trading of financial instruments, attracting large investments by foreign financial institutions. This has meant that within the European Union London remains easily the most important financial centre; it has also enabled UK financial institutions, since 1979, to increase significantly their international activities, in terms of loan portfolios or financial assets.

As for influence on economic policy, it is also clear that, diverse though the City's interests are, it has always been united especially in seeking continued freedom from controls and a reasonably stable exchange rate, which are seen as essential to London's role as a leading world financial centre. Since the advent of monetarism in 1976, the City has consistently supported its main policy precepts of quantitative monetary targets, cuts in public expenditure and reliance on the rate of interest as the main discretionary policy instrument. It has also demanded and won the 'self-regulation' of financial markets. City economists have come to dominate debate in the mass media, and the Bank of England continues to dictate the Treasury view on major issues such as the UK's departure from the European Monetary System's exchange rate mechanism in 1992.

However, the conventional critique is on much weaker ground when it comes to the relations between the City and industrial capital. Clearly, there is a fundamental opposition between the two in so far as the City lends and industry borrows; but so long as industry remains a major part of productive capital as a whole, there is also a fundamental unity, since the interest and dividends accruing to the financial sector come out of profits earned in production. Thus, Fine and Harris (1985) argue that the City, despite its primary concern with financial markets is, nevertheless, also concerned about the health of British industry: it is just that their preferred medicine for its ills is market discipline, rather than state aid. Equally, they insist (*ibid.*: 66–71) that, despite its overseas orientation, the City's financial health does ultimately depend on the health of the whole British economy.

Taking first the role of the City in providing finance, Fine and Harris (1985) and Thompson (1977) argue (as did the Wilson Committee) that for the most part the financial needs of industry *are* met. Banks provide short-term loans, and the 'institutions' (life insurance companies, pension funds, investment and unit trusts) provide long-term funds where retained profits are insufficient. The problem is that industry does not *demand* funds on different terms or in greater quantity. In addition, throughout the post-war period, but especially since the merger boom of the mid-1960s (repeated notably in the early 1970s and mid to late 1980s), merchant banks and institutional investors have played a major role in the restructuring of industrial capital. High levels of self-financing overall should not obscure the crucial role of outside long-term finance, both in accelerating accumulation for individual firms, and in organising the centralisation of capital. In addition, since the mid-1970s, and especially since 'Big Bang', competition among banks has led to a growing provision of longer-term industrial finance.

However, the critique can be reformulated as a more structural problem. Industrial capital has made few demands on the City, certainly when compared with other capitalist countries, and these demands have been, by and large, satisfied. The weakness in the linkage, from the standpoint of an acceleration of industrial investment, is that it has allowed banking capital to exercise to the full its predilection for security and liquidity, and that neither industry nor the City have ever felt the need to call upon the British state to take the lead in developing German or Japanese style investment banking (Fine and Harris, 1985: ch. 4). Thus, if industry is content with the provision of finance, this is because the structures and practices of UK business and government have evolved in a particular way – the 'Anglo-Saxon model' of capitalism.

In this model, ownership is widely dispersed among disinterested institutional owners whose preference is for high and stable dividends; the interests of owners are enforced through company laws which exclude the claims of other 'stakeholders'; companies are therefore dominated by financial management aimed at maximising the return on equity and avoiding takeover or liquidation. This is the essence of the recent reformulation of the critique as a problem of short-termism and 'corporate governance' (Goodhart and Grant, 1988; Labour Party, 1992). The critics look to the Continental or Japanese models in which 'committed' ownership forms the basis of long-term industrial investments in high technology, and hostile take-overs and excessive dividends are absent; or as Hutton (1993) puts it, there is a 'culture of production' rather than a 'culture of finance'.

This reformulated critique is still open to some questions. First, it is not clear whether the 'Continental' model is a cause or a consequence of the comparative industrial success of Germany or Japan. Close and harmonious relations between finance and industry are much more likely if accumulation is rapid and profitable. Secondly, the recent problems at Deutsche Bank concerning the crises at Metalgesellschaft and Schneider have shown how difficult it can be for money capital to disengage from production in this model: more generally, restructuring between sectors may be more difficult (Meyer, 1993: 18). Thirdly, the Anglo-Saxon model has the distinct political and ideological advantage, from a capitalist point of view, of drawing a large proportion of middle-class savings into the circuits of private capital: outside the Anglo-Saxon countries, most savers hold their wealth in government bonds, or in postal or savings banks which either in turn finance public spending, or immobilise capital in family housing. Fourthly, globalisation is eroding the Continental model: thus Daimler-Benz seeks a listing in New York to help it tap into cheaper US funds to finance its North American and Pacific expansion – but has to adopt New York's 'Anglo-Saxon' accounting and disclosure conventions. Lastly, the much-heralded Cadbury report, in concentrating so much on the role of outside directors, shows that UK business wants to strengthen the Anglo-Saxon model of dispersed outside control, not to move towards an insider model.

If the structures and practices of company finance give the City so much power over UK industry, has the City directed or encouraged the overseas investments of industry, at the expense of investment in domestic modernisation? In the previous section, it was argued that the two are not in any case direct substitutes: as Fine and Harris point out (1985: ch. 4), British industrial capitalists have themselves been unwilling to invest more in Britain, for their own perfectly good capitalist reasons – notably, low profit prospects. However, the City has been a crucial part of the structures and practices that *enable* UK firms to respond to low UK profitability by investing abroad. The unparalleled international reach and flexibility of UK banking and finance has offset their relative weakness in technology and production, allowing them to establish powerful bridgeheads first in Western Europe, and more recently in the USA. The internationalisation of banking has also supported the internationalisation of UK property companies, accountancy firms, advertising agencies, construction companies, etc. The City has also been a cornerstone for the dominant role of Anglo-Saxon institutions, practices and culture in global business and finance.

In conclusion, there is no doubt that in the 'Anglo-Saxon' model, financial institutions are less directly involved in the affairs of industry; nevertheless they have been an important part of the nexus of forces that have shaped the continuing backwardness of UK-located industry. The global character of the City does not intrinsically conflict with the interests of UK industrial and commercial firms, since the latter have historically been highly global also. The City of London and industrial capital located in Britain collectively form British-based finance capital, of mixed British and foreign ownership; while British-owned capital has taken full advantage of the international scope of the British financial system to operate increasingly at a global level.

V   Policy implications: is there an alternative?

The traditional left view of the links between industrial decline, foreign investment and the dominance of the City over industry can thus be reformulated as a more complex structural problem. But what consequences does this have for the development of alternative policies?

In the first place, our reformulation opens up the possibility of a particular form of relative industrial *recovery*. For most of the Thatcher period the left tended to locate the main cause of industrial decline in the government's economic policies, concluding that as long as the policies continued unchanged, so would the decline. On the other hand, the Thatcher policies could be seen as promoting a process of adjustment to 'new realities' of international competition. The sustained attack on the unions, for example, opens the way for the installation of Japanese-style ('post-Fordist') management methods, making Britain's relatively low wages attractive to footloose multinationals. At the same time, the sharp rise in personal disposable incomes of those in work has made Britain a more attractive market, and Britain remains an attractive base for the wider European market in many sectors, as the recent recovery of inward direct investment shows. Deregulation and privatisation then provide the flexibility required to continue the recovery beyond a cyclical recovery. Meanwhile, the City of London is able to maintain its role in the world's financial markets, with British capitals in this arena being willing to concede substantial participation to foreign financial institutions, but able at the same time to expand abroad in more dynamic areas.

However, this remains a very peculiar, selective and fragile recovery. First of all, both unemployment and inequality have worsened enormously, and are constantly reinforced by continuing deregulation of labour markets and cuts in direct taxation. Secondly, although North Sea oil has become less important as an influence on macroeconomic balances, the exhaustion of reserves remains a long-term concern.

But the arguments of the previous section suggest two more specific criticisms. First, inward investment and better export performance may not amount to success by 'UK industry' as a locational category, but rather the success of UK-based subsidiaries of MNCs, whether British- or foreign-owned, since it is well established that they are responsible for the bulk of UK manufactured exports. This 'success' depends crucially not on a substantial core of UK-centred investment and innovation, but on the *international corporate integration* of UK economic activity. Secondly, the deepening of external financial integration renders UK production ever more vulnerable to the fluctuations and fancies of global financial markets – which of course also transmit the consequences of government policies in our major trading 'partners'.

This leads to the question of alternatives. Traditionally, these have centred on some variant of national industrial planning, coupled with the reform or reregulation of the City and of trade and capital flows (see for example Costello *et al.*, 1989, or Cowling and Sugden, 1990). Criticism of such proposals within the left has tended to focus on the *politics* of winning electoral support and then implementing them. But important questions are also raised by the changed character of the UK economy. Firstly, if that economy is now fragmented and externally integrated, as I have argued, it is hard to see what possible system of incentives and controls could ensure a coherence of interests *including* 'industrial capital' around a programme of national industrial expansion. At the very least, substantial powers would be required to compel MNCs to carry out investments in accordance with a national plan. Secondly, because the City is in fact closely tied to industry and trade (if in its own peculiar ways), it cannot be treated as a distinct economic sphere merely requiring reregulation, or the provision of incentives aimed at redirecting capital flows towards domestic industry. The City's global scope is central to the competitiveness of UK-owned MNCs, which despite their relative disengagement from UK production, remain central to it.

The traditional left alternative is thus torn in two directions. One of these is to retreat from political confrontation with capital. In this case, the structures of global integration impose very narrow limits on reform, and the left risks remaining locked within the logic of international competition, attempting to pit 'British' manufacturing against Japanese, American or German (or South Korean?) manufacturing. The current emphasis in the political centre ground on training and infrastructure investment can certainly attract support from British industrialists, but it will still not shift the structures of British capitalism as a whole towards a production-centred model. In particular, the City's leaders can rest secure in the knowledge that no challenge to their influence over those government policies which are central to their interests is likely to come from within their own class, given British industry's common interest in global integration.

The second alternative within the traditional framework of debate is to reassert an active role for the state in the strategic direction of economic affairs, but going beyond the 'national industrial planning' approach of the last thirty years. An approach which challenged the rule of capital would include, at the least, controls on international capital flows, the subordination of monetary policy to government rather than the City, and the reregulation, if not renationalization, of large parts of the productive sector. However, when envisaged as a *national* political programme - often on the basis of a supposed political realism - the logic of greater state intervention pushes rapidly towards a utopian and historically-discredited 'socialism in one country'.

A more real, and realistic, alternative for the left has to start by rejecting the logic of international competition, and seek to subordinate the market to social needs at all levels. Locally, control by external capital and a remote central government has created space for democratic movements to redefine the objectives of economic development, away from the logic of competing for limited resources from outside towards mobilising local resources. Nationally, the economic and social divisions that beset the UK bear witness to an increasing disjuncture between the national economy and British capital; business, so visibly preoccupied with financial speculation, 'downsizing' and massive pay rises for top managers, has never been less popular.

So far, so good: a programme along such lines would command significant public support in Britain today. But without an *international* dimension, not just bolted on top but as an integral part of the politics and economics of the left, any attempt to articulate the many discontents of the post-Thatcher era will be frustrated by the corrosive powers of the world market. If we look again at the deepening global economic integration which has undermined both 'national' British capitalism and the traditional progressive alternative, we can see that this integration also creates a common experience across different countries, and therefore a common agenda in which cooperation makes more sense than competition. Internationalism becomes a matter of practical economics, and not merely of utopian politics. For all their many faults, the European Union and the United Nations continue to embody ideals that are completely absent from foreign exchange markets and jet-setting management consultants: they are much more susceptible to a progressive agenda than the tired and conservative British state. At the same time, there has been a massive growth in grass-roots internationalism in progressive social movements of all kinds. The left should reassert the ideals of socialist internationalism and aim seriously to develop a progressive global politics. *That* would begin to offer a real alternative.

Notes

1. In the period 1980–83, 52% of outward direct investment flows (excluding oil companies) went to the USA alone, compared to a meagre 5% for the whole of Western Europe; in 1990–91, 18% went to the USA and over 50% to Western Europe.
2. Rowthorn and Wells (1987: 15–23) insist that it is not necessary to invoke Engel's Law by arguing that with high incomes, demand shifts to services. In their view, the statistical evidence for this is distorted by quality improvements in manufactured goods.
3. In addition, the trend given in Young *et al.*'s data on this disappears once an exceptional massive disinvestment in motor vehicles is omitted (*op. cit.*: 72).

Part 6

The state

The literature we have so far surveyed in the collection has given centre-stage, as causes of UK economic under-performance to labour, to capital and to culture – to non-political causes of economic decline. Now we reach a series of arguments which focus on the character and role of the UK state, and the policies of successive UK governments, as key factors in economic failure. We begin with an extract from *David Marquand's* powerful survey of why and how the UK failed to develop a 'developmental state' on Japanese lines or a 'consensual' one of the German/Swedish kind. Marquand's survey attaches particular importance to the corrosive impact on UK political and economic development of the persistence of liberal ideas on state and economy. 'Possessive individualism' is, for Marquand, the key damaging component of the UK's dominant political culture, an antipathy to state activity consolidated in the nineteenth century and increasingly anachronistic in the twentieth. As he puts it, 'in the age of the industrial laboratory, the chemical plant and later of the computer' the UK 'stuck to the mental furniture of the age of steam'.

Peter Hall focuses directly on the role of state intervention in contributing to Britain's economic underperformance. He concentrates on three activities of the state, namely the growth of public expenditure, macroeconomic management and industrial policy. On the size of the state he finds little evidence to support the existence of a causal connection between public sector growth and economic decline. Not only is the timing of the expansion of the state sector out of line with the prior decline of British economic performance but also, contrary to the Bacon-Eltis hypothesis, he argues that comparative studies show a significant positive correlation between the expansion of the public sector and the rate of economic growth in the post-war period. Hall also notes that the costs of the welfare state in the form of increased taxation were not excessive in Britain compared to better performing international competitors; nor is there evidence to link a high public sector borrowing requirement with lower levels of private investment.

This leads Hall to ask why the government did not intervene more to transform the market conditions associated with slow growth. As far as macroeconomic policy is concerned he accepts that, until the 1970s, a major imperative was the desire to maintain a high exchange rate. He reviews the debate that such a policy orientation impaired the performance of the economy and concludes that to blame macroeconomic policies is to mistake the source of the problem. He then turns to industrial policy and discovers that, unlike in countries such as France and Japan, the approach was voluntaristic and tended to enhance rather than diminish the structural rigidities of many markets.

Thus the British state has not pursued effective policies for restoring the profitability, productivity and growth of the economy. The roots of the problem, according to Hall, lie in the structural setting of the British state – the position of Britain within the international economy, the organisational configuration of British society, the institutional structure of the state itself and the nature of the wider political system. Together these variables have affected the willingness and ability of the state to adopt a more developmental role. Hall concludes that, while the state is not primarily responsible for economic decline, its inertia has derived from the institutional rigidities of the system in which it has been embedded. This implies that whereas the state can transform the economic system it must first transform itself.

One element of the constellation of consequences set in train by possessive individualism, imperial grandeur and the downplaying of civilian industrial policy was the heavy involvement of the post-war UK state in military expenditure. That too, according to *Malcolm Chalmers*, made its own contribution to economic underperformance. It did so by cutting away at investment in civilian industry, by absorbing a disproportionate amount of scarce high technology inputs, and by adversely affecting the economy's balance of international payments. Chalmers ties this disproportionate concern with military expenditure back to the period of Empire, implying that the UK's economic decline can be located in patterns of imperial over-reach and the neglect of domestic needs that have brought empires to their knees before: viz Spain in the seventeenth century, and arguably the USA in this.

The contradictions of imperial dominance surface too in *David Cameron*'s critique of the Olson thesis of institutional sclerosis. The extract by Cameron is included here for two reasons. One is the quality and brevity of the historical sweep it contains; the second is the way in which it demonstrates how vital such a historical perspective is to any adequate analysis of contemporary UK economic underperformance. What connects the past to the present are what Cameron calls 'factors involving international economics and politics': the international political economy, Britain's evolving role within the world economy, the policy responses through which governments sought to perpetuate or alter that role, and the constraints that role imposed on domestic economic policy. In other words, if the Cameron approach has any validity, the key to economic underperformance has to be sought in some complex international political economy. It will not be found in any simplistic political sociology, or in any knee-jerk return to the 'certainties' of unregulated markets.

Finally, *Kevin Theakston* reviews the suitability of the UK state as an agent for economic modernisation. He notes that the character of Britain's mandarin elite has been a target for declinist critics – the higher civil service has been condemned for its generalist outlook, its anti-interventionist ethos and its lack of understanding of and sympathy towards the needs of manufacturing industry. Far more important than these attitudinal problems, according to Theakston, is the fragmentation and instability of the industrial policy community inside Whitehall. This has militated against the development and implementation of a coherent approach to the needs of manufacturing industry. Not only is there a network of government departments responsible for industrial policy but also there has been a continual shifting of responsibilities between different departments. Further, standing at the centre of the Whitehall machine is the Treasury which has consistently opposed a positive and interventionist industrial policy. The result has been a lack of coordination and continuity in the government's approach to industrial policy. Theakston examines various attempts to adopt a more strategic approach to industry, such as the Ministry of Technology in the 1960s, but the general picture in the post-war period is one of incoherence and instability – reinforcing Hall's point that although the activities of the UK state may not be the necessary condition bringing about economic underperformance, the latter is unlikely to be cured without the sufficient condition of a state-led industrial strategy.

CHAPTER 24

Doctrine and reality*

David Marquand

In at least three related respects, twentieth-century Britain has been the prisoner of her nineteenth-century past. She was the first industrial society in history, the pathfinder to the modern world. The values and assumptions of her élites, the doctrines disseminated in her universities and newspapers, the attitudes and patterns of behaviour of her entrepreneurs and workers were stamped indelibly by this experience. But because she was the pathfinder because she made the passage to industrialism early, at a time when the technology was still primitive, when the skills it required were still rudimentary and when it could still be managed efficiently by the small-scale, fragmented structures of liberal capitalism – the experience taught the wrong lessons.

Britain had become the pathfinder in the first place because she had broken more decisively than any other country in the world with the values and assumptions of what Harold Perkin has called the 'Old Society' (Perkin, 1972). The notions that property has duties as well as rights, that consumers owe producers a just price while producers owe consumers just dealing, that the community is a whole greater than the sum of its parts, that high and low are bound together by a chain of reciprocal obligation, that man is placed on earth by God to serve greater ends than the satisfaction of his own wants – all these were victims of a cultural revolution, which preceded and made possible the industrial revolution. More thoroughly than any other country in Europe, Britain's culture was permeated with the individualism which her intellectuals codified and justified, and to which the astounding growth of her economy gave the sanction of success. To the British, it seemed almost self-evident that industrialism must be the child of individualism, that 'progress' could come only through setting individuals free to pursue their own interests and to make what use they wished of their own property, without reference to society or interference from the state, but although these attitudes suited the conditions of primitive industrialism, they did not suit the sophisticated, science-based and organised industrialism which

---

* Reproduced with permission from *The Unprincipled Society*, Cape, 1988.

slowly superseded it. With suitable modifications, the communal ethic of the 'Old Society' has turned out to be better adapted to the capital- and skill-intensive industrialism of the twentieth century than the individualistic ethic of the industrial revolution; and it is in societies where something of the old ethic survived the transition to modernity that sophisticated industrialism has flourished most. Having made one cultural revolution in the seventeenth and eighteenth centuries, however, Britain has been unable to make another in the twentieth. In the age of the industrial laboratory, the chemical plant, and later of the computer, she stuck to the mental furniture of the age of steam.

Much of that furniture was arranged around her extraordinary role in the outside world. Not only was she the first industrial society in history, she was also the first world power in history, the guarantor as well as the midwife of the world-wide trading system which the guns of the Royal Navy had made possible. But she was a world power of a very odd kind. In Andrew Gamble's phrase, she was the 'World Island' (Gamble, 1981), the centre of an informal network of trading relationships and capital movements, of which her formal empire was merely a part. This network was permeated with the same individualism that permeated her economy. It was not managed from London, in the interests of the imperial state. In an important sense, it was not managed at all. It depended on the spontaneous, unplanned activities of private entrepreneurs and investors, looking for profit wherever they could find it. They were not agents of some overarching imperial mission; they pursued their own private interests, not the interests of the empire in general or of the mother country in particular. Here too, what had been an asset in the days of Britain's industrial supremacy became a handicap as others overtook her. British entrepreneurs failed to compete with the Germans and Americans in the new technologies of the late-nineteenth and early-twentieth centuries because, in the short term, they could survive and prosper by selling more of their existing products in their traditional markets in Latin America and the colonies. Meanwhile, capital which might have been invested in modernising British industry flowed abroad instead. The same theme sounded repeatedly between the wars and after 1945. This external network, moreover, created a powerful nexus of internal interests with a stake in its survival. Partly because of this, successive governments gave higher priority to the world role, financial or military, than to the home economy. Examples include the return to the gold standard in 1925, the high expenditure on overseas military bases in the 1950s and 1960s and the sacrifice of the National Plan to the $2.80 sterling parity in 1966. And although the long post-script to world power ended with Britain's belated entry into the European Community in the early 1970s, it was plain that her political class found it exceptionally hard to adjust to membership.

The legacy of the nineteenth century does not end there. One reason why British politicians and officials cannot easily adapt to EEC membership is that the 'Westminster Model' of parliamentary government rests on the doctrine – heavily influenced by the utilitarian individualism of Jeremy Bentham and his followers who thought that sovereignty was inherently unlimited and who dismissed the notion of fundamental rights as 'nonsense on stilts' – that the Crown-in-Parliament must be absolutely and inalienably sovereign. An obvious corollary is that British governments cannot share power with other tiers of government, sub-national or supra-national. In its day, the 'Westminster Model' was a remarkable example of successful adaptation. The accommodations and concessions which gave birth to it made possible Britain's peaceful transition to democracy, and the peaceful incorporation of the Labour Movement into the political order. Here too, however, assumptions born of successful adaptation in the past impede adaptation to more recent changes. Not only do we live in an interdependent world, in which absolute national sovereignty is an illusion and transnational power sharing inevitable, we also live in an interdependent society, dense with organised and unorganised groups, whose co-operation in the productive process is essential to the smooth running of the economy. In practice, governments have either to break the power of these groups – a costly and uncertain business, itself inimical to the health of the economy – or to share power with them. Thus, in fact even if not in form, they too have ended the Westminster monopoly of sovereignty. Buttressing the doctrine of absolute parliamentary supremacy, moreover, are the twin assumptions that the courts should not limit the freedom of action of the sovereign Parliament, and that there is in any case no need to limit it since informal restraints and political processes provide adequate safeguards against the abuse of power. Yet, in an increasingly diverse society, in which deference to customary authority is waning, these assumptions have become recipes for mistrust and alienation.

Half a century of social change has, in short, invalidated the doctrines which are supposed to underpin the political order. This, in turn, has undermined public confidence in its equity, and made it more difficult for governments to mobilise consent for the changes without which economic adjustment is impossible.

II

[At the heart of British political culture, in both governing circles and more popularly, is] the orthodox Anglo-American economic tradition, whose paradigm of a properly working economy is still – whether consciously or unconsciously – the atomistic, market economy which the eighteenth- and nineteenth-century British founders of the tradition saw around them. Britain was the workshop of the world, the implicit argument goes, in the days when she obeyed the rules of market liberalism. Since she no longer obeys them, that must be why her economy has declined since. Thus, many have found the origins of Britain's economic decline in a 'counter-revolution of values', which led the manufacturing bourgeoisie of the late-nineteenth century to abandon the hard-driving, risk-taking entrepreneurialism of the heroic age of British industry in favour of an anti-industrial ethos disseminated by the old universities and public schools.

Others have found them in the early emergence of trade unions and cartels, strong enough to 'distort' the working of the market. Others again have found them in the conversion of the governing class to a flabby and soft-hearted liberalism, dominated by a concern for social welfare.

I think the explanation is more complex than this. It is true that changes have taken place since the early-nineteenth century. It is true that some of them have played a part in Britain's relative economic decline. But the changes are more complicated than they seem; and, in any case, they are less significant than the continuities. The notion that the roots of Britain's economic decline lie in her failure to stick to the early-nineteenth-century, market-liberal model of a successful economy rests on the assumption that adjustment can only be market-led. In reality, there are at least three models of successful adjustment, not one. Market-led adjustment, on the pattern of Industrial-Revolution Britain, represents one way of coping with economic change. But state-led adjustment, on the Japanese pattern, and negotiated or corporatist-consensual adjustment, on the pattern of central Europe and Scandinavia, represent others. It is true that Britain abandoned the market-led model. But it does not follow that that is why her economy declined: when her decline began, she was closer to it than were her more successful rivals. Her real predicament is that, having abandoned it, she has been unwilling or unable to adopt either of the other two models. And, by a strange paradox of cultural conservatism, the reason is that the 'ethos' of market liberalism – the web of assumptions, values, understandings and experiences which gave the market-led model its emotional power – survived long after the doctrine was abandoned.

At the heart of that ethos lies a set of attitudes to the role of public power, and to the relationship between public power and private freedom, which is unique in Europe. The developmental states, which first followed and then overtook Britain on the path to industrialism, deliberately repudiated the orthodox classical and neo-classical theories of international trade and the political assumptions underlying them. Their approach to international trade differed in at least four ways from the orthodox classical approach. For them, the world economy was made up of nations, not of individuals. These nations sought wealth as a means to power; they wished to maximise their power in the long term, even if it meant sacrificing individual satisfactions in the short term. They were not content with a pattern of comparative advantages which condemned them to permanent inferiority to the world's economic pacemakers. It was the task of the state to change the pattern.

However, Britain did not follow suit. The notion of a welfare state was slowly accepted. The notion of a developmental state, using its power to give its citizens a more sophisticated set of comparative advantages so that it could compete more effectively with other states, met dogged and uncomprehending resistance. At most, the state's job was to distribute wealth. It was not supposed to create it. The public sector came to be seen as the domain of the non-economic – of the fair, the concerned and the tender-hearted in the eyes of its supporters, and of the sloppy, the profligate and the uncompetitive in the eyes of its opponents.   The notion that it might be the ally of, or even a spur to, competitiveness remained alien to both.   Even when governments began to intervene in the supply-side, first in the 1930s and more systematically in the hands-on phase of Keynesian social democracy, essentially welfare considerations – the protection of existing jobs and existing industries – characteristically predominated over developmental ones.

The implications go wide.   In a path-breaking essay, Alexander Gerschenkron once observed that the more 'backward' the society undergoing industrialisation, and the wider the gap between its level of technological sophistication and the level of the most advanced economies of the time, the more industrialisation depends on public authorities (Gerschenkron, 1966).   Thus, the German state intervened in the economy more than the British, and the Russian and Japanese more than the German.   Gerschenkron's insight underlines a paradox which echoes through the last century of British economic history like a tolling bell. The minimalist state of late-eighteenth and early-nineteenth-century England was appropriate for an industrial pioneer, in which economic development could take place slowly and gradually, through a series of small, piecemeal steps within the capacity of a decentralised private sector.   Once Britain's old followers had begun to overtake her, however, roles were reversed.   She was no longer a pioneer, and began to fall into relative backwardness herself.   But the values and assumptions of her pioneering days still survived, inhibiting her from overcoming her backwardness in the way that her imitators of the previous generation had overcome theirs ...

Yet it can scarcely be argued that Britain would not have profited from developmental intervention.   In theory, no doubt, different forms of private organisation – for example, a banking system on the German model, attuned to the needs of industrial development and willing to put long-term growth ahead of short-term profit – might have enabled her to break out of the pattern of decline without government intervention.   But if her private sector had been so organised, she would not have been caught in the pattern in the first place. Moreover, some of her economic handicaps – above all, her backward education systems and the comparatively poor quality of her human capital – sprang directly from the minimalist view of the state, and could have been put right only by adopting a different view.   By the same token, there is no reason to believe that the British were, for some reason, technically incapable of creating as entrepreneurial a state apparatus as existed elsewhere.   The British administrative machine managed the wartime economies of 1914–18 and 1939–45 with great skill.   In the Second World War, Britain may well have been the most efficiently mobilised of all the belligerents – partly, of course, because American aid made it possible to ignore balance of payments considerations.   The civil-service élite which had wearily resisted the Lloyd George-Mosley programme of home development on the grounds that the roads it envisaged could not be built in time to make any difference to the unemployment figures now ran a quasi-totalitarian command economy with flair and drive. The barrier to such behaviour in peace-time was not technical. What was it?

At first sight, the obvious answer is that it was the extraordinary longevity of market liberalism among the British political class. But there are two weaknesses in that. The first is that it is not so much an answer as another way of formulating the question. It is a characteristic illusion of intellectuals to imagine that doctrines convert societies ...

The second weakness is that, in any event, only some market-liberal doctrines continued to carry conviction. Logically, market liberalism is as hostile to the welfare state as to the developmental state: to the Social Liberal programme of 1906–14 as to the Social Imperialist programme of Joe Chamberlain and the tariff reformers. Yet, British politicians and administrators accepted the idea of a welfare state without much difficulty. If they could come to believe that the state had an obligation to maintain its citizens through sickness and unemployment, why did they not also come to believe that it had an obligation to develop the economy?

Part of the explanation, of course, lies in nineteenth-century Britain's unique place in the world economy, and in the web of interests, values, assumptions and loyalties which grew up around it. The developmental states of that era were trying, quite consciously, to break away from economic subordination to her, just as many of the developmental states of the twentieth century have been anxious to break away from economic subordination to the United States. It is not surprising that she found it hard to emulate them when she eventually lost her pre-eminence and when, as a result, the logic of her own internal development began to conflict with the logic of the world-wide trading and financial system which she had brought into existence. For, in a sense true of no other country before or since, she was the child of that system, as well as its midwife. The British state, the British governing class, the British civil service, the British education system, the British economy and the British capital market were all shaped by its imperatives. It was because Britain was committed to free trade and the gold standard, because individual British citizens exported huge quantities of capital all over the world, because the Royal Navy maintained the *pax Britannica*, because British trading posts and naval bases girdled the globe, that the world-wide system came into being; and it was because Britain had been the pivot of that system for so long that later British politicians and opinion leaders could not emancipate themselves from its assumptions. Of course, she would have been better off if she had put the needs of the domestic economy ahead of the claims of the world-wide system, as most of the developmental states of the nineteenth and twentieth centuries have done. That theme has run through a long succession of lost opportunities, from Joe Chamberlain's defeat at the hands of the free traders in the early 1900s and the rejection of the Lloyd George-Mosley programme under the second Labour government to the abandonment of the National Plan in 1966. But the British governments which acted in this way did not do so out of caprice. They were listening to ancestral voices of enormous

262 UK Economic Decline

power. They could have given precedence to internal development instead only by breaking with the tradition which had made them and their countrymen what they were.

Yet this is only part of the explanation. The developmental states also had histories; and their histories also created obstacles to modernisation and adjustment. Looking back from the vantage point of the late-twentieth century it is easy to see that there were strands in the cultural inheritances of Meiji Japan, or early-nineteenth-century Prussia or Gaullist France which favoured the emergence of developmental states, with the will and power to modernise their economies. But it is easy to see this because we know that developmental states in fact emerged. Before they did so, the obstacles to modernisation – the backwardness and poverty of Japan, the archaic militarism of the Prussian Junkers, the political instability of France – all loomed quite large. If we want to understand Britain's failure to emulate them, it is not enough to know that ancestral voices counselled against doing so. We also need to know why the ancestral voices were listened to.

Andrew Shonfield's contrast between the French official, eagerly embracing administrative discretion, and the British official, desperate to pretend that he does not have any, provides an important clue. For the developmental state is inherently discretionary, in a sense in which the welfare state is not. In a welfare state, the authorities treat precisely specified categories of citizens in precisely specified ways. Once the rules have been laid down, the system is 'rule-governed'. The developmental state cannot be rule-governed in that way; flexibility is the whole essence of the developmental *économie concertée*. In it, the state browbeats, bribes and bargains with private economic agents, favouring some at the expense of others, in varying ways and according to varying criteria – choosing from among a panoply of interventionist devices those that seem most appropriate at any given moment. In Britain, that kind of flexibility seems faintly improper; and when governments have engaged in it, as in the 1930s and the 1960s, their efforts have been half-hearted and lacking in legitimacy. The crucial question, then, is why? Why has Britain's political culture been consistently hostile to the notion, not so much of an interventionist state as of a discretionary one?

The answer lies deep in the experiences which shaped that culture. Thanks to the upheavals of the seventeenth century – thanks, in particular, to the victory of the English landed class over the Stuart kings – one cannot speak of a 'British state' in the way that one speaks of a 'French state' or, in modern times, of a 'German state'. The United Kingdom is not a state in the continental sense. It is a bundle of lands (including such exotica as the Channel Islands and the Isle of Man, which are not even represented at Westminster), acquired at different times by the English crown, and governed in different ways. Its inhabitants are not citizens of a state, with defined rights of citizenship. They are subjects of a monarch, enjoying 'liberties' which their ancestors won from previous monarchs. Executive power is still, in an odd way, private rather than public. It lies with named individuals – ministers of the Crown, legally responsible for the activities of their departments – not with the state. The civil servants who advise the minister and implement his decisions are, in constitutional theory, simply that: individual 'servants', hired technicians in administration, not a corporate body with a corporate responsibility to the public and a corporate obligation to pursue the public interest. The political culture which all this reflects and sustains can tolerate reactive intervention, designed to respond to pressures which have already made themselves felt or to buy off trouble which is patently in the offing. It cannot provide a moral basis for discretionary intervention – for intervention designed, in Shonfield's suggestive phrase, to serve 'the community's needs before the community itself has recognised them'.

To be sure, most of the nation-states of mainland Europe started in the same way. Germany was still a patchwork quilt of kingdoms, principalities and city states more than half-way through the nineteenth century. Even France – in many ways the paradigm case of the European nation-state – became a united monarchy much later than England. But by the early nineteenth-century, the Bourbons, the Jacobins and Napoleon had hammered the lands of the French Crown into the French state, while the Hohenzollerns had hammered the Prussian state out of their bleak, unpromising inheritance and the conquests they added to it. Over most of mainland Europe, modernity came by the same route. Weak and fissiparous medieval kingdoms slowly evolved into absolute, but still patrimonial, monarchies. The old medieval estates were neutered or pushed aside. As in the middle ages, however, there was no real distinction between the monarch as a person and the monarch as a ruler. Under the pressure of war, financial exigency and the ideas of Roman law and the Enlightenment, the patrimonial monarchies of the early modern period then evolved into the benevolent despotisms of the eighteenth century, in which the monarch could boast with Frederick II that he was 'the first servant of the state' – the caretaker or trustee of a public power, above and beyond his own person and, by the same token, above and beyond the persons of his subjects. Sometimes monarchies gave way to republics and sometimes not. But from our point of view, that made little difference. What mattered was that, monarchies and republics alike, patrimonial power was transformed into state power, and that, in republics no less than in monarchies, the state was assumed to be more than the sum of the citizens who made it up.

From the seventeenth century, Britain followed an aberrant path. The Stuarts, like their contemporaries on the European mainland, tried to create an absolute, patrimonial monarchy, strong enough to impose its will on the medieval corporations and the nobility and gentry. For a brief moment, it looked as if Cromwell's Protectorate might take an alternative, republican route to the same destination. But all of these attempts trenched on the freedom of the landed class to do what it wished with its own, and all of them broke on the instinctive resistance of the landowners of the Country Party to the ambitions of a centralising Court. The Revolution Settlement of 1688 marked their final defeat. Instead of being suppressed, the medieval particularism of the past blended with the 'possessive individualism' of emergent capitalism. The old liberties, the old corporations, the old, precedent-bound common law, the old houses of parliament all survived; and they, not the will of a reforming monarch, became the conduits of modernity. The end product was a political culture suffused with the values and assumptions of whiggery, above all with the central Lockean assumption that individual property rights are antecedent to society. In such a culture, the whole notion of a public power, standing apart from private interests, was bound to be alien. Yet without that notion, it is hard to see how a developmental state, with the capacity to form a view of the direction the economy ought to take, and the will and moral authority to put its view into practice, can come into existence.

CHAPTER 25

The state and economic decline*

Peter A. Hall

Just as the rise of the British economy was one of the miracles of the nineteenth century, so its decline has been one of the enigmas of the twentieth. Although her absolute rate of growth improved during world-wide expansion after World War II, Britain's performance relative to other industrial competitors, in both efficiency and output terms, has been one of continuous deterioration since the 1880s.

Britain's economic problems have been structural rather than conjunctural. Whatever the contribution of international fluctuations or relative factor endowments to growth, the British economy does not employ its resources as effectively as do overseas competitors. In particular, its industries have been characterised by low levels of investment, a reluctance to innovate or expand, and outmoded forms of work organisation at both the managerial and shop floor levels. Such factors are the proximate causes of economic decline. However, the presence of these conditions in Britain must still be explained.

This chapter is concerned with the contribution of public policy to those conditions. What was the role of the state in Britain's economic decline? To answer that question, we examine three aspects of the state's activities that might have alleviated or contributed to Britain's economic problems: the growth of the public sector, macroeconomic management, and industrial policy.

The size of the state

There are three variations to the view that the expansion of the British state itself is the principal source of Britain's economic problems. The first suggests that the growth of the public sector diverted critical resources from more productive pursuits in the private sector. The second variant argues that the growth in public

---

* Reproduced with permission from B. Elbaum and W. Lazonick (eds), *The Decline of the British Economy*, Oxford University Press, 1986.

spending, especially in the transfer payments of the welfare state and correlative increases in taxation, impaired growth by reducing the incentives of private sector actors to put more work effort and investment into the economy. A third view maintains that the rising public sector borrowing requirement associated with increased levels of public expenditure began to 'crowd out' private investment in the 1960s.

All of these positions begin from the incontrovertible fact that the share of national resources being channelled through the public sector has increased dramatically in the period since World War II. In Britain, public expenditure as a share of GNP rose from 32 per cent in 1950 to 45 per cent in 1980. The critical issue, however, is one of causation. Did the expansion of public activity actually limit the growth of the private sector in Britain? There is little evidence to support the existence of a causal connection between public sector growth and economic decline. First, the timing of the two occurrences is not coincident. The performance of the British economy relative to that of her trading partners began to decline at least fifty years before the public sector began to grow appreciably. In absolute terms, British growth rates actually improved during the period when most public sector expansion took place. This implies that the growth of the welfare state may have enhanced economic performance.

Comparative analysis also suggests that the growth of the public sector had little to do with Britain's relatively poor economic performance. In many European nations whose rates of growth exceeded that of Britain over the post-war period, including Germany, France, Sweden, Norway, the Netherlands, and Austria, government spending as a portion of GNP was equal to or higher than the British level. Recent studies have found a significant positive correlation between the expansion of the public sector and rates of growth over the post-war period.

Careful attempts to analyse the causal relation between public sector expansion and economic performance in Britain itself have also produced negative results. Hadjimatheou and Skouras (1979) call into question both the premises and empirical data of Bacon and Eltis (1976). The rather physiocratic contention that public sector activity is 'unproductive' neglects the contribution that health policy, education, and infrastructure make to national production; and the argument that public sector growth in the 1970s squeezed the manpower resources available to the private sector seems implausible given the high levels of unemployment that prevailed during much of the period.

Similar considerations cast doubt on the view that the costs of the welfare state impaired British economic performance. In all of the faster-growing nations cited above, taxes consumed a substantially greater portion of GNP than in Britain, and in many, marginal rates of tax were also higher for most income levels. Empirical studies have found that the impact of personal taxation on work effort is negligible, and that the incidence of corporate taxation in Britain actually fell over the post-war period.

Finally, while the large portion of institutional funds currently being invested in government gilt rather than industrial capital may be a cause for concern, no satisfactory evidence has been found to link a high PSBR with lower levels of private investment. Most studies suggest that government borrowing has not squeezed the funds available to industry, and that investment in Britain responds much more strongly to expectations of demand and profitability than to changes in the interest rate induced by the PSBR. Public sector deficits still seem more likely to expand investment through their impact on demand than to restrict it via monetary effects.

In general, no search for the causes of British economic decline should turn too quickly to the state. Relative decline must be seen, in the first instance, as one of the central consequences of the market itself. After all, Britain has had one of the most unconstrained market economies in the world. She was the first European nation to develop a self-regulating market system, and her markets have been free from state intervention to a degree that has no continental parallel. From the repeal of the Corn Laws in 1846 to the tariff measures of the 1930s, Britain remained the principal defender of free trade in the international system. Her governments stayed with this policy throughout the Great Depression of 1876–90 when most other nations enacted substantial trade barriers; and during the 1930s, when many countries employed public works programmes to secure reflation, Britain relied on the market system to revive the economy. Even the Keynesian system of demand management pursued after World War II was welcomed by both political parties because it seemed to free them from the need to intervene directly in industrial markets. Government interference into industry was so rare and restrained in this period that Shonfield (1958) could conclude that Britain had an 'arm's-length state'.

In such a context, we can ask why did the government not do more to transform the market conditions associated with slow growth? Many theories of the state suggest that it could have been expected to provide the necessary correctives, whether as the custodian of the public interest or as the 'ideal collective capitalist'. A central problem is to explain why it did not. Two broad areas of policy are relevant: those of macroeconomic management and microeconomic intervention.

The role of macroeconomic policy

Macroeconomic policy in Britain, from 1918 to the floating of the pound in 1972, was dominated by a concern to maintain the value of sterling on the foreign exchanges ...

By the end of World War II a profound transformation had taken place in the economic philosophy guiding British policy-makers. They embraced a variant of Keynesianism which suggested that variations in fiscal and monetary policy could be used to attain their new goal of full employment. Despite this development, however, the maintenance of a high exchange rate remained an overriding priority for successive governments.   When aggregate demand was expanded, rising levels of imports produced a deficit in the balance of payments; and rather than devalue the exchange rate to correct this imbalance, British governments chose to deflate the domestic economy.   Hence, expansion gave way to a famous series of 'stop-go' cycles.   The timing of the 'stops' indicates they were not the result of Keynesian moves to moderate the fluctuations of the business cycle but a direct consequence of attempts to protect the value of sterling.

How much impact did this pattern of macroeconomic policy have on the performance of the British economy?   Many commentators attribute the poor performance of British industry directly to macroeconomic policy.   Although the effect of alternative policies is ultimately a hypothetical issue, we can gain considerable insight by examining recent experience with alternative policies and comparing Britain's stance with that of other nations.

Essentially, there are four respects in which macroeconomic policy may have impaired the performance of the British economy.   First, the timing or intensity of demand management in the post-war period may have been destabilising for the economy.   Second, the particular monetary instruments on which the government relied for demand management in the post-war decades and the frequency with which they were applied may have been especially disruptive to investment. Third, it can be argued that failure to devalue often impaired the competitiveness of British products on world markets.   Finally, British policy over the entire period may have been more deflationary than necessary, thus needlessly inhibiting the growth of investment, output, and productivity.

The notion that demand management was destabilising has been the subject of considerable debate.   Although British policy remained the least stabilising of the seven nations usually studied, recent evidence suggests that post-war policy was positively destabilising only if the investment of public enterprise is considered a component of policy.   Policy was also more correctly timed in the years after 1965.   In comparative terms, overall variations around the trend of output and investment, including the impact of demand management, have still not been as great in Britain as in many nations with faster growth; and one finds plenty of instances of destabilising policy in such nations.

Similarly, the contention of British reliance on monetary instruments for demand management had an adverse effect on industry is contradicted by recent studies that have failed to find any convincing relationship between interest rates and the level of investment in Britain.   Many industrialists have testified that short-run changes in such instruments had no effect on their long-term investment plans; and it now seems likely that post-war controls on bank lending did not effectively restrict the money supply.   Although nominal interest rates have been slightly higher in the UK over the post-war period, the real rate of interest on long-term loans has been lower than in most other industrialised nations.   In these terms, British monetary policy has not been unduly restrictive.

The consequences of Britain's high exchange rate policies have also been widely debated. Moggridge (1972) and Pressnell (1978) argue that, if Britain had adopted a lower parity for the pound in the 1920s, her share of world exports would not have declined so dramatically in that decade. However, the temporary advantages gained from the 1931 devaluation were soon offset when other nations followed suit; and Britain's real wage costs were so high relative to those of other nations, and the price elasticity of demand for British exports so low in the 1920s, that a moderate devaluation would probably have had only a small effect on exports and economic growth.

Devaluation might also have been considered between 1949 and 1967 when Britain's competitiveness fell steadily, but the post-1968 experience must render one less sanguine about its advantages. The case for devaluation rests on an optimistic reading of four parameters: (1) and (2) the price elasticities for British exports and foreign imports in Britain, (3) the propensity of British exporters to utilise price advantages for profit-taking versus reorganisation and higher volume production, and (4) the rapidity with which real wages adjust to the domestic price inflation that devaluation entails (Posner and Steer, 1979). Recent experience suggests that there are few grounds to assume that developments on any of these fronts would make devaluation work. In particular, the apparent absence of 'money illusion' among British unions means that wage costs rise rapidly in the wake of a devaluation; and the price advantages of the 1967 devaluation had disappeared by 1971. If the export price advantages last only until lagging real wages adjust, a series of devaluations would have been required to maintain competitiveness over the post-war period. When this policy was pursued in 1972–79, Britain's share of world exports did increase after falling by 7 per cent in the preceding thirteen years, but the increase was marginal, and by no means did it eliminate balance of payments problems or render deflation unnecessary.

Moreover, one should question any strategy that depends on depressing real wages, because the more recent problem is not real wage rates, which have increased far less in Britain than in most European nations: it is lower levels of productivity growth that render British goods less competitive on world markets. Devaluation simply limits the impact of low productivity on exports – it does not remedy the causes of the problem. The long-term effect of the strategy would have been to render Britain even more dependent on low-wage industries and low productivity for its national income at a time when most industrialised nations prospered by concentrating on high-wage and high-value-added industries in the face of increased competition from the developing world. Indeed, as quality considerations came to play an increasing role in export competitiveness, it would have been particularly short-sighted for Britain to focus on price competitiveness. In short, while devaluation in the early 1920s or 1960s might have made a contribution to the competitiveness of British industry, it was unlikely to be a panacea for the underlying problems of the economy.

To deal with the contention that British policy has been overly deflationary, we must distinguish between the interwar and post-World War II periods. During the interwar years Britain pursued policies that seem to have unnecessarily restricted growth and adjustment, especially during the 1920s, when both fiscal and monetary policy were highly contractionary. Howson (1975: 63) argues that 'technical progress and structural factors are not independent of aggregate demand and with one million unemployed there could have been more expansion ... if aggregate demand had been growing sufficiently to create profit expectations favourable to investment in the new industries'. Although monetary policy was loosened in the 1930s, Britain's growth rates remained low by international standards, perhaps because she failed to adopt the expansionary fiscal policies that accompanied more rapid growth in Sweden, Germany, and the United States.

It is more difficult to assess the effects of British policy in the post-war period. The gap between actual GDP and potential GDP (assuming full factor use) between 1955 and 1973 was only slightly higher in Britain than the European average or the gap in nations, such as Germany, Austria, Belgium, and the Netherlands, which achieved much higher rates of growth. Similarly, the aggregate impact of British budgetary policy on demand was low by European standards but only slightly less than that in France, Sweden, and Belgium over the 1955–77 period. The British stance was not greatly out of line with those of many high-growth nations, and given the underlying buoyancy of consumption, there may have been little room for more expansionary policy.

A highly reflationary policy would have been possible only if, as a by-product, it altered the relatively high income elasticity for imports and low trend rate of productivity growth in Britain which rapidly imposed balance of payments constraints on expansion. Even those who argue that expansion should be used for this purpose, however, admit that it would have to be accompanied by stringent controls on imports and incomes. Such a strategy runs serious risks, beyond the possibility of foreign retaliation. Protection could fuel domestic inflation and shift resources into the least efficient sectors of the economy without forcing them to rationalise, as the tariff of 1932 seems to have done.

In short, these results suggest that more frequent devaluation or further expansion would have had a marginal impact at best on British rates of growth. To blame Britain's problems primarily on her macroeconomic policies is to mistake the source of the problem; and to look to better macroeconomic management alone for the solution is to overestimate the impact that alternative policies could have had on a stagnant economic base.

The pattern of industrial policy

Only in conjunction with an activist industrial policy could more expansionary macroeconomic policies have begun to address the underlying problems of the economy. Yet industrial policy remains a neglected feature of most analyses. All too often it is viewed as no more than a set of funding programmes for industry. Every industrial policy, however, contains three components: the volume of funds it channels to industry; the set of criteria that governs the choice of sectors, firms, and projects to be supported; and the degree of government pressure that is brought to bear on the reorganisation and reallocation of resources within industry. Since 1918, British policy has followed a pattern that is distinctive in each of these components.

The amount of money that British governments were willing to spend on industry was negligible until the 1960s. Despite some advances under the Trade Facilities Act of 1921, the Treasury kept a tight hold on the public purse strings during the interwar period. Instead, tariffs were used to augment the public coffers and protect the private sector. By contrast, Sweden, Japan, Germany, and even the United States spent considerable sums on guaranteed loans, industrial subsidies, and public works in this period. As late as 1961, the British state spent over £270 million on aid to agriculture and less than £50 million on industry and employment. Modest tax allowances were the principal investment incentive. In the 1960s, however, subsidies replaced tax allowances, and they increased during the 1970s as successive governments began to rescue firms hit by the post-1974 recession. Between 1971 and 1979, the government spent £9,290 million in subsidies to the private sector as well as large sums on the nationalised industries. By the 1970s, therefore, Britain was spending almost the same percentage of GDP on industrial grants as France or Germany (Dechery, 1980).

The set of criteria that guided British industrial support remained more distinctive. A substantial portion of British aid has been devoted to regional development programmes whose object is not to promote specific firms or sectors but to transfer resources to the depressed regions of the country. Britain was a pioneer of such policies, implementing the Special Areas Act in 1934, the Town and Country Planning Act in 1947, the Regional Employment Premium of 1968, and the Industry Acts of 1972 and 1975. Although regional policy was not notably successful until the 1960s, even then its effect was more to shift the location of investment than to stimulate new investment to rationalisation. Many British legislators favoured this form of policy precisely because it was voluntary, non-selective among firms, and likely to have little impact on the structure of industry. In 1979 the portion of public expenditure devoted to regional aid was twice as great in Britain as in most other European nations.

British policy has also emphasised research and development, which consumed almost 50 per cent of public spending on industry since 1970. Although the programme is seemingly analogous to continental efforts, British funds were put to far more restricted uses. Since the 1960s, well over 70 per cent of state spending on R & D has gone to the defence, aerospace, and nuclear sectors. By contrast Germany, France, and Japan spent equivalent sums on a broader spectrum of promising industries, including chemicals, electrical goods, transportation, and machine tools.

Finally, the British criteria have tended to channel the remaining selective aid to unprofitable firms and declining sectors. For instance, over £500 million of the £600 million allocated to the National Enterprise Board, which the Labour government established in 1975 to rejuvenate British industry, was spent to rescue a few large firms such as British Leyland, Rolls-Royce, Ferranti, and Alfred Herbert. At first glance this seems eminently reasonable: unprofitable firms most need support. In a few cases, the policy enabled a sound firm to survive; in most cases it sent vast resources to firms or sectors where Britain's prospects could never have been too promising. While most nations began some rescue operations after the 1974 recession, France, Japan, and Germany have been more inclined to focus aid on profitable firms in sectors targeted for long-term growth.

The third component of industrial policy, after the volume of funding and the criteria for support, involves the degree of public pressure used to inspire rationalisation within manufacturing sectors. The object is generally to consolidate existing firms into units of the most efficient size, to improve the level of investment or technology, to alter work practices or product specialisation, and to reallocate resources within and between industrial sectors. State intervention of this sort can take many different forms, however, and it is important to distinguish those in which the government enforces reform on particular firms and industries from those in which state-supported schemes are essentially directed by the private sector. The striking feature of British intervention has been its reliance on the latter. With the exception of an occasional nationalisation, compulsory schemes have been avoided in favour of an approach that has been highly consensual, or 'quasi-corporatist', to use Samuel Beer's (1969: 297) term.

Since 1918, industries in Britain have essentially been asked to rationalise themselves. The government initially encouraged sectors to form trade associations so as to have a partner with whom to bargain. When a sector seemed in need of reorganisation, the government then authorised these associations to negotiate common pricing policies, mergers, production quotas, and investment or marketing schemes with their members; in order to facilitate such schemes, it made public resources available, either in the form of tariff protection during the 1930s or in the form of subsidies, tax concessions, or import quotas during the post-war period. While these resources were often presented as inducements, they were rarely used as sanctions, and the government's role in reorganisation remained limited. Such a consensual approach to industrial policy stands in striking contrast to the more *dirigiste* policies of France or Japan, where sectoral plans were drawn up by the state rather than industry, where individual firms were the direct object of much policy, and where a host of public sanctions was employed to enforce implementation...

The Economist (15 June 1940, cited in Harris, 1972) described interwar industrial policy as:

> a set of notions that sees its ideal of an economic system in an orderly organisation of industries, each ruled feudally from above by the business firms already established in it, linked in associations and confederations and, at the top, meeting on terms of sovereign equality with such other Estates of the Realm as the Bank of England and the Government. Each British industry, faithful to the prescription, has spent the past decade in delimiting its fief, in organising its baronial courts, in securing and entrenching its holdings and administering the legal powers of self-government conferred on it by a tolerant State.

By 1956, over 2,550 restrictive agreements had been made public, and many others undoubtedly remained underground.

Collusive practices were viewed less benevolently in the 1950s, but the general thrust of policy did not change. The Industrial Development and Organisation Act of 1947, which might have begun a process of active economic planning in Britain, left the initiative to form development councils up to private sector actors, with the result that only four were ever established. Apart from belated action on restrictive practices and the introduction of investment allowances, whose impact was marginal at best, the government's principal effort was on regional development. In 1962 the Conservatives established a National Economic Development Council ('Neddy') to discuss economic policy with the Trades Union Congress and Federation of British Industries. Although some policy-makers hoped the Council would become a vehicle for economic planning on the French model, it never assembled the sanctions that put teeth into the French plans. Neddy remained a body for tripartite consultation between government and industry.

The Labour government of 1964–70 tried to introduce a more *dirigiste* industrial policy by establishing a Department of Economic Affairs to formulate national plans, a Ministry of Technology to foster research and development, the Industrial Reconstruction Corporation to facilitate mergers and modernisation in the private sector, and a National Prices and Incomes Board to encourage productivity agreements between industry and labour. However, the DEA failed in the face of Treasury resistance; and the other institutions did not begin to move beyond consensualism until the last eighteen months of their existence. Although these programmes represented a brief attempt to go beyond the existing patterns of policy, they supplied too little too late.

Under the Conservatives in 1970–74 and Labour in 1974–79, industrial policy reverted to its normal course, marked only by larger sums of aid for declining sectors. After an abortive switch to investment allowances, the Industry Act of

1972 restored a system of subsidies, but almost all went to regional development grants or the industrial bail-outs of British Leyland, Rolls-Royce, and Cammell Laird. The industrial policies of the Labour government were very similar. Only one of the 'planning agreements' that the 1973 programme advertised as a scheme for imposing investment plans on industry was ever negotiated; and the National Enterprise Board became little more than a source of capital for ailing firms whose redundancies the government was unwilling to tolerate. The 'new industrial strategy' of November 1975 created thirty-nine sectoral working parties (SWPs) operating by consensus at the sectoral level, much like the state-sponsored cartels of the 1930s.

What were the effects of this pattern of industrial policy? In political terms the answer is clear. Despite the growth of the state apparatus and the nominal extension of intervention, British policy tended to reinforce the power of private sector actors *vis-à-vis* the government. The result was 'less the domination of public over private powers than their interpenetration leading to the creation of a board area of shared authority' (Beer, in Blank, 1973: xi). The principal effect of the SWPs, for instance, was to enhance the capacity of industrial actors to lobby the government for various forms of protection. This suggests that we must be careful to distinguish between different forms of 'state intervention'. The form of the state involvement in the economy that emerged in Britain was fundamentally different from that in France, and it had different consequences. In particular, it was characterised more by the growth of bargaining between the government and the two sides of industry than by the growth of unilateral state control.

Similarly, analyses that treat the British case as the diametrical opposite of a corporatist system may have to be corrected. We should distinguish between the two dimensions of policy-making that 'corporatism' often conflates. When the term refers to a process whereby policy is formulated in a highly centralised fashion by peak associations that can impose agreements on their constituencies, it applies very rarely to the British case. However, to the extent that the term denotes a form of policy-making in which a great deal of policy is the product of bargaining between the state and producers' groups, it clearly applies to Britain more than many other nations. The process is simply less centralised in Britain.

The economic effects of industrial policies are harder to assess. On balance, British policy seems to have reinforced the ability of existing firms to resist market pressure for reorganisation. By providing subsidies, authorisation for price fixing, production quotas, or import protection to these sectors, without at the same time bringing sufficient pressure in favour of rationalisation to bear on the individual firms in an industry, British policy tended to enhance rather than reduce the structural rigidities of many markets. That is reflected in the middling results that have followed from these schemes. For instance, the tariffs and state-sponsored cartelisation of the 1930s kept prices high in many sectors, but did little to tackle the underlying inefficiency of the firms. By contrast, the more activist policies of Germany contributed to the dramatic improvement of its manufacturing base from an even worse situation.

Similarly, most studies of post-war policy conclude that insufficient resources were devoted to the problem, that policy was not sustained enough to produce results, or that it had very little impact on the investment and allocation decisions of private sector actors.   Although British policy cushioned the impact of contraction in declining sectors, it seems to have had little effect on the most serious problem underlying poor economic performance, namely, productivity. Only in the one period when industrial policy veered towards *dirigisme*, under the Labour government of 1964–70, did the growth of the capital–labour ratio and output per person begin to approach continental levels. The experience of other nations, such as France and Japan, suggest that in order to tackle underlying productivity problems Britain would have needed an industrial policy based less on voluntarism and more on rationalisation enforced directly by the state.

The roots of policy

Like British markets, the British political setting was shaped by two of the formative experiences in British history: early industrialisation and empire. Britain's experiences as the 'first industrialiser' and as an imperial power left her with a peculiar set of international relations, financial institutions, producers' organisations, and governmental structures that were revised in the ensuing two centuries but never entirely replaced.

Britain's international position

Although Britain's macroeconomic stance had only a limited impact on her relative economic performance, the government's persistent defence of the pound drew attention and resources away from the problems of the domestic economy. This approach to policy was rooted in the experience of empire. During the interwar period, a clear-cut set of international concerns and obligations pressed policy-makers into the return to gold. Even after British hegemony had declined, however, the imperial legacy continued to influence policy.

One aspect of this legacy was an overhang of foreign sterling balances. The net holdings in sterling and short-term sterling assets of foreigners grew to a considerable size because a major portion of world trade was once conducted in sterling. These balances continued to average £3.5 billion for most of the post-war period, rising at times to as much as £6 billion. They intensified the possibility that any weakening in the exchange rate, or balance of payments deficit, could lead to massive sales of sterling and a precipitous drop in the value of the currency. This heightened the pressure on policy-makers to respond with deflation to any balance of payments crisis; and the latter became a kind of hair-trigger inducing the periodic 'stop-go' cycles of macroeconomic management.

Along with this financial legacy came a diplomatic one. Most of the overseas balances were held in the official reserves of nations who once belonged to the old sterling area. Any fall in the British exchange rate would reduce the value of these reserves and have serious diplomatic repercussions. As a result, British policy-makers were inclined to see devaluation as a form of default on Britain's international obligations. The impact of this consideration influenced civil servants and politicians alike. Although the Bank of England is often portrayed as the only agency resisting devaluation, the Bank itself suggested a floating exchange rate in 1952. The scheme, known as 'Operation Robot', might have left Britain with a more advantageous parity at a critical time in her post-war recovery. However, it was vetoed by the Cabinet on the grounds that any drop in the exchange rate would mean abdication of Britain's duty to the overseas holders of sterling.

Similarly, overseas spending to meet Britain's extensive military and diplomatic obligations intensified pressure on the balance of payments. For most of the post-war period, private sector transactions across the external account were in surplus, but the public sector ran a sufficient deficit to throw the entire balance of payments off and trigger periodic 'stop-go' cycles.

Because Britain had been one of the principal suppliers of capital to the rest of the world, her governments also became accustomed to relying on a surplus in the invisible account, derived primarily from repatriated profits and shipping fees, to make up for a growing deficit in traded goods. When exports began to decline during the interwar period, this cushion reduced the pressure on the state for action to revive manufacturing. Moreover, when Britain was deprived of the surplus by World War II (in which she lost overseas assets worth £100 million a year to the balance of payments and acquired significant external liabilities), the nation was bound to face recurring balance of payments problems. A series of post-war governments had to face the consequences of relying far too long on the financial advantages of imperial power.

Finally, the experience of empire left Britain with a set of financial institutions that were heavily oriented towards overseas lending. Therefore, the City became a powerful lobby against devaluation, which was widely expected to weaken international confidence in British financial markets, and a proponent of deflation in the face of balance of payments crises. A pertinent contrast is Germany, where the bank's equity position in domestic industry and the country's less developed international role gave them a stronger interest in policies that would expand German industry and exports. The German financial sector agitated successfully to keep the Deutschmark undervalued on the world exchanges.

Societal structure

There are those who discount the effect that society can have on public policy because they point, quite properly, to the ability of the state to resist societal pressure. However, this view neglects the fact that, in the era of the managed economy, public policy is implemented to a great extent through societal rather than state organisations. Therefore, differences in the organisation of society may, on the one hand, affect the problems with which states are forced to deal, and on the other hand, may affect their capacity to implement policies that tackle these problems. In these respects, two features of British society had profound consequences for economic policy.

The nature of British financial institutions and their relationship to industrial capital was one such feature. Partly because the nation industrialised during the textile era, when start-up costs were low, British manufacturers came to depend primarily on internally generated funds and public issues of equity for finance. Therefore, Britain did not develop the large investment banks common to the Continent. Because the latter held long-term debt or equity in most sectors, they became interested in industrial modernisation, capable of financing it, and influential enough to enforce it on recalcitrant firms. Since Britain acquired no such co-ordinating agents, the tasks facing the British state were greater than those in many other nations.

In addition, the organisation of British financial markets limited the state's ability to control the flows of funds in the banking system in order to finance or induce compliance with a more aggressive industrial policy. Industry was relatively independent from the banks because it borrowed only over the short term and relatively sparingly from them; and, in any event, the banks were insulated from government control by the powerful Bank of England. Even after nationalisation in 1949, the Bank used its quasi-autonomous status to resist any reforms that might adversely affect the City. Its sponsorships of the Bankers Industrial Development Co. in 1930, the Industrial and Commercial Finance Corporation in 1945, and the Finance Corporation for Industry in 1946 were all undertaken to forestall the more radical attempts of a Labour government to establish public investment banks.

The relevant counter-case is that of France, where the long-term lending practices of the banks gave them considerable leverage over industry, and the detailed control that the Ministry of Finance exercised over the flows of funds in the financial sector through the subordinate Bank of France allowed it to orchestrate the investment strategies of entire industrial sectors long before President Mitterrand came to office. These institutions, rather than those of the Planning Commission, were the real key to the *économie concertée*.

The form of organisation of British labour and employers placed another set of constraints on state economic policy. Britain had developed a strong labour movement by 1918, when over four million people were affiliated to a trade union, and by 1975 union membership covered 50 per cent of the work force. Since large portions of labour were organised along craft lines, however, the Trades Union Congress remained a loose federation without much central control over its members. Employers' associations took a similar form: organisation was extensive, but most national associations were merely loose confederations of smaller units.

The organisational strength of the unions forced the government into negotiating with them to secure industrial peace, initially during World War I and then in the interwar period. The Ministry of Labour expanded more than any other agency in this era; and these early attempts to bargain with the representatives of labour and capital set a pattern for most subsequent policies in the industrial arena. The British state passed up unilateral action in favour of negotiating the path of subsequent arrangements with organised labour and capital.

If the strength of the unions *vis-à-vis* the government initially pressed the state into a particular pattern of policy *formulation* based on bargaining, however, the internal weakness of union and employer organisations, *vis-à-vis* their members, limited the options facing the government for policy *implementation*. In particular, it prevented the state from using these associations to impose industrial reorganisation on their members, as nations with more corporatist arrangements were able to do. Thus the Mond-Turner talks of 1928, several agreements with the CBI, and a series of incomes policies broke down in the face of rank-and-file defections. The organisational features of Britain's unions and employers' associations rendered them more effective as veto groups than as positive contributors to an active industrial policy.

State structure

Finally, Britain was governed throughout this period by a state that had a particular institutional structure, imparting a consistent bias to policy. Just as the shape of a market influences the behaviour of individuals in it, so the structure of the state affects the set of incentives, balance of power, and flow of information facing individuals at different positions within it. This, in turn, influences the kind of policies they are likely to implement. Because policy is the product of a collective process, the particular form of aggregation that each state uses influences the outcome.

The British state contained a particularly powerful central bank, which was a private corporation until 1949 and even afterwards retained the right to hire its own staff, deal directly with the prime minister, and take public positions at variance with government policy.

Because Bank officials saw themselves as spokesmen for an internationally oriented financial community, custodians of the exchange rate, and financiers for the public debt, they tended to oppose devaluation, alterations to the financial system, and expansionary measures that might lead to higher borrowing or balance of payments difficulties. Therefore, they acted as a powerful force for fiscal conservatism in both the interwar and post-war periods.

The other institution at the heart of British policy apparatus has been HM Treasury. For most of the period, it supervised all departmental promotions and every spending proposal going to the Cabinet. As a result, the 'Treasury view' exercised a pervasive influence throughout the civil service. One Minister of Labour, for instance, complained that his departmental staff lacked 'the necessary audacity of imagining schemes which they felt would certainly be frowned on by the Treasury' (Lowe, 1978: 283).

The Treasury emerged from the nineteenth century as an institution dedicated to the control of public expenditure. Until a few changes were made in 1975, its officials had virtually no familiarity with, or direct concern for, the progress of British industry. Therefore, they were far more likely to suggest reductions, rather than expansion, in the funds being spent on industry. Just as the Treasury opposed granting spending powers to the industrial commissions of the 1930s, so it opposed the National Enterprise Board in 1975. Moreover, Gladstone existed uneasily beside Keynes. The Treasury rejected fiscal expansion in the 1920s and 1930s in order to protect the exchange rate and public debt; and many post-war officials, with one eye on rising expenditure totals, were relieved to be able to use balance of payments problems as an excuse for reducing public spending. As late as 1962 there were still no more than a dozen economists in the Treasury: its principal focus remained the control of expenditure, yet it has continued to dominate economic policy-making. The British case stands in contrast to that of France or Germany, where one of the principal preoccupations of the Ministry of Finance and Economics is the economic conditions facing industry, or that of Japan, where the Ministry of International Trade and Industry is far more powerful in such matters than the Ministry of Finance.

The organisation of the British civil service also reduces the state's capacity to pursue innovative economic policies. Its upper echelons are staffed almost exclusively with personnel who spent their life in the service; information and advice is channelled to political leaders through a few individuals at the top of the hierarchy; and promotion is dependent on the approval of these civil servants rather than that of elected officials. Most economic decisions are made in great secrecy, and few official documents are ever exposed to public scrutiny. As a result, the access of political leaders to alternative sources of advice is limited; power is concentrated in the hands of those with the greatest interest in long-standing approaches to policy. The character of the civil service system and the politics-administration nexus in Britain may thus contribute to the extraordinary continuity that has characterised her economic and industrial policies.

The political system

Does this mean there was no room for change in the British system? In many nations, a coalition of social groups, forged by political elites around a new set of policies, has been the agency for a major change in direction. Why did we not see the emergence of such a coalition dedicated to a more activist industrial policy in Britain? To answer this question we must consider the institutional features of the wider political system, including both the political parties and interest intermediaries in Britain who would have had to organise such a coalition.

In the first place, the nature of the constituent groups who would form the building-blocks of such coalitions was different in Britain from that in many other nations. Early commercialisation of agriculture, marked by widespread enclosures and the rapid spread of industrialisation, reduced the independent farmers to very small numbers by 1918. Unlike the Social Democrats in Sweden and the Democrats in the United States, therefore, the Labour Party in Britain lacked the option of forming a workers-farmers' alliance around farm supports and reflationary policies. Similarly, the more pronounced divisions between industrial entrepreneurs and the financial sector in Britain meant that business pressure on both parties was more heavily weighed towards the concerns of international finance than in many other nations.

If a new social coalition were to take power in Britain, it would also have to do so through the party system. However, party organisations develop deeply rooted doctrines which become central to their existence and resistant to change because they link leaders to followers and the parties' present actions to their past ones. In Britain, these doctrines contained long-standing lines of thought that tended to militate against more coercive state intervention. In addition, the close ties that British parties developed with particular interest groups also limited their range of action.

Within the Conservative Party, two strains of thought existed uneasily side by side. One segment, associated with the Tory democracy of Disraeli, was prepared to condone a measure of intervention, in the form of regulations or transfer programmes to limit the effects of the market on the populace. In the 1930s, for instance, a small group of MPs associated with Harold Macmillan agitated for industrial reorganisation, but they sought statutory authority only for schemes that had the support of a substantial majority of the firms in an industry. During the post-war period, these ideas were pressed most strongly by a group of MPs around R. A. Butler, who persuaded the party to accept the basic programmes of the welfare state. However, in the industrial sphere, the most they were willing to advocate were consultative mechanisms such as those mentioned in the Industrial Charter of 1947.

Even these proposals encountered opposition from the other strain of thought that ran through party doctrine. Its proponents defended the unimpeded operation of market mechanisms and opposed most forms of state intervention altogether. Their influence within the party can be traced to the *laissez-faire* sentiments that many businessmen defecting from the Liberals brought to the party at the turn of the century; but they became particularly powerful in the mid-1950s and again after Mrs Thatcher assumed the leadership in 1975. Neither stream of Conservative thought condoned state intervention of the sort that right-wing governments in France frequently practised. Moreover, the proposals of

Tory democrats were always susceptible to defeat within the party by a coalition of free market ideologists and the business leaders who were respected advisors to the party on such issues. Macmillan's schemes for industrial reorganisation in the 1930s lost to just such a coalition.

In some respects, the Labour Party seems a more appropriate vehicle for an activist industrial policy. Its post-war programme of nationalisation certainly reflected a clear-cut willingness to intervene. However, the long-standing ideology of the party centred on precisely this – nationalisation – and not on how the state might be used to revive private industry. Labour MPs were reluctant to use public funds for schemes that raised profits; they were more interested in reducing unemployment in declining sectors. For instance, Labour members attacked the British Sugar (Subsidies) Bill of 1924 on the grounds that it was inappropriate for the government to subsidise any private industry. In a mixed economy, however, an efficient industrial policy must often direct funds away from declining sectors to more promising, and perhaps already profitable, sectors and firms. The highly effective and interventionist industrial policies of France and Japan were conducted during long periods of *conservative* rule. In Sweden and Austria, socialist governments were careful to adapt their policies to a mixed economy.

The close ties between British political parties and particular interest intermediaries also constrained their action. It is often observed that Britain has a 'strong' state, or one relatively impervious to direct pressure from organised interest groups; and it is true that the British executive dominates the legislature, employs a highly insulated bureaucracy, and concentrates power in the hands of the Cabinet. However, British political parties have enjoyed no such insulation. The trade unions pay most of the Labour Party's expenses and dominate its annual conference; many Conservative MPs not only depend on business interests for their electoral funds but continue to devote a substantial portion of their time to employment in the City or industry while in office. Therefore, while both parties have a degree of independence that derives from their need to appeal to a broad cross-section of society, their policies have been heavily influenced by the groups on whom they depend for finance, advice, and personnel. These groups were also inclined to oppose state intervention in the industrial area.

In contrast to many socialist parties in Europe, which embraced Marxism and interventionist doctrine before they formed an alliance with the trade unions, the Labour Party was created to defend the independence of the labour movement. The formative experiences of the British trade unions, which pitted them against a state attempting to break their power, left them staunch opponents of any policies that seemed to limit their autonomy to determine wages and working conditions through collective bargaining. The lessons of Taff Vale and the Osborne decision remained alive in the memories of many trade unionists. So the Labour governments that came to power in the interwar period strove not so much to revive British manufacturing as to protect the industrial power of the unions. This goal lent their economic policies a non-interventionist cast.

In the post-war era, Labour's approach to industry was again primarily consultative. Representatives who urged more activist policies at the annual conference often met stiff opposition from a coalition of party leaders (influenced by the structural constraints of Government and electoral appeal) and trade unionists who saw such policies as a threat to their autonomy in the workplace.

Within the Conservative Party, the influence of City interests, concerned about international confidence rather than industrial modernisation, has been particularly strong. Even the employers' associations remained defenders of the status quo structure of industry. They did not become the agents for a rationalising alliance between the most dynamic sections of capital and the state that the French CNPF became in the 1970s. Although a few businessmen, such as Sir Alfred Mond, were willing to consider such an alliance, the British employer's associations were never ready to endorse an interventionist policy. Because they were trying to assemble a broad membership, ever ready to desert to competing associations, they usually refrained from any action that might disturb the vested interests of their members. Therefore, just as the unions waged bitter battles against industrial relations legislation in 1968 and 1971, the employers fought to remove selective inducements from the Coal Mines (Reorganisation) Act of 1930, the Industrial Organisation and Development Bill of 1954, and the Industry Act of 1972.

The two post-war conjunctures

The inertia of the political system became most important during the critical conjunctures that followed the two world wars. Many European nations seized these moments to change direction. Although Britain did not suffer the trauma that accompanied defeat, these were periods of widespread disillusionment with the old order and rising aspirations for the future. The extension of intervention during the war also provided a precedent on which the state might have built a new industrial policy. Why did the political system not respond?

The prospects for change after World War I depended heavily on the possibility that an interventionist coalition might emerge around Lloyd George. As Minister of Munitions and Prime Minister during the war, Lloyd George masterminded Britain's first serious steps toward state direction of industrial resources. He drew to his side Winston Churchill and the most interventionist of the Conservatives, such as Austen Chamberlain, Lord Birkenhead, Arthur Balfour, and Stanley Salvadge; and it was widely believed that they might form a Fusion Party. Drawing on the intellectual legacy of Joseph Chamberlain and Randolph Churchill, such a party might have built a programme around the extension of tariffs, the welfare state, and the enforced rationalisation of industry.

However, Lloyd George was viewed as a dangerous maverick, and the chances for fusion faded when Bonar Law's followers threw their support to the Conservatives rather than trust his machinations. Adroit manoeuvring by Stanley

Baldwin, which committed the Conservative Party to protection before Lloyd George could draw support on that issue, sealed the fate of the Fusionists. Britain's future would lie with the Conservatives or Labour.

At a second critical conjuncture, after World War II, Labour secured a majority in Parliament and inherited a system of physical controls that might have been adapted, as in France, to industrial planning. After implementing the nationalisation proposals of its 1945 manifesto, however, the government did little else to influence the direction of industry. Precisely the sort of factors outlined above inhibited further action. The trade unions opposed any extension of manpower planning, and opposition from business associations scuttled Stafford Cripps' attempt to establish tripartite development councils in most industries. The desperate state of the balance of payments preoccupied economic policy-makers, and inhibited any attempts to reorganise the financial sector. With one eye on the export earnings of insurance, for instance, the Treasury opposed Aneurin Bevan's plans to nationalise the industrial assurance companies; and the nationalisation of the Bank of England remained a technical exercise. It retained control of the Bank rate, and the rest of the financial sector remained untouched. Despite the reforms in other areas, the post-war Labour government missed its opportunity to take control over the domestic flows of capital within the financial sector. The French case suggests that such a move would have been necessary if a more active industrial policy or effective system of planning were to have been implemented.

Instead, the remaining energies of the Labour government went into the creation of the social programmes, such as unemployment insurance, superannuation, and the National Health Service, that we now associate with the welfare state. They were a remarkable achievement, and one around which support could be rallied much more readily within both the party and the electorate, who were more interested in social reform than in socialism. On the economic side of its platform, the party needed most of all a plank that seemed to make full employment possible. Its leaders were gradually won over to the view that a version of Keynesianism, based on the management of aggregate demand, could accomplish this task. This was an important step. Since Keynesianism seemed to provide a technique for achieving full employment without the need for more detailed intervention into the decisions of industrial sectors, it was instrumental in persuading both parties that they could abandon economic planning without sacrificing economic performance. As such, Keynesianism played a major role in the victory of the 'revisionists' within the Labour Party, and contributed to the convergence in party politics known as 'Butskellism'. The nation that most avidly embraced Keynesianism also adopted the most arm's-length industrial policy in Europe. In that respect, while Keynes's doctrine solved many of the parties' political problems, it by no means solved Britain's economic problems.

Conclusion

This analysis suggests that the state is not primarily responsible for Britain's economic decline. But it is not an innocent bystander. If the principal causes of economic decline lie elsewhere, successive British governments did little to address them. There were alternatives. The French experience in the post-war period suggests that a state can transform the operation of its economic system, but first it must transform itself. The British have found that difficult because institutional rigidities affected the actions of the British state, just as such rigidities influenced the operation of the British economy. The structure of Britain's international position, state, and society pushed policy-makers in a particular direction by influencing the perceived costs and benefits that accrued to any one policy.

This observation has important implications for contemporary theories of the state. None of the main theoretical alternatives quite fits the British case. Those who explain state action as a response to the dictates of capital or the functional imperatives of capitalism cannot explain the inadequacies of British policy from the point of view of capital or the great variation in policies across capitalist nations. Pluralists who view the state as a respondent to the concerns of competing social groups miss the fact that policy-makers had interests and inclinations of their own and that the biases inherent in their institutional setting precluded an equal response to all groups. And the more recent group of state-centric theorists who view the state as a free-floating actor, generating its preferences in relative autonomy from the rest of society, cannot explain how the preferences of the state are generated. They imply that the policy preferences of the state are relatively unaffected by the configuration of society; yet if there is one lesson to be learned from the course of British economic policy, it is that policy is not made from a *tabula rasa*; policy-makers are profoundly influenced by societal factors.

In short, this case suggests that we need a theory of the state that recognises that policy-makers' actions are deeply conditioned by the institutional structures within which they operate. We already know that the structure of the state and its position in the international system can affect the preferences of policy-makers and their capacity to act. Here we see that these preferences and capacities can also be affected by the configuration of societal institutions such as trade unions and banking systems, as well as the institutional memory embedded in the organisations of the wider political system. Nowhere is this more true than in Britain.

The very stability of the British political system, so long a valued asset, has become something of a liability in an era of rapid economic change. The consequences have been grave because economic failure in the modern age is also political failure. After several decades in which politicians claimed credit for every economic success, electorates have begun to hold them responsible for every economic failure. Consequently, Britain's economic crises engendered a crisis of political authority. One of the results has been a profound disruption in the party system, marked by increasing electoral volatility, partisan dealignment, and the rise of a new party. Another has been the election of a government that rejected the Keynesianism on which post-war consensus was built.

Margaret Thatcher was elected in 1979 because many sections of the electorate were dissatisfied not only with the performance of the economy but also with the rising level of conflict between trade unions and the state. Such conflict invariably appeared during the penultimate stage of tripartite bargains about incomes policy, which had become an indispensable supplement to the Keynesian techniques of successive post-war governments. It was often disruptive enough to defeat the government at the next election. In that sense, an 'industrial relations cycle' has been as important as the political business cycle in Britain. In short, the Thatcher government came to power as much because of a backlash against the system of functional representation which had become central to economic policy-making in Britain as because that system produced poor economic results.

Under Thatcher, the Conservatives mounted an electoral appeal that spoke directly to dissatisfaction with the tripartite bargaining of the past. Drawing on the *laissez-faire* strain of Conservative thought, Thatcher repudiated the consensualist Keynesianism which had dominated the economic thinking of both parties for forty years. Her advisors adapted monetarist economic theory into a highly political creed that promised economic prosperity without the need for either corporatist bargaining or state intervention in much the same way that Labourites had adapted Keynesianism for another purpose thirty years before.

Perhaps because this version of monetarism has such an affinity with the neo-classical economics of the 1920s, the course of policy under the Thatcher government has closely resembled policy in that decade. The pursuit of a lower borrowing requirement, spending reductions, lower taxes on the upper incomes, a tight monetary policy, and initially a high exchange rate have all been rationalised in very similar terms; and once again these policies reflect a greater sensitivity to the concerns of the City than to those of British industry. In these respects, there has been a real continuity between Mrs Thatcher's macroeconomic policies and those of the interwar period. Some would argue there has also been a continuity of result.

The object of the Thatcher government [was] to reinforce the operation of market mechanisms in the hope that they will rejuvenate the economy with a minimum of state intervention. Its goal [was] to begin a new period of *laissez-faire*. Paradoxically, however, the task required a great deal of state intervention in order to alter many long-standing practices and institutions in the economy. The Thatcher regime [was] characterised by what Andrew Gamble termed 'the strong state in a weak economy' (Gamble, 1979). The government attacked the power of the trade unions by limiting their rights to strike, enforcing lay-offs in the nationalised industries, and limiting wage settlements in the public sector. To enforce public spending reductions, far-reaching changes [were] made in relationships with the local authorities and the programmes of the welfare state. Several firms have been denationalised; and the movement of capital has been decontrolled.

These measures altered many aspects of the British economy. As a result of government pressure and rising levels of unemployment, the unions have been forced to accept lay-offs, de-skilling, and the reorganisation of work. An austere economic climate drove many small firms out of business and compelled the large enterprises to contract. The British economy has been put on a diet, and some of its operations are undoubtedly slimmer. In this light the government's policies can be seen as a break with the recent past. They represent one, classically conservative, strategy for tackling Britain's problems.

However, there are many defects in such a strategy. Policies aimed primarily at the unions tackle rigidities on only one side of the economic system. The Thatcher government did little to correct the defects in management, supply of investment, organisation of production, and distribution that are more significant obstacles to the effective performance of British capitalism. Moreover, the trade unions are not going to disappear, and the Thatcher policies provided no basis for constructive dealings with them over the long term.

Second, these policies are based on the premise that self-regulating markets can be relied upon to restore British industry to a healthy international status. However, attempts to secure industrial adjustment exclusively through market mechanisms are likely to fail. Even with unions at their weakest, British industries do not move naturally towards international competitiveness. The monetarist vision depends on a neo-classical image of self-equilibrating markets that simply does not conform to reality.

Finally, Thatcher's economic policy relied on the sanctions of economic austerity to enforce changes in behaviour. As such, it exacted costs that threatened to destroy much of Britain's industrial base before rendering it more efficient. The kind of efficiencies secured under Thatcher derived from losses of labour rather than from a more fundamental reorganisation of the productive apparatus. As such, they imposed tremendous human hardship yet provided few long-term benefits. Similarly, most of the government's economies [were] secured by cuts in spending on capital programmes rather than in current expenditure, and so ran down the social infrastructure on which further growth depends.

The Thatcher experiment, however, indicated that political parties remain vehicles for innovation in economic policy. Institutional analysis of the polity, as of the economy, underlines the magnitude of the obstacles that stand in the way of reform; but it also reminds us that economic performance is not entirely a matter of fate or the product of iron laws in economics. The institutions that affect the performance of the economy are ultimately shaped by political action, and from time to time we may recast them.

CHAPTER 26

Military spending and the British economy[*]

Malcolm Chalmers

Military spending has contributed to Britain's relative economic decline in three interrelated ways. First, it has taken place at the expense of investment, rather than consumption. As a result, the capacity for future production (and consumption) has risen relatively slowly. Secondly, it has used a disproportionate amount of scarce high-technology inputs. These have not been available for civilian use, and the rate of technical progress outside the military sector has been slowed as a result. Thirdly, it has harmed the UK balance of payments, both through diversion of resources from industries, and by the high level of overseas military expenditure. This has in turn resulted in policies of economic management which have damaged investment, and thus long-term growth potential.

Military spending and investment

The main cause of Britain's low level of growth in productivity and output has been a persistently low level of productive investment ...

Arms spending competes directly with civilian investment for scarce resources both in the equipment production sector and in research and development. The competition for the resources of the equipment production sector was particularly important in the period after the outbreak of the Korean war in 1950, when a programme of rearmament led to arms spending almost trebling in two years – from £286 million in 1950–51 to £524 million in 1952–53 ...

The diversion of machine tools to the defence sector resulted in a cut in civilian deliveries of about one-third, despite increased deliveries from the US, and subsequently led to reductions in investment and export performance. In

---

[*] Reproduced with permission from *Paying for Defence*, Pluto Press, 1985.

1959, Denis Healey noted that Britain's engineering industry, crucial to its exports, had been 'particularly hard hit by rearmament' while its commercial rivals, especially West Germany, were not similarly hampered (Healey, 1959) ...

Probably as important as the strain on the capacity of the engineering industry was the demand for the limited resources for R & D, and in particular for first-rate research personnel. The concentration of R & D effort in the defence sector was particularly marked in the 1950s as Britain sought to keep up with the technological arms race between the superpowers. Germany and Japan were capturing one market after another in steel, ship-building, machinery, etc., while British scientists and engineers were concentrated in fields such as aircraft, atomic energy, and radar. Military R & D grew from £71 million in 1950–51 to £204 million in 1956–57. By the latter year, 40 per cent of all professionally qualified scientists and engineers engaged in R & D were working on defence projects. In 1955–56 almost 60 per cent of national R & D was financed from defence funds, and nearly two-thirds of the research done by private industry was on defence contracts. At the same time the mechanical engineering industry, shipbuilding and steel had scarcely any graduate engineers in any positions before the 1960s, in marked contrast to the prominent place they held in German industry ...

In the 1980s, Britain's high level of arms spending continues to deprive civilian industry of the scarce skilled personnel that are necessary for technical innovation, productivity growth and efficient investment. The opportunities lost are particularly costly in growing new areas such as 'information technology' ...

'Spin-off'

An important argument for arms production has been that there will be 'spin-offs' benefiting technical progress in civilian products. It is an argument which can clearly be countered by pointing out that it would almost certainly be possible to use R & D resources more effectively were they to be applied directly to the advance of civilian technology. Chance by-products of military R & D can at best reduce, not eliminate, the cost to the civilian economy.

In the period we are considering, however, there are two further important objections. The first is that some investment in 'spin-off' civilian sectors has itself been an uneconomic use of resources and thus a further cost, not a benefit, to the economy. The second is that modern military technology has increasingly diverged from civilian technology, and therefore the scope for spin-off has been reduced.

The British aerospace industry produces both military and civilian products, and provides a good example of 'negative spin-off'. The production and export of civilian aircraft and parts depends to some extent on knowledge and skills acquired in military production, and vice versa. This has meant that considerable subsidies have been given for the maintenance of the civil aerospace industry, the funds provided for the survival of Rolls-Royce and the cost of Concorde being two good examples. In a 1976 report to the Department of Industry, N. K. Gardiner estimated that over £1,500 million (at 1974 prices) of government finance had been invested in *civil* aerospace since 1945 for a return of under £150 million. Despite these subsidies, however, the enormous economies of scale in the aerospace industry ensured that the US, with its much larger investments, would remain supreme in world markets. Other medium-sized nations, such as Germany and Japan, avoided aerospace, concentrating their research efforts in products in which they had a greater long-run comparative advantage ...

The need to maintain and develop civilian products, in which other nations have a clear comparative advantage, so as to build or keep a capacity for military production, thus constituted an indirect cost of arms spending and defence policy, and resulted in the concentration of R & D in a relatively small number of sectors.

The second objection to the spin-off arguments rests on the proposition that modern military technological development increasingly puts an emphasis on custom-built, highly sophisticated, low volume production in direct contrast to the emphasis on high volume inexpensive products for civilian markets ...

The arms trade

Successive governments have claimed that the export of armaments constitutes a valuable spin-off from Britain's investment in its arms industry. Whatever else one might think about the wisdom or morality of such a trade, it must be conceded that some benefit to Britain's balance of payments does accrue because of the £2,400 million of annual military exports. The hidden costs of this are, however, substantial. Given the scale of resources devoted to arms production, the return is relatively poor. Italy, with a level of defence spending less than 40 per cent that of the UK, had a roughly equal share of the world arms market in 1979–83. And France, whose total defence budget is comparable to Britain's, exported two and a half times as much during the same period ...

Finally, while arms exports may provide a limited plus for the balance of payments, this is outweighed (for arms exports as a whole) by their economic and political costs. A truer measure of their costs can only be obtained by asking: how would the volume of exports be changed if the resources used were re-deployed elsewhere in the economy? Since over a quarter of total R & D (government and civilian) is spent on defence, yet only 3½ per cent of visible exports are provided, it would be surprising if the answer was favourable for the arms trade. It is clear that the existence of a British arms industry cannot be justified by the contribution it makes to the balance of payments. At best, arms exports offset only a small part of the costs of that industry. More probably, they add a further burden, and contribute Britain's part in the rapid militarisation of the Third World.

Military spending and the balance of payments

Military spending indirectly affected the balance of payments by (i) diverting production from industries – such as engineering – whose production could otherwise have been used for export, (ii) reducing the rate of modernisation in civilian sectors, thus harming their long-run international competitiveness in both domestic and overseas markets ...

In addition to these indirect effects, there was, and is, the direct effect of overseas military spending. First, Britain maintained bases in the Middle and Far East for part or all of this time which were costly in foreign exchange – Suez, Aden, Singapore, Hong Kong, etc. Secondly, its forces were almost continuously engaged in 'limited' counter-insurgency conflict in the Empire, and also in occasional larger wars. Finally, as a result of the commitment in 1954 to maintain permanently a substantial peacetime force in West Germany, a considerable proportion of the British Army and Air Force is stationed in that country, adding further to foreign exchange costs.

Together, these overseas commitments have added a considerable burden to the balance of payments ... [and] contrasted with the substantial surpluses of countries – such as Germany and Japan – which benefit, economically at least, from the presence of foreign troops. British spending in Germany alone, some £957 million in 1984–85, constitutes a substantial transfer from the balance of payments of a weak industrial nation to that of its main European competitor. Indeed, an examination of the statistics shows that government overseas expenditure – of which military spending has been the most important component – may in itself help to explain Britain's persistent balance of payments crisis. For the period 1958–81, Britain had accumulated commercial surplus of £16,710 million offset by a government deficit of £30,330 million. Of this, £9,790 million was the deficit in military spending overseas. Although part of the government deficit was accounted for by aid to less developed countries, Britain's record in this area was by no means exceptionally generous. It is in military spending that Britain had a particularly large deficit.

The costs of the world role

There is thus considerable evidence that Britain's high level of military spending since the Second World War has been an important contributory factor in its relative economic decline. As important as the direct effects of military spending, however, have been the indirect effects of a foreign policy that has consistently given preference to the attempt to retain a world rule above domestic economic performance. Indeed, Samuel Brittan, in a seminal study of post-war Treasury policy, concluded that:

The excessive 'overseas' orientation among the upper reaches of British policy-makers ... gave priority to the maintenance of a world role the country could no longer carry ... While British leaders rushed from capital to capital on self-appointed international peace-keeping missions, the rest of the world was more conscious of the rustle of their begging bowl, their utter dependence on the USA, their repeated humiliation by de Gaulle ... The best that governments can do to help recover a healthy patriotism and sense of national pride is to concentrate on the welfare of the inhabitants of these isles. (Brittan, 1969)

This priority has been reflected in a number of ways – the commitment to sterling's reserve role, the high levels of overseas investment, the failure to join the European Community at an earlier moment, and, not least, the high level of military spending ...

A particularly damaging consequence of the world role was the continuing export of capital on a massive scale. During 1946–59 the outflow of British capital amounted to £4,000 million, most of it to Overseas Sterling Area countries. This was an annual rate of £280 million, or between a quarter and a third of domestic net investment. The export of capital on this scale was actively encouraged by the government despite the long-run damage to domestic growth and its contribution in the short run to balance of payments deficits. Without a military presence to protect British overseas investment, the level of capital flow would have been considerably lower. There appears to be a clear falling off in UK investment in areas where British military withdrawal took place. Thus overseas military spending not only directly hurt the current account but indirectly ensured a deterioration in the capital account.

Nor was the British military commitment confined to the maintenance of bases. Inevitably it also involved participation in a series of limited conflicts, some of which proved extremely costly ...

Overseas military spending, therefore, was an essential component of a set of interrelated circumstances which resulted from a failure to adjust to the political disintegration of the British Empire and the diminished economic strength of the UK. Without it, the level of overseas investment would have been lower and the Sterling Area would have been wound up sooner – both of which could have done the domestic economy no harm.

CHAPTER 27

A critique of Olson[*]

David Cameron

Among the many nations from which Olson draws support for his theory, none is more frequently mentioned or alluded to than Britain. The coincidence in Britain of an old and (allegedly) stable political system, a proliferation of narrow interest groups (particularly within the labour movement), and a relatively low rate of growth in the post-war era apparently provides strong confirmation of the theory. Applying his 'logic' to the British case, Olson states:

> Countries that have had democratic freedom of organisation without upheaval or invasion the longest will suffer the most from growth-repressing organisations and combinations. This helps to explain why Great Britain, the major nation with the longest immunity from dictatorship, invasion, and revolution, has had in this century a lower rate of growth than other large, developed democracies ... With age British society has acquired so many strong organisations and collusions that it suffers from an institutional sclerosis that slows its adaptation to changing circumstances and technologies (Olson, 1982: 778)

Olson's interpretation of the British experience is problematic in several ways. For one thing, it is by no means obvious (to a sceptical reader, at least) that Britain suffers more than other countries from 'growth-repressing organisations'. Nor is it obvious that so many special-interest organisations exist in Britain that it suffers from 'institutional sclerosis' (although, since Olson did not define the term, it is difficult to assess the argument). And it is simply incorrect to argue that Britain has had the lowest rate of growth among the major capitalist democracies in the twentieth century. In regard to this last point, the

---

[*] Reproduced with permission from 'Distributional coalitions and other causes of economic stagnation', *International Organisation*, **42**: 592–604, 1988.

comparative data demonstrate that while Britain's gross domestic product did grow slowly in the years immediately before and after World War I, its growth was about average in the 1920s and was well above average in the 1930s, in spite of the Depression. In fact, it emerged from the Depression sooner than most nations, and in the late 1930s it experienced a growth rate well above those of France, Italy, Canada, the Low Countries, and Scandinavia (although the unemployment rate exceeded 10 per cent throughout the interwar period). In the early and middle 1940s, through World War II, Britain experienced an aggregate growth rate well above those of France and Germany. In short, although Britain's growth rate was quite low throughout the twentieth century, it was not until the post-war period that its rate of growth began to deviate significantly from those of other major nations.

More important than these several problems of definition and data is the possibility that, as with Germany and other countries, Olson's attribution of growth rates to the characteristics of group life in Britain constitutes an impressive exercise in spurious correlation. It may well be the case that Britain's highly fragmented labour movement, some segments of which have enduring traditions of militancy (for example, the miners), has contributed to the stagnation of the post-war era. But it is equally plausible that union militance represents, as Bacon and Eltis argue, an effect rather than a cause of slow growth and stagnation (Bacon and Eltis, 1976).

It would be presumptuous to pretend that we could, in a few paragraphs, identify and assess the relative importance of all the possible sources of Britain's historic experience of slow growth in various periods over the last century. As Gamble says of that experience,

It has become the most observed and analysed decline in modern history, provoking a speculative literature of enormous dimensions. Few explanations have not been proffered, few causes not dissected, few remedies not canvassed at least twice. (Gamble, 1981: xxi)

But it is nevertheless possible to extract from that literature several essential factors that may account for the low rate of growth in Britain over the last century and, in particular, over the last four decades, none of which involves the proliferation of narrow, 'growth-repressing' special-interest organisations.

Among the most important of the many factors that may account for the relatively low rate of growth in Britain, especially in the post-war period, are these:

1. The absence after the war (as well as for several decades before the war) of a large pool of unproductive and cheap labour, such as existed in France, Italy, Japan, and (because of the inflow of refugees and expelled persons) Germany. Britain's early industrialisation and its highly labour-intensive phase in the

nineteenth century, accompanied as it was by the massive flow of population into the industrial cities, eliminated that source of under-utilised labour much earlier than in nations where industrialisation began later and was more partial in its development. Thus, in contrast to Britain, in which by 1870 less than one-quarter of the labour force worked in agriculture and in which by 1945 less than one-tenth was so employed, in France, Italy, and Japan approximately one-third of the work force was still in agriculture after World War II.

2. The simultaneous rapid industrialisation, during the last half of the nineteenth century, of several nations which sought to protect domestic markets from British (and other foreign-produced) goods while challenging British domination in the world economy.

3. The relatively low rate of capital formation in Britain during much of the last century, reflecting in large part the combined effects of substantial capital outflow throughout the period and domestic stagnation.

4. The gradual obsolescence of British plant and equipment and production processes, relative to those of later-industrialising nations which sought to obtain competitive advantages by telescoping technological change.

5. The loss in the wars of the twentieth century of a considerable portion of the stock of human capital – capital that was, because of Britain's longer experience as an industrial economy, more highly developed than in many of its competitors.

6. The loss, after World War II, of colonies in Africa, South Asia, and the Caribbean, with their cheap sources of raw material, cheap labour, and captive markets. Of these, India, with a population ten times of Britain, was of particular importance as a market in which Britain enjoyed a privileged position.

7. The refusal to join the European Economic Community at its founding – in spite of the large prospective market it offered – as governing elites sought to preserve a special status for Britain *vis-à-vis* Europe.

8. The pervasive after-effects on British fiscal and monetary policy of its dominant role in the world economy throughout the nineteenth and early twentieth centuries, in spite of the diminution of that role, particularly after World War II.

What is most noteworthy about this abbreviated list of possible sources of slow growth in Britain is the inclusion of several factors that involve international economics and politics. If Britain's slow growth reflected (among other things) its early industrialisation, relative to other nations, the rise of later-industrialising challengers, the outflow of capital, the costs of war, the loss of colonies, the effects of delayed entry into the EEC, and the international constraints on domestic economic policy, then the explanation of that growth would have to be cast in terms that would encompass the nation's historic and evolving position in the world economy, and the policy responses through which that position was maintained or altered, rather than the purely domestic, social organisational characteristics emphasised by Olson. Since, as we noted above, Olson relies heavily upon the British case for confirmation of his theory, it is useful to elaborate this alternative, internationalist explanation in some detail.

Many observers view British domination, or hegemony, in the world economy as a nineteenth-century phenomenon associated with its industrial pre-eminence, but it is important to note that the imperium began more than a century before, in the mid-seventeenth century, with the several defeats of the Dutch, the seizure of Jamaica, and the passage of the Navigation Acts and other legislation that can only be termed mercantilist. And it is important to note that its development as the first (and, therefore, dominant) industrial nation after the Napoleonic Wars and in the wake of the sustained industrialisation that had begun in the third quarter of the eighteenth century was, itself, a product of that commercial and trading empire, as the wealth accumulated from trade with colonies and external markets circulated through the merchant banks of London and the provincial banks and provided the means by which factors of production (most notably, new technologies and plentiful labour) could be better organised to take advantage of the large available markets.

After the defeat of Napoleon and before the unification of Germany and industrialisation of Russia, Japan, and the United States, Britain with its colonial possessions in India, Africa, Canada, the Caribbean, and the Pacific dominated the world economy. With that position of dominance, coupled with its lead in industrialisation, came an awareness of the benefits that accrue to a dominant power from an international system (regime) of free trade, such as access to markets in which its goods would enjoy technological, qualitative, and price advantages. Eventually, that realisation gave rise to legislation committing Britain to free (or at least freer) trade, epitomised by the repeal of the Corn Laws in 1846 and the Navigation Acts in 1851.

The commitment to free trade represented, in a sense, the high-water mark of the Empire. With the commitment the seeds of the imperial power's decline were planted, for just as Britain gradually exposed its dominant position in world markets to potential competitors a historically unique reorganisation of the state system and the economies of several of those states occurred. Within the space of a few decades, new regimes in a half-dozen large countries took power and began to pursue a course of sustained industrialisation: Germany, recently unified in the North German Confederation and then the Empire but still founded on Prussian authoritarian principles and using Bismarck's policy of political repression and protectionism, as typified by the 'iron and rye' coalition, to support industry; Italy, also recently unified (although differing from the German case in that the state-forming impulse came from Piedmont, the most economically developed section of the nation); France, under the authoritarian rule of Louis Bonaparte's Second Empire, during which the state and the banks provided much of the investment in the infrastructure necessary for industrial development; Russia, with the abolition of serfdom creating a pressure upon the peasantry to emigrate to the cities and providing the cheap labour for new industry that was largely financed by the state and foreign investment; Japan, where the Meiji Restoration gave rise to a strategy of rapid state-led industrialisation and closure of the domestic market to the West; and the United States, where the Civil War ended slavery and the labour-repressive economy that had provided Britain with the cheap raw material for its principal industry (textiles), and provided the stimulus for industrialisation by creating a demand for railroads and armaments.

In all cases, the industrialising latecomers which challenged Britain's pre-eminence in world markets instituted tariffs that were raised several times in the last decades of the nineteenth century. Even in its colonies, Britain faced a challenge. In India, for example, the first textile plant was built in 1853, and by World War I India was self-sufficient in cheap cottons, produced two-thirds of its consumption of cotton yarn and one-half of its consumption of cotton cloth, and was exporting as much cotton as Britain! With the appearance of these challengers in the international economy, Britain no longer enjoyed unimpeded entry in captive markets. Its position of dominance in world markets was being undercut by producers in other nations (such as Germany) in which wage costs were significantly lower, and it even faced a danger within its home market from foreign producers.

At the same time, the rate of return on investment in Britain began to decrease and to pale in comparison with those found in the colonies and in other countries. In addition, Britain 'enjoyed' an excessively high level of savings – the product, as Hobson argued in *Imperialism,* of a highly skewed distribution of income and wealth that provided too little for popular consumption and too much to property owners. For these three reasons – declining rates of return for domestic investment, high rates of return abroad, and excessively high levels of savings available for investment – Britain experienced a high and increasing rate of investment abroad in the late nineteenth century, at precisely the time that the growth rate began to drop. By 1914, 50 per cent of Britain's total fixed investment was overseas and had a cumulative worth of some 4 billion pounds, almost as much as the combined foreign investments of Germany, France, Italy, and the United States. By that time net foreign investment had risen from about 2 per cent of GNP in the first half of the nineteenth century to 8 per cent, and in the last year before the war it exceeded domestic investment. As Edelstein has said, 'Never before or since has one nation committed so much of its national income and savings to capital formation abroad' (Edelstein, 1981: 70).

As important as the deprivation of capital from domestic investment may have been in contributing to the diminution of the rate of economic growth after the early 1870s (a subject about which economic historians do not agree), the outflow of capital in the late nineteenth and early twentieth centuries from Britain, occurring as it did with the simultaneous development of industry in regions of a half-dozen nations, had an even more important effect on the British economy, one that contributed to the characteristic pattern of slow growth in the twentieth century. That effect involved a fundamental shift in the nature of British capitalism. Just as Britain's industrial capitalism grew out of the accumulation of wealth from colonies and markets acquired in the earlier era of commercial capitalism, so too the development of challengers to Britain's dominance in industrial production, accompanied by the movement of capital from London throughout the world, shifted the balance of power within the capitalist class and within the economy away from industry and towards finance.

Industry and industrialists did not become unimportant, of course. But financiers, the City, and financial interests did become more important, while industry and industrialists became somewhat less so. And as interest and influence within the heart of British capitalism shifted from industry towards finance, as Britain emerged as the financial centre of a world economic system in which industrial production was dispersed among several nations that enjoyed cheap labour, proximity to raw materials, and large markets, and as its role changed from that of workshop of the world to that of banking house of the world the domestic economic priorities of Britain shifted from the promotion of industrial production and exports to the maintenance of the value of the pound. As Britain's financial stake overseas grew, more concern was given to maintaining the value of overseas assets and diminishing the purchase price of additional assets – even if the pound were overvalued, even if the nation suffered endemic or recurring deficits in the balance of payments.

The commitment to a stable, although overvalued, currency, reflected in an aversion to devaluation and to inflation – even at the cost of losses in production, exports, and employment – was pervasive during much of the interwar period, as well as during the years after World War II. One reason this commitment was such a powerful force – one reason the 'national interest' was so easily defined in ways that were compatible with financial, rather than industrial, interests – was its long-standing nature. One can find traces of it a century ago; as Lewis notes, Britain probably should have devalued the pound in the mid-1880s, in order to stave off the erosion in the balance of trade caused by the reduction in the rate of growth in exports and the continued rise in imports (Lewis, 1978). But the pound was not devalued – an unobtrusive indicator, perhaps, that financial interests had supplanted exporters in defining the priorities of economic policy. Instead, the pound remained tied to gold (and to other currencies) at a fixed rate throughout the last decades of the nineteenth century and first years of the twentieth. As a result, instead of promoting exports and contributing to production, employment, and growth, the transformation in interest within British capitalism – the product of the evolving role of the nation in the world economy – led to the maintenance of the value of the pound, even when over-valued and even when a consequence was the loss of exports and production, slower growth, and unemployment.

After World War I, the pound floated, it is true. But the Treasury and the Bank of England sought a return to the gold standard at the 1914 rate of exchange and, instead of devaluing to eliminate the payments deficits (which by then were chronic), sought to finance the deficits by raising the bank rate and pursuing a tight money policy. Simultaneously, the Treasury sought to prevent the war debt from entering the money supply by converting it to longer-term debt, via the inducement of high interest rates. And it sought to reduce the overall magnitude of the debt by running budget surpluses. In 1925, the nation returned, as the Treasury and Bank wished, to the gold standard at the pre-war exchange rate, with the overvalued pound supported by the tight monetary and fiscal policy. The domestic consequences of this policy package of high interest rates, tight money, and budget surpluses were, quite predictably, a relatively low rate of growth (especially of industrial production, as the overvalued pound priced exports out of foreign markets and made imports cheap) and a high rate of unemployment that ranged between 7 and 15 per cent throughout the interwar period.

After World War II and the creation of the IMF, with the American dollar serving as the reserve currency, the pound no longer played that role in the system of world trade and finance. But Britain nevertheless retained its traditional commitment to a fixed, and overvalued, exchange rate (broken only once, in 1949, when the Labour government devalued the pound from $4.03 to $2.80) and for the next two decades, until late 1967, chancellors and prime ministers of both major parties accepted the arguments of the City of London against devaluation. In spite of recurrent payments crises, as British exports continued to lose market share to those produced by the rebuilt economies of the post-war era, successive governments refused to devalue and, instead, responded to runs on the pound with fiscal and monetary contraction (the 'stop' in 'stop-go'). In order to prevent further deterioration of reserves (and, after 1973, further depreciation of the pound), one government after another sought to tighten credit and reduce the fiscal stimulus of government in order to reduce consumption of imports and lower the relative price of export goods. Thus, instead of committing itself to growth, production, and employment, British economic policy acted as a recurrent brake, reducing domestic consumption and investment, reducing the ability of one export sector after another to compete in the world economy and thus contributing to the de-industrialisation of the economy, creating a relatively low average rate of growth that masked a pattern of frequent surge and slump, and creating a large pool of permanently unemployed and underemployed labour.

This brief review of the British experience suggests that the international political economy, Britain's evolving role within the world economy, the policy responses through which governments sought to perpetuate or alter that role, and the constraints that role imposed on domestic economy policy are essential components of an explanation of the relatively low rate of economic growth in the twentieth century. This does not mean that the explanation of low growth in Britain is exclusively international, of course, just as it does not mean that the special-interest groups and 'distributional coalitions' had no impact whatsoever on the rate of growth. But it does suggest the extent to which the explanation of growth of the type offered by Olson – grounded as it is in purely domestic social organisational characteristics and activities – is, at best, incomplete and, more likely, simply incorrect.

CHAPTER 28

Whitehall and British industrial policy*

Kevin Theakston

'The orderly management of decline', was how the then-Head of the Civil Service, Sir William Armstrong, described the task of the civil service in 1973 (Hennessy, 1989: 76). The economic and industrial record since then, together with its social and political fall out, hardly merits the tag 'orderly'. The policy switches and U-turns of recent decades, and the related organisational tinkering and redesign, speak more of a desperate search for quick results than a rational analysis of problems and options or a careful review of the impact of the last round of changes (though politicians rather than mandarins are the real culprits here). Andrew Marr recently mused that 1992 was not a good year for the British system: 'Westminster has been a lesser place, one of squabbling that most of the country finds irrelevant and distasteful. Whitehall has been a venue for scandal (Matrix-Churchill) and incompetence (pit closures). This is not even the genteel, well-ordered decline cynics said we were good at. This is tacky' (*Independent*, 28.12.92). But how much of the blame for Britain's long economic decline do our governing arrangements really deserve? Is Whitehall part of the problem rather than part of the solution? Have the people and the institutions that run the country contributed powerfully and directly to our economic and industrial malaise – such that their reform is a precondition for economic recovery – or are they just a set of convenient scapegoats?

The Whitehall culture

The character of Britain's mandarin elite is a favourite target of 'declinist' critics. It is no accident, they suggest, that the civil service took on broadly its modern

---

* Specially commissioned for this volume. A fuller version of this chapter is available as Discussion Paper No 4 (1993) from the Centre for Industrial Policy and Performance, University of Leeds.

form at the same time – the end of the nineteenth century – as Britain's economic decline set in. The public school/Oxbridge anti-industrial culture was the breeding ground for the new corps of administrators who were 'almost without exception lacking in scientific, mechanical, technological or commercial training or experience' (Macdonagh, quoted in Weiner, 1981: 24). The mandarins were 'essay-writers rather than problem-solvers', in Corelli Barnett's (1986: 215) dismissive phrase. 'The ethos of the British senior civil servant is that of the adviser-regulator, not of the original-thinker-doer', according to Peter Hennessy. This meant that 'the British Civil Service in similar conditions could not have done what the Japanese or, particularly, the French bureaucracies did so brilliantly after the war on the economic and industrial fronts ... because [it] was not designed for the purpose' (Hennessy, 1989: 717). Hennessy in fact contends that Whitehall's failure after 1945 to fashion the peacetime equivalent of the army of 'irregulars' – the businessmen, scientists, engineers and other 'temporaries' who had helped to make the wartime civil service 'a world-beating bureaucracy' – represented 'probably *the* greatest lost opportunity in the history of British public administration' (see Hennessy, 1989: chs 3 and 4).

Wilks' (1990: 173) view that 'higher civil servants have little training in, familiarity with, or, one suspects, sympathy for manufacturing industry' is one that is widely shared. The mandarin who confessed that it had never occurred to him to visit a factory – 'What were they like?' – was not the fictional Sir Humphrey but a real-world senior official quoted in *The Financial Times* in early 1993 (*Financial Times,* 21.1.93)! There is indeed a wide gulf of understanding between Whitehall and the private sector, arising from a difference in culture, a merchant banker seconded for a spell into the DTI told Hennessy (1989: 523): 'The civil servant is thinking of his public duty, his responsibility upwards to ministers, whereas the private sector person is thinking of how to get their company to survive in a competitive environment'. 'Ruthless and single-minded maximisers of world market share or gross national product' is not the civil service ideal, Corelli Barnett (1986: 221) complained, a view shared by Tony Benn in his 1960s technocratic phase: 'our present Civil Service is not interested in growth. It is geared to care and maintenance' (Benn, 1987: 264). Whitehall just does not understand the profit motive, argue some critics. Lord Chandos (a Conservative minister in the 1950s) believed that 'civil servants regard with suspicion and distaste illiterate and vulgar men who have made a lot of money' (quoted in Theakston and Fry, forthcoming). An official who had been out on secondment to business confessed: 'Civil servants often have bad feelings about contractors – they are viewed as "money-grabbing" and that is seen as contemptible. I now realise that making money is all right so long as abnormal profits are not being made' (Gosling and Nutley, 1990: 52).

Sir Leslie Murphy (who was chairman of the National Enterprise Board 1977–79, and who has experience of both Whitehall and private business) agreed that 'civil servants had no industrial experience and did not understand industrial problems'. But his was not a blanket condemnation: 'Civil servants were not good at running a large state industrial holding company or dealing with large businesses like BL and Rolls-Royce. However, they were better at handling requests [for financial assistance] under the Industry Acts where social and other considerations had to be taken into account' (Murphy, 1981: 26, 28). This balancing or arbitrating role is, of course, the classic 'generalist' function. Within the DTI itself the generalist ethos dominates, officials' 'career moves might well take them from active involvement in the affairs of a sector of manufacturing industry to a post concerned with tourism or the recondite formulae of the General Agreement on Tariffs and Trade' (Blackstone and Plowden, 1988: 129). But the generalist's lack of in-depth expertise is a key factor in the reactive and arm's-length administrative style marking government's relations with industry. Abromeit's work on government and the British Steel Corporation led her to link lack of expertise with government passivity and policy inertia:

> Frequent changes leave no incentive to civil servants to enter wholeheartedly into the problems they deal with in each position, nor do they allow for commitment to programmes, or for a sense of responsibility for programme results. Instead, civil servants tend to define their tasks in very limited terms ('administering the statutes') and, because of the limited base of knowledge they operate from, to take the 'safe course' of avoiding risks and postponing decisions – hence to cling to the status quo. (Abromeit, 1986: 95–6)

Generalist mandarins seem particularly vulnerable to the charge of 'amateurism' when dealing with high technology projects, perhaps one reason why government's role has so often been that of a 'milch cow' in that field (Dell, 1973: 165). How else can one explain the behaviour of the Ministry of Aviation official who, faced with the original estimate of £60m for Concorde, blithely added another £40m 'for the sake of not getting things wrong' (Bruce-Gardyne and Lawson, 1976: 13)? A case-study of the Alvey project also revealed 'the limited ability of non-expert officials in central departments to assess high technology proposals' (Keliher, 1990: 67). A Treasury official described his department's approach:

> We often subject what the DTI submits to us by way of these key technology proposals to a "Red Jelly Test". If we can substitute "Red Jelly" for, say, opto-electronics without any damage to their case, then we don't think DTI has presented a very good case because it doesn't discriminate between one technology and another ... It's a good exercise to go through because you come up with statements like "We should support Red Jelly because the Red Jelly producers are risk averse" or "There are fantastic externalities from Red

Jelly". Bullshit. We want to know precisely what it is you are claiming for
this technology as opposed to any other technology.

But another Treasury mandarin explained, 'We wouldn't ask much about the
technicalities because we wouldn't be able to judge even if someone told us'
(Keliher, 1990: 69).

The former Labour minister, Edmund Dell, has similarly noted the way in
which the reluctant attitude of the civil service to government intervention in
industry, together with lack of substantial experience of industry, has conditioned
the form of that intervention when it has occurred:

> Civil servants will know from bitter experience that politically intervention is
> more likely to be an embarrassment than a triumph. Therefore their protective
> attitude to ministers as well as to the government service will recommend
> caution ... Where the political risks are so grave and the possibilities of
> national advantage so questionable, why get involved? If one has to get
> involved, why get involved too deeply? Why take management responsibility
> that can reasonably be left to others? ... A rescue operation by the government
> may bring in a political dividend. But why get involved voluntarily? Why
> convert what sometimes may be a reluctant necessity into a positive policy of
> intervention, when the dangers are so great and prospective gains so doubtful?
> (Dell, 1973: 159–60)

Benn in the 1970s declared that 'the idea that somehow you could solve the
problem by having more qualified civil servants is rubbish. If I had ten thousand
PhDs in Business Studies in my Department of Industry, it would contribute
absolutely zero to our productivity' (Benn, 1989: 242). Whitehall, however, *has*
made efforts to improve its economic and industrial expertise, but deep-rooted
attitudes and practices are not easily changed. There is, though, a sense in which
it cannot win because closer links with industry fuel left-wing suspicions of a
political bias in the civil service in favour of business values – seen in the
reactions to retired officials taking jobs in business (Doig, 1986). Amazingly,
there were only about a dozen professional economists working in Whitehall in
1960 but, following the creation of the Government Economic Service in 1964,
the number was almost 200 by 1970 and about 400 by 1976, though the 1980s
saw major cutbacks in the government's economics capability: the Economist
Group was just 116 strong in 1988 (7 of these in the DTI), growing to 183 (16 in
the DTI) by 1992.

Attempts have been made via secondments and exchanges to give civil
servants direct experience of industry and to fill the skills gap in government by
bringing in outside expertise. However, these programmes are not large-scale

(280 outward/189 inward movements in 1986, for instance), involve the financial sector and consultancy firms more than manufacturing companies, and departments often waste the experience officials gain by posting them to unrelated jobs on 're-entry' (Gosling and Nutley, 1990). DTI in particular has acknowledged that the formulation and implementation of industrial policy can require expertise not available in Whitehall (it accounted for 82 of the total of 469 interchanges in 1986 noted above – the Ministry of Defence accounted for 204). Industrial advisers have been brought in on short-term contracts since the 1960s. The Industrial Development Unit (IDU) formed in 1972 to appraise projects and handle applications for selective financial assistance was, from the start, staffed predominantly by secondees from accountancy firms, banks and industry. The Alvey directorate established in 1983 to fund IT research brought together civil servants and managers loaned from IT companies (Mueller, 1985: 107). But the scale of this influx must be kept in proportion: DTI staff totalled over 11,000 in 1992, secondments thus involving less than 1 per cent of its personnel at any one time.

The government machine

The fragmentation and institutional instability of the industrial policy community in British government have worked against the development and implementation of a coherent industrial policy. The departmental set-up in the fields of financial and macroeconomic policy has been relatively stable (and marked by Treasury predominance); in contrast, the departments dealing with industry and trade have experienced continual reorganisation and upheaval, with their number, size and responsibilities changing sometimes quite abruptly and for short-term political reasons (Hogwood, 1988). As Hennessy (1989: 432) puts it, 'Success, in terms of sustained growth in the British economy, might have brought stability. Relative failure did not'. Activity, as seen in regular departmental reorganisations, became a substitute for – perhaps even a further barrier to – achievement, as measured in the statistics of economic and industrial performance.

Industrial policy is not something that is formulated and implemented by a single industry department but instead by a network of government departments (involving also a range of paragovernmental agencies linked to Whitehall, local-level bodies and – increasingly – the European Commission). The main departmental 'players' with industry-related functions include the Department of Trade and Industry, the Treasury, the regional departments for Scotland, Wales and Northern Ireland, the Department of Employment, the Department of Transport and (until its abolition in 1992) the Department of Energy. In addition the Ministry of Agriculture (which now has a bigger budget than DTI), dealing with the farming and food sectors, the Department of Health (the drugs industry), and the Ministry of Defence (industry's biggest single customer, with its Procurement Executive spending around £8bn a year on equipment for the armed forces), also come into the picture. Other departments' policies can impact on industry too. Wilks (1990: 173) gives the example of the Home Office: its 'preference for an annual registration suffix ... helps the police identify vehicles. Unfortunately it also distorts the whole pattern of vehicle demand, boosting August sales when factories tend to have reduced holiday production, and allowing continental factories to shift their stocks to Britain'. This pattern of overlapping responsibilities, and the need to secure the active co-operation of a number of organisational actors in order to make progress, produces frequent calls for 'improved coordination' but, as Hogwood (1982: 36–7) notes, this is really 'a statement of the problem rather than a description of the solution'. The concept of coordination is actually very problematic and, in practice, there are a variety of mechanisms through which it can be attempted (with different degrees of success).

The policy-involvement of top politicians at the Cabinet/prime ministerial level is on the whole spasmodic and *ad hoc* or crisis-driven, though fundamentally important in a broad 'climate-setting' sense. Myths about 'prime ministerial government' are easily punctured: in the Alvey case, for instance, 'Thatcher's interventions ... were either counter-productive in terms of the PM's own objectives or were quickly evaded by the bureaucracy and organized interests at the implementation stage' (Keliher, 1990: 61). Individual industrial crises (e.g. bail-outs or rescue operations) tend to be handled by different combinations of ministers, depending on the case, often in an *ad hoc* committee, and with 'political' factors decisive in the outcome (Wilks, 1983: 129–30). During his time in the political wilderness in the late 1980s, Michael Heseltine called for a powerful industrial policy committee of the Cabinet, chaired by the Industry Secretary, with a strengthened DTI ranking on a par with the Treasury (Heseltine, 1987). His argument did not wash with Mrs Thatcher, but Major has set up a standing industrial policy committee, though with the 'neutral' Lord Privy Seal in the chair (*Financial Times*, 20.5.92).

The Treasury has long been a favourite bogey figure for those seeking to explain Whitehall's role in economic decline and deindustrialisation. For Pollard (1982: 159), in particular, it institutionalises that 'contempt for production' that makes the government machine 'a powerful contributory cause of our decline'. Its responsibility for public expenditure control ensures that it will generally be hostile to increased state spending on programmes directed at industry (looking for cuts wherever it can find them, even if that means sacrificing productive investment). And its macroeconomic management role, it is argued, together with its close links with the Bank of England and the City, invariably lead it to give priority to short-term and financial considerations (the exchange rate, the balance of payments, the rate of inflation), introducing measures (e.g. interest rate changes) which can affect industry more than any number of DTI 'supply-side' measures. It is said to be deeply committed to a free-market approach and sceptical of anything like a positive and interventionist industrial policy. Condemned by the critics for having virtually no direct contacts with or knowledge of industry, the Treasury nevertheless dominates economic policy-making in government. Although it no longer controls top-level civil service postings, it remains one of the elite departments, powerfully influencing Whitehall's values and culture. It has seen off all challengers, defeating the Department of Economic Affairs in the 1960s and ensuring that the National Economic Development Council was marginalised (and eventually killed off in 1992 at the Treasury's instigation); its power has grown under the Conservative governments that have been in office since 1979. All this is in marked contrast to the position in other systems, such as France and Germany where the central economics ministries do not stand back from industrial policy questions, or Japan where the powerful Ministry of International Trade and Industry has more clout than the Ministry of Finance.

In the mid-1970s it looked as if the Treasury could begin to play a more constructive role in industrial policy-making, with Chancellor of the Exchequer Healey and official opinion becoming more interested in 'supply side' problems. The Treasury created its own Industrial Policy Group and worked closely with the Department of Industry (after Varley replaced Benn); the inter-departmental Industrial Strategy Steering Group (chaired by the Treasury) shaped the thinking behind Labour's 1975 'Industrial Strategy' and tried to get non-economic departments (e.g. Education, Environment) to address the industrial implications of their policies (Grant, 1982: 28; Middlemas, 1991: 69–70). The failure of senior ministers to keep up their initial level of interest and the fall out from the 1976 IMF crisis meant that the Strategy slipped down the Treasury's agenda, however (Middlemas, 1991: 127). And after 1979, the Thatcher government's ideological hostility to the idea of an industrial strategy reinforced the traditional Treasury view.

The case against the Treasury should not, though, be exaggerated. Thain (1984) believes that there is only 'limited scope for blaming the Treasury for decline'. He argues that there is no monolithic 'Treasury line', that the Treasury's priorities have been determined by the political decisions of ministers, and that other Whitehall departments and outside interest groups limit its room for manoeuvre. The consensus on foreign economic policy (the 'sterling lobby'), for instance, extended far beyond the Treasury. And the long-term growth in the total of public spending is testimony to the limits on its power. Its failure to stop the Concorde project, for instance, was described as 'a saga of unrelieved humiliation for the Treasury' (Bruce-Gardyne and Lawson, 1976: 163). The Treasury is undoubtedly a key player in the economic and industrial policy machine, Thain suggests, but it is not an all-powerful one.

Over a long period of time the Board of Trade was one of the central departments dealing with industry. During the war, its officials had developed a clear (and pessimistic) analysis of Britain's industrial backwardness and its post-war competitive prospects, but ministers and Whitehall had balked at creating a full-blown 'Ministry of Industry' to push through some of the radical ideas then being floated (e.g. for an Industrial Commission) (Middlemas, 1986). Instead, the Board's traditional *laissez-faire* or hands-off approach was confirmed and in the 1950s and early 1960s it 'sought to operate industrial policies *neutrally*, giving firms and industries as little special treatment as possible' (Young and Lowe, 1974: 27). Industry was to operate on its own within a framework provided by government (e.g. legislation relating to restrictive trade practices and monopolies was passed), with the Board of Trade acting as 'a referee rather than a player' (*ibid.*: 12). The contrast with the attitude and practices of, for instance, the Ministry of Supply and military production departments is stark, as Edgerton (1992) notes. In the early 1960s, the 'dash for planning' and the establishment of the National Economic Development Council (NEDC) and the National Economic Development Office (NEDO), which had an industrial division working on sectoral issues, represented the first moves towards a more active government involvement with industry, but the key developments came, first, after the election of Harold Wilson's Labour government in 1964, and second, with the arrival of Edward Heath's Conservative administration in 1970.

Labour's ill-fated Department of Economic Affairs failed to break the Treasury's predominance over economic policy, handicapped as it was by an ill-thought-out division of functions between it and the Treasury and by a lack of direct executive powers on key issues, primarily because of political decisions giving priority to the defence of the exchange rate which ensured that the Treasury would inevitably come out on top in the inter-departmental struggle.

The establishment and subsequent expansion of the Ministry of Technology was a more successful innovation (Coopey, 1991). Wilson wanted to redirect the national technological effort away from military and 'prestige' (aerospace and nuclear) projects to boost industrial production generally. And by 1969 he had built up MinTech as a super ministry for industry, transferring to it responsibilities from the Board of Trade (of which he had a low opinion) and the DEA, and allowing it to gobble up the functions of the Ministry of Aviation and the Ministry of Power, the result being that it had 'wider responsibilities for public and private industry than have ever been enjoyed by an industry department since' (Grant, 1988: 88) – according to Edgerton (1991a: 105), next to MinTech, 'Japan's much-vaunted MITI is a minnow by comparison'. Although it was not staffed by a new breed of technocrats, MinTech was a pioneer in trying to breach the monopoly of the Whitehall generalist, opening up senior posts to scientists and engineers.

Young and Lowe (1974: 28) argue that the significance of MinTech was the 'institutionalisation of the principle of discrimination', and the overturning of Whitehall's traditionally 'neutral' stance – though, as Edgerton (1991b: 163) points out, this description only makes sense if the history of the state's role in procurement is ignored. Young and Lowe quote its permanent secretary: 'from the start the Ministry of Technology insisted on being selective', and also a former Board of Trade official: 'with the arrival of MinTech, the judgement of the bureaucrat has replaced the judgement of the market'.

Grant's judgement (1982: 88–9) is that 'the MinTech experience ... did help to nurture something of an interventionist culture among civil servants who were later to occupy senior positions in subsequent industry departments. That is not to say that they believed in massive state intervention, but they did believe in trying to create a working relationship with industry'. But he argues that this period saw 'essentially a reinforcement and development of an earlier clientilistic conception of government's relationship with industry, rather than a predilection for a replacement of the market by the state'. Certainly, MinTech's ministers did not believe that their department represented any sort of challenge to the Treasury, and they complained that macroeconomic policy was formulated without reference to what MinTech was doing (Contemporary Record, 1991: 142–3). And it must be said that whatever its *potential*, MinTech's record in practice was not impressive, both in terms of shifting technological and R&D priorities and in industrial support and restructuring. Symptomatic of this was the continuation of Concorde, and the conversion of Sir Richard Clarke from being a powerful critic of the project at the Treasury to an enthusiastic and successful advocate for it when he took over as MinTech's permanent secretary (Bruce-Gardyne and Lawson, 1976: 18).

Wilson also established the Industrial Reorganisation Corporation (IRC) in 1966, giving it the role of assisting and promoting mergers with the aim of creating bigger companies able to compete internationally (and IRC also acted in a number of rescue cases). Acting as something like a state merchant bank, IRC's personnel came from the private sector, and it had considerable operational independence (reporting in the first instance to the DEA and later to MinTech), which meant that parliament was able to exercise little detailed control over it (Young and Lowe, 1974). A small, unbureaucratic, active, fast-moving, commercially oriented body, IRC's value as a catalyst for industrial development was limited in two ways. First, because the government failed to relate its work to any clear and detailed long-term industrial strategy (*ibid.*: 87). And second, because in its interventions in a number of important cases, 'economic nationalism and social factors seemed more important than any buccaneering pursuit of industrial efficiency', for example its role in the formation of BL and in aiding Rolls-Royce and Cammell Laird (Fry, 1981: 100–101). In the event, however, the IRC experiment was cut off just as it was building up steam.

Heath in 1970 abolished the IRC (it did not fit into his 'disengagement' philosophy) and dismantled MinTech, allocating its aircraft procurement functions (the largest in staff terms) to the MoD and merging the rump of the ministry with the Board of Trade to form the giant Department of Trade and Industry (DTI), bringing together responsibility for industry and responsibility for export promotion and trade policy. Hogwood (1988: 219) argues that the creation of the DTI provided an organisational container for more coherent policies: 'it removed the organizational excuse for ineffective policies'. However, DTI's very wide policy scope made it bureaucratically unwieldy, with serious problems of internal coordination exacerbated by the continuance of different traditions – Trade's free-trade outlook, and on the Industrial (former-MinTech) side a more interventionist impulse (Radcliffe, 1991: ch. 6). And the political and economic crises of the Heath years meant that the government's approach soon became a reactive rather than a strategic one. The 1972 U-turn saw the establishment of the Industrial Development Unit inside DTI (mentioned earlier) and the appointment of a second DTI Cabinet minister (for prices, consumer affairs and trade). Heath's departmental pattern unravelled soon after. A separate Department of Energy had been carved out even before the return of a Labour government in 1974 saw DTI broken up to form three ministries – Industry, Trade, Prices and Consumer Protection – for reasons of party management and political balancing between left and right in the Cabinet (with Wilson particularly keen to deny Benn, whose interventionist ambitions he opposed, a major departmental power base). In 1979, Mrs Thatcher abolished Prices and Consumer Protection, but kept Trade and Industry as separate departments. However, DTI's 'common services' (personnel, finance, economics, statistics, legal, accountancy, information) had been maintained after 1974, as were a common staffing structure (permitting cross-postings) and integrated regional offices, a 'shadow DTI' thus existing in the 1974–83 period (Hogwood, 1988: 221–2). In 1983, to complete the narrative, the Departments of Trade and Industry were merged again, DTI reabsorbing Energy in 1992.

On a more disaggregated level, the scene has also been unstable with responsibility for particular industries or sectors shifting across departmental boundaries and between different branches or groupings within departments. Hogwood (1979) charted thirteen changes in the location of responsibility for shipbuilding between 1959 and 1977, for instance, including six inter-departmental shifts. He concluded that this frequent moving of the administrative furniture imposed 'disruption costs' and reduced government's ability to deal with the industry. Fashionable functions can become political footballs: in 1985 DTI lost a battle to keep responsibility for small firms which Lord Young insisted on taking charge of as newly appointed Employment Secretary. When he moved across to become Industry Secretary in 1987, small businesses stayed with Employment, however, only to be returned to DTI after the 1992 election.

The underlying civil service approach to industry seems to have been more resilient than the departmental architecture. As Grant (1988: 89) put it: 'in the 1970s, the successive industry departments ... operated under a guiding bureaucratic philosophy which held as a core value that the department should do its best, within the framework of public policy, for its industrial clients'. The Department of Industry was very unhappy about Benn's proposals for planning agreements. William Plowden (1985: 26), then a senior official in DoI, recalled that 'there was considerable reluctance on the part of the department – to use a collective noun – to implement to the hilt some of the things that Labour ministers were trying to do in relation to industrial policy because, as the department saw it, these policies would damage the private sector of industry'. An embattled Tony Benn felt his department was simply a 'mouthpiece for the

CBI' (Benn, 1989: 139), and complained about what he saw as civil service sabotage of the manifesto (including what amounted to a public signal of opposition to his support for workers' co-ops via the leaking of an accounting officer's minute). In reality, of course, Benn's main problem was that he was out of step with his political colleagues and the prime minister and Labour Cabinet were not committed to his radical interventionist policies. Certainly, the National Enterprise Board (NEB), established in 1975, turned out to be a very different creature from that intended by the Labour left, operating as a 'hospital for lame ducks' (Mitchell, 1982: 47) rather than spearheading an active socialist industrial policy. The DoI and the Treasury tried to emphasise commercial viability as the key criteria in government rescue cases, but ministers' political needs could be paramount (Wilks, 1983: 141). For instance, the Chrysler bail-out – with the government trying to shore-up its political position in Scotland – killed off any chance of developing a coherent policy for the motor industry of the sort the Central Policy Review Staff (which took an interest in industrial policy throughout its existence 1971–83) had sketched in 1975 (Blackstone and Plowden, 1988: 136–9).

Taking over the Industry Department in 1979, the new Conservative minister, Sir Keith Joseph, handed over a reading-list so that officials could educate themselves in the new thinking about markets and frame policy advice accordingly. His special adviser, David (later Lord) Young, suspected that some officials hoped that the Conservatives would be only temporary residents in government for reasons of institutional self-interest – under a Labour government there is more money to spend and decisions to take (Young, 1990: 46). Joseph was much given to agonised musings about whether his department should be abolished but there were in fact continuities with the pre-1979 approach, with continuing massive aid to BL, for instance, after the Cabinet over-ruled its hapless Industry Secretary. Under his successor, Patrick Jenkin (Industry Secretary 1981–83), the idea that DoI could play some sort of constructive role surfaced in the support given to the information technology sector (Kenneth Baker being appointed as IT minister in 1981). But the government's general ideological hostility to state intervention, together with the Treasury's axe-wielding on public spending and pursuit of macroeconomic policies damaging to industry, left DoI/DTI without much of a role. Staff fell from 16,000 in 1978/79 to 12,800 in 1987, and departmental spending plummeted from over £3bn a year in the early 1980s to £2bn in 1987/88 (measured in 1991/92 prices: Treasury, 1993: 39). Other departments made the running on the government's key 'supply side' initiatives: the Treasury on privatisation, the Cabinet Office and Employment on deregulation, Employment on training and small businesses, Environment on inner cities (taken over by DTI after 1987). Regional policy (long one of the department's main functions) was downgraded and over large parts of its bailiwick – competition policy, regional aid, R&D support, trade negotiations, etc. – the European Commission loomed ever larger as a body to respond to or negotiate with (Wilks, 1989). A series of rapid ministerial changes added to the gloom and the feeling of loss of purpose.

The arrival of Lord Young as minister in 1987 saw an attempt to revitalise and reorient the department (Wilks, 1989; Flynn, 1989). Young (1990: 237) felt DTI had lost its way and had become 'a Department of Disasters' and he wanted to change its role and image, putting it back into the political limelight as the 'Department of Wealth Creation'. From being 'the vet's surgery of the British economy' (Hennessy, 1989: 431), it would become the champion of free-market competition, the facilitator of the enterprise economy, encouraging small business and trying to change attitudes (DTI's advertising budget rose dramatically). The talk was of 'an enterprise strategy' rather than 'an industrial policy', the government's line was that 'industry is responsible for its own destiny' (DTI, 1988), and Young dismissed old-style government intervention, the idea of 'picking winners' or the need to give priority to manufacturing industry.

Signalling the new regime, Young abolished DTI's sponsorship divisions. Sponsorship divisions provided a point of contact within government for every industry (not all industries falling under DTI's wing, of course), acting as a channel of communication between the industry and Whitehall and also to some extent as internal lobbyists within the machine for the interests of 'their' industry. Wilks (1990: 173) argues that sponsorship divisions (at least in the case of the motor industry) actually communicated badly with companies and that sponsorship was just a 'passive, best-endeavour sort of relationship ... involv[ing] no planning and little policy-implementation capability' (Wilks, quoted in Judge, 1990: 60). The official view was that 'departments need to be critical lobbyists because, at the end of the day, government is interested in total economic performance and a department just acting as a protectionist lobby is unlikely to be contributing to improved performance' (Mueller, 1985: 101). Young was adamant that they had to go, however. 'The danger is that "sponsorship" can give the impression of "responsibility" for particular sectors of industry', his 1988 white paper argued (DTI, 1988: 38). He feared that officials who spent a few years in a particular division before moving on would simply end up as the creatures of the trade associations and a conduit for more claims on the public purse (Young, 1990: 240, 257). A National Audit Office investigation of DTI assistance to industry showed that there was something in that suspicion: applications for aid on projects over £2m, vetted by the IDU, resulted in lower percentage level grants than smaller projects examined only by sponsoring divisions. The NAO concluded that the 'shallower investigations' conducted by sponsoring divisions may have led to more aid given than was strictly necessary to ensure that the projects concerned went ahead (NAO, 1987: 14–16).

'Market' divisions replaced the DTI's sponsorship divisions, focusing on 'the markets for particular goods and services rather than specific supplier industries ... [and designed to] tackle broad policy issues affecting all the suppliers and customers in the market in question, rather than dealing with particular industries' (DTI, 1988: 38–9). Grant (1989: 93) deprecated the end of the 'sponsorship' function: other countries saw the value of specialist industry divisions as a source of expertise and a means of keeping in contact. He also detected a 'hidden agenda': destroying part of the administrative apparatus that a future interventionist government would need. In the event, the vertically organised market divisions did not last long. Young's successor, Nicholas Ridley, replaced them with 'horizontal units, e.g., "manufacturing technology", responsible for delivering DTI services of a particular kind to many types of businesses, though responsibility for some industrial sectors –vehicles, aerospace, shipbuilding – was located in units called "Business Task Forces"' (Connelly, 1992: 36).

The arrival of Michael Heseltine after the 1992 election saw further changes. 'Sponsorship' divisions were now revived, with the aim of encouraging closer contacts with industry (DTI was apparently not in touch with 60% of Britain's companies), but the minister indicated that he did not want them to be channels for special pleading and ruled out the return of subsidies and bail-outs – indeed, DTI's budget was set to fall further (*Sunday Times*, 7.6.92; *Guardian*, 4.7.92). Heseltine tried to combine the rhetoric of free enterprise *and* that of selective intervention. 'If I have to intervene to help British companies ... then ... I'll intervene before breakfast, before lunch, before tea and before dinner. And I'll get up the next morning and I'll start all over again', he told the 1992 Conservative Party conference (*Guardian*, 8.10.92). John Major, the prime minister, also appeared to back the idea of 'a more co-operative, problem-solving partnership with industry', trying simultaneously to distance himself from the negative attitude of the Thatcher administration towards manufacturing industry while saying there was no question of a return to 'interventionist policies' (*Independent*, 2.1.93). The sight of the Treasury flexing its muscles and scoring a point against Heseltine by abolishing the NEDC, together with the fiasco of the pit closures programme announced in late 1992, hardly augurs well for this new-style industrial policy, however.

Conclusions

Making sense of Britain's economic and industrial travails requires a multi-causa not a mono-causal explanation. 'The state is not primarily responsible fo Britain's economic decline', argued Peter Hall (1986: 67). 'However it has no been an innocent bystander.' Walter Williams (1989: 251) agreed that 'an ailin; machinery of government is not the primary cause of Britain's problems Exogenous facts beyond the control of British government no doubt dominate al controllable factors'. William Keegan and Rupert Pennant-Rea (1979: 9) mak the point more vividly: 'the economic policy machine of ministers and official has given the impression of permanently trying to run up the downwar; escalator'.

Quizzed by Peter Hennessy, the economist David Henderson rather pooh poohed the idea that a country's economic success depended crucially on th quality of its civil service: 'I'm not sure that in the British case it's been a major influence on economic performance. Insofar as it has been, it has been to do with ideas that were held outside the Civil Service as well ... The British Civil Service has something to answer for in its closed nature and the way it has not reacted to evidence. But it's very easy to overdo the extent to which you can blame economic performance on the administrators' (Hennessy, 1989: 688).

But as Sir John Hoskyns (1983, 1984) has argued, it is not the individual bits and pieces of the British system of government that matter so much as the system as a whole – the total 'configuration'. The British state has developed, historically, as a 'Pontius Pilate' rather than a 'Bismarckian' state (Wilks, 1986: 40). Its permanent officials are remote from industry and their traditions are of arm's-length regulation rather than interventionist and discriminatory. Its politicians react to short-term crises rather than articulating long-term modernisation strategies. Its administrative machinery gives a greater priority to financial and macroeconomic policy than to any sort of coordinated and coherent industrial policy.

'A state can transform the operation of its economic system, but first it must transform itself', argues Peter Hall (1986: 68), citing the French experience in the post-war period (but the French, of course, had the advantage of a deep-rooted *dirigiste* state tradition). Walter Williams cautions that modernising the British government system does not 'guarantee the curing of the British disease', but nevertheless believes that without 'an institutional great leap', the 'continuing pre-modern anti-modern British central government seems likely to doom the nation to economic decline and political instability' (Williams, 1989: 251, 259). Wilks too (1986: 45) is clear that Britain 'does not require a policy, it requires an upheaval in the institutions of economic life ... The need is for basic reform of the institutions, policy-making processes and some of the traditional features of economic structure'.

But Britain cannot simply transplant a Japanese-style MITI and a French-style breed of technocratic officials. The traditions, constitutions and political environments of French and Japanese government are very different from those of Britain. It is also clear that administrative reform is not something that involves a 'big bang' implementation of a critic's blueprint but is instead a process of piecemeal adaptation, as seen with developments since the 1960s – in terms of personnel (civil service reform) and machinery (the emergence of the DTI). The problem is, of course, that change at this pace is probably not enough to arrest, let alone reverse, economic and industrial decline quickly, and that will make the task much more difficult and politically perilous. If 'the orderly management of decline' is no longer a viable long-term option – not least because it cannot be kept a politically and socially orderly process indefinitely – we are still a long way from developing the political and governmental apparatus that may be a necessary but not sufficient condition of economic regeneration.

BIBLIOGRAPHY

Abromeit, H. (1986), *British Steel*, Berg.

Ackrill, M. (1988), 'Britain's managers and the British economy, 1870s to 1880s', *Oxford Review of Economic Policy*, **4**: 59–73.

Addison, J. (1985), 'What do unions really do?', *Industrial and Labor Relations Review*, **38**: 245–63.

Allen, G. C. (1976), *The British Disease*, Institute of Economic Affairs.

Anderson, A. (1987), 'Adult training: private industry and the Nicolson letter', in Education and Training UK 1987, in A. Harrison and J. Gretton (eds), *Policy Journals*.

Anderson, P. (1987), 'The figures of descent', *New Left Review*, **161**: 20–77.

Anthony, V. (1979), *Banks and Markets*, Heinemann.

Arrow, K. (1962), 'The economic implications of learning by doing', *Review of Economic Studies*, June: 155–73.

Atkinson, J. (1984), 'Manpower strategies for flexible organisations', *Personnel Management*, August: 28–31.

Bacon, R. and Eltis, W. (1976), *Britain's Economic Problem: Too few producers*, Macmillan.

Bank of England, (1989), 'London as an international financial centre', *Bank of England Quarterly Bulletin*, **29**: 516–28.

Barnett, C. (1972), *The Collapse of British Power*, Alan Sutton.

Barnett, C. (1975), *The Human Factor and British Industrial Decline*, David Higham and Associates.

Barnett, C. (1986), *The Audit of War*, Macmillan.

Barratt Brown, M. (1970), *After Imperialism*, 2nd ed, Merlin Press.

Barratt Brown, M. (1988), 'Away with all great arches: Anderson's history of British capitalism', *New Left Review*, **167**: 22–52.

Beer, S. H. (1969), *Modern British Politics*, Faber.

Benn, T. (1987), *Out of the Wilderness: Diaries 1963–67*, Hutchinson.

Benn, T. (1989), *Against the Tide: Diaries 1973–76*, Hutchinson.

Bennett, A. and Smith-Gavine, A. N. (1988), 'The percentage utilisation of labour index', in D. Bosworth (ed.), *Working Below Capacity*, Macmillan.

Bishop, T. J. and Wilkinson, R. (1967), *Winchester and the Public School Elite: A statistical analysis*, Faber.

Blackaby, F. (ed.) (1979), *Deindustrialization*, Heinemann.

Blackstone, T. and Plowden, W. (1988), *Inside the Think Tank*, Heinemann.

Blanchflower, D. and Oswald, A. (1988), 'The economic effects of trade unions', *Employment Institute*.

Blank, S. (1973), *Government and Industry in Britain*, Saxon House.

Brittan, S. (1969), *Steering the Economy*, Secker & Warburg.

Brittan, S. (1978), 'How British is the British sickness?', *Journal of Law and Economics*, **21**: 245–68.

Broadberry, S. N. and Crafts, N. F. R. (1990), 'Explaining Anglo-American productivity differences in the mid-twentieth century', *Oxford Bulletin of Economics and Statistics*, **52**: 275–402.

Broadberry, S. N. and Fremdling, R. (1990), 'Comparative productivity in British and German industry', *Oxford Bulletin of Economics and Statistics*, **52**: 403–21.

Bruce-Gardyne, J. and Lawson, N. (1976), *The Power Game*, Macmillan.

Buxton, T., Chapman, P. and Temple, P. (eds) (1994), *Britain's Economic Performance*, Routledge.

Cairncross, A. (1988), 'Britain's industrial decline', *Royal Bank of Scotland Review*, **159**: 5–17.

Cameron, D. (1988), 'Distributional coalitions and other causes of economic stagnation', *International Organisation*, **42**: 592–604.

Caves, R. (1980), 'Productivity differences among industries', in R. Caves and L. Krause (eds), *Britain's Economic Performance*, Brookings Institute.

Central Policy Review Staff (CPRS) (1975), *The Future of the British Car Industry*, HMSO.

Chalmers, M. (1985), *Paying for Defence*, Pluto Press.

Chandler, A. D. (1976), 'The development of modern management structure in the US and UK', in L. Hannah (ed.), *Management Strategy and Business Development*, Macmillan.

Chandler, A. D. (1977), *The Visible Hand*, Harvard University Press.

Chandler, A. D. (1990), *Scale and Scope: The dynamics of industrial capitalism*, Harvard University Press.

Clark, K. (1980), 'The impact of unionisation on productivity: a case study', *Industrial and Labor Relations Review*, **33**: 451–69.

Coakley, J. and Harris, L. (1992), 'Financial globalisation and deregulation', in J. Michie (ed.), *The Economic Legacy 1979–1992*, Academic Press.

Coates, D. (1994), *The Question of UK Decline*, Harvester Wheatsheaf.

Coates, D. and Hillard, J. V. (eds) (1986), *The Economic Decline of Modern Britain: The debate between Left and Right*, Harvester.

Coates, D. and Hillard, J. V. (eds) (1987), *The Economic Revival of Modern Britain: The debate between Left and Right*, Edward Elgar.

Coleman, D. C. (1973), 'Gentlemen and players', *Economic History Review*, **26**: 92–116.

Coleman, D. C. (1987), 'Failings and achievements: some British businesses 1910–1980', *Business History*, **29**: 1–17.

Coleman, D. C. (1988), 'Review', *Business History*, **30**: 130–1.

Connelly, P. (1992), *Dealing With Whitehall*, Century Business.

Contemporary Record (1991), 'Witness Symposium: the Ministry of Technology 1964–70', *Contemporary Record*, **5**: 128–48.

Coopey, R. (1991), 'The white heat of scientific revolution', *Contemporary Record*, **5**: 115–27.

Costello, N., Michie, J. and S. Milne (1989), *Beyond the Casino Economy*, Verso.

Cowling, K. G. (1986), 'The internationalization of production and deindustrialization', in A. Amin and J. Goddard (eds), *Technological Change: Industrial Restructuring and Regional Development*, Allen & Unwin.

Cowling, K. G. and Sugden, R. (eds) (1990), *A New Economic Policy for Britain*, Manchester University Press.

Crafts, N. F. R. (1988), 'The assessment: British economic growth over the long run', *Oxford Review of Economic Policy*, **4**: i–xxi.

Crafts, N. F. R. (1991), 'Reversing relative economic decline? The 1980s in historical perspective', *Oxford Review of Economic Policy*, **7**: 81–98.

Cross, M. (1988), 'Changing work practices in UK manufacturing 1981–1988', *Industrial Relations Review and Report*, **415**: 2–10.

Cutler, T. *et al.* (1989), *1992: The Struggle for Europe*, Berg.

Cutler, T. *et al.* (1991), 'Building Europe? Jacques Delors and his plan for EMU', *Thames Paper in Political Economy*, 3.

Cutler, T. (1992), Vocational training and British economic performance: a further instalment of the British labour problem?', *Work, Employment and Society*, **6**: 161–83.

Daly, A., Hitchens, D. and Wagner, K. (1985), 'Productivity, machinery and skills in a sample of British and German manufacturing plants', *National Institute Economic Review*, February: 48–61.

Daniel, W. (1987), *Workplace Industrial Relations and Technical Change*, Pinter.

Dechery, B. (1980), 'Quelque commentaires sur les politiques industrielles de la France et de la RFA', Commissariat General au Plan.

Dell, E. (1973), *Political Responsibility and Industry*, Allen & Unwin.

Dintenfass, M. (1988), 'Entrepreneurial failure reconsidered: the case of the interwar coal industry', *Business History Review*, **62**: 1–34.

Dintenfass, M. (1992), *The Decline of Industrial Britain, 1870–1970*, Routledge.

Doig, A. (1986), 'A question of balance: business appointments of former senior civil servants', *Parliamentary Affairs*, **39**: 63–78.

DTI (1988), *DTI – the department for Enterprise*, Cm 278, HMSO.

DTI (1994), *Competitiveness: Helping Business to Win*, Cmnd. 2563, HMSO.

Eatwell, J. (1982), *Whatever Happened to Britain?: The economics of decline*, Duckworth.

Edelstein, M. (1981), 'Foreign investment and Empire 1860–1914', in R. Floud and D. McCloskey (eds), *The Economic History of Britain since 1700: volume 2, 1860–*, Cambridge University Press.

Edgerton, D. (1991a), *England and the Aeroplane*, Macmillan.

Edgerton, D. (1991b), 'Liberal militarism and the British state', *New Left Review*, **185**: 18–169.

Edgerton, D. (1992), 'Whatever happened to the British Warfare State? The Ministry of Supply 1945–1951', in H. Mercer, N. Rollings and J. D. Tomlinson (eds), *Labour Governments and Private Industry*, Edinburgh University Press.

Elbaum, B. (1986), 'The steel industry before World War I', in B. Elbaum and W. Lazonick (eds), *The Decline of the British Economy*, Oxford University Press.

Elbaum, B. and Lazonick, W. (1984), 'The decline of the British economy: an institutional perspective', *Journal of Economic History*, **44**: 567–83.

Elbaum, B. and Lazonick, W. (eds) (1986), *The Decline of the British Economy*, Oxford University Press.

Elger, T. (1990), 'Technological innovation and work reorganisation in British manufacturing in the 1980s: continuity, intensification or transformation?', *Work, Employment and Society*, Special Issue, May: 67–102.

Evans, S., Ewing, K. and Nolan, P. (1992), 'Industrial relations and the British economy in the 1990s: Mrs Thatcher's legacy', *Journal of Management Studies*, **29**: 571–89.

Feinstein, C. (1988), 'Economic growth since 1870: Britain's performance in international perspective', *Oxford Review of Economic Policy*, **4**: 1–13.

Fine, B. and Harris, L. (1985), *The Peculiarities of the British Economy*, Lawrence & Wishart.

Fine, B., O'Donnell, K. and Prevezer, M. (1985), 'Coal before nationalisation', in B. Fine and L. Harris, *The Peculiarities of the British Economy*, Lawrence & Wishart.

Finegold, D. and Soskice, D. (1988), 'The failure of training in Britain: analysis and prescription', *Oxford Review of Economic Policy*, **4**: 21–53.

Flynn, A. (1989), 'The changing management of central government: the case of the DTI', *Teaching Public Administration*, **9**: 8–23.

Foster, C. D. (1971), *Politics, Finance and the Role of Economics: An essay on the control of public expenditure*, Allen & Unwin.

Frankel, M. (1957), *British and American Manufacturing Productivity*.

Freeman, R. B. and Medoff, H. (1979), 'The two faces of unionism', *The Public Interest*, **57**: 69–93.

Freeman, R. B. and Medoff, H. (1984), *What Do Unions Do?*, Basic Books.

Frobel, F., Heinrichs, J. and Kreye O. (1980), *The New International Division of Labour*, Cambridge University Press.

Fry, G. (1981), *The Administrative 'Revolution' in Whitehall*, Croom Helm.

Gaffikin, F. and Nickson, A. (1984), *Jobs Crisis and the Multinationals: The case of the West Midlands*, Birmingham Trade Union Resource Centre.

Gamble, A. (1979), 'The free economy and the strong state', in R. Miliband and J. Saville (eds), *The Socialist Register 1979*, Merlin.

Gamble, A. (1981), *Britain in Decline*, Macmillan.

Gapper, J. (1988), '£500,000 scheme to boost training in tourist sector', *Financial Times*, 17 March.

Gerschenkron, A. (1966), *Economic Backwardness in Historical Perspective*, Harvard University Press.

Glyn, A. and Sutcliffe, B. (1972), *British Capitalism, Workers and the Profits Squeeze*, Penguin.

Goodhart, D. and Grant, C. (1988), *Making the City Work*, Fabian Society Tract no. 528.

Gosling, R. and Nutley, S. (1990), *Bridging the Gap: Secondments between government and business*, Royal Institute of Public Administration.

Grant, W. (1982), *The Political Economy of Industrial Policy*, Butterworths.

Grant, W. (1988), *Government and Industry: A comparative analysis of the US, Canada and the UK*, Edward Elgar.

Greenhalgh, C. (1988), *Employment and Structural Change: Trends and policy options*, mimeo, Oxford.

Gregg, P., Machin, S. and Metcalf, D. (1993), 'Signals and cycles? Productivity growth and changes in union status in British companies 1984–89', *Economic Journal*, **103**: 894–907.

Gregg, P. and Yates, A. (1991), 'Changes in trade union and wage setting arrangements in the 1990s', *British Journal of Industrial Relations*, **29**: 361–76.

Hadjimatheou, G. and Skouras, A. (1979), 'Britain's economic problem: the growth of the non-market sector', *Economic Journal*, **89**: 392–401.

Hahn, F. H. and Matthews, R. C. O. (1964), 'The theory of economic growth: a survey', *Economic Journal*, December: 779–902.

Hakim, C. (1990), 'Core and periphery in employers' workforce strategies: evidence from the 1987 E.L.U.S. survey', *Work Employment and Society*, **4**: 157–88.

Hall, P. (1986), *Governing the Economy*, Polity.

Hannah, L. (1976), 'Strategy and structure in the manufacturing sector', in L. Hannah (ed.), *Management Strategy and Business Development*, Macmillan.

Hannah, L. (1980), 'Visible and invisible hands in Great Britain', in A. D. Chandler and H. Daem (eds), *Managerial Hierarchies: Comparative perspectives on the rise of the modern industrial enterprise*, Harvard University Press.

Hannah, L. (1983), 'New issues in British business history', *Business History Review*, **107**: 165–74.

Harris, N. (1972), *Competition and the Corporate Society*, Methuen.

Hayek, F. A. (1980), *Unemployment and the Unions*, Institute of Economic Affairs.

Healey, D. (1959), 'Britain and NATO', in K. Knorr (ed.), *NATO and American Security*, Princeton University Press.

Hennessy, P. (1989), *Whitehall*, Secker & Warburg.

Heseltine, M. (1987), *Where There's a Will*, Hutchinson.

Hill, C. (1982), *Finance and British Economic Policy* (paper to the House Committee on Banking and Urban Affairs, Washington DC).

Hillard, J. V. (1986), 'Thatcherism and decline', in D. Coates and J. V. Hillard (eds), *The Economic Decline of Modern Britain*, Harvester.

Hirschman, A. O. (1970), *Exit, Voice and Loyalty*, Harvard University Press.

Hobsbawm, E. (1968), *Industry and Empire*, Weidenfeld and Nicolson.

Hogwood, B. (1979), *Government and Shipbuilding*, Saxon House.

Hogwood, B. (1982), 'In search of accountability: the territorial dimension of industrial policy', *Public Administration Bulletin*, **28**: 22–39.

Hogwood, B. (1988), 'The rise and fall and rise of the Department of Trade and Industry', in C. Campbell and B. G. Peters (eds), *Organizing Governance: Governing organizations*, University of Pittsburgh Press.

Hoskyns, Sir J. (1983), 'Whitehall and Westminster: an outsider's view', *Parliamentary Affairs*, **36**: 137–47.

Hoskyns, Sir J. (1984), 'Conservatism is not enough', *Political Quarterly*, **55**: 3–16.

Howson, S. (1975), *Domestic Monetary Management in Britain 1919–38*, Cambridge University Press.

Hunter, L. and MacInnes, J. (1992), 'Employers and labour flexibility: the evidence from case studies', *Employment Gazette*, June: 307–15.

Hutton, W. (1993), 'Rhineland resists westward drift', *Guardian*, 24 April.

Ingham, G. (1984), *Capitalism Divided: The City and industry in British social development*, Macmillan.

Judge, D. (1990), *Parliament and Industry*, Dartmouth.

Kaldor, N. (1966), *Causes of the Slow Rate of Growth of the United Kingdom*, Cambridge University Press.

Keegan, W. and Pennant-Rea, R. (1979), *Who Runs the Economy?*, Temple Smith.

Keliher, L. (1990), 'Core executive decision making in high technology issues: the case of the Alvey Report', *Public Administration*, **68**: 61–82.

Kirby, M. W. (1991), 'The economic record since 1945', in T. Gourvish and A. O'Day (eds), *Britain Since 1945*, Macmillan.

Kirby, M. W. (1992), 'Institutional rigidities and economic decline: reflections on the British experience', *Economic History Review*, 637–48.

Knell, J. (1993), 'Labour force skills and human resource management: A local economy perspective', *Personnel Review*, **22**: 30–44.

Labour Party (1992), *Making Britain's Future*.

Lamont, N. (1993), *The Performance of British Industry*, Conservative Research Department.

Landes, D. (1969), *The Unbound Prometheus*, Cambridge University Press.

Lazonick, W. (1981), 'Production relations, labour productivity and choice of technique', *Journal of Economic History*, September: 491–516.

Lazonick, W. (1993), *Business Organisation and the Myth of the Market Economy*, Cambridge University Press.

Lewis, W. A. (1978), *Growth and Fluctuations 1870–1913*, Allen & Unwin.

Leys, C. (1985), 'Thatcherism and British manufacturing: a question of hegemony', *New Left Review*, **151**: 5–25.

Leys, C. (1986), 'The formation of British capital', *New Left Review*, **160**: 114–20.

Lorenz, E. and Wilkinson, F. (1986), 'The shipbuilding industry 1880–1965', in B. Elbaum and W. Lazonick (eds), *The Decline of the British Economy*, Oxford University Press.

Love, J. H. (1989), 'External takeover and regional economic development: a survey and critique', *Regional Studies*, **23**: 417–29.

Lowe, R. (1978), 'The erosion of state intervention in Britain 1917–1924', *Economic History Review*, **31**: 270–86.

Lynn, R. (1988), *Educational Achievement in Japan*, Macmillan.

MSC/NEDO (1984), *Competence and Competition: Training in the Federal Republic of Germany, the United States and Japan*, NEDO.

Machin, S. and Wadwhani, S. (1991), 'The effects of unions on organisational change and employment', *Economic Journal*, **101**: 835–54.

Marquand, D. (1988), *The Unprincipled Society*, Cape.

Mathieson, M. and Bernbaum, G. (1988), The British Disease: a British tradition', *British Journal of Educational Studies*, **26**: 126–66.

Mathewson, S. B. (1931), *Restriction of Output Among Unorganized Workers*, Viking Press.

Matthews, R. C. O. (1988), 'Research on productivity and the productivity gap', *National Institute Economic Review*, May: 66–71.

Maynard, G. (1988), *The Economy Under Mrs Thatcher*, Blackwell.

McConnell, J. (1985), *The English Public Schools*, Herbert.

McGregor, A. and Sproull, A. (1992), 'Employers and the flexible workforce', *Employment Gazette*, May: 225–34.

McWilliams, D. (1994), 'Manufacturing is special: myth or reality?', *Bulletin*, Foundation for Manufacturing and Industry, April: 3–8.

Meeks, G. (1977), *Disappointing Marriage: A study of the gains from merger*, Cambridge University Press.

Melitz, J. (1980), *A Report on the Issue of Exchange Rate Determination*, OECD.

Metcalf, D. (1989a), 'Water notes dry up: the impact of the Donovan proposals and Thatcherism at work on labour productivity in British manufacturing industry', *British Journal of Industrial Relations*, **27**: 1–31.

Metcalf, D. (1989b), 'Trade unions and economic performance: the British evidence', *LSE Quarterly*, **3**: 21–42.

Metcalf, D. (1990a), 'Union presence and labour productivity in British manufacturing industry: a reply to Nolan and Marginson', *British Journal of Industrial Relations*, **28**: 249–66.

Metcalf, D. (1990b), 'Can unions survive in the private sector?', in J. Philpott (ed.), *Trade Unions and the Economy: Into the 1990s*, Employment Institute.

Meyer, C. (1993), 'Ownership: an inaugural lecture', Warwick Economic Research Paper no. 402.

Middlemas, K. (1986), *Power, Competition and the State, vol. 1: Britain in Search of Balance, 1940–61*, Macmillan.

Middlemas, K. (1991), *Power, Competition and the State, vol. 3: The End of the Postwar Era: Britain since 1974*, Macmillan.

Mitchell, D. (1982), 'Intervention, control and accountability: the National Enterprise Board', *Public Administration Bulletin*, **38**: 40–65.

Moggridge, D. E. (1972), *British Monetary Policy 1924–31*, Cambridge University Press.

Muellbauer, J. (1986), 'The assessment: productivity and competitiveness in British manufacturing', *Oxford Review of Economic Policy*, **2**: 1–25.

Mueller, A. (1985), 'A civil servant's view', in D. Englefield (ed.), *Today's Civil Service*, Longman.

Murphy, Sir L. (1981), 'Reflections on the National Enterprise Board', in *Allies or Adversaries? Perspectives on government and industry in Britain*, Royal Institute of Public Administration.

Murrell, P. (1983), 'The comparative structure of the growth of West German and British manufacturing industry', in C. Mueller (ed.), *The Political Economy of Growth*, Yale University Press.

Nairn, T. (1977), 'The twilight of the British state', *New Left Review*, **101–2**: 3–61.

Nairn, T. (1979), 'The future of Britain's crisis', *New Left Review*, **113–14**: 43–70.

Namier, L. (1975), 'The social foundations', in D. Baugh (ed.), *Aristocratic Government and Society in Eighteenth Century England*, New York.

NAO (1987), *Department of Trade and Industry: Assistance to industry under section 8 of the Industrial Development Act 1982*, HC 329, 1986/87.

Nettl, J. P. (1965), 'Consensus or elite domination: the case of business', *Political Studies*, **13**: 22–44.

New, C. C. and Myers, A. (1986), *Managing Manufacturing Operations in the UK 1975–85*, Institute of Manpower Studies.

Nichols, T. (1986), *The British Worker Question*, Routledge and Kegan Paul.

Nichols, T. (1989), 'Thatcherism, industrial relations, and British manufacturing', mimeo.

Nickell, S., Wadhwani, S. and Wall, M. (1989), 'Unions and productivity growth: evidence from UK company accounts data, 1972–86', London School of Economics, *Centre for Labour Economics Discussion Paper, 353*.

Nolan, P. (1989a), 'The productivity miracle?', in F. Green (ed.), *The Restructuring of the UK Economy*, Harvester.

Nolan, P. (1989b), 'Walking on water? Performance and industrial relations under Thatcher', *Industrial Relations Journal*, **20**: 81–92.

Nolan, P. and Marginson, P. (1990), 'Skating on thin ice? David Metcalf on trade unions and productivity', *British Journal of Industrial Relations*, **28**: 227–47.

Nolan, P. and O'Donnell, K. (1991), 'Flexible specialisation and UK manufacturing weakness: a comment on Hirst and Zeitlin', *Political Quarterly*, **62**: 106–24.

OECD (1985), *Education and Training After Basic Schooling*, Paris.

Olson, M. (1982), *The Rise and Decline of Nations*, Yale University Press.

Ormerod, P. (1994), *The Death of Economics*, Faber & Faber.

Pavitt, K. (ed.) (1980), *Technical Innovation and British Economic Performance*, Macmillan.

Payne, P. (1979), *Colvilles and the Scottish Steel Industry*, Oxford University Press.

Perkin, H. (1972), *The Origins of Modern English Society 1780–1880*, Routledge and Kegan Paul.

Phelps, N. A. (1993), 'Branch plants and the evolving spatial division of labour: a study of material linkage change in the Northern region of England', *Regional Studies*, **27**: 87–101.

Plowden, W. (1985), 'The culture of Whitehall', in D. Englefield (ed.), *Today's Civil Service*, Longman.

Pollard, S. (1982), *The Wasting of the British Economy*, Croom Helm.

Porter, M. E. (1990), *The Competitive Advantage of Nations*, Macmillan.

Porter, S. (1975), *The Lion's Share*, Macmillan.

Posner, M. and Steer, A. (1979), 'Price competitiveness and the performance of manufacturing industry', in F. Blackaby (ed.), *De-industrialisation*, Heinemann.

Postlethwaite, N. (1988), 'English last in science', *Guardian*, 1 March.

Prais, S. J. (1981), *Productivity and Industrial Structure*, Cambridge University Press.

Prais, S. J. (1987), 'Educating for productivity: comparisons of Japanese and English schooling and vocational preparation', *National Institute Economic Review*, February: 40–53.

Prais, S. J. and Steedman, H. (1986), 'Vocational training in France and Britain: the building trades', *National Institute Economic Review*, May: 45–55.

Prais, S. J. and Wagner, K. (1983), 'Some aspects of human capital investment: training standards in five occupations in Britain and Germany', *National Institute Economic Review*, August: 46–65.

Prais, S. J. and Wagner, K. (1985), 'Schooling standards in England and Germany', *National Institute Economic Review*, May: 53–76.

Prais, S. J. and Wagner, K. (1988), 'Productivity and management: the training of foremen in Britain and Germany', *National Institute Economic Review*, August: 34–47.

Prais, S. J. and Wagner, K. (1989), 'Productivity and vocational skills in services in Britain and Germany: hotels', *National Institute Economic Review*, November: 52–72.

Pratten, C. F. (1976), *Labour Productivity Differentials within International Companies*, Cambridge University Press.

Pressnell, L. S. (1978), '1925: the burden of sterling', *Economic History Review*, **31**: 67–88.

Prigigone, I. and Nicolis, G. (1989), *Exploring Complexity*, Freeman.

Radcliffe (1959), *Report of the Committee on the Working of the Monetary System*, Cmnd. 827, HMSO.

Radcliffe, J. (1991), *The Reorganisation of British Central Government*, Dartmouth.

Radice, H. (1988), 'Keynes and the policy of practical protectionism', in J. V. Hillard (ed.), *J.M. Keynes in Retrospect*, Edward Elgar.

Radice, H. (1989), 'British capitalism in a changing global economy', in A. MacEwan and B. Tabb (eds), *Instability and Change in the World Economy*, Monthly Review Press.

Ray, G. (1987), 'Labour costs and international competitiveness', *National Institute Economic Review*, May: 71–4.

Reddaway, W. B. (1968), *The Effects of UK Direct Investment Overseas: Final report*, Cambridge University Press.

Reddaway, W. B. (1983), 'Problems and prospects for the UK economy', *Economic Record*, **59**: 220–31.

Reddaway, W. B. (1992), 'Introduction', in J. Michie (ed.), *The Economic Legacy 1979–1992*, Academic Press.

Reder, M. (1985), 'What do unions do? Review symposium', *Industrial and Labor Relations*, **38**.

Rees, A. (1963), 'The effects of unions on resource allocation', *Journal of Law and Economics*, **6**: 69–78.

Reid, G. L. (1980), 'The research needs of British policy-makers', in A. McIntosh (ed.), *Employment Policy in the UK and US*, John Martin.

Roderick, G. and Stephens, M. (eds) (1982), *The British Malaise: Industrial performance, education and training in Britain today*, Falmer Press.

Rosecrance, R. (1979), 'The Pax Britannica and British foreign policy', in I. Kramnick (ed.), *Is Britain Dying? Perspectives on the current crisis*, Cornell University Press.

Rowthorn, B. (1986), 'Deindustrialisation in Britain', in R. Martin and B. Rowthorn (eds), *The Geography of Deindustrialisation*, Macmillan.

Rowthorn, B. (1994), 'Brave new world of services exports is folly', *Guardian*, 23 May.

Rowthorn, R. E. and Wells, J. R. (1987), *Deindustrialization and Foreign Trade*, Cambridge University Press.

Rubinstein, W. D. (1990), 'Cultural explanations of Britain's economic decline', in B. Collins and K. Robbins (eds), *British Culture and Economic Decline*, Weidenfeld and Nicolson.

Saunders, C. T. (1978), *Engineering in Britain, West Germany and France: Some statistical comparisons*, Sussex European Research Centre.

Sayers, R. S. (1976), *The Bank of England 1891–1944*, Oxford University Press.

Select Committee on Trade and Industry (1994), *Competitiveness of UK Manufacturing Industry*, House of Commons.

Shepherd, D., Silberston, A. and Strange, R. (1985), *British Manufacturing Investment Overseas*, Methuen.

Shonfield, A. (1958), *British Economic Policy since the War*, Penguin.

Singh, A. (1977), 'UK industry and the world economy: a case of de-industrialisation?', *Cambridge Journal of Economics*, **1**: 113–36.

Singh, A. (1987), 'Manufacturing and de-industrialization', in J. Eatwell, M. Milgate and P. Newman (eds), *The New Palgrave: A Dictionary of Economics*, Macmillan.

Smith, M. (1986), 'UK manufacturing: output and trade performance', *Midland Bank Review*, Autumn: 8–16.

Spence, M. (1985), 'Imperialism and decline: Britain in the 1980s', *Capital and Class*, **25**: 117–39.

Stanworth, P. and Giddens, A. (eds) (1974), *Elites and Power in British Society*, Cambridge University Press.

Steedman, H. (1988), 'Vocational training in France and Britain: mechanical and electrical craftsmen', *National Institute Economic Review*, November: 57–71.

Steedman, H. and Wagner, K. (1987), 'A second look at productivity and skills in Britain and Germany', *National Institute Economic Review*, November: 84–95.

Steedman, H. and Wagner, K. (1989), 'Productivity, machinery and skills: clothing manufacture in Britain and Germany', *National Institute Economic Review*, May: 40–57.

Steer, P. and Cable, J. R. (1978), 'Internal organisation and profit: an empirical analysis of large UK companies', *Journal of Industrial Economics*, **27**: 13–30.

Streeck, W. (1985), 'Industrial relations and industrial restructuring in the motor industry', Industrial Relations Research Unit, Warwick University, mimeo.

Streeck, W. (1991), 'On the institutional conditions of diversified quality production', in E. Matzner and W. Streeck (eds), *Beyond Keynesianism: The socio-economics of production and full employment*, Edward Elgar.

Thain, C. (1984), 'The Treasury and Britain's decline', *Political Studies*, **32**: 581–95.

Theakston, K. and Fry, G. (forthcoming), 'The Conservative Party and the Civil Service', in A. Seldon (ed.), *The Conservative Party in the Twentieth Century*, Oxford University Press.

Thompson, E. P. (1963), *The Making of the English Working Class*, Gollancz.

Thompson, G. (1977), 'The relationship between the financial and industrial sectors of the UK economy', *Economy and Society*, **6**: 235–83.

Tolliday, S. (1986), 'Steel and rationalisation policies 1918–1950', in B. Elbaum and W. Lazonick (eds), *The Decline of the British Economy*, Oxford University Press.

Toporowski, J. (1989), 'The financial system and capital accumulation in the 1980s', in F. Green (ed.), *The Restructuring of the UK Economy*, Harvester Wheatsheaf.

Treasury (1993), *Public Expenditure Analyses to 1995–96*, Cm 2219, HMSO.

Turok, I. (1993), 'Inward investment and local linkages: how deeply embedded is "Silicon Glen"?', *Regional Studies*, **27**: 401–17.

Verdoorn, P. J. (1949), 'Factors governing the growth of labour productivity', *L'Industria*. Translated in A. P. Thirlwall and G. Thirlwall, *Research in Population and Economics*, Autumn 1979.

Wadhwani, S. (1990), 'The effect of unions on productivity growth, investment and employment: a report on some recent work', *British Journal of Industrial Relations*, **28**: 371–85.

Warwick, P. (1985), 'Did Britain change?: an inquiry into the causes of national decline', *Journal of Contemporary History*, **20**: 99–133.

Walker, W. (1993), 'National innovation systems: Britain', in R. Nelson (ed.), *National Innovation Systems: A comparative analysis*, Oxford University Press.

Weiner, M. J. (1981), *English Culture and the Decline of the Industrial Spirit, 1850–1980*, Cambridge University Press.

Wells, J. (1991), 'Britain in the 1990s: the legacy of Thatcherism', in J. Cornwall (ed.), *The Capitalist Economies: Prospects for the 1990s*, Edward Elgar.

Wells, J. (1992), 'The economy after ten years: stronger or weaker?', in N. M. Healey (ed.), *Britain's Economic Miracle: Myth or reality?*, Routledge.

Wells, J. (1994), 'De-industrialization', in P. Arestis and M. C. Sawyer (eds), *The Elgar Companion to Radical Political Economy*, Elgar.

Wilensky, H. and Turner, L. (1987), *Democratic Corporatism and Policy Linkages*, Institute of International Studies, Berkeley.

Wilks, S. (1983), 'Liberal state and party competition: Britain', in K. Dyson and S. Wilks (eds), *Industrial Crisis*, Martin Robertson.

Wilks, S. (1986), 'Has the state abandoned British industry?', *Parliamentary Affairs*, **39**: 31–46.

Wilks, S. (1989), 'The Department of Trade and Industry under Lord Young', *Public Money and Management*, **9**: 43–6.

Wilks, S. (1990), 'Institutional insularity: government and the British motor industry since 1945', in M. Chick (ed.), *Governments, Industries and Markets*, Edward Elgar.

Williams, K., Williams, J. and Haslam, C. (1990), 'The hollowing out of British manufacturing', *Economy and Society*, **19**: 456–90.

Williams, W. (1989), 'Central government capacity and the British Disease', *Parliamentary Affairs*, **42**: 250–64.

Wilson Committee Hearings (1978), *Evidence on the Financing of Industry and Trade*, HMSO.

Wood, D. (1987), 'The Conservative member of parliament as lobbyist for constituency economic interests', *Political Studies*, **35**: 393–409.

Young, A. (1928), 'Increasing returns and economic progress', *Economic Journal*, December: 527–42.

Young, Lord (1990), *The Enterprise Years*, Headline Books.

Young, S. and Hood, N. (1992), 'Transnational corporations and policy dilemmas: the problems of the machine-tool industry in the United Kingdom', *Transnational Corporations*, **1**: 77–92.

Young, S. and Lowe, A. V. (1974), *Intervention in the Mixed Economy*, Croom Helm.

Young, S., Hood, N. and Hamill, J. (1988), *Foreign Multinationals and the British Economy: Impact and policy*, Croom Helm.

Zysman, J. (1983), *Governments, Markets and Growth*, Basil Blackwell.